Kaplan Publishing are constantly finding new w... difference to your studies and our excitin... offer something different to students look...

This book comes with free MyKaplan onlin... study anytime, anywhere. **This free online ... separately and is included in the price of ...**

Having purchased this book, you have access to the following online study materials:

CONTENT	ACCA (including FBT, FMA, FFA)		FIA (excluding FBT, FMA, FFA)	
	Text	Kit	Text	Kit
Electronic version of the book	✓	✓	✓	✓
Check Your Understanding Test with instant answers	✓			
Material updates	✓	✓	✓	✓
Latest official ACCA exam questions*		✓		
Extra question assistance using the signpost icon**		✓		
Timed questions with an online tutor debrief using clock icon***		✓		
Interim assessment including questions and answers	✓		✓	
Technical answers	✓	✓	✓	✓

* Excludes BT, MA, FA, FBT, FMA, FFA; for all other papers includes a selection of questions, as released by ACCA
** For ACCA SBL, SBR, AFM, APM, ATX, AAA only
*** Excludes BT, MA, FA, LW, FBT, FMA and FFA

How to access your online resources

Kaplan Financial students will already have a MyKaplan account and these extra resources will be available to you online. You do not need to register again, as this process was completed when you enrolled. If you are having problems accessing online materials, please ask your course administrator.

If you are not studying with Kaplan and did not purchase your book via a Kaplan website, to unlock your extra online resources please go to www.mykaplan.co.uk/addabook (even if you have set up an account and registered books previously). You will then need to enter the ISBN number (on the title page and back cover) and the unique pass key number contained in the scratch panel below to gain access. You will also be required to enter additional information during this process to set up or confirm your account details.

If you purchased through the Kaplan Publishing website you will automatically receive an e-mail invitation to MyKaplan. Please register your details using this email to gain access to your content. If you do not receive the e-mail or book content, please contact Kaplan Publishing.

Your Code and Information

This code can only be used once for the registration of one book online. This registration and your online content will expire when the final sittings for the examinations covered by this book have taken place. Please allow one hour from the time you submit your book details for us to process your request.

Please scratch the film to access your unique code.

Please be aware that this code is case-sensitive and you will need to include the dashes within the passcode, but not when entering the ISBN.

KAPLAN PUBLISHING

ACCA Diploma in Financial and Management Accounting (RQF Level 3)

Paper MA2

Managing Costs and Finance

STUDY TEXT

British library cataloguing-in-publication data

A catalogue record for this book is available from the British Library.

Published by:
Kaplan Publishing UK
Unit 2 The Business Centre
Molly Millars Lane
Wokingham
Berkshire
RG41 2QZ

ISBN 978-1-78740-849-4

Printed and bound in Great Britain.

Acknowledgements

These materials are reviewed by the ACCA examining team. The objective of the review is to ensure that the material properly covers the syllabus and study guide outcomes, used by the examining team in setting the exams, in the appropriate breadth and depth. The review does not ensure that every eventuality, combination or application of examinable topics is addressed by the ACCA Approved Content. Nor does the review comprise a detailed technical check of the content as the Approved Content Provider has its own quality assurance processes in place in this respect.

We are grateful to the Association of Chartered Certified Accountants and the Chartered Institute of Management Accountants for permission to reproduce past examination questions. The answers have been prepared by Kaplan Publishing.

CONTENTS

Quality and accuracy are of the utmost importance to us so if you spot an error in any of our products, please send an email to mykaplanreporting@kaplan.com with full details.

Our Quality Co-ordinator will work with our technical team to verify the error and take action to ensure it is corrected in future editions.

INTRODUCTION

This is the new edition of the FIA study text for MA 2 – *Managing Costs and Finance,* fully updated and revised according to the examiner's comments.

Tailored to fully cover the syllabus, this Study Text has been written specifically for FIA students. A clear and comprehensive style, numerous examples and highlighted key terms help you to acquire the information easily. Plenty of activities and self-test questions enable you to practise what you have learnt.

At the end of most of the chapters you will find practice questions. These are exam-style questions and will give you a very good idea of the way you will be tested.

ACCA SUPPORT

For additional support with your studies please also refer to the ACCA Global website.

SYLLABUS AND STUDY GUIDE

Position of the examination in the overall syllabus

Knowledge of MA1, *Management Information*, at the introductory level is required before commencing study for MA2.

This examination provides the basic techniques required to enable candidates to develop knowledge and understanding of how to prepare, process and present basic cost information to support management in planning and decision making in a variety of business contexts.

Candidates will need a sound understanding of the methods and techniques introduced in this examination to ensure that they can take them further in subsequent examinations. The methods introduced in this examination are revisited and extended in FMA, *Management Accounting.*

SYLLABUS

A Management information **Chapters 1, 2, 3, 19 and 20**

1 Management information requirements

2 Cost accounting systems

3 Cost classification

4 Information for comparison

5 Reporting management information

B Cost recording **Chapters 4 to 7**

1 Accounting for materials

2 Accounting for labour

3 Accounting for other expenses

C Costing techniques **Chapters 8 to 12**

1 Absorption costing

2 Marginal costing

3 Job and batch costing

4 Process costing

5 Service costing

D Decision making **Chapters 13 to 15**

1 Cost- volume- profit analysis

2 Factors affecting short term decision making

3 Principles of discounted cash flow

E Cash management **Chapters 16 to 18**

1 Nature of cash and cash flow

2 Cash management

3 Cash budgets

4 Investing and financing

Study guide

A MANAGEMENT INFORMATION

1 Management information requirements **Chapter 1**

(a) Describe the purpose of management information: planning, control and decision making. [K]

(b) Describe the features of useful management Information. [K]

(c) Describe the nature, source and importance of both financial and non-financial information for managers. [K]

(d) Describe management responsibilities for cost, profit and investment and their effect on management information and performance measurement. [k]

(e) Explain the role of information technology in management information. [K]

(f) Explain the role of the trainee accountant. [K]

2 Cost accounting systems **Chapter 2**

(a) Explain the relationship between the cost/management accounting system and the financial accounting/management information systems (including interlocking and integrated bookkeeping systems). [K]

(b) Describe the process of accounting for input costs and relating them to work done. [K]

(c) Identify the documentation required, and the flow of documentation, for different cost accounting transactions. [S]

(d) Explain and illustrate the use of codes in categorising and processing transactions (including sequential, hierarchical, block, faceted and mnemonic coding methods. [K]

(e) Explain and illustrate the concept of cost units. [S]

(f) Describe the different methods of costing final outputs and their appropriateness to different types of business organisation. [S]

(g) Describe methods of capturing, processing, storing and outputting cost and management accounting data by computer. [K]

3 Cost classification **Chapter 3**

(a) Describe the variety of cost classifications used for different purposes in a cost accounting system, including by responsibility, function, direct/indirect, behaviour. [K]

(b) Explain and illustrate the nature of variable, fixed, stepped fixed and mixed (semi-variable) costs. [S]

(c) Use the high-low method to separate semi-variable costs. [S]

(d) Use variable, fixed and semi-variable costs in cost analysis. [S]

(e) Analyse the effect of changing activity levels on unit costs. [S]

4 Information for comparison **Chapter 19**

(a) Explain the purpose of making comparisons. [K]

(b) Identify relevant bases for comparison: previous period data, corresponding period data, forecast/budget data. [S]

(c) Explain the forecasting/budgeting process and the concept of feed forward and feedback control. [K]

(d) Explain and illustrate the concept of flexible budgets. [S]

(e) Use appropriate income and expenditure data for comparison. [S]

(f) Calculate variances between actual and historical/forecast data which may or may not be adjusted for volume change. [S]

(g) Identify whether variances are favourable or adverse. [S]

(h) Identify possible causes of variances. [S]

(i) Explain the concept of exception reporting. [K]

(j) Explain factors affecting the decision whether to investigate variances. [K]

5 Reporting management information — Chapter 20

(a) Identify suitable formats for the presentation of management information according to purpose. [S]

(b) Describe methods of analysing, presenting and communicating information. [K]

(c) Identify suitable formats for communicating management information according to purpose and organisational guidelines including: informal business reports, letter and email or memo. [S]

(d) Identify the general principles of distributing reports (e.g. procedures, timing, recipients) including the reporting of confidential information. [K]

(e) Interpret information presented in management reports. [S]

B COST RECORDING

1 Accounting for materials — Chapter 4 and 5

(a) Describe the main types of material classification. [K]

(b) Describe the procedures and documentation required to ensure the correct authorisation, coding, analysis and recording of direct and indirect material costs. [K]

(c) Explain, illustrate and evaluate the FIFO, LIFO and periodic and cumulative weighted average methods used to price materials issued from inventory. [S]

(d) Describe and illustrate the accounting for material costs. [S]

(e) Calculate material input requirements, and control measures, where wastage occurs. [S]

(f) Describe the procedures required to monitor inventory and to minimise discrepancies and losses. [K]

(g) Explain and illustrate the costs of holding inventory and of being without inventory. [S]

(h) Explain, illustrate and evaluate inventory control levels (minimum, maximum, reorder). [S]

(i) Calculate and interpret optimal order quantities. [S]

(j) Explain the relationship between the materials costing system and the inventory control system. [K]

2 Accounting for labour — Chapter 6

(a) Explain, illustrate and evaluate labour remuneration methods. [S]

(b) Describe the operation of a payroll accounting system. [K]

(c) Distinguish between direct and indirect labour costs. [K]

(d) Describe the procedures and documentation required to ensure the correct coding, analysis and recording of direct and indirect labour. [K]

(e) Describe and illustrate the accounting for labour costs. [S]

(f) Explain the relationship between the labour costing system and the payroll accounting system. [K]

(g) Explain the causes and costs of, and calculate, labour turnover. [S]

(h) Describe and illustrate measures of labour efficiency and utilisation (efficiency, capacity utilisation, production volume and idle time ratios). [S]

3 Costing of other expenses — Chapter 7

(a) Describe the nature of expenses by function. [K]

(b) Describe the procedures and documentation required to ensure the correct authorisation, coding, analysis and recording of direct and indirect expenses. [K]

(c) Describe and calculate capital and revenue expenditure and the relevant accounting treatment. [K]

(d) Calculate and explain depreciation charges using straight-line, reducing balance, machine hour and product units methods. [S]

(e) Explain the relationship between the expenses costing system and the expense accounting system. [K]

C COSTING TECHNIQUES

1 Absorption costing Chapter 8 and 9

(a) Explain the rationale for absorption costing. [K]

(b) Describe the nature of production and service cost centres and their significance for production overhead allocation, apportionment and absorption. [K]

(c) Describe the process of allocating, apportioning and absorbing production overheads to establish product costs. [K]

(d) Apportion overheads to cost centres using appropriate bases. [S]

(e) Reapportion service cost centre overheads to production cost centres using direct and step down methods. [S]

(f) Justify, calculate and apply production cost centre overhead absorption rates using labour hour and machine hour methods. [S]

(g) Explain the relative merits of actual and predetermined absorption rates. [K]

(h) Describe and illustrate the accounting for production overhead costs, including the analysis and interpretation of over/under absorption. [S]

(i) Describe and apply methods of attributing non-production overheads to cost units. [S]

(j) Calculate product costs using the absorption costing method. [S]

2 Marginal costing Chapter 9

(a) Explain and illustrate the concept of contribution. [S]

(b) Prepare profit statements using the marginal costing method. [S]

(c) Prepare profit statements using the absorption costing method. [S]

(d) Compare and contrast the use of absorption and marginal costing for period profit reporting and inventory valuation. [K]

(e) Reconcile the profits reported by absorption and marginal costing. [S]

(f) Explain the usefulness of profit and contribution information respectively. [K]

3 Job and batch costing Chapter 10

(a) Identify situations where the use of job or batch costing is appropriate. [K]

(b) Calculate unit costs in job and batch costing. [S]

(c) Describe the control of costs in job and batch costing. [K]

(d) Apply cost plus pricing in job costing. [S]

4 Process costing Chapter 11

(a) Identify situations where the use of process costing is appropriate. [K]

(b) Explain and illustrate the nature of normal and abnormal losses/gains. [S]

(c) Calculate unit costs where losses are separated into normal and abnormal. [S]

(d) Prepare process accounts where losses are separated into normal and abnormal. [S]

(e) Account for scrap and waste. [S]

(f) Distinguish between joint products and by-products. [K]

(g) Explain the accounting treatment of joint products and by-products at the point of separation. [K]

(h) Apportion joint process costs using net realisable values and weight/volume of output respectively. [S]

(i) Discuss the usefulness of product cost/profit data from a joint process. [K]

(j) Evaluate the benefit of further processing. [S]

5 Service costing Chapter 12

(a) Describe the characteristics of service costing. [K]

(b) Describe the practical problems relating to the costing of services. [K]

(c) Identify situations (cost centres and industries) where the use of service costing is appropriate. [S]

(d) Illustrate suitable cost units that may be used for a variety of services. [S]

(e) Calculate service unit costs in a variety of situations. [S]

D DECISION MAKING

1 Cost/volume/profit analysis — Chapter 13

(a) Calculate contribution per unit and the contribution/sales ratio. [S]

(b) Explain the concept of break-even and margin of safety. [K]

(c) Use contribution per unit and contribution/sales ratio to calculate breakeven point and margin of safety. [S]

(d) Analyse the effect on break-even point and margin of safety of changes in selling price and costs. [S]

(e) Use contribution per unit and contribution/sales ratio to calculate the sales required to achieve a target profit. [S]

(f) Interpret break-even and profit/volume charts for a single product or business. [S]

2 Factors affecting short term decision-making — Chapter 14

(a) Explain the importance of the limiting factor concept. [K]

(b) Identify the limiting factor in given situations. [S]

(c) Formulate and determine the optimal production solution when there is a single resource constraint. [S]

(d) Solve make/buy-in problems when there is a single resource constraint. [S]

(e) Explain the concept of relevant costs. [K]

(f) Apply the concept of relevant costs in business decisions. [S]

3 Principles of discounted cash flow — Chapter 16

(a) Explain and illustrate the difference between simple and compound interest, and between nominal and effective interest rates. [S]

(b) Explain and illustrate compounding and discounting. [S]

(c) Explain the distinction between cash flow and profit and the relevance of cash flow to capital investment appraisal. [K]

(d) Explain and illustrate the net present value (NPV) and internal rate of return (IRR) methods of discounted cash flow. [S]

(e) Calculate present value using annuity and perpetuity formulae. [S]

(f) Calculate payback (discounted and non-discounted). [S]

(g) Interpret the results of NPV, IRR and payback calculations of investment viability. [S]

E CASH MANAGEMENT

1 Nature of cash and cash flow — Chapter 16

(a) Define cash and cash flow. [K]

(b) Outline the various sources of cash receipts and payments (including regular/exceptional revenue/capital receipts and payments, and drawings). [K]

(c) Describe the relationship between cash flow accounting and accounting for income and expenditure. [K]

(d) Distinguish between the cash flow pattern of different types of organisations. [S]

(e) Explain the importance of cash flow management and its impact on liquidity and company survival (note: calculation of ratios is not required). [K]

2 Cash Management — Chapter 17

(a) Outline the basic treasury functions. [K]

(b) Describe cash handling procedures. [K]

(c) Outline guidelines and legislation in relation to the management of cash balances in public sector organisations. [K]

(d) Describe how trends in the economic and financial environment can affect management of cash balances. [K]

3 Cash budgets **Chapter 18**

(a) Explain the objectives of cash budgeting. [K]

(b) Explain and illustrate statistical techniques used in cash forecasting including moving averages and allowance for inflation. [S]

(c) Prepare a cash budget/forecast. [S]

(d) Explain and illustrate how a cash budget can be used as a mechanism for monitoring and control. [S]

4 Investing and financing **Chapter 17**

(a) Explain how surplus cash and cash deficit may arise. [K]

(b) Explain the following types of short term investments and the associated risks/returns. [K]:

  (i) bank deposits

  (ii) money- market deposits

  (iii) certificates of deposit

  (iv) government stock

  (v) local authority stock

(c) Explain different ways of raising finance from a bank and the basic terms and conditions associated with each financing. [K]

NOTE:

Outcomes marked with a [K] are areas where knowledge is needed. This means that you might be asked to explain the area, but you would never have to apply it in a question.

Outcomes marked with an [S] are areas where some practical skills will be needed. So you may need to apply the skill to a brief exam scenario

THE EXAMINATION

Format of the examination

	Number of marks
50 objective test questions	100

Computer Based Exam (CBE)

The syllabus is examined via an on-demand CBE. The exam will contain 50 questions. Each question is worth two marks each and can take one of four formats:

- multiple choice questions (this is where a candidate must choose one of four options, A through to D)
- multiple response questions (this is where the candidate must select more than one response from the options provided by clicking the appropriate tick boxes).
- multiple response matching questions (this is where the candidate must match together related items. For example, statements on activity based costing might have to be categorised as either TRUE or FALSE)
- number entry questions (this is where the candidate will be provided with an on-screen box into which he/she must enter the correct number)

The ACCA provide the following guidance for attempting questions in the CBE:

- Read each question carefully.
- When you answer a question, your answer will automatically be saved.
- You can revisit questions and change your answers at any time during the exam.
- The only permitted characters for numerical answers are:
  - Numbers
  - One full stop as a decimal point if required
  - One minus symbol at the front of the figure if the answer is negative. For example: –10234.35
  - No other characters, including commas, are accepted

Questions assess all parts of the syllabus and will include both computational and non-computational elements.

Pass mark: 50%
Total time allowed: 2 hours

Tips for sitting CBEs

The ACCA have provided the following advice for sitting a CBE:

In a CBE you are presented with one question at a time. Displaying only one question at a time helps you focus on each question. Research tells us that the way we read information presented on a computer is different to how we read on paper. On the computer our eyes tend to jump around the screen rather than read it systematically as we would a printed page. Remember to take time to read the question carefully to ensure you don't miss any important information. Once you have entered your answer for a question, it is important to click on the 'Submit' button for your answer to be saved. You can revisit questions and change answers at any time until the exam duration has been reached – however, remember to click on 'Submit' to save your new answer once you have changed it.

Do not spend a lot of time on questions you are unsure of; instead, move on and come back to these questions at the end of the exam.

To make CBEs as user-friendly as possible we have incorporated features that will guide you through the exam. Part of the screen has been reserved for tools that will help you navigate between questions. In addition, questions that you have not attempted will be highlighted by an asterisk in the drop-down list of questions and you can quickly move to these questions by clicking on the relevant question number in the list. The exams also include a timer to show you how much time is remaining.

Preparing for the exam

- You can take a CBE **at any time during the year** –the exams are conducted at centres which are licensed by ACCA and there is lots of flexibility as to when the exam can be attempted.

- Be sure you **understand how to use the software** before you start the exam. If in doubt, ask the assessment centre staff to explain it to you. **Questions are displayed on the screen** and **answers are entered using keyboard and mouse**.

- Don't panic if you realise you've answered a question incorrectly – **you can always go back and change your answer.**

- Read the questions carefully and work through any calculations required. If you don't know the answer, eliminate those options you know are incorrect and see if the answer becomes more obvious. Remember that only one answer to a multiple-choice question can be right!

- At the end of the examination, **you are given a certificate showing the result** you have achieved.

STUDY SKILLS AND REVISION GUIDANCE

Set your objectives

Before starting to study decide what you want to achieve – the type of pass you wish to obtain. This will decide the level of commitment and time you need to dedicate to your studies.

Devise a study plan

Determine which times of the week you will study.

Split these times into sessions of at least one hour for study of new material. Any shorter periods could be used for revision or practice.

Put the times you plan to study onto a study plan for the weeks from now until the exam and set yourself targets for each period of study – in your sessions make sure you cover the course, course assignments and revision.

If you are studying for more than one examination at a time, try to vary your subjects as this can help you to keep interested and see subjects as part of wider knowledge.

When working through your course, compare your progress with your plan and, if necessary, re-plan your work (perhaps including extra sessions) or, if you are ahead, do some extra revision/practice questions.

Effective studying

Active reading

You are not expected to learn the text by rote, rather, you must understand what you are reading and be able to use it to pass the exam and develop good practice. A good technique to use is SQ3Rs – Survey, Question, Read, Recall, Review:

(1) **Survey** the chapter – look at the headings and read the introduction, summary and objectives, so as to get an overview of what the chapter deals with.

(2) **Question** – whilst undertaking the survey, ask yourself the questions that you hope the chapter will answer for you.

(3) **Read** through the chapter thoroughly, answering the questions and making sure you can meet the objectives. Attempt the exercises and activities in the text, and work through all the examples.

(4) **Recall** – at the end of each section and at the end of the chapter, try to recall the main ideas of the section/chapter without referring to the text. This is best done after a short break of a couple of minutes after the reading stage.

(5) **Review** – check that your recall notes are correct.

You may also find it helpful to re-read the chapter to try to see the topic(s) it deals with as a whole.

Note-taking

Taking notes is a useful way of learning, but do not simply copy out the text. The notes must:

- be in your own words
- be concise
- cover the key points
- be well-organised
- be modified as you study further chapters in this text or in related ones.

Trying to summarise a chapter without referring to the text can be a useful way of determining which areas you know and which you don't.

Three ways of taking notes:

Summarise the key points of a chapter.

Make linear notes – a list of headings, divided up with subheadings listing the key points. If you use linear notes, you can use different colours to highlight key points and keep topic areas together. Use plenty of space to make your notes easy to use.

Try a diagrammatic form – the most common of which is a mind-map. To make a mind-map, put the main heading in the centre of the paper and put a circle around it. Then draw short lines radiating from this to the main subheadings, which again have circles around them. Then continue the process from the sub-headings to sub-sub-headings, advantages, disadvantages, etc.

Highlighting and underlining

You may find it useful to underline or highlight key points in your study text – but do be selective. You may also wish to make notes in the margins.

Revision

The best approach to revision is to revise the course as you work through it.

Also try to leave four to six weeks before the exam for final revision. Make sure you cover the whole syllabus and pay special attention to those areas where your knowledge is weak. Here are some recommendations:

Read through the text and your notes again and condense your notes into key phrases. It may help to put key revision points onto index cards to look at when you have a few minutes to spare.

Review any assignments you have completed and look at where you lost marks – put more work into those areas where you were weak.

Practise exam questions under timed conditions.

If you are stuck on a topic find somebody (e.g. your tutor or, where appropriate, a member of Kaplan's Academic Support team) to explain it to you.

Ensure you **know the structure of the exam** – how many questions and of what type you will be expected to answer. During your revision attempt all the different styles of questions you may be asked.

MATHEMATICAL TABLES

Present value table

Present value of 1 i.e. $(1+r)^{-n}$

where r = discount rate

n = number of periods until payment

Periods (n)	1%	2%	3%	4%	5%	6%	7%	8%	9%	10%	
	Discount rate (r)										
1	0.990	0.980	0.971	0.962	0.952	0.943	0.935	0.926	0.917	0.909	1
2	0.980	0.961	0.943	0.925	0.907	0.890	0.873	0.857	0.842	0.826	2
3	0.971	0.942	0.915	0.889	0.864	0.840	0.816	0.794	0.772	0.751	3
4	0.961	0.924	0.888	0.855	0.823	0.792	0.763	0.735	0.708	0.683	4
5	0.951	0.906	0.863	0.822	0.784	0.747	0.713	0.681	0.650	0.621	5
6	0.942	0.888	0.837	0.790	0.746	0.705	0.666	0.630	0.596	0.564	6
7	0.933	0.871	0.813	0.760	0.711	0.665	0.623	0.583	0.547	0.513	7
8	0.923	0.853	0.789	0.731	0.677	0.627	0.582	0.540	0.502	0.467	8
9	0.914	0.837	0.766	0.703	0.645	0.592	0.544	0.500	0.460	0.424	9
10	0.905	0.820	0.744	0.676	0.614	0.558	0.508	0.463	0.422	0.386	10
11	0.896	0.804	0.722	0.650	0.585	0.527	0.475	0.429	0.388	0.350	11
12	0.887	0.788	0.701	0.625	0.557	0.497	0.444	0.397	0.356	0.319	12
13	0.879	0.773	0.681	0.601	0.530	0.469	0.415	0.368	0.326	0.290	13
14	0.870	0.758	0.661	0.577	0.505	0.442	0.388	0.340	0.299	0.263	14
15	0.861	0.743	0.642	0.555	0.481	0.417	0.362	0.315	0.275	0.239	15

(n)	11%	12%	13%	14%	15%	16%	17%	18%	19%	20%	
1	0.901	0.893	0.885	0.877	0.870	0.862	0.855	0.847	0.840	0.833	1
2	0.812	0.797	0.783	0.769	0.756	0.743	0.731	0.718	0.706	0.694	2
3	0.731	0.712	0.693	0.675	0.658	0.641	0.624	0.609	0.593	0.579	3
4	0.659	0.636	0.613	0.592	0.572	0.552	0.534	0.516	0.499	0.482	4
5	0.593	0.567	0.543	0.519	0.497	0.476	0.456	0.437	0.419	0.402	5
6	0.535	0.507	0.480	0.456	0.432	0.410	0.390	0.370	0.352	0.335	6
7	0.482	0.452	0.425	0.400	0.376	0.354	0.333	0.314	0.296	0.279	7
8	0.434	0.404	0.376	0.351	0.327	0.305	0.285	0.266	0.249	0.233	8
9	0.391	0.361	0.333	0.308	0.284	0.263	0.243	0.225	0.209	0.194	9
10	0.352	0.322	0.295	0.270	0.247	0.227	0.208	0.191	0.176	0.162	10
11	0.317	0.287	0.261	0.237	0.215	0.195	0.178	0.162	0.148	0.135	11
12	0.286	0.257	0.231	0.208	0.187	0.168	0.152	0.137	0.124	0.112	12
13	0.258	0.229	0.204	0.182	0.163	0.145	0.130	0.116	0.104	0.093	13
14	0.232	0.205	0.181	0.160	0.141	0.125	0.111	0.099	0.088	0.078	14
15	0.209	0.183	0.160	0.140	0.123	0.108	0.095	0.084	0.074	0.065	15

Annuity table

Present value of an annuity of 1 i.e. $\frac{1-(1+r)^{-n}}{r}$

where r = discount rate

n = number of periods

Periods					Discount rate (r)						
(n)	1%	2%	3%	4%	5%	6%	7%	8%	9%	10%	
1	0.990	0.980	0.971	0.962	0.952	0.943	0.935	0.926	0.917	0.909	1
2	1.970	1.942	1.913	1.886	1.859	1.833	1.808	1.783	1.759	1.736	2
3	2.941	2.884	20829	2.775	2.723	2.673	2.624	2.577	2.531	2.487	3
4	3.902	3.808	3.717	3.630	3.546	3.465	3.387	3.312	3.240	3.170	4
5	4.853	4.713	4.580	4.452	4.329	4.212	4.100	3.993	3.890	3.791	5
6	5.795	5.601	5.417	5.242	5.076	4.917	4.767	4.623	4.486	4.355	6
7	6.728	6.472	6.230	6.002	5.786	5.582	5.389	5.206	5.033	4.868	7
8	7.652	7.325	7.020	6.733	6.463	6.210	5.971	5.747	5.535	5.335	8
9	8.566	8.162	7.786	7.435	7.108	6.802	6.515	6.247	5.995	5.759	9
10	9.471	8.983	8.530	8.111	7.722	7.360	7.024	6.710	6.418	6.145	10
11	10.37	9.787	9.253	8.760	8.306	7.887	7.499	7.139	6.805	6.495	11
12	11.26	10.58	9.954	9.385	8.863	8.384	7.943	7.536	7.161	6.814	12
13	12.13	11.35	10.63	9.986	9.394	8.853	8.358	7.904	7.487	7.103	13
14	13.00	12.11	11.30	10.56	9.899	9.295	8.745	8.244	7.786	7.367	14
15	13.87	12.85	11.94	11.12	10.38	9.712	9.108	8.559	8.061	7.606	15

(n)	11%	12%	13%	14%	15%	16%	17%	18%	19%	20%	
1	0.901	0.893	0.885	0.877	0.870	0.862	0.855	0.847	0.840	0.833	1
2	1.713	1.690	1.668	1.647	1.626	1.605	1.585	1.566	1.547	1.528	2
3	2.444	2.402	2.361	2.322	2.283	2.246	2.210	2.174	2.140	2.106	3
4	3.102	3.037	2.974	2.914	2.855	2.798	2.743	2.690	2.639	2.589	4
5	3.696	3.605	3.517	3.433	3.352	3.274	3.199	3.127	3.058	2.991	5
6	4.231	4.111	3.998	3.889	3.784	3.685	3.589	3.498	3.410	3.326	6
7	4.712	4.564	4.423	4.288	4.160	4.039	3.922	3.812	3.706	3.605	7
8	5.146	4.968	4.799	4.639	4.487	4.344	4.207	4.078	3.954	3.837	8
9	5.537	5.328	5.132	4.946	4.772	4.607	4.451	4.303	4.163	4.031	9
10	5.889	5.650	5.426	5.216	5.019	4.833	4.659	4.494	4.339	4.192	10
11	6.207	5.938	5.687	5.453	5.234	5.029	4.836	4.656	4.486	4.327	11
12	6.492	6.194	5.918	5.660	5.421	5.197	4.988	4.793	4.611	4.439	12
13	6.750	6.424	6.122	5.842	5.583	5.342	5.118	4.910	4.715	4.533	13
14	6.982	6.628	6.302	6.002	5.724	5.468	5.229	5.008	4.802	4.611	14
15	7.191	6.811	6.462	6.142	5.847	5.575	5.324	5.092	4.876	4.675	15

Chapter 1

MANAGEMENT INFORMATION

This chapter describes the nature and purpose of management information, and the use of accounting information within a management information system. It also describes the use of responsibility accounting, with cost centres, profit centres and investment centres, and the role of IT in the provision of management information. This chapter covers syllabus areas A1.

CONTENTS

LEARNING OUTCOMES

At the end of this chapter you should be able to:

- describe the purpose of management information: planning, control and decision making
- describe the features of useful management information
- describe the nature, source and importance of both financial and non-financial information for managers
- describe management responsibilities for cost, profit and investment and their effect on management information and performance measurement
- explain the role of information technology in management information
- explain the role of the trainee accountant.

1 PURPOSE OF MANAGEMENT INFORMATION

1.1 THE ROLE OF MANAGERS

Managers within any organisation are decision-makers. They have to make decisions about what should be done, and then issue instructions based on the decisions they have taken.

Decisions can be categorised as planning decisions and control decisions.

- **Planning decisions** are about what should be done. These can be decisions for the long-term or for the shorter-term. Many organisations try to work within the framework of an annual plan or budget. Much planning is done on a day-to-day or week-by-week basis and some planning, known as strategic planning, can be for longer periods ahead.

- **Control decisions** relate to monitoring what is actually happening, and if anything seems to be going wrong, deciding what should be done to correct the problem.

Many organisations produce or revise their forward planning annually, in the form of a budget. The budget cycle is illustrated in the following diagram.

The budget cycle

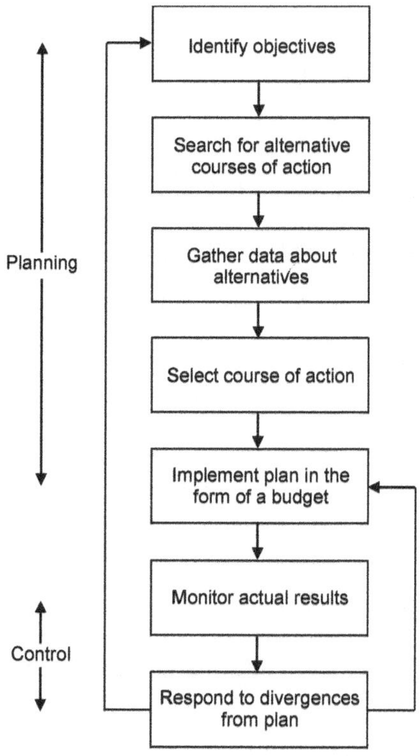

Identifying objectives

The first stage in a planning process is to identify the objectives; in other words, it is important to decide what the organisation is trying to achieve. Should it be trying to increase sales and profits, and if so by how much? Which products or services should it be trying to sell?

Assessing alternative action plans and selecting the preferred plan

There might be several ways of achieving the objectives. For example, sales and profits can be increased by raising selling prices, cutting costs or introducing new products or services to sell to customers. Alternative courses of action should be identified and evaluated. When they have been compared and evaluated the preferred course of action is selected and implemented.

EXAMPLE

Suppose the objective of an organisation is to increase production by 10%. The following alternative courses of action might be identified to achieve the 10% increase.

(a) Increase the workforce by 10% and introduce a night shift. Premium wage rates would have to be paid to the night-shift workers. Machinery servicing and maintenance costs will probably increase.

(b) Replace the existing machines with modern machines with a higher capacity and train existing staff how to use the new machines.

Information would be gathered for each of these alternatives. In particular, management would want to know how much each option would cost. Much of the information will be financial (the effect on costs) but some important information will be non-financial in nature (e.g. the attitude of the workforce to shift working, or to using new machines).

Implement plan

A long-term plan usually communicates an organisation's objectives and how they are to be achieved over a 5–10 year period. This plan is then broken down into annual targets or budgets, and annual budgets might be broken down further into month-by-month plans and targets. The budget communicates detailed plans to managers within the organisation.

Monitoring actual results

When the plan is put into action, actual results should be monitored and compared with the targets. Managers need to know whether the targets will be achieved (or exceeded) and if not, by how much are actual results short of budget, and for what reasons.

The results obtained by the comparison of actual and budget performance are reported to management as part of a 'feedback' process.

Responses to divergences: taking control action

When actual results differ significantly from the budget or plan, a manager responsible for achieving the results should be required to take control measures. Control is an integral part of the planning cycle.

1.2 INFORMATION AND DECISION MAKING

Management need information to help them to make decisions.

- Information for planning comes from a variety of sources, both inside and outside the organisation. Information about what the organisation has achieved in the past is often a starting point for making plans for the future. For example, knowing what a process or operation has cost in the past can be very useful for estimating the likely costs in the future.

- Information for control is largely obtained from internal sources within the organisation. Managers need to know what actual results have been achieved, in order to compare what has happened so far with what had been planned, and also in order to re-think what is likely to happen in the future unless corrective measures are taken.

A large amount of management information is financial in nature, although non-financial information can be just as important. In particular, managers need to know how much activities cost, and how much it costs to make and sell the products or services that the organisation provides to its customers.

This text will look at the nature of information about costs: how it is gathered, analysed and presented to management to help them with decision making. Cost accountants or management accountants have the job of providing information to managers about costs and profits. For the purpose of this text, cost accounting and management accounting can be taken to mean the same thing, which is the provision of management information about costs and profits.

2 DATA AND INFORMATION

A distinction can be made between data and information.

- Data is a collection of unprocessed facts or opinions.

- Information is data that has been processed so that it has a purpose and meaning.

Managers need information not data. The cost accountant processes data about expenditures into meaningful figures about the costs of products, services and processes. A simple example might help to illustrate the difference between data and information.

EXAMPLE

Suppose that a departmental manager wants to know how many of the department's staff have been employed for three years or longer.

The raw data for obtaining this information would come from the employment records of each of the department's employees, which should show when the individual started in the job. This raw data would then be processed to identify how many have been employed for three years or longer, and the information presented to the departmental manager might be: '25 out of 50 of the department's employees have been in their job for over three years, representing 50% of the department's staff'.

In cost accounting, raw data consists of expenditure transactions and sales invoices, and management information consists of items such as the costs of manufacturing an item or providing a service, the profitability of a product or the cost per unit of an item, and so on.

Data has no value to management, whereas information should have a value. However, there is a cost involved in processing data into management information.

3 QUALITIES OF USEFUL MANAGEMENT INFORMATION

Information is provided to management to assist them with planning, control and decision making. Management decisions are likely to be better when they are supported by better quality information.

'Good quality' information has several characteristics.

- It should have a **purpose**, and be **relevant** for that purpose.

  There is no point in providing a manager with a report if the manager does not know why he has been given it, or what he is expected to do with it. Similarly, the information within a report should be relevant to its purpose and should not contain details that can be ignored.

- It should be **timely**. This means that it should be provided to a manager in time for the manager to do something with it. For example, suppose that a business produces monthly performance reports for its cost centres, and that in May the manager of cost centre X receives a report about actual costs incurred by the centre in January. This information would be over three months old, and the cost centre manager is likely to ignore it because it is not relevant to his current situation.

  Similarly, suppose that a senior management team want to decide on their strategy for overseas expansion, and ask for a report on market conditions in Southern Africa. If they want to make their decision in February, a report submitted in March will be of no value, because the decision will already have been taken.

- It should be **understandable**. A manager should be able to understand what the information is telling him. If he doesn't understand it, he will not use it to make a decision. If he misunderstands it, he might make a bad decision. There can be a particular problem with the use of technical language ('jargon'), and accountants should always be careful about the way in which they present financial information to non-financial managers.

- Information should be **as accurate as it needs to be**. The degree of accuracy required will depend on the reason why the information is needed. A problem in accounting can be that reports are produced showing figures to the nearest pound or dollar, when managers are only interested in figures to the nearest hundred thousand or ten thousand. On the other hand, when calculating the cost of a unit of product manufactured in a factory, managers might want the cost to be accurate to the nearest penny or cent.

- Information should be **as complete as it needs to be**, but it should **not be excessive**. Managers should be given all the information they need to make their decisions, but it is often helpful to draw their attention to what seems significant. In control reports, for example, actual results might be compared with planned results, with differences between actual and plan reported as 'variances'.

  A report that highlights the most significant information, such as the biggest variances, can help to draw management attention to what is important. Sometimes, management only want to be informed when something exceptional or out-of-the-ordinary has happened. Reporting on this basis is called **reporting by exception**.

- Information should be **communicated to the right person**. Within a business, management information should be directed to the manager or managers who can use it and do something with it. For example, information about costs and revenues should be reported to the manager responsible, who is in a position to control them. There is little value to be gained in reporting costs to a manager who has no control over them.

- Information should be **communicated by an appropriate channel**. A 'channel' of information refers to the method by which the information is given, such as verbally, in a formal report, in an informal report, by email, by electronic file transfer, and so on. It also refers to the individual or department or external organisation that provides the information.

  The appropriate channel of communication varies according to circumstances and the nature of the information. For example, it will depend on how quickly it is needed, how much information has to be communicated, how far the information has to be sent and the costs of sending it in different ways.

  Here are some examples.

Information	*Channel of communication*
A fire breaks out in the stores area.	The information must be transmitted immediately, using a fire alarm, internal and external telephone.
A cutting machine becomes badly adjusted and starts to produce components that are too short.	The machine operator must communicate verbally with his or her superior immediately. It would be wasteful to wait for the routine daily or weekly inspection.
An accounts clerk is processing petty cash vouchers from several departments that have not been properly authorised by the office manager.	The most efficient method of communicating information to several people internally, as is required in this case, is by email. However, before sending out an email, the effect on people's behaviour must be estimated. It would usually be appropriate to see people individually first in order to explain company policy.
Summary results of a subsidiary company in India need to be sent to the head office in the UK for consolidation.	A data file can be sent by email or a hard copy report could be sent by facsimile (fax).
A telephone order clerk needs to check the availability of an item of inventory before accepting a customer order.	One of the most efficient methods is to give the clerk a keyboard and screen connected to the computer system, which allows for direct interrogation of inventory levels.

3.1 THE VALUE OF INFORMATION

Another quality of good management information is that the value of the information to management should exceed the cost of producing it.

Management information has a value because it helps a manager to make decisions. If a decision by a manager is different from what it would have been without the information, the value of the information could be measured by the amount of money that has been saved as a result. The **value of information** results from actions by decision makers who use the information to improve profitability.

Here are some examples.

Reducing unnecessary costs	An investigation into the causes of unexpectedly high costs may uncover inefficiencies and wastage that can be eliminated in future. If a manager is not even informed that costs are running in excess of what they should be, he will not take any corrective action, and the excess spending will carry on.
Adopting better marketing strategies	Modern point-of-sales terminals in stores and supermarkets provide detailed analysis of sales by product. This information can be used to direct management attention to the products and store locations with the highest profit potential.
Better analysis of 'cost drivers'	With detailed information about the causes of costs and the factors which 'drive costs', more realistic budgets can be set. This in turn should result in scarce resources being applied in the most profitable way.

Information has a value as a strategic resource, and an efficient management information system can give a company a strategic advantage over its competitors. Information has no value if it is not used. Neither has it any value if it is known already (no 'surprise value'). In order to assess the value of information, the following questions can be asked:

- Who uses the information?
- What is it used for?
- How often is it used?
- How often is it provided but not used?
- What is achieved by its use?
- Are there alternatives to this source of information?

3.2 THE COST OF INFORMATION

The cost of producing information includes:

- the cost of gathering data
- the cost of processing data
- the cost of storing data and information
- the costs of providing the information
- the opportunity cost of management time.

In a business, management information systems can be very expensive, with large computer systems and databases, and large numbers of employees whose job it is to process and provide the information. These include management accountants. There might also be external costs, such as the cost of using a market research agency or a firm of management consultants.

4 SOURCES OF DATA FOR MANAGEMENT ACCOUNTING

Data for preparing management information comes from a variety of sources, both within the organisation (internal sources) and from outside the organisation (external sources).

4.1 INTERNAL SOURCES

There are many internal data sources for management accounting, not all of which are part of the accounting system. The boundaries of an accounting system are not always clearly defined, particularly in management accounting. The following internal accounting sources may be used.

Source	*Information obtainable from the data*
Sales ledger system	Number and value of invoices Volume of sales Value of sales, analysed by customer or product Receivables by age
Purchase ledger system	Number and value of invoices Value of purchases, analysed by supplier Payables by age
Payroll system	Number of employees Hours worked Time lost through sickness Wages earned Tax deducted
Records of non-current assets	Date of purchase Initial cost Location Depreciation method and rate Service history Production capacity

In addition the following internal, non-accounting sources may be used.

Source	*Information available from the data*
Production records	Machine breakdown times Output achieved Number of rejected units
Sales and marketing records	Types of customer Market research results Demand patterns, seasonal variations, etc.
Employees	Wage demands Working conditions

4.2 EXTERNAL SOURCES

In addition to the internal information sources, information can be obtained from a wide range of external sources, as illustrated below.

Source	*Information*
Suppliers	Product prices Product specifications
Newspapers, journals	Share price Information on competitors Technological developments
Government	Industry statistics Taxation policy Inflation rates
Customers	Product requirements Price sensitivity

ACTIVITY 1

Suppose that you are a manager in a general hospital.

List some of the cost information that you might want to know about and have reported to you.

For a suggested answer, see the 'Answers' section at the end of the book.

4.3 FINANCIAL AND NON-FINANCIAL INFORMATION

It should be noted that much of the data collected will be of a non-financial nature. For example, if you examine the information coming from the payroll system above we can divide this as follows:

Financial Information	*Non-Financial Information*
Wages earned	Number of employees
Tax deducted	Hours worked
	Time lost through sickness

Both elements are of equal importance to managers for their planning, control and decision making purposes.

5 COST CENTRES, PROFIT CENTRES AND INVESTMENT CENTRES

The nature of internal reporting systems will vary according to the way the organisation is structured, and the responsibilities that different managers are given. Within businesses, the focus of attention is largely on profit, and managers are held accountable for the revenues earned by their team or department, or the costs they incur.

5.1 RESPONSIBILITY ACCOUNTING

Definition **Responsibility accounting** is a system of providing financial information to management, where the structure of the reporting system is based on identifying individual parts of a business which are the responsibility of a single manager.

Definition **Responsibility centre.** A responsibility centre is an individual part of a business whose manager has personal responsibility for its performance.

Many businesses are structured into a hierarchy of responsibility centres. These might be called cost centres and revenue centres, profit centres and investment centres.

- At the 'lowest level' of structured financial reporting, there are cost centres and revenue centres. Their managers are responsible for the costs incurred by their centre or the revenues earned by the centre.
- At a higher level, there might be profit centres. Their managers are responsible for both the revenues and the costs of the centre, and so are accountable for the profit or loss the centre makes.
- At the highest level in the reporting hierarchy, there might be investment centres. In a large group of companies, an investment centre might be an entire subsidiary company, or even several subsidiary companies (a 'strategic business unit'). The manager is responsible not only for the revenues, costs and profits of the centre, but also for its capital investments and the return on investment it achieves.

5.2 COST CENTRE

Definition A **cost centre** can be defined as 'a production or service location, function, activity or item of equipment whose costs may be accumulated and attributed to cost units'.

For example, cost centres in a manufacturing company might be the machining department, the assembly department and the finishing department. Other cost centres might be order handling and despatch, stores and warehousing, and transport. Within the accounting system, the costs incurred by a cost centre are charged to that centre, so that information can be gathered about the total costs it has incurred.

The performance of a cost centre manager is judged on the extent to which cost targets have been achieved.

5.3 REVENUE CENTRE

Definition A **revenue centre** is a part of the organisation that earns sales revenue. Its manager is responsible for the revenue earned, but not for the costs of the operation.

Revenue centres are therefore generally associated with selling activities, and within a company, the sales teams under each regional sales manager might be treated as responsibility centres. Each regional manager would have sales targets to reach, and would be held responsible for the achievement of those targets.

The management information system must therefore be capable of tracing all sales revenue earned to the individual revenue centres.

5.4 PROFIT CENTRE

Definition A **profit centre** is a part of the business for which both the costs incurred and the revenues earned are identified.

The performance of a profit centre manager is measured in terms of the profit made by the centre. The profit centre performance can also be measured in terms of profit per unit, profit margins and by comparing actual profit with target profit. The manager must therefore be responsible for both costs and revenues, and in a position to plan and control both. He or she is therefore likely to have a substantial amount of authority.

Profit centres are often found in large organisations with a divisionalised structure, and each division is treated as a profit centre. Within each profit centre, there could be several cost centres and revenue centres.

When a business has a profit centre structure, data for revenues and costs must be collected and attributed to the appropriate profit centres. This data is then used to measure profit trends, profit per unit, profit margins and to compare actual profit with target profit.

5.5 INVESTMENT CENTRE

Definition The CIMA *Official Terminology* defines an **investment centre** as 'a profit centre with additional responsibilities for capital investment and possibly for financing, and whose performance is measured by its return on investment'.

An investment centre might include several profit centres.

Managers of investment centres are responsible not just for decisions affecting revenues and costs, but also for investment decisions. They should therefore be accountable not just for profits, but also for the performance of the capital invested. Performance is measured in terms of the profit relative to the level of investment. In its simplest form, this means monitoring return on capital employed (ROCE).

$$\text{ROCE} = \frac{\text{Profit}}{\text{Capital employed}}$$

To operate an investment centre system, it is necessary to collect data to provide information on costs, revenues and amounts invested (assets less liabilities).

EXAMPLE

An investment centre has recorded the following information:

	20X5 ($000)	*20X6* ($000)
Profit	180	234
Capital employed	1,000	1,200
Sales	2,000	2,400

The performance of the investment centre can be measured by calculating the ROCE and the secondary ratios, net profit margin and asset turnover.

	20X5		*20X6*	
ROCE	$\frac{180}{1,000}$	= 18%	$\frac{234}{1,200}$	= 19.5%
Net profit margin	$\frac{180}{2,000}$	= 9%	$\frac{234}{2,400}$	= 9.75%
Asset turnover	$\frac{2,000}{1,000}$	= 2	$\frac{2,400}{1,200}$	= 2

The return earned by the investment centre has increased from 18% to 19.5%. This has been achieved by increasing the net profit margin from 9% to 9.75%, either by increasing sales or by reducing costs. The asset turnover has remained the same at 2, which means that the same sales are being generated for each $ of capital employed.

Overall performance could be compared with other similar investment centres.

5.6 THE LINK BETWEEN ROCE, NET PROFIT MARGIN AND ASSET TURNOVER

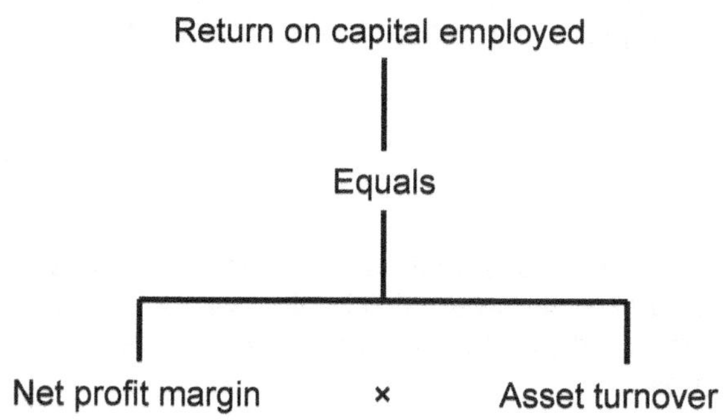

ROCE = net profit margin × asset turnover

For example, we can calculate the ROCEs using the information in the previous paragraph as follows:

20X5 ROCE = 9% × 2 = 18% (as calculated above).

20X6 ROCE = 9.75% × 2 = 19.5% (as calculated above).

5.7 THE IMPACT OF RESPONSIBILITY ACCOUNTING ON MANAGEMENT INFORMATION AND APPRAISAL

The way in which an organisation is structured, into a hierarchy of cost centres and revenue centres, profit centres and investment centres, affects the nature of management reporting. Data has to be gathered and information provided to management that will enable managers to plan and control their area of the business, and the activities for which they are responsible.

In addition, managers will recognise that their performance as a manager will be assessed in terms of costs, revenues, profits or returns on investment for their centre. Individual managers will therefore be likely to take whatever decisions seem appropriate to optimise the results of their centre.

6 IT AND MANAGEMENT ACCOUNTING

Computer technology has transformed management information systems. Many years ago, when computers were comparatively slow and with limited storage capacity, there were severe limitations to the quantity of data that could be collected, stored and analysed. Computers were able to produce regular reports, such as monthly budget performance reports, but it was difficult for managers to interrogate a system on-line and extract up-to-date information.

Today, businesses can develop information systems with enormous processing and storage capacity, providing access to vast stores of internal and external data (e.g. through the Internet). The challenge, however, is to produce information systems that:

- are designed to provide the information that managers need, both in routine reports and through ad hoc enquiries
- provide information that has value in excess of the cost of providing it.

Small businesses might limit themselves to simple systems, to avoid the cost.

6.1 FEATURES OF IT SYSTEMS

Several features of IT systems are worth noting, in the context of management information systems.

- **Data collection**. In many businesses, data can be collected electronically, which means that large volumes of data can be gathered for analysis. For example, in stores and supermarkets, point of sale (POS) systems gather data about the goods that customers purchase, mainly through bar code readers. This data is stored and analysed to provide management with information about sales volumes for each product, for each group of products, for each storage shelf in the store or for each day and for each part of each day. This can be used to analyse customer buying patterns and preferences, and to calculate the profitability of each product sold.
- **Data files**. Computer systems can have a vast storage capacity, which means that large quantities of data can be held at a relatively small cost. With database systems, data can be structured and organised so as to make it readily accessible. Data mining techniques might also be used to extract more information from databases.

- **Speed of communication and networks**. Data can be transmitted quickly to remote locations. The Internet and more particularly business intranet systems, allow managers to access business data from a laptop computer anywhere in the world. Managers can have constant access to information.

- **Processing capability**. Data can be processed quickly. Managers with on-line access to the information systems of their business might therefore be able to ask for and obtain instant 'ad hoc' information for planning, control or ad hoc decision making purposes.

- **Computer software**. Managers have access to a wide range of software for processing data and preparing management information. In particular, spreadsheet software is used extensively for planning and forecasting. Software packages are also available for financial accounting, stores control, statistical forecasting and so on.

7 THE ROLE OF THE TRAINEE ACCOUNTANT

As part of the cost accounting team, the trainee accountant is likely to be involved in gathering and processing data to measure the costs of an organisation's activities, products or services. For example, in a manufacturing business, the trainee accountant could be involved in measuring and analysing:

- the cost of raw materials used in product manufacture
- the value of raw materials inventory
- the valuation of work-in-progress and finished goods – in other words, what are the costs of production;
- the costs of the labour used/employed in each period
- the costs of other expenses in the period
- overhead costs for each cost centre
- overhead absorption rates
- the total cost of each type of product made by the business
- the cost per unit sold
- the profitability of each product.

CONCLUSION

Measuring costs and revenues is an important first step in providing management with information to assist them with planning and control decisions. A variety of costing methods and techniques are described in the following chapters.

KEY TERMS

Responsibility accounting – a system of providing financial information to management, where the structure of the reporting system is based on identifying individual parts of a business which are the responsibility of a single manager.

Responsibility centre – an individual part of a business whose manager has personal responsibility for its performance.

Cost centre – a location, function, activity or item of equipment for which costs are accumulated and attributed to cost units.

Profit centre – a part of the business for which both the costs incurred and revenues earned are identified.

Investment centre – a profit centre which is also responsible for capital investment.

SELF TEST QUESTIONS

		Paragraph
1	What is the purpose of management information?	1.2
2	What is the difference between data and information?	2
3	List six qualities of good information.	3, 3.1
4	Define responsibility accounting.	5.1
5	Define a cost centre.	5.2
6	Define a profit centre.	5.4
7	Define an investment centre.	5.5

EXAM-STYLE QUESTIONS

1 A profit centre is:

A the profit attributable to a business unit

B a business unit whose manager is responsible for operating costs and revenues from the activities of the unit

C a unit of product or a service for which costs and revenues are measured

D a business unit whose manager is responsible for investment decisions within the unit.

2 Which of the following is always a desirable quality of information?

A Instant availability

B Complete accuracy

C Brevity

D Understandability

3 Which of the following is an example of data?

A A graph showing sales by product for the previous year

B A list of employees of an organisation

C A report showing the percentage of rejects by machine

D A table showing inflation projections by business sector

4 Information should be produced if:

(i) Its cost exceeds its value

(ii) It is relevant and timely

(iii) It has always been produced

Which of the above statements are true?

A (ii) only

B (ii) and (iii)

C (i) and (iii)

D All of them

For the answers to these questions, see the 'Answers' section at the end of the book.

Chapter 2

COST ACCOUNTING SYSTEMS

This chapter explains the framework for a cost accounting system, and how data is captured and processed to produce information about costs for management. The features of a cost accounting system outlined in this chapter will be explained in more detail in subsequent chapters. This chapter covers syllabus area A2.

CONTENTS

LEARNING OUTCOMES

At the end of this chapter you should be able to:

- explain the relationship between the cost/management accounting system and the financial accounting/management information systems (including interlocking and integrated bookkeeping systems)
- describe the process of accounting for input costs and relating them to work done
- identify the documentation required, and the flow of documentation, for different cost accounting transactions
- explain and illustrate the use of codes in categorising and processing transactions, and the importance of correct coding (including sequential, hierarchical, block, faceted and mnemonic coding methods)
- explain and illustrate the concept of cost units
- describe the different methods of costing final outputs and their appropriateness to different types of business organisation
- describe methods of capturing, processing, storing and outputting cost and management accounting data by computer.

1 A COST ACCOUNTING SYSTEM

Definition A **cost accounting system** is a system used by an organisation to gather, store and analyse cost data. The purpose of a cost accounting system is to provide management information about costs and profits.

A cost accounting system is often the basis for a management accounting system. The terms 'cost accounting' and 'management accounting' are often used to mean the same thing, although strictly there are some differences.

- A cost accounting system is concerned with gathering internal data about costs and revenues, whereas a management accounting system is also concerned with gathering and analysing data from external sources.
- A cost accounting system is concerned mainly with measuring actual costs and revenues, whereas a management accounting system is also concerned with providing management with forward-looking estimates and predictions.
- A cost accounting system is often based on a system of double-entry ledger accounting, whereas a management accounting system can exist without a cost ledger.

1.1 COST ACCOUNTING AND FINANCIAL ACCOUNTING SYSTEMS

Financial accounting systems have a nominal ledger, sales ledger and purchase ledger, and books of prime entry for recording transaction data before entering the data in the ledger accounts.

The cost ledger is either integrated with the nominal ledger system or supplementary to the nominal ledger system.

Definition **Integrated accounts** are a set of accounting records which provides both financial and cost accounts using a common input of data for all accounting purposes. (*CIMA, Official Terminology*)

Definition **Interlocking accounts** are a system in which the cost accounts are distinct from the financial accounts, the two sets of accounts being kept continuously in agreement by the use of control accounts or reconciled by other means. (*CIMA, Official Terminology*)

- The nominal ledger in a financial accounting system contains accounts for assets, liabilities, owners' capital, income and expenses.
- The cost ledger in a cost accounting system contains accounts for recording input elements of cost and building up the cost of items produced and sold by the organisation.

The accounts in the cost ledger take the information from the nominal ledger, and analyse it into greater detail in order to establish the costs of products, services or processes.

1.2 THE FINANCIAL LEDGER CONTROL ACCOUNT

An interlocking system will mean that there are two systems running in parallel – the financial ledger (which will be used to prepare the financial accounts) and the cost ledger (which will be used to provide more detail than the simple costing information recorded in the financial ledger). In an interlocking system only costing information is recorded – items such as revenue, payments to suppliers, bank and cash transactions etc. that would normally be recorded in a financial ledger system are not necessary in the costing system. This means that there will be no accounts in the costing system for elements such as receivables and payables, for example.

In the cost ledger the accountant will therefore create a financial ledger control account. This will act as the other part of the double entry for accounts that are not maintained in the cost ledger control account. So, for example, in an integrated system when materials are purchased for cash the double entry would be to debit the stores ledger control account and credit the cash account. But because a cash account is not maintained in an interlocking system the double entry would be to debit the stores ledger control account and to credit the financial ledger control account. Likewise, when wages are paid to staff the double entry would be to debit the wages control account and credit the financial ledger control account.

This means that the financial ledger control account represents all of the transactions that would normally have been made to other accounts (such as bank, payables, receivables and cash accounts) in an integrated accounting system. The account works to record the missing double entry when there is no account in the cost ledger system. It may also be called the cost ledger control account.

1.3 DIRECT COSTS AND INDIRECT COSTS

Cost accounting systems make a distinction between direct costs and indirect costs. A direct cost is an item of cost that is directly attributable to a particular cost unit, such as a particular product, service or job. An indirect cost is an item of expense that cannot be attributed directly to a specific cost unit. Indirect costs are known as **overheads**.

Overhead costs within a manufacturing organisation are commonly categorised into:

- **production overheads**, which are indirect costs relating to production activities
- **administration overheads**, which are indirect costs relating to general administration activities
- **selling and distribution overheads**, which are indirect costs relating to selling, marketing and distribution activities.

Overhead costs in a service organisation may also be categorised into functional elements in a similar way.

We will be looking at direct costs and indirect costs in more detail in the next chapter.

1.4 THE PROCESS OF ACCOUNTING FOR INPUT COSTS

Materials costs, labour costs and other expenses

There are three basic components of cost:

- materials costs
- labour costs
- other expenses.

In a cost accounting system, **transactions involving materials costs** are recorded in a **stores ledger control account**. These transactions are mainly the purchase of stores items and the issue of materials to various departments within the organisation. The stores ledger control account also records the value of opening inventory and closing inventory of materials at the beginning and end of each period. Inventory may be raw materials in a manufacturing environment or material inputs in a service environment.

Transactions involving labour costs are recorded in a **wages and salaries control account**. This account records the total cost of wages and salaries, and is used to charge these costs to different departments, as either direct labour costs or indirect labour costs (overheads).

If we assume for simplicity that all other expenses are treated as indirect costs or overheads, **transactions involving other expenses** are recorded in an overhead costs account.

Building up costs of final outputs

There are also accounts within a cost ledger for building up the costs of production and the cost of sales of the products manufactured or jobs carried out for customers. The accounts that are used to do this are:

- the **work-in-progress account**, which records the costs of items manufactured. The account records costs in total, but the costs might be broken down into the costs of individual jobs or processes or the costs of individual products. The opening balance and closing balance on this account at the start and end of a period represent the total cost of unfinished production

- the **finished goods account**, which records the cost of finished production that has not yet been sold to a customer

- the **cost of sales account**, which records the cost of finished production that has been sold to customers.

Similar accounts may be used to collect the cost of providing a service but there will be no finished goods account as it is not possible to hold inventory of finished services.

1.5 THE MAIN ACCOUNTS IN THE COST LEDGER

To understand a cost accounting system, you need to be familiar with the principles of double entry bookkeeping. The following example illustrates how the double entry in a cost ledger would be carried out. Work through this to gain an overview of the approach and revisit this example after studying Chapters 3 to 8 which give you more detail on each individual account.

EXAMPLE

Note that this example is longer than any question that could be asked for in an exam. But it should explain all the possible entries that you could be asked to make.

A company has the following information:

Opening balances of:	Raw materials	$2,000
	Work-in-progress	$1,500
	Finished goods	$8,000
Transactions recorded in the period		
Material purchases		$40,000
Direct materials issued to production		$21,000
Indirect materials issued to production		$3,000
Indirect materials issued to administration		$6,000
Indirect materials issued to selling		$5,000
Gross wages		$30,000
Of which direct wages are		$11,000
Indirect wages in production are		$7,000
Indirect wages in administration are		$4,000
Indirect wages in selling are		$8,000
Indirect production expenses		$7,500
Indirect administration expenses		$10,000
Indirect selling expenses		$3,000
Overheads charged to production		$17,500
Production completed		$49,000
Production cost of goods sold		$52,000

This information can be used to prepare the cost accounts.

The main accounts in the cost ledger are illustrated below. There are different types of account.

- Asset accounts such as the stores ledger control account, work-in-progress (WIP) account and finished goods account. These record the transactions relating to raw materials, partly finished goods and completed goods in a period. Often there is inventory of raw materials, partly finished goods and finished goods at the end of a period which results in a closing balance and a corresponding opening balance for the beginning of the next period. In our example you can see the opening balances recorded on the debit side of the accounts. Once all of the other transactions for the period have been recorded in these accounts, the closing balance can be calculated as a balancing figure on the credit side.

- Expense accounts such as wages and overheads accounts. The stores ledger control account also records any purchases of raw materials in the period. Total costs for the period are debited to these accounts. The costs are then analysed according to whether they are direct or indirect costs. Direct costs are transferred to the WIP account and indirect costs are passed to the relevant overhead accounts. Normally you would not expect to see a closing balance on a wages account as all of the labour costs incurred are allocated in the period. In our example you can see the costs incurred in the period debited to the stores, wages and overhead accounts. The analysis into direct and indirect costs and the resulting accounting treatment will be covered in more detail in later chapters.

In the example you can see that the WIP account collects all of the costs relating to the production of the cost units in the period. As the goods are completed the value of the finished goods is credited to the WIP account and debited to the finished goods account.

The cost of goods sold is then credited to the finished goods account and debited to the cost of sales account.

Stores ledger control account

	$		$
Opening inventory	2,000	Work-in-progress	21,000
Material purchases*	40,000	*(Direct materials issued to production)*	
		Production overheads	3,000
		Admin overheads	6,000
		Selling/dist'n overheads	5,000
		(Indirect materials consumed)	
		Closing inventory	7,000
		(Balancing figure)	
	42,000		42,000

Wages and salaries control account

	$		$
Gross wages paid*	30,000	Work-in-progress	11,000
(*Total wages and salaries costs*)		*(Direct wages costs)*	
		Production overheads	7,000
		Admin overheads	4,000
		Selling/dist'n overheads	8,000
		(Indirect labour costs)	
	30,000		30,000

Production overheads account

	$		$
OVERHEADS INCURRED		OVERHEADS ABSORBED TO PRODUCTION**	
Stores ledger control account	3,000	Work-in-progress	17,500
(*Indirect production materials costs)*			
Wages and salaries control	7,000		
(Indirect production labour costs)			
Other indirect expenses*	7,500		
	17,500		17,500

****Note:** As we shall see in a later chapter, the total amount of overheads absorbed or charged to production is often different from the total amount of overhead costs actually incurred, and there are under-absorbed or over-absorbed overhead costs.

Administration overheads account

	$		$
Stores ledger control account *(Indirect materials costs)*	6,000	Statement of profit or loss	20,000
Wages and salaries control *(Admin labour costs)*	4,000		
Indirect admin expenses*	10,000		
	20,000		20,000

Selling and distribution overheads account

	$		$
Stores ledger control account *(Indirect materials costs)*	5,000	Statement of profit or loss	16,000
Wages and salaries control *(Sales and distribution labour costs)*	8,000		
Indirect selling expenses*	3,000		
	16,000		16,000

Work-in-progress (WIP) account

	$		$
Opening inventory *(Unfinished production)*	1,500	Finished goods *(Production completed)*	49,000
Stores ledger control account *(Direct materials costs)*	21,000		
Wages and salaries control *(Direct labour costs)*	11,000		
Production overhead account *(Indirect production costs)*	17,500	Closing inventory *(Unfinished production – Balancing figure)*	2,000
	51,000		51,000

Finished goods account

	$		$
Opening inventory *(Unsold finished production)*	8,000	Cost of sales *(Production cost of finished goods sold in the period)*	52,000
Work-in-progress *(Production completed in the period)*	49,000	Closing inventory *(Unsold finished production – Balancing figure)*	5,000
	57,000		57,000

Cost of sales account

	$		$
Finished goods *(Production cost of finished goods sold in the period)*	52,000	Statement of profit or loss	52,000
	52,000		52,000

***Note:** In an interlocking system the other entry for these entries would be in the financial ledger control account.

2 DOCUMENTATION FOR THE SOURCE DATA

The details of costs incurred are obtained from source data and recorded in the costing system. The nature of the source documentation used varies between organisations. Source documents include:

Cost incurred	**Documents**	**Reason for the document**
For materials purchased	Goods received note Purchase invoice	Confirming receipt into stores Details of purchase costs
For materials used	Materials requisition note Job cost card	For materials issued to a particular department To record materials used in a particular job
Expenses	Purchase invoices	
Costs of production	Job cost cards Production analysis sheets	
Labour costs	Payroll records Job cost cards Job sheets/ job time cards	Total labour costs, analysed between departments Details of labour time/costs on particular jobs Details of time spent on different activities and costs of the time spent

Source documents will be described in more detail in later chapters.

3 COST UNITS

3.1 COST UNITS

Definition A **cost unit** is a unit of production or a unit of activity in relation to which a cost is measured. In other words, a cost unit is an item for which an output cost or an activity cost is measured.

Cost units are measured for several reasons:

- to establish how much it has cost to produce an item or perform an activity
- to measure the profit or loss on the item
- to value closing inventories of the item

- to compare actual costs of the item with budgeted costs
- to plan future costs, by basing future costs on historical costs
- to decide on a selling price for the item, where the selling price is derived by a 'cost plus' formula
- to monitor changes in costs over time.

In a manufacturing business, the cost units that are used will depend on the nature of the manufacturing process.

- When the firm manufactures different products or standardised batches, the cost unit will be a unit of the product, and each product will have a different cost unit.
- When a firm carries out jobs, batches or contracts for customers, the cost unit will be the cost of each specific job, batch or contract.

With service industries, or for measuring the cost of activities, cost units will vary according to the nature of the work. Here are some examples:

Activity	*Cost unit*
Road haulage	Tonne-mile delivered
Passenger transport	Passenger-mile
Canteen services	Meal
Hospital services (in-patient services)	Patient-day
Hotel accommodation	Guest-night
Electricity generation	Kilowatt hour generated

An average cost per unit can be calculated by dividing the total costs by the total number of units. Cost units for service industries are often composite measures, and can be difficult to identify.

4 RECORDING AND CODING OF COSTS

4.1 RECORDING COSTS

When costs are recorded, analysed and reported to management, it is important that costs should be reported to the managers or departments responsible for the spending. In other words, the reporting of cost information should ideally be based on a system of responsibility accounting and responsibility centres.

- Direct material costs can be charged directly to the production department or the job that uses the materials.
- Similarly, direct labour costs can be charged directly to the production department or the job where the work is carried out.
- Overheads, which cannot be traced directly to an output product or job, can be traced directly to a department or unit of the organisation. In other words, indirect costs can be traced to responsibility centres within the organisation.

When costs are recorded in a cost accounting system, it should therefore be possible to identify the cost with a particular production department, product, job, process or responsibility centre. Having recorded costs in this way, the process of measuring and reporting costs of output can begin.

4.2 COST CODES

When an organisation operates a cost accounting system, the system is likely to be computer-based. Transactions are recorded by input to a computerised cost accounting system (which is usually integrated with the financial accounting system). To simplify the process of entering data into the system, and subsequently analysing output costs, coding systems will be used.

Definition A **code** is a system of symbols designed for application to a classified set of items, to give a brief accurate reference. Codes facilitate the entry of data to a system, and the collation and analysis of the data.

Cost codes are used in a costing system.

4.3 CODING SYSTEMS

There are many ways to cost codes. Here are some of the more popular methods:

Sequential Code

This is the most basic type of code. It simply means that each code follows a numerical or alphabetical sequence. Planning is needed to determine how many codes might be needed in total.

For example, let's assume we are making a coding list for different types of expenses. We could give our first category, say Motor Expenses, code 001. Our next type of expense, say Electricity, would get code 002. Each expense would then follow in sequence. This allows us to have as many as 999 different types of expenses as we are using a three digit sequential code.

Block Code

Block codes are often used to categorise sequential codes together. For example, an accounting system might have the following block codes:

0000 – Expenses

1000 – Revenue

2000 – Non-current assets

3000 – Current assets

4000 – Long term liabilities

5000 – Equity

The 3000 'Block' is allocated to Current assets. This means that it is possible to classify up to 1,000 different current assets (such as different types of inventories and bank accounts) using this block.

Hierarchical Code

This text uses a hierarchical code. Each section is given a number and each sub-section is given an added decimal number. For example, we have seen

1 A COST ACCOUNTING SYSTEM

- 1.1 COST ACCOUNTING AND FINANCIAL ACCOUNTING SYSTEMS
- 1.2 DIRECT COSTS AND INDIRECT COSTS
- 1.3 THE PROCESS OF ACCOUNTING FOR INPUT COSTS
- 1.4 THE MAIN ACCOUNTS IN THE COST LEDGER

This allows for infinite expandability. For example, if we decided to further sub-divide section 1.2 we might get the following:

- 1.2 DIRECT COSTS AND INDIRECT COSTS
  - 1.2.1 DIRECT COSTS
  - 1.2.2 INDIRECT COSTS

Each sub-category simply gets a further decimal coding.

Faceted Code

A faceted code is one that is broken down into a number of facets or fields, each of which signifies a unit of information.

Consider the following simplified table which has been extracted as a sample from the faceted code used by a large international manufacturer:

Code	Region	Code	Department	Code	Expense
01	Europe	01	Sales	0244	Salaries
02	Asia	02	Production	0245	National insurance
03	USA	03	Personnel and Finance	0246	Pension contributions
04	Africa	04	Administration	0247	Bonuses

In this example, there are three facets, or fields, to the code:

Facet 1 is the region, and is 2 digits long

Facet 2 is the department, and is 2 digits long

Facet 3 is the type of expense, and is 4 digits long

If we wanted to post an expense for a bonus paid to the production department of the USA region, the code would be:

03020247

That is: 03 (for USA), 02 (for Production) and 0247 (for Bonuses).

It can be seen that a faceted system is a complicated one and requires lots of training and possibly a table such as the one above to be used for interpretation of codes. But it does allow for more sub-divisions and a greater number of codes.

Mnemonic Code

Mnemonic means something that aids the memory or understanding. This uses an alphabetical coding rather than a numerical coding system. It is often used to abbreviate or simplify information. For example, in accounting we might use:

Code	Meaning
NCA	Non-current assets
EXP	Expenses
REV	Revenue

Mnemonic codes are a way of quickly expressing information and making that information easily understood. However, this coding method makes it very difficult to use sub-categories or to have too much information. Mnemonic coding is likely to struggle to categorise 999 different types of expenses, for example.

Conclusion A **cost code** is designed to analyse and classify the costs of an organisation in the most appropriate manner for that organisation. There are no set methods of designing a cost code and the cost code of a particular organisation will be that which best suits the operations and costs of that business.

ACTIVITY 1

Suppose that a cost coding system is such that the first two letters of the code represent the cost centre, the third letter the type of expense and the fourth letter the detail of the expense.

Codes are as follows:

S Salesman's expenses

ED Eastern Division

P Petrol

Code an Eastern Division's salesman's petrol expenses.

For a suggested answer, see the 'Answers' section at the end of the book.

4.4 PURPOSE OF COST CODES

The main purposes of cost codes are to:

(a) assist precise information: costs incurred can be associated with pre-established codes, so reducing variations in classification

(b) facilitate electronic data processing: computer analysis, summarisation and presentation of data can be performed more easily through the medium of codes

(c) facilitate a logical and systematic arrangement of costing records: accounts can be arranged in blocks of codes permitting additional codes to be inserted in logical order

(d) simplify comparison of totals of similar expenses rather than all of the individual items

(e) incorporate check codes within the main code to check the accuracy of the postings.

ACTIVITY 2

The following is a short extract from an organisation's code structure.

Cost centres	*Code*
Factory	
Machine shop A	301
Machine shop B	302
Boiler house	303
Etc.	
Administration	
Accounts department	401
Secretary	402
Security officers	403
Etc.	
Selling	
South area	501
North area	502
East area	503
Etc.	
Type of expense	
Materials	
Machine lubricants	001
Cleaning supplies	002
Stationery	003
Etc.	
Wages	
Supervisor's salary	051
Cleaning wages	052
Etc.	
Expenses	
Depreciation of machinery	071
Insurance of machinery	072
Etc.	

How would the following items be coded?

(a) A stores requisition for an issue of machine lubricant to machine shop B.

(b) The salary of an East area sales supervisor.

(c) The depreciation expense for the machine shop A machinery.

For a suggested answer, see the 'Answers' section at the end of the book.

5 COMPUTER SYSTEMS AND COST ACCOUNTING

5.1 INTRODUCTION

Cost accounting data is likely to be collected, processed and analysed using computer systems. The main elements of computer systems are:

- hardware
- software, and
- in many cases, communications links, including links to the Internet.

5.2 HARDWARE

The term 'hardware' is used to describe the equipment in a computer system, including the computer itself.

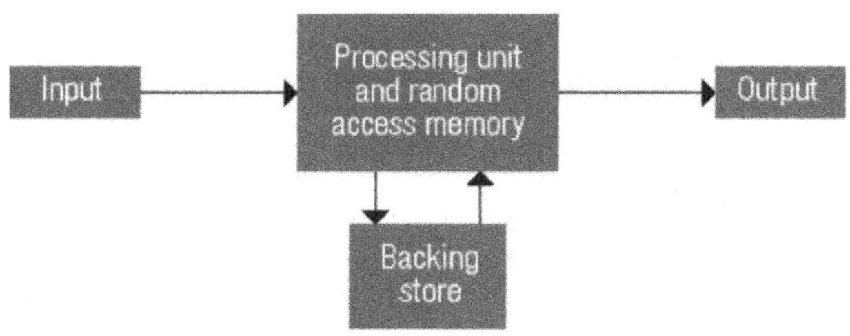

The diagram shown above can represent all computers. Data is entered through input devices, or data may be used from the backing store, and output is produced. Records on the backing store may also be updated.

Peripherals are hardware devices other than processors or networks. The term peripherals commonly refers to input, output and communication hardware. Some of these devices are covered below.

5.3 INPUT DEVICES

Examples of input hardware devices include keyboard and mouse, bar code reader, touch screen, optical mark reading, optical character recognition and a scanner.

You may be familiar with many of these devices and how they may be used to capture management accounting data.

Keyboard and mouse

A keyboard and mouse are commonly used input devices in office systems, in conjunction with visual display screens (VDUs). Many office workers, including managers, have a personal computer (PC) or other terminal on their desk top, with keyboard and mouse (or tracker ball) and the VDU for input and output.

Using a mouse is usually quicker than a keyboard, and input errors are fewer, when the computer system provides a **graphical user interface** (GUI) such as Windows.

However, both keyboard input and input with a mouse are slow methods of input, since they are dependent on the speed of the human operator. They are inappropriate input devices for high volume, high-speed automated processing systems and, where possible, faster input methods should be preferred.

Bar code reader

A bar code is a pattern of black and white stripes representing a code, often an inventory item code.

The code is read by a scanner or light pen, which converts the bar code image into an electronic form acceptable to the computer. Bar codes are used widely at checkout points in supermarkets and shops (**point of sale systems** or **POS systems**). They allow the point of sale system to recognise the item being purchased and to add its price to the customer's total bill. They speed up the checkout process and reduce the risk of input error by the checkout clerk.

A Quick Response (QR) code is similar to a bar code. It is a machine-readable code consisting of an array of black and white squares, typically used for storing data for reading by a camera on a smartphone or similar device. QR codes can store over 200 more lines of data than a bar code.

QR codes are used for many things such as storing the details of a passenger on an airline boarding pass.

Touch screen

A touch screen is another form of point of sale device, which might be used in a cafeteria or restaurant. The screen displays a range of items that are available for sale, and the salesperson inputs the customer's order by touching the appropriate icon with a finger. The screen recognises the instruction and converts it into an electronic command for the computer.

Optical mark reading (OMR)

Optical mark reading (OMR) involves making marks, usually with a pencil or pen, on a standard document. The document is then read by an optical mark reader, and the positioning of the mark or marks on the document can be interpreted as data for processing by the computer.

Optical character recognition (OCR)

With optical character recognition (OCR), a reader can recognise hand-written characters from their shape, and convert them into electronic data format. OCR applications have included meter reading forms for electricity and gas meters.

Scanner

A scanner is a device that can read any form of image and convert it into an electronic form for acceptance by a computer system. Scanners can therefore be used to input diagrams and pictures, signatures and other visual images, as well as images of text.

5.4 OUTPUT DEVICES

Output from a computer system is often stored, in which case the output is transferred to a storage device. The other most common forms of output are printer and VDU screen.

Printers

Different types of printer are available. The most commonly used are now either:

- ink-jet printers for smaller computers and low-volume output, and
- laser printers, which are capable of faster output and so can handle much higher print volumes, with high print quality.

Printers can be used for the output of diagrams and pictures as well as text, and have widespread applications in business. In some computer systems, output can be printed on the standard pre-printed stationery, to produce documents such as sales invoices and statements.

VDU screen

Output to a VDU screen is temporary, whereas printed output is more permanent. However, many computer systems rely on output to VDU, where the computer user can simply read the information provided. There are many examples of VDU output, but examples are:

- email messages, which can be printed out but are more usually read on screen
- customer service centres, where customer sales orders and queries by telephone can be handled by a customer service representative with access to central computer records through keyboard, mouse and VDU screen.

Other output devices

The other most commonly used output devices are for storing data in electronic form, and include DVDs and external storage devices (explained in the next section).

5.5 STORAGE DEVICES

Storage devices are devices for holding data or information (and programs) in electronic form. They are used for both input of data into a computer system and for output of data and information for storage. A distinction is made between:

Internal storage

Data and programs can be stored in the internal RAM of the computer, or in a hard disk.

RAM (random access memory) is volatile memory (i.e. the contents are lost when the computer is turned off) but it is accessible directly by the computer.

ROM (read-only memory) is non-volatile memory (i.e. the contents are not lost when the computer is turned off). ROM is a memory chip which has data permanently written onto it, hence its name (read-only memory). New data cannot be written into this memory and the original data cannot be changed.

Hard disks provide the permanent storage in a computer. The contents of memory remain intact without the need for power supply, but there is a small time delay involved in accessing data and files stored on the disks. DVDs can also provide disk storage, although DVD drives are needed to read and write to this storage medium.

External storage

The main types of external storage are USB flash drives, discs, flash memory cards and external hard drives.

Storage capacity is measured in bytes. A byte is a unit of eight binary digits or bits, and can be used to represent one character (one number, one letter or one punctuation mark, etc).

A kilobyte (kb) is about 1,000 bytes (it is actually 1,024 bytes).

A megabyte (mb) is about 1,000,000 bytes (it is actually 1,024 × 1,024 bytes).

A gigabyte (gb) is about 1,000 megabytes.

A terabyte (tb) is about 1,000 gigabytes.

Different devices will be able to store more data. A dvd disc can, for example, only hold 4.7gb of data whilst external hard drives can often hold two or three tbs.

5.6 THE CENTRAL PROCESSING UNIT (CPU)

The central processing unit (CPU) is the computer itself. It consists of several component elements:

- a control unit, which supervises and co-ordinates all the computer's processing, in accordance with its programmed instructions
- an arithmetic and logic unit, which carries out mathematical computations and logic tests on data
- internal storage or memory.

The central computer must have a small amount of ROM and some RAM. It will also have some instantly accessible permanent storage, commonly referred to as the **hard drive**.

The CPU controls all the input, output and storage devices of the computer, holds the program that is currently being worked on and executes the program instructions.

5.7 OPERATING SYSTEMS SOFTWARE

The operating system is the most important piece of software in any computer system, as without it the system will not work at all. It consists of a number of tools to allow the following functions:

- communication between the operator and the computer
- control of the processor and storage hardware
- the management of files
- the use of peripherals such as printers and modems.

When the computer is multi-tasking, and running several application programs simultaneously, the operating system allocates internal storage space to each application, chooses which programs should be run in which order of priority and decides how much CPU time to give to each application.

There are many different types of operating systems, the most commonly used are:

- Windows, created by Microsoft, which has a commonly used interface which allows a reduction in the amount of training required to use the system, and prevents the selection of invalid or unreasonable options or instructions.
- macOS created by Apple which allows much easier integration between computer and mobile hardware (such as cell phones)
- Android created by Google which was initially created for mobile devices but is now available on Chromebook laptops

5.8 APPLICATIONS SOFTWARE

Many computer users have the same applications. For example, any business has to have systems for word processing, payroll, sales ledger, bought ledger and inventory control. Very often the requirements for these applications are similar for a wide range of companies. An application package is a standard program, or suite of programs, designed to perform a specific task. It saves users from having to develop application programs that are essentially the same as those already developed.

Examples of applications software include spreadsheets, word processing, databases, accounting and communications packages.

Integrated packages

Some programs, or packages of programs, can perform more than one task e.g. office administration packages that comprise word processing, creating and using a database, spreadsheets and business graphics. These are called integrated packages because they bring these varied tasks together. Examples of integrated software packages include Microsoft Office® and AppleWorks®. The applications will have a common user interface and will be designed to work easily together (for example, data from a spreadsheet can be easily brought into a presentation document).

Accounting packages

At their simplest level, accounts packages can be considered as electronic ledgers, with the routine transactions recorded on a computer system, rather than on paper, and the general principles of double entry bookkeeping being incorporated in the software.

There are many advantages in computerising an accounts system e.g. the software package **Sage Instant Accounts®** includes sales invoicing, inventory control and report generation, as well as the basic sales, purchase and nominal ledgers. The format of invoices can be set by the user as pre-printed forms and other features that can be expected from even the simplest packages would include some form of security and auditing controls. More advanced, and more expensive, packages would be expected to provide such options as payroll, multiple currency accounts, and cheque production facilities with integrated word processors and spreadsheets so that information can be used anywhere in the system and incorporated into financial modelling routines and reports or letters as required.

Desk Top Publishing (DTP)

DTP packages such as CorelDraw® and InDesign® are popular as they let a user combine text and art to present reports in a much more professional-looking way. Applications for a DTP package include:

- output of financial reports, incorporating the use of high quality graphics
- the preparation of financial accounts that requires a high quality of printout
- reports used in consultancy work, which may incorporate graphs, charts, etc.

5.9 COMPUTER COMMUNICATIONS

Where an organisation has several locations, it may be more effective to process data locally rather than at one central installation. By doing this, individual managers will be able to schedule their own processing and will have more control over the contents of their database systems. Any system that requires computers to communicate with each other will need specialised hardware and software such as:

- modems
- communication programs
- local area networks (LANs).

The modem is the interface between the computer and the telephone system. In addition communications software is needed to handle the communications process.

Communication through a modem uses the public telecommunications system. This may be unnecessarily elaborate for an organisation that simply needs its own computers to be able to communicate with each other or to share a piece of expensive hardware. In these circumstances, a local area network (or LAN) may be more suitable. This consists of a circuit, which connects the computers to each other and contains the hardware needed for efficient communication (often in the form of expansion cards that plug directly into the computers' circuitry), and software to run the network.

5.10 INTERNET AND OTHER FORMS OF COMMUNICATION

Access to the Internet is invaluable for many businesses.

Information can be obtained from other organisations quickly. Examples of external information include published financial information by companies (and other investor information), government guidelines and statistics and information about the products and services of other suppliers and competitors.

An organisation can provide information about itself on its own website, including information about its products or services. Customers might be able to place orders via the Internet and even pay for the order. E-commerce, a term for buying and selling via the Internet, continues to grow rapidly.

Intranets

An intranet is a 'private' computer network operated by an organisation, usually consisting of several local area networks linked to each other by telecommunications links and in which one or more Internet servers provide a link between the network and the Internet.

Email

Electronic mail (email) allows messages and data files to be transmitted between users instantly, without the need for paper or disks as transmission media. When users are allowed to send and receive email messages to computers outside the network, the system uses the Internet.

Electronic Data Interchange (EDI)

Electronic Data Interchange or EDI is a system for enabling the computer systems of different organisations to communicate without the need for paperwork. Typically, it is used to link the purchasing and invoicing systems of suppliers and their customers. EDI is used predominantly by large business organisations.

CONCLUSION

Cost accounting systems are likely to be computerised systems, in which cost and revenue transactions are entered with identifying cost codes. Individual transactions will be traced to cost centres, and identified by type of cost. Total costs are built up within a double entry cost bookkeeping system.

Cost accounting systems vary between organisations. This chapter has introduced the main elements of these systems, which will be explained in greater detail in later chapters of this text.

KEY TERMS

Cost accounting system – a system used by an organisation to gather, store and analyse cost data.

Stores ledger control account – debited with the cost of raw material purchases and credited with materials issued.

Work-in-progress account – debited with the cost of production and credited with the cost of finished goods.

Finished goods account – debited with the cost of finished goods and credited with the cost of goods sold to customers.

Production overhead account – debited with the overhead cost incurred and credited with the overhead cost absorbed. Any balance on the account is under or over absorbed overhead.

Cost unit – a unit of production or activity for which a cost is measured.

Computer hardware – the equipment in a computer system, including input devices, output devices, the central processing unit and storage devices.

Computer software – the systems used to run the computer, including operating systems and application software.

SELF TEST QUESTIONS

		Paragraph
1	What is a cost accounting system?	1
2	Which account in a cost ledger is used to record the cost of materials purchased?	1.4
3	Which account in a cost ledger is used to record the cost of items manufactured?	1.4
4	What double entry accounting record is needed for recording the cost of completed production?	1.5
5	What double entry accounting record is needed for recording the cost of indirect materials used in production?	1.5
6	Which source document might be used to record the cost of materials taken from stores by a cost centre or for a particular job?	2
7	What is a cost unit?	3.1
8	What is the purpose of calculating the cost of cost units?	3.1
9	What is a typical cost unit for a passenger transport service?	3.1
10	What is a cost centre code?	4.3

EXAM-STYLE QUESTIONS

1 If the direct labour costs in a manufacturing company are $95,000 in March, the costs would be recorded in the cost ledger as:

A Debit Work-in-progress $95,000, credit Wages and Salaries $95,000

B Debit Work-in-progress $95,000, credit Production Overheads $95,000

C Debit Wages and Salaries $95,000, credit Work-in-progress $95,000

D Debit Production Overheads $95,000, credit Work-in-progress $95,000.

2 Which of the following is an example of a cost unit?

A Department 234

B A cost per labour hour in department 234

C Stationery costs in the administration department

D A service provided to a customer

3 A firm operates an integrated cost and financial accounting system.

The accounting entries for an issue of direct materials to production would be:

A DR work-in-progress control account, CR stores ledger control account

B DR finished goods account, CR stores ledger control account

C DR stores ledger control account, CR work-in-progress control account

D DR cost of sales account, CR work-in-progress control account.

4 During a period $35,750 was incurred for indirect labour. In a typical cost ledger, the double entry for this is:

A	Dr Wages control $35,750	Cr Overhead control $35,750
B	Dr WIP control $35,750	Cr Wages control $35,750
C	Dr Overhead control $35,750	Cr Wages control $35,750
D	Dr Wages control $35,750	Cr WIP control $35,750

5 Which of the following is an example of computer hardware?

A Operating system

B Spreadsheet package

C Modem

D Graphical user interface

For the answers to these questions, see the 'Answers' section at the end of the book.

Chapter 3

COST CLASSIFICATION AND COST BEHAVIOUR

This chapter explains that costs can be classified in different ways, according to the purpose for which the cost information is required. Several different methods of classifying costs are described. The chapter then goes on to explain that one important method of classifying costs is according to how the amount of the cost varies as the volume of output or level of activity changes. This is classifying costs according to 'cost behaviour'. Where possible, costs are classified by behaviour into either fixed or variable costs, and one technique that needs to be learned for identifying fixed and variable cost elements is the high-low method. This chapter covers syllabus area A3.

CONTENTS

LEARNING OUTCOMES

At the end of this chapter you should be able to:

- describe the variety of cost classifications used for different purposes in a cost accounting system, including by responsibility, function, direct/indirect, behaviour
- explain and illustrate the nature of variable, fixed, stepped fixed and mixed (semi-variable) costs
- use the high-low method to separate semi-variable costs
- use variable, fixed and semi-variable costs in cost analysis
- analyse the effect of changing activity levels on unit costs.

1 CLASSIFICATION OF COSTS

Cost classification is the analysis of costs into logical groups so that they may be summarised into meaningful information for management.

Costs can be classified in different ways, according to the purpose for which they are to be used. Some of the methods of classifying costs are to separate them into:

- functional costs
- expense type, such as materials costs, labour costs and other expenses
- direct and indirect costs (overheads)
- fixed and variable costs, that is analysis by cost behaviour.

1.1 FUNCTIONAL ANALYSIS OF COSTS

In cost accounting, costs are often analysed by function, and categories of functional costs commonly used are:

- manufacturing costs
- administration costs
- selling and distribution costs (or marketing costs)
- possibly, research and development costs.

The functions used for costing will depend on the type of organisation. For example, there are no manufacturing costs in a service business. The reasons for classifying costs by function might be to:

- produce a statement of profit or loss
- decide which costs should or should not be used to value inventory
- apply cost control. Costs of each function can be compared with a budget and the manager responsible for those costs held accountable for any inefficient or wasteful spending. For example, the production manager will be held responsible for production costs and the sales manager for selling costs.

1.2 MATERIALS, LABOUR AND EXPENSES

Another basic classification of costs widely used in cost accounting is to classify costs by element. This distinguishes costs between the cost of materials, such as raw materials or components, the cost of labour and other expenses. We shall look at materials, labour and expenses in more detail in the chapters which follow.

1.3 DIRECT AND INDIRECT COSTS, PRIME COST AND OVERHEADS

The classification of costs into direct and indirect costs is a very important technique which is used to build up the full cost of a cost unit. A cost unit may be a product or service, a job or a contract. Cost units may be produced in batches or through a series of processes, in which case the full cost of the batch or process is collected and the cost per cost unit is found by dividing by the number of units of output.

- A **direct cost** is expenditure that can be directly identified with a specific cost unit. For example, direct material costs in a product are the costs of the materials that go into making that product. Direct labour costs of a product are the costs of the labour engaged directly in the manufacture of the product. Direct expenses are not so common for products, but the cost of a job or a contract could include the direct expenses of equipment hired to do the work or the direct cost of sub-contractors.

  Some costs may, technically, be direct costs but be so small in value that it is not economical to trace the expenditure to the cost unit. For example, the cost of sewing thread when making clothes, the cost of nails for a building job. These costs may be classified as indirect costs because the cost of recording them exceeds the value of the increased accuracy that would be gained.

- **Prime cost** is the total of direct materials cost, direct labour cost and direct expenses.

- **Indirect costs** or **overheads** are expenditure which cannot be directly identified with a specific cost unit and must be 'shared out' on an equitable basis. For example in a manufacturing company, the cost of indirect materials include the cost of materials used to clean and maintain machinery. Indirect labour costs of a product are the costs of labour that does not spend a measurable amount of time directly on making the product. Indirect expenses usually include all general expenses, such as the costs of building rental, heating and lighting and so on.

The **total production cost** or **full factory cost** of a cost unit is its prime cost or direct cost, plus its share of production overheads, consisting of indirect materials, indirect labour and indirect expenses.

The methods used to attribute a share of overhead costs to cost units are explained in a later chapter.

Summary

	$
Direct materials	X
Direct labour	X
Direct expenses (occasionally)	X
	—
Prime cost	X
Production overhead	X
	—
Full factory cost	X
	—

Note: In a business there will also be non-manufacturing overheads such as administration and selling and distribution.

ACTIVITY 1

Classify

A company manufactures and retails clothing.

Group the costs (1) – (10) below into the classifications (i) to (viii) (each cost is intended to belong to only one classification).

Costs

(1) lubricant for sewing machines

(2) new software for general office computer

(3) wages of operatives in the cutting department

(4) telephone rental plus metered calls

(5) interest on bank overdraft

(6) performing rights society charge for music broadcast throughout the factory

(7) market research undertaken prior to a new product launch

(8) wages of security guards for factory

(9) carriage on purchases of basic raw material

(10) royalty payable on number of units of product XY produced

Classifications

(i) direct materials

(ii) direct labour

(iii) direct expenses

(iv) production overhead

(v) research and development costs

(vi) selling and distribution costs

(vii) administration costs

(viii) finance costs

For a suggested answer, see the 'Answers' section at the end of the book.

2 COST BEHAVIOUR

Cost behaviour means the way that a cost changes as the volume of activity or output rises. For example, if a company manufactures widgets, we would expect the total cost of making and selling 10,000 widgets to be more than the total cost of making and selling 5,000 widgets. In other words, total costs should rise as the volume of output and sales rises.

However, not all individual items of expense will incur higher costs as the output level rises and if they do it may not be in direct proportion.

Cost behaviour analysis is concerned with how costs change with the 'level of activity' and by how much. Individual items of cost can be classified according to their cost behaviour. There are many different cost behaviour 'patterns', but many costs can be classified according to behaviour as:

- fixed costs
- variable costs
- semi-variable (and semi-fixed) costs
- stepped-fixed costs.

2.1 FIXED COSTS

Definition **Fixed costs** are costs that are not affected in total by the level of activity, but remain the same amount regardless of how much or how little work is done in a period.

An example is the rent of a factory, which is a constant amount each period regardless of how much or how little is manufactured inside it.

The rent paid on a factory may be $5,000 per month whether 2 widgets or 200 widgets are made, as in the diagram below.

Fixed costs in total

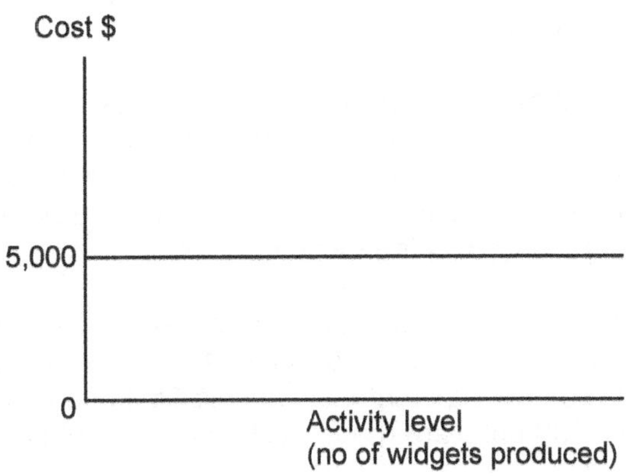

In reality, there must be a level of activity so large that more than one factory must be rented and rent is no longer a fixed cost (but a stepped-fixed cost). However, as long as we are only considering a reasonable range of activity, rent can be considered to be a fixed cost. This reasonable range of activity is known as the **relevant range**. If an organisation's normal output is within the relevant range, then rent can be considered to be a fixed cost.

Note that a fixed cost is not a cost that necessarily stays the same over a period of time. The key is that it doesn't vary with activity. So, for example, heating costs are generally considered to be fixed as they must be paid regardless of the level of production. These costs will be higher in winter than in summer.

If an item of cost is fixed in total, then the cost per unit must fall as the activity level increases, as in the diagram that follows.

Fixed cost per unit

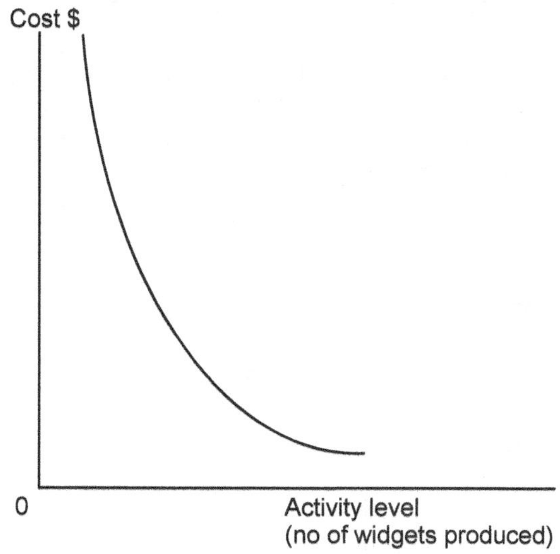

If 2 widgets are made the fixed cost per unit is $\frac{\$5,000}{2}$, i.e. \$2,500 per widget.

If 200 widgets are made the fixed cost per unit is $\frac{\$5,000}{200}$, i.e. \$25 per widget.

Conclusion As the activity level increases, fixed costs remain the same in total, but the cost per unit of activity falls.

2.2 VARIABLE COSTS

Definition **Variable costs** are costs that change in direct proportion to the level of activity.

An example is direct materials costs. Each additional unit produced of a product needs the same quantity of materials, which costs the same. Similarly, direct labour is sometimes treated as a variable cost, because each extra unit produced needs the same time as the previous units and, if labour is costed on a time basis, each additional unit therefore costs the same in labour.

Variable costs in total change at the same rate as the level of activity. For example, if the cost of direct materials is two kilograms at \$2 per kg for each widget, this amounts to \$4 per widget. So, the total materials cost is \$4 if one unit is made, \$8 if 2 units are made and \$800 if 200 units are made, as in the diagram below.

Variable costs in total

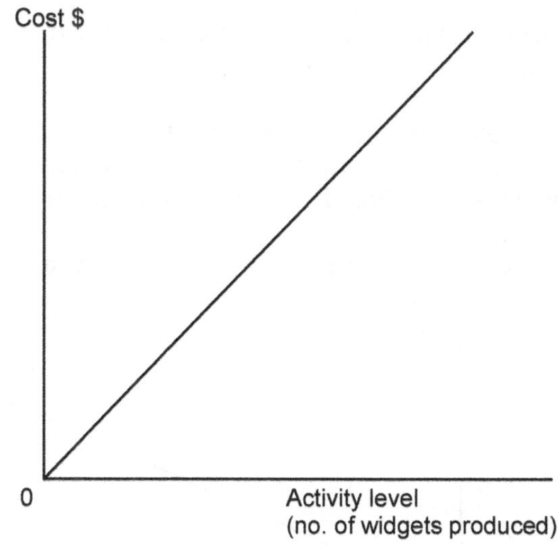

In practice, as the activity level increases, there might be changes in the additional cost of each unit. For example, as an organisation buys ever greater quantities of materials, it might be able to negotiate a bulk discount from its suppliers, so that the materials cost per unit of product falls. However, within a reasonable range of activity levels, it is often found that the variable cost per unit of output remains much the same. This is illustrated in the diagram below.

Variable cost per unit

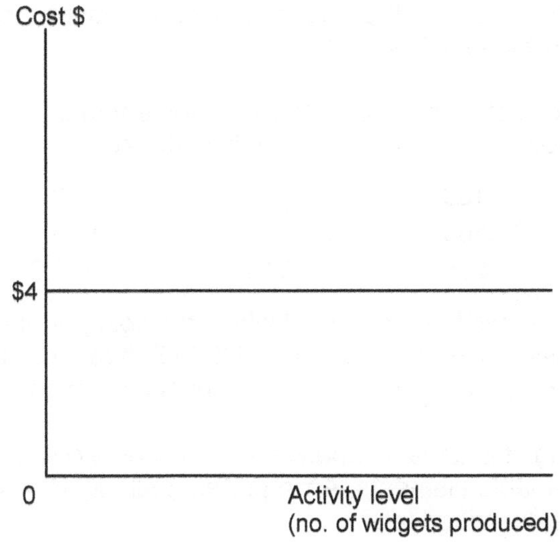

Conclusion As the level of activity increases, total variable costs increase in direct proportion to the increase in activity, but the variable cost per unit of activity remains the same.

2.3 SEMI-VARIABLE COSTS

Definition **Semi-variable costs** are those that have both fixed and variable elements.

An example is telephone costs, which consist of a fixed period rental and charges for calls made. Since call charges tend to vary with the volume of activity, telephone charges are roughly semi-variable in relation to the volume of production and sales.

A semi-variable cost, e.g. telephone charges

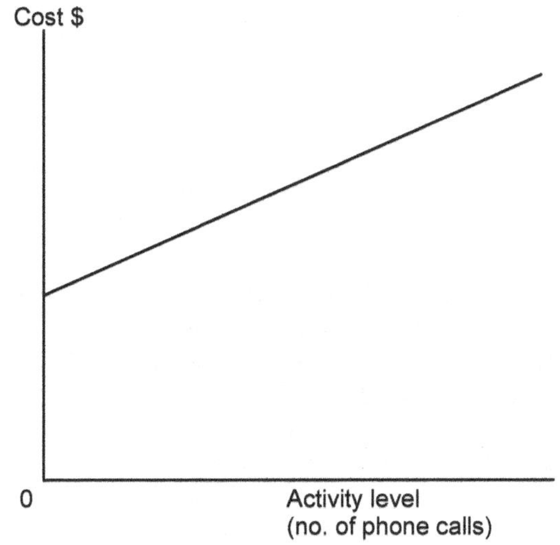

With semi-variable costs, as the level of activity increases the cost per unit falls. This can be demonstrated as follows.

If a semi-variable cost is made up of a fixed element of $2,000 and a variable element of $5 per unit, then the cost per unit will fall as the activity level rises as follows:

Activity level	100	200	300	400
Total cost	$2,500	$3,000	$3,500	$4,000
Cost per unit	$25	$15	$11.67	$10

The table above shows that the rate at which the cost per unit falls as the activity level rises is a decreasing one i.e. it falls from $25 to $15 (a $10 fall per 100 units) then from $15 to $11.67 (a fall of $3.33 per 100 units) and so on.

In cost accounting, it is usual to analyse semi-variable costs by separating them into their fixed and variable elements. An important technique for doing this is the high-low method, which is described later.

2.4 STEPPED-FIXED COSTS

Definition **Stepped-fixed costs**, also called **step** costs, are costs that are constant for a range of activity levels, and then change, and are constant again for another range.

An example is the cost of supervisors' salaries. For example, for production of up to 50 widgets, it might be sufficient to have just one supervisor, whereas if 50 to 100 are made two supervisors would be necessary and so on.

The key feature of stepped-fixed costs is that they are fixed within a limited range of activity, but then go up a step as the activity level rises beyond a certain level.

Stepped-fixed costs, e.g. supervisors' salaries

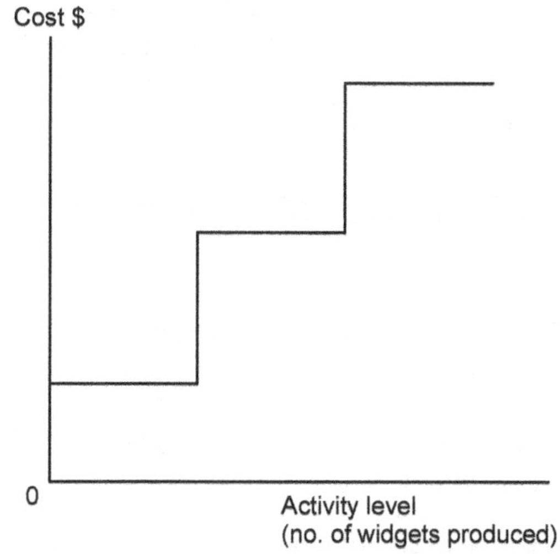

The stepped-fixed cost per unit is not constant and as the level of activity increases within a given range of activity the stepped-fixed cost per unit falls. This is very similar to the way in which the fixed cost per unit falls as activity levels increase. The main difference is that each time the fixed cost goes up in a 'step' the fixed cost per unit will be at its highest and then as the level of activity increases in the given range, the stepped-fixed cost per unit will fall until the cost goes up in another 'step' again. This can be demonstrated in the table shown below for a stepped-fixed cost that increases by $5,000 as the activity level increase by 100 units.

Activity level in units (range)	0-100	101-200	201-300	301-400
Stepped-fixed cost	$5,000	$10,000	$15,000	$20,000
Cost per unit	1 unit = $5,000 50 units = $100 100 units = $50	101 units = $99 150 units = $67 200 units = $50	201 units = $75 250 units = $60 300 units = $50	301 units = $66.5 350 units = $57 400 units = $50

2.5 USING FIXED AND VARIABLE COSTS

The distinction between fixed and variable costs might be used:

- in product costing (for example in marginal costing, which is explained later)
- to help to analyse profitability
- to help managers to make decisions about increasing or decreasing activity levels
- to estimate future costs (forecasting and budgeting)
- to estimate what costs should have been (for budgetary control) and performance assessment.

Semi-variable costs are usually divided into their fixed and variable components. The fixed portion is included in fixed costs for the period and the variable portion included within total variable costs.

Knowing about stepped-fixed costs can be important for decision-makers, who need to know whether as a result of any decision they take some costs might rise or fall a step. In practice, however, it is often possible to treat stepped-fixed costs as either fixed costs for the period (on the assumption that activity will remain within a range that keeps the cost on the same level) or variable costs, where there are a large number of small steps as activity increases.

3 ESTIMATING FUTURE COSTS WITH COST BEHAVIOUR ANALYSIS

A knowledge of fixed and variable costs is important in cost accounting, because cost behaviour analysis can be used for a variety of purposes. Two of these purposes are:

- estimating what future costs should be, given an estimated volume of activity, for example in budgeting
- comparing actual costs with the cost expected for the actual level of activity achieved (the **flexed budget**). This is a feature of control reports in cost accounting.

EXAMPLE

A company manufactures two products, X and Y. The following costs have been estimated.

	Product X	*Product Y*
Direct materials cost per unit	$14	$12
Direct labour hours per unit	1.5 hours	2.5 hours
Direct labour cost per hour	$10	$10
Variable overhead costs per hour	$2	$2

Fixed costs for the period are expected to be $220,000, and it is expected that 5,000 units of Product X and 2,000 units of Product Y will be manufactured.

What is the total expected costs for the period?

SOLUTION

	Product X 5,000 units	*Product Y* 2,000 units	*Total*
Variable costs	$	$	$
Direct materials	70,000	24,000	94,000
Direct labour	75,000	50,000	125,000
Variable overhead costs	15,000	10,000	25,000
Total variable costs	160,000	84,000	244,000
Fixed costs			220,000
Total costs			464,000

ACTIVITY 2

A business makes two products, C and D, with the following sales prices and cost data.

	C	*D*
Sales price per unit	\$25	\$30
Direct material cost per unit	\$8	\$7
Direct labour cost	\$6 per unit	0.5 hours \$8 per hour
Variable overhead	\$1 per unit	\$2 per direct labour hour

Fixed costs are \$40,000 per month.

Given this information, what is the forecast of total costs and profits for a month when the business expects to make and sell 1,200 units of product C and 1,800 units of product D.

For a suggested answer, see the 'Answers' section at the end of the book.

Estimates of future costs may be shown as a cost function:

y = a + bx where y = total cost

a = total fixed cost

b = variable cost per unit

x = number of units of output

If all but one piece of information is known this can be found by rearranging and solving the formula. The complete formula can then be used to forecast future costs.

EXAMPLE

An organisation's cost function is known to be:

y = a + bx where y = total cost

a = total fixed cost

b = variable cost per unit

x = number of units of output

The total cost for output of 1,000 units is \$3,950 and the total variable cost is \$1,350.

Required:

(i) Calculate the fixed cost for the period.

(ii) Calculate the total cost if output were 1,250 units.

(iii) Calculate the cost per unit if output were 900 units.

SOLUTION

(i) Total cost = fixed cost + variable cost

$3,950 = fixed cost + $1,350

Therefore fixed cost = $3,950 – $1,350 = $2,600

(ii) The variable cost per unit = $1,350/1,000 = $1.35 per unit

The cost function is:

y = 2,600 + 1.35x

If x = 1,250 then total cost = 2,600 + (1.35 × 1,250) = $4,287.50

(iii) If x = 900 then total cost = 2,600 + (1.35 × 900) = $3,815

The cost per unit = $3,815/900 = $4.24 (to 2 d.p.)

4 HIGH-LOW METHOD

The high-low method estimates fixed and variable costs by comparing the costs of the highest and lowest activity levels and analysing the difference between them.

- We take the cost information for the highest activity level and for the lowest activity level, from the data available. The assumption is that the total cost line goes through these two points.
- Assuming that fixed costs are the same at both activity levels, the difference in total cost between the highest and the lowest activity levels must be attributable to variable costs entirely. The difference must be the variable cost for the number of units of activity between the lowest and the highest points.
- This allows us to calculate a variable cost per unit. Having done this, we can apply the variable cost value to either the low cost or the high cost data, to calculate the fixed costs.

This method of analysis is based on historical data for costs at different activity levels. If there has been inflation in costs over the time periods covered by this data, all the costs should be re-stated at a common price level.

To illustrate the high-low method, the data below will be used as an example.

EXAMPLE

Inspection costs for the six months to 31 December 20X8 are as follows:

Month	*Units produced*	*Cost*
		$
July	340	2,260
August	300	2,160
September	380	2,320
October	420	2,400
November	400	2,300
December	360	2,266

Use the high-low method to calculate the fixed costs per month and the variable cost per unit.

SOLUTION

The variable element of a cost item may be estimated by calculating the unit cost between high and low volumes during a period.

Note: Take the highest and lowest **activity volumes**. These might not be the highest or lowest costs.

High month = October (420). Low month = August (300).

	Units	*Total cost*
		$
High	420	2,400
Low	300	2,160
	120	240

Variable cost per unit = $240/120 = $2.

Having calculated the variable cost per unit, we can calculate the fixed costs from either the high or the low activity level costs.

420 units	$
Total cost	2,400
Less: Variable cost (420 × $2)	840
Therefore fixed cost	1,560

Inspection costs are therefore estimated as $1,560 per month plus $2 per unit produced.

Advantages and limitations of the high-low method

The high-low method has the enormous advantage of simplicity. It is easy to understand and easy to use.

The limitations of the high-low method are as follows.

- It relies on historical data, assuming that (i) activity is the only factor affecting costs and (ii) historical costs reliably predict future costs.
- It uses only two values, the highest and the lowest, which means that the results may be distorted because of random variations in these values.

ACTIVITY 3

Use the high-low method to calculate the fixed and variable elements of the following costs:

	Activity	$
January	400	1,050
February	600	1,700
March	550	1,600
April	800	2,100
May	750	2,000
June	900	2,300

For a suggested answer, see the 'Answers' section at the end of the book.

CONCLUSION

Accurate classification of costs is often an important first step in cost accounting techniques. The use of direct/indirect costs and knowledge of cost behaviour is fundamental to the syllabus and you should learn the definitions carefully and be prepared to use them.

KEY TERMS

Direct cost – expenditure which can be directly identified with a specific cost unit or cost centre.

Prime cost – the aggregate of direct materials cost, direct labour cost and direct expenses.

Indirect costs – expenditure which cannot be directly identified with a specific cost unit or cost centre. Also called **overheads**.

Cost behaviour – how costs vary as the level of activity (e.g. output or sales) varies.

Fixed costs – costs which are not affected in total by the level of activity.

Variable costs – costs which change in total in direct proportion to the level of activity.

Semi-variable costs – costs which have both fixed and variable elements.

Stepped-fixed costs – costs which are constant for a range of activity levels, and then change and are constant again for another range. Also called step costs.

SELF TEST QUESTIONS

		Paragraph
1	Define a direct cost.	1.3
2	What is a prime cost?	1.3
3	Give an example of an indirect cost.	1.3
4	Sketch a graph of total fixed cost.	2.1
5	What is the relevant range?	2.1
6	Sketch a graph of total variable cost.	2.2
7	Explain how the high-low method is used.	4

EXAM-STYLE QUESTIONS

1 Which is NOT an example of a functional analysis of costs?

A Overheads

B Marketing costs

C Selling costs

D Manufacturing costs

2 Which of the following would be classed as indirect labour?

A Assembly workers

B A stores assistant in a factory store

C Plasterers in a building company

D An audit clerk in an accountancy firm

3 Direct costs are:

A costs that can always be identified with a single cost unit

B costs that can be expensed to the Statement of profit or loss

C costs that can be attributed to an accounting period

D costs that change in direct proportion to the number of units produced.

4 A firm is trying to find a relationship between its sales volume in a quarter and its telephone expense that quarter.

If a sales volume of 2 million units corresponds to a telephone expense of $5,000 and sales volume of 4 million units corresponds to a telephone expense of $6,000, then if the sales volume is 5 million units, the telephone expense is likely to be:

A $2,500

B $6,500

C $7,000

D $7,500

5 Which of the following graphs depicts the cost per unit of fixed cost?

A

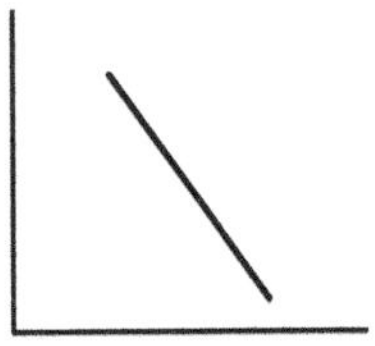

B

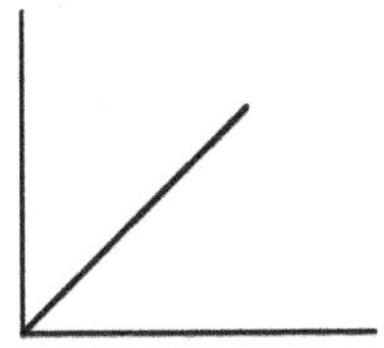

C

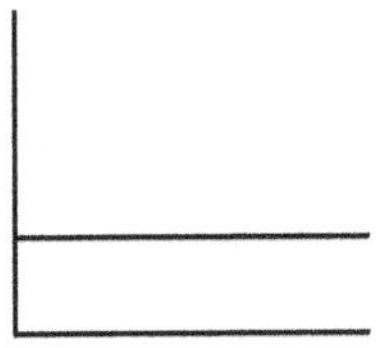

D

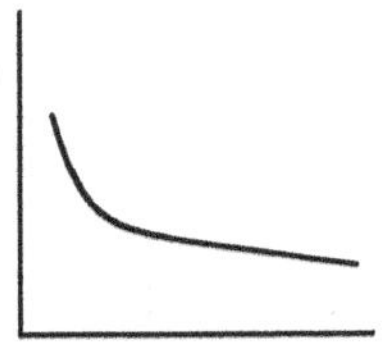

6 The following data are records of output levels and overhead costs.

	January	*December*
Hours worked	18,000	21,000
Total costs	$86,800	$97,438

There was 3% inflation between January and December. The variable cost per hour worked, at January price levels and to the nearest $0.01, is:

A $4.52

B $2.68

C $3.55

D $2.60

7 The 'high-low' method of cost estimation can be used to:

A calculate the forecast cost for a given volume of activity

B calculate the highest and lowest cost in the period

C measure the actual cost of an activity

D predict the range of costs expected in a period.

8 The following information relates to the overhead costs of the production department:

Units of output	5,000	7,000
Overheads	$21,100	$26,100

The variable overhead rate per unit is $2.50. The amount of fixed overhead is:

A $5,000

B $8,600

C $13,600

D $21,100

9 Bronze recorded the following costs for the past six months.

Month	*Activity level* Units	*Total cost* $
1	80	6,586
2	60	5,826
3	72	6,282
4	75	6,396
5	83	6,700
6	66	6,054

Calculate the estimated total costs of producing 90 units.

A $6,966

B $6,844

C $7,222

D $6,886

10 The following unit costs are incurred in producing 4,000 units of a product in January:

	$ per unit
Variable costs	4.12
Semi-variable costs	2.36
Fixed costs	3.00
Total costs	9.48

$1 of the semi-variable costs are fixed costs.

Production for February is budgeted to be 5,000 units. The budgeted total production cost for February is:

A $32,400

B $36,600

C $43,400

D $47,400

For the answers to these questions, see the 'Answers' section at the end of the book.

Chapter 4

ACCOUNTING FOR MATERIALS

This chapter is the first of several that explain how the elements of cost are calculated and accounted for. The elements of cost are materials, labour and expenses. These can be either direct costs or indirect costs. This chapter covers syllabus area B1 (a) to (e).

CONTENTS

LEARNING OUTCOMES

At the end of this chapter you should be able to:

- describe the main types of material classification
- describe the procedures and documentation required to ensure the correct authorisation, coding, analysis and recording of direct and indirect material costs
- explain, illustrate and evaluate the FIFO, LIFO and periodic and cumulative weighted average methods used to price materials issued from inventory
- describe and illustrate the accounting for material costs
- calculate material input requirements, and control measures, where wastage occurs.

1 DIRECT AND INDIRECT MATERIALS

In cost accounting, materials are commonly classified as either direct materials or indirect materials

Definition **Direct materials** are the materials that can be directly attributed to a unit of production, or a specific job, or a service provided directly to a customer.

In a manufacturing business, direct materials are therefore the raw materials and components that are directly input into the products that the organisation makes. For example the many different components that make up a motorcar are the direct materials of the car.

Definition **Indirect materials** are other materials that cannot be directly attributed to a unit of production.

An example of indirect materials might be the oil used for the lubrication of production machinery. This is a material that is used in the production process but it cannot be directly attributed to each unit of finished product.

In a manufacturing business, the **cost of direct materials** can be charged directly to the cost unit that uses the materials. In a jobbing business or a contracting business, direct materials costs are charged directly to the job or contract for which they are used.

The **costs of indirect materials** are charged to the cost centre that requisitions them from the stores department and uses them.

2 PROCEDURES AND DOCUMENTATION FOR MATERIALS

The stores department is responsible for the receipt, storage and issue of materials and components.

- **Receipt of materials into store**. When materials are received from suppliers, they are normally delivered to the stores department. The stores personnel must check that the goods delivered are the ones that have been ordered, in the correct quantity, of the correct quality and in good condition.

- Once the materials have been received they must be **stored** until required by user departments.

- **Issue of materials from store**. When cost centres require materials, they submit a requisition for the materials to the stores department.

- **Recording receipts and issues**. Receipts of materials into store and issues of materials must be controlled and recorded. Oddly perhaps, the responsibility for recording receipts and issues of materials is divided between the stores department and the costing department. Each of these departments could maintain its own separate inventory records, although there should ideally be one integrated inventory control system. The stores department should monitor the quantities of materials received and issued, and ensure the safety and security of the physical inventory. The costing department is responsible for recording the cost of materials received into stores and for putting a value to the cost of direct and indirect materials issued from store.

2.1 PROCEDURES AND DOCUMENTATION FOR RECEIPTS OF MATERIALS

It is useful to have an overview of the departments involved in the purchasing process.

Stores department	Notifies the purchasing department of the need to buy materials, using a purchase requisition/inventory reorder form.
Purchasing department	Orders goods from external supplier using a purchase order.
External supplier	Delivers goods to the stores department. The goods are accompanied by a delivery note. The external supplier also sends a purchase invoice to the accounts department, asking for payment for the goods.
Stores department	Raises goods received note (GRN) from the delivery note details. The goods received note is used to update the inventory records with the quantities of goods received.
Costing department	The costing department records the cost of the materials received, using the delivery note and the purchase invoice details.

2.2 PROCEDURES AND DOCUMENTATION FOR THE ISSUE OF MATERIALS

Requests for materials to be issued from stores to a production department or other department are initiated and then authorised by a **materials requisition note**. This document performs two functions: it authorises the storekeeper to release the goods and acts as a source record for updating the stores records.

An example of a materials requisition document is shown below.

MATERIAL REQUISITION Serial No: ....

Charge Job/
Cost Centre No: .... Date: ....

Code No.	Description	Quantity or weight	Cost office only				
			Rate	Unit	$	$	Stores ledger

Authorised by:	Storekeeper:	Price entered by:
Received by:	Bin card entered:	Calculations checked:

Notes:

1 Every item of inventory has a unique identity code. The materials requisition note is filled in to show both the code and the description of the materials requisitioned.

2 The materials requisition note also identifies the job or cost centre for which the materials are issued.

3 The materials issued from stores must be given a price or value. The task of pricing materials issued from stores is the responsibility of the costing department. A copy of the requisition is sent to the costing department, which calculates and enters the costs.

2.3 STORES RECORDS

In any inventory control system, there should be a continual record of the current quantities of each item of inventory held in store. Receipts into store and issues from store must be recorded, so that the current inventory balance can be kept up-to-date.

When the stores control system is a paper-based system, there could be two separate inventory records:

- a **bin card system**, in which a stores record (a 'bin card') is kept for each item of inventory. The bin card is held in the stores department, and is used to record the **quantities only** of inventory received and issued and the current inventory balance

- an **inventory ledger system**, in which a record is kept for the cost ledger for each item of inventory. In a paper-based system, there is a stores ledger control account for each item of inventory. This is kept up-to-date by the costing department, and **records both the quantity and value** of items received into stores, issued from stores and the current balance held in stores.

STORES LEDGER CARD

Description .... Unit .... Location .... Code ....

Maximum .... Minimum .... Reorder level .... Reorder quantity ....

Receipts			Issues			On order			
Date/ ref	Quantity	$	Date/ ref	Quantity	$	Physical balance	Date/ ref	Quantity	$

Note: The purchase cost of materials excludes any Sales Tax. It includes any costs associated with buying the materials that the business is required to pay, notably the costs of freight and delivery ('carriage inwards' costs).

When an inventory **control system is computerised**, there will be just one stores ledger record system. For each item of inventory, there is a computer record similar to a stores ledger control account, showing both the quantities and the value of items received and issued, and the current inventory balance.

3 PRICING ISSUES OF MATERIALS

When materials are purchased, the process of giving them a value is fairly straightforward. The purchase cost of the items is the price charged by the supplier (excluding any Sales Tax) plus any carriage inwards costs. The cost should be net of any trade discount given.

When materials are issued from store, a cost or price has to be attached to them.

- When a quantity of materials is purchased in its entirety for a specific job, the purchase cost can be charged directly to the job.
- More commonly however, materials are purchased in fairly large quantities (but at different prices each time) and later issued to cost centres in smaller quantities. It would be administratively extremely difficult, if not impossible, to identify specific units of material that have been purchased with units issued to cost centres. Consequently, when issues of materials from store are being valued/priced, we do not try to identify what the specific units actually did cost. Instead, materials issued from store are valued/priced on the basis of a valuation method.

A business might use any of several valuation methods for pricing stores issued. Four such methods are:

- First in first out (FIFO)
- Last in first out (LIFO)
- Cumulative weighted average cost (AVCO)
- Periodic weighted average

EXAMPLE

The same example will be used to illustrate each of these methods.

In November 1,000 tonnes of inventory item 1234 were purchased in three lots:

3 November	400 tonnes at $60 per tonne
11 November	300 tonnes at $70 per tonne
21 November	300 tonnes at $80 per tonne

During the same period four materials requisitions were completed for 200 tonnes each, on 5, 14, 22 and 27 November.

3.1 FIRST IN FIRST OUT (FIFO) METHOD

With the first in first out method of valuation, it is assumed that materials are issued from store in the order in which they were received. In the example above, it would be assumed with FIFO that the 400 tonnes purchased at $60 each on 3 November will be used before the 300 tonnes bought on 11 November, and these in turn will be used before the 300 tonnes bought on 21 November.

The closing inventory at the end of November is 200 units. These consist of 200 of the most recently purchased units.

The stores ledger account for inventory item 1234 is summarised below.

Date	*Receipts*	*Issues*	*Balance*	
			No.	$
3 Nov	400 × $60		400	24,000
5 Nov		200 × $60	200	12,000
11 Nov	300 × $70		500	33,000
14 Nov		200 × $60	300	21,000
21 Nov	300 × $80		600	45,000
22 Nov		200 × $70	400	31,000
27 Nov		100 × $70		
		100 × $80	200	16,000

Note that each successive consignment into stores is exhausted before charging issues from stores at the next price.

Using this method the total value of materials issued is $53,000 and the value of closing inventory is $16,000.

3.2 LAST IN FIRST OUT (LIFO) METHOD

With the last in first out method of pricing, it is assumed that materials issued from stores are the units that were acquired the most recently of those still remaining in inventory.

In this example, the 200 tonnes issued on 5 November will therefore consist of materials purchased on 3 November, the 200 tonnes issued on 14 November will consist of materials purchased on 11 November and the 200 tonnes issued on 22 November will consist of materials purchased on 21 November. The materials issued on 27 November will consist of the remaining 100 tonnes bought on 21 November and the 100 tonnes bought on 14 November.

The closing inventory at the end of November consists of 200 of the tonnes bought on 5 November.

The stores ledger control account for item 1234 using LIFO would be as follows.

Date	*Receipts*	*Issues*	*Balance*	
			No.	$
3 Nov	400 × $60		400	24,000
5 Nov		200 × $60	200	12,000
11 Nov	300 × $70		500	33,000
14 Nov		200 × $70	300	19,000
21 Nov	300 × $80		600	43,000
22 Nov		200 × $80	400	27,000
27 Nov		100 × $80		
		100 × $70	200	12,000

Using this method the total value of materials issued is $57,000 (more than under FIFO) and the closing inventory value is $12,000 (less than FIFO). When prices are rising this will always be the case.

3.3 CUMULATIVE WEIGHTED AVERAGE COST (AVCO) METHOD

With the cumulative weighted average cost method of pricing material issues, all quantities of an item of inventory are valued at a weighted average cost. A new weighted average cost is calculated each time that there is a new delivery into stores. A weighted average price is usually calculated to the nearest cent.

Cumulative weighted average price =

$$\frac{\text{Inventory value of items in stores + Purchase cost of units received}}{\text{Quantity already in stores + Quantity received}}$$

The price so calculated is used to value all subsequent issues until the next consignment of the inventory is received into stores and a new weighted average cost is calculated.

Item 1234				
	Receipts (issues)			*Weighted average price*
Date	*Quantity*	*Purchase price*	*Value*	*(issue price)*
		$	$	$
3 Nov	400	60	24,000	60
5 Nov	(200)		(12,000)	60
	———		———	———
	200		12,000	60
11 Nov	300	70	21,000	
	———		———	
Balance	500		33,000	66 (W1)
14 Nov	(200)		(13,200)	66
	300		19,800	66
21 Nov	300	80	24,000	
	———	———	———	
Balance	600		43,800	73 (W2)
22 Nov	(200)		(14,600)	73
27 Nov	(200)		(14,600)	73
	———		———	———
30 Nov (bal)	200		14,600	73
	———		———	———

A new average cost price calculation is required after each new receipt.

Workings:

(W1) $33,000/500 = $66

(W2) $43,800/600 = $73

Using this method the total value of materials issued is $54,400 and the closing inventory value is $14,600. These figures are between the FIFO and LIFO valuations.

A variation on the AVCO method is the **periodic** weighted average cost method.

3.4 PERIODIC WEIGHTED AVERAGE COST METHOD

With the periodic weighted average cost method of pricing inventory an average price is calculated at the end of the period which is then used to price all issues.

Periodic weighted average price =

$$\frac{\text{Cost of opening inventory + Cost of all receipts in the period}}{\text{Units in opening inventory + Units received}}$$

The stores ledger control account for the item 1234 would be as follows:

Item 1234
Receipts (Issues)

Date	*Quantity*	*Purchase price*	*Value*	*Periodic Weighted Average price (issue price)*
3 Nov	400	60	24,000	
11 Nov	300	70	21,000	
21 Nov	300	80	24,000	
	1,000		69,000	69.00
5 Nov	(200)		(13,800)	69.00
14 Nov	(200)		(13,800)	69.00
22 Nov	(200)		(13,800)	69.00
27 Nov	(200)		(13,800)	69.00
30 Nov (bal)	200		13,800	69.00

Using this method the total value of materials issued is $55,200 and the closing inventory value is $13,800. Note that using this method the cost of issues cannot be calculated until the end of the period.

ACTIVITY 1

You are given the following information about one line of inventory held by Tolley plc.

Assuming that there are no further transactions in the month of May, what is the value of the issues made on 1 March and 1 May and what would be the inventory valuation, using (i) the FIFO valuation method (ii) LIFO and (iii) AVCO (iv) Periodic weighted average pricing?

How does the inventory pricing method used impact on the profit made on sales?

		Units	*Cost*	*Sales price*
			$	$
Opening inventory	1 January	50	7	
Purchase	1 February	60	8	
Sale	1 March	40		10
Purchase	1 April	70	9	
Sale	1 May	60		12

For a suggested answer, see the 'Answers' section at the end of the book.

3.5 COMPARISON OF VALUATION METHODS – THE EFFECT ON PROFIT OF THE INVENTORY VALUATION METHOD SELECTED

A business can choose whichever method of inventory valuation it wants to use. FIFO and weighted average costs are both acceptable for financial reporting, whereas LIFO is not. However, in cost accounting, the rules of financial reporting do not apply, and businesses can use LIFO should they wish.

If the purchase price of materials stayed the same indefinitely, every inventory valuation method would produce the same values for stores issues and closing inventory. Differences between the valuation methods is usually only significant during a period of price inflation, because the choice of valuation method can have a significant effect on the value of materials consumed (and so on the cost of sales and profits) and on closing inventory values.

The relative advantages and disadvantages of FIFO, LIFO and AVCO are therefore discussed below, particularly in relation to **inflationary situations**.

Method	*Advantages*	*Disadvantages*
FIFO	• Produces current values for closing inventory.	• Produces out-of-date production costs and therefore potentially overstates profits. • Complicates inventory records as inventory must be analysed by delivery.
LIFO	• Produces realistic production costs and therefore more realistic/prudent profit figures.	• Produces unrealistically low closing inventory values. • Complicates inventory records as inventory must be analysed by delivery.
Weighted average price	• Simple to operate – calculations within the inventory records are minimised.	• Produces both inventory values and production costs which are likely to differ from current values.

Whichever method is adopted it should be applied consistently from period to period.

4 ACCOUNTING FOR MATERIALS COSTS

Within the inventory control system, there is a stores ledger control account for each item held in stores.

This stores ledger control account records details of all receipts of the material as well as all issues of the material to production.

The information in a stores ledger account can be presented in the form of a T account, for double entry bookkeeping purposes, as follows.

Stores ledger control account – item 2345

	$		$
Opening balance b/d	X	Issues	X
Receipts	X	Closing balance c/d	X
	X		X
Balance b/d	X		

There is an account for each item of inventory in the inventory control system, but in the cost ledger accounting system, there is a **stores ledger control account** for all items of inventory in total. In other words, the materials cost ledger account shows in total all of the entries that have taken place in the individual stores ledger control accounts. The materials cost ledger account therefore records the total materials purchases for the organisation, and the total value of materials issued to production as direct materials or to cost centres as indirect materials.

4.1 PURCHASE OF MATERIALS

When materials are purchased and the purchases are recorded in the cost accounts, the credit side of the entry will be to either cash (cash purchases) or creditors (credit purchases). The debit entry is in the stores ledger control account, recording the purchase cost of the materials.

EXAMPLE

Ogden Ltd is a small company that was set up at the beginning of May 20X4 by the issue of $20,000 of shares for cash. Ogden Ltd purchases three types of material: A, B and C. During the month of May 20X4 the purchases of each type of material were as follows:

Material A	
3 May	$2,000
24 May	$9,000
Material B	
6 May	$5,000
10 May	$3,000
21 May	$7,000
Material C	
1 May	$4,000
7 May	$4,000
28 May	$4,000

Purchases of materials A and B are for cash and material C is on credit of 45 days.

Record these transactions in the individual stores ledger control accounts as well as the cash and creditor accounts.

SOLUTION

Stores ledger control account Material A

	$		$
3 May	2,000		
24 May	9,000		

Stores ledger control account Material B

	$		$
6 May	5,000		
10 May	3,000		
21 May	7,000		

Stores ledger control account Material C

		$		$
1 May		4,000		
7 May		4,000		
28 May		4,000		

Cash account

		$		$
1 May	Share capital a/c	20,000	3 May Material A	2,000
			6 May Material B	5,000
			10 May Material B	3,000
			21 May Material B	7,000
			24 May Material A	9,000

Payables account

	$		$
		1 May Material C	4,000
		7 May Material C	4,000
		28 May Material C	4,000

Note: The stores ledger control account would include all of the entries for Materials A, B and C.

4.2 ISSUES OF MATERIALS

Materials issued from stores are recorded as a credit entry in the stores ledger control account. The value or cost of the materials issued is determined by whichever valuation method is used (FIFO, LIFO, weighted average cost, etc).

The corresponding double entry is to:

- a work-in-progress account, for direct materials
- an overhead account, for indirect materials. (This can be a production overhead, administration overhead or selling and distribution overhead, according to the function of the cost centre that obtains the materials.)

Continuing the example from paragraph 4.1, now suppose that Ogden Ltd made the following issues of materials in June:

Material A	Direct material to production	$7,000
Material B	To selling and distribution	$3,000
	To administration	$4,000
Material C	Indirect material to production	$3,000

The ledger accounts would be completed as follows.

Stores ledger control account

	$		$
Opening balance	38,000	WIP (Material A)	7,000
		Selling and distribution overhead (Material B)	3,000
		Administration overhead (Material B)	4,000
		Production overhead (Material C)	3,000
		Closing balance (bal. fig.)	21,000
	38,000		38,000

Work-in-progress (WIP)

	$		$
Stores control	7,000		

Production overhead control

	$		$
Stores control	3,000		

Administration overhead

	$		$
Stores control	4,000		

Selling and distribution overhead

	$		$
Stores control	3,000		

5 INVENTORY LOSSES AND WASTE

5.1 MATERIAL INPUT REQUIREMENTS

In some manufacturing processes, there is wastage or loss of inventory. When wastage is expected during processing, the department using the materials should allow for the losses when it orders materials.

Wastage is usually measured as a percentage of the quantities of materials input.

Input – Wastage = Output

For example, if wastage is 3% of input, output will be 97% of input. In formula terms:

$$\text{Input} = \text{Output} \times \frac{100\%}{(100\% - \text{wastage rate percentage})}$$

So if the required output is 500 units, the input material requirements are:

$$\text{Input} = 500 \text{ units} \times \frac{100}{(100 - 3)}$$

= 515.5 units, say 516 units.

ACTIVITY 2

In a production process, there is usually a wastage rate of 5% of input. Materials cost $8 per kilogram. The required output is 1,520 kilograms.

What quantity of input materials should be required, and what will they cost?

For a suggested answer, see the 'Answers' section at the end of the book.

5.2 CONTROL MEASURES

If wastage is a normal part of the production process, control measures (i.e. expected or targeted levels of waste) should be calculated and actual wastage rates compared to the control measures to check that the wastage rates are as expected. If wastage is greater or less than expected, the reasons why this has happened must be investigated and action taken as necessary.

Wastage may be greater than expected:

- if labour is less experienced than expected and make more mistakes when using the material
- if a machine is old or poorly maintained and there are more breakdowns and errors than expected
- if the production process has changed
- if the estimate of the control rate for wastage was too low.

EXAMPLE

A business expects wastage to be 5% of material input. In a period actual material input was 250 kg and 230 kg of finished output was produced.

Compare the actual wastage rate with the expected wastage rate.

SOLUTION

The actual wastage rate is 20/250 × 100% = 8%

This is higher than the expected wastage rate of 5% and the reasons for the difference should be investigated.

CONCLUSION

This chapter has explained in detail the procedures concerned with ordering, receiving, storing and issuing materials. It has illustrated the accounting techniques used to value materials. For your examination, it is important to have a working knowledge of the inventory valuation methods, particularly FIFO, LIFO and AVCO. You should also be able to compare these methods, particularly during a period of rising or falling prices.

KEY TERMS

Direct materials – materials that can be directly attributed to a unit of production, or a specific job or a service provided directly to a customer.

Indirect materials – materials that cannot be directly attributed to a unit of production.

FIFO – first in first out method of inventory valuation.

LIFO – last in first out method of inventory valuation.

AVCO – weighted average method of inventory valuation.

SELF TEST QUESTIONS

		Paragraph
1	Distinguish between direct materials and indirect materials.	1
2	Which document is used to record materials issued from stores?	2.2
3	Under the LIFO method of inventory valuation at what price is closing inventory valued, the most recently or the earliest-purchased units of the item of inventory?	3.2
4	What are the advantages and disadvantages of the weighted average price method of inventory valuation?	3.5
5	What double entry is used to record the issue of materials from stores to a production overhead cost centre?	4.2
6	What formula can be used to calculate the required quantity of input materials, given a required output quantity and a wastage rate expressed as a percentage of input quantities?	5.1

EXAM-STYLE QUESTIONS

1 ABC Ltd had an opening inventory of $880 (275 units valued at $3.20 each) on 1 April.

The following receipts and issues were recorded during April:

8 April	receives 600 units at $3.00 each
15 April	receives 400 units at $3.40 each
30 April	issues 925 units

Possible inventory values:

A $2,935

B $4,040

C $2,932

D $2,850

(i) What would be the value of the issues under LIFO?

(ii) What would be the total value of issues under AVCO?

(iii) What would the total value of issues under FIFO?

2 W Ltd has closing inventory at 31 July of 400 units valued at $10,000 using LIFO. Inventory movements in July were:

5 July	300 units bought for $25/unit
10 July	500 units issued
15 July	400 units bought for $22/unit
20 July	200 units issued

What was the value of the opening inventory?

A $11,200

B $10,000

C $9,400

D Cannot be found

The following information relates to Questions 3, 4, 5 and 6.

Inventory movements of component AB1 for the month of March were as follows:

8 March	4,000 received, total cost $20,000
15 March	3,900 issued
19 March	1,200 received, total cost $7,200
21 March	1,100 issued
24 March	2,800 received, total cost $21,000

3 What is the inventory valuation at 31 March on a LIFO basis?

A $22,100

B $22,500

C $15,000

D $18,000

4 What is the value of the issue made on 21 March using a FIFO basis?

A $6,600

B $5,500

C $8,250

D $6,500

5 What is the inventory valuation at 31 March on a cumulative weighted average basis?

A $18,075

B $18,500

C $22,185

D $22,046

6 A company uses FIFO inventory pricing and has a high level of inventory turnover. In a period of rising prices, the closing inventory valuation is:

A close to current purchase prices

B based on the prices of the first items received

C much lower than current purchase prices

D lower than if LIFO inventory pricing were used.

7 A and B are in business, buying and selling goods for resale. During September 20X3 the following transactions occurred:

September	1	Balance brought forward NIL
September	3	Bought 200 units at $1.00 each
September	7	Sold 180 units
September	8	Bought 240 units at $1.50 each
September	14	Sold 170 units
September	15	Bought 230 units at $2.00 each
September	21	Sold 150 units

The value of inventory using the cumulative weighted average method of inventory valuation to the nearest $) is:

A $174

B $285

C $314

D $340

For the answers to these questions, see the 'Answers' section at the end of the book.

Chapter 5

MATERIAL INVENTORY CONTROL

The previous chapter looked at how transactions involving direct and indirect materials are recorded and valued. This chapter looks at the control of inventory levels as a means of controlling the costs of stores administration. This chapter covers syllabus area B1 (f) to (j).

CONTENTS

LEARNING OUTCOMES

At the end of this chapter you should be able to:

- describe the procedures required to monitor inventory and to minimise inventory discrepancies and losses
- explain and illustrate the costs of holding inventory and of being without inventory
- explain, illustrate and evaluate inventory control levels (minimum, maximum, re-order)
- calculate and interpret optimal order quantities
- explain the relationship between the materials costing system and the inventory control system.

1 MONITORING INVENTORY AND INVENTORY LOSSES

1.1 STOCKTAKING

Inventory records are kept on bin cards (in a manual stores control system) or in a computerised inventory control system. These record quantities purchased, quantities issued and the current balance held in inventory.

In practice, the records could become inaccurate. There are several reasons for this.

- There could be errors recording the quantities received or issued.
- A receipt into stores or an issue from stores might not be recorded at all, due to an oversight.
- Items of inventory might have to be thrown away, because they have deteriorated, and the write-off might not be recorded in the accounts.
- Inventory might get lost or stolen.

Inventory records should be kept as up-to-date as possible, and from time-to-time, there should be a physical count of the inventory actually held in store (a 'stocktake'). Actual quantities counted should be compared with the balances that should be in inventory, according to the records. Discrepancies should be investigated, and any errors in the accounts should be rectified.

Definition A **stocktake** is the counting and recording of the physical quantities of each item of inventory.

Periodic stocktakes are carried out at a specified time, for example at the end of the accounting year. This can be very disruptive to production as it may involve closing the stores for several days. This approach also means that there are long periods between inventory checks and substantial discrepancies may build up.

Continuous stocktakes involve checking items on a rotating basis. All items are checked at least once a year but items which are of high value or are used frequently can be checked more often.

1.2 ACTION TO BE TAKEN

Once the reasons for the difference have been identified then the appropriate action must be taken.

- If errors have been made when writing up the bin card or items omitted then the bin card must be corrected.
- If items of inventory were stored in the wrong place then they must be moved and a new total of actual inventory held should be calculated.
- If items have been stolen then security arrangements must be reviewed and the cost of the items stolen accounted for as an expense of the business.
- If inventory is being lost because it has deteriorated and has to be thrown away, measures for improving storage conditions might be considered, in order to reduce losses.

2 COSTS OF HOLDING INVENTORY AND STOCKOUTS

Inventory is held so that sales can be made and profits can be earned. When inventory is held, a wider variety of products can be offered, customer demand can be satisfied immediately and production is not delayed waiting for a new delivery of raw materials. However, holding inventory can be expensive. The objective of an inventory policy should be to minimise the total annual costs associated with inventory.

The total costs associated with inventory include the following costs:

- purchase costs
- inventory holding costs
- inventory ordering costs
- stockouts (i.e. the costs of being without inventory when it is needed).

Holding inventory is expensive. Holding costs include interest on capital, the costs of storage space and equipment, administration costs, and losses from deterioration, pilferage and obsolescence. Holding costs can be reduced by keeping inventory levels to a minimum. This suggests that there ought to be a policy of purchasing materials in small-sized orders, which would have to be placed at frequent intervals.

Order costs are incurred every time inventory is purchased from a supplier. Order costs include the buyer's time spent contacting the supplier, and the storekeeper's time spent checking the goods received. Order costs can be reduced by placing orders only at infrequent intervals. However, this means that order quantities need to be large, to reduce the total overall order costs for the year. Such a policy would result in high average levels of inventory, which increases holding costs.

There is a conflict between:

- the desire to minimise holding costs, by ordering in small quantities at frequent intervals; and
- the desire to minimise order costs, by placing large orders at infrequent intervals.

An inventory ordering and holding policy that minimises the total costs of holding inventory and ordering inventory combined (given a constant purchase price per unit of material regardless of order quantity) is to purchase materials in their **economic order quantity** (EOQ). The EOQ is the purchase order quantity that minimises total order costs plus inventory (stock) holding costs.

Running out of inventory (known as a **stockout**) also incurs costs. Customers might go elsewhere if finished goods are not in inventory when they want to buy them. Similarly, production will be disrupted if raw materials inventory is not on hand when required due to a stockout. **Buffer inventory (or buffer stock) which is also known as safety inventory (or safety stock),** is a basic level of inventory held to cover unexpected demand or uncertainty of lead time for the item of inventory. A further problem for management could be to decide how much buffer inventory to hold for each inventory item, to minimise the combined costs of:

- stockouts if the buffer inventory is not held; and
- the additional inventory holding costs that arise from having buffer inventory.

Clearly it is important to think carefully about the right level of inventory to hold so as to minimise the total associated costs.

Three questions about inventory control have to be resolved:

- in what quantities to order an item of inventory
- when to re-order
- what system to use for monitoring inventory levels.

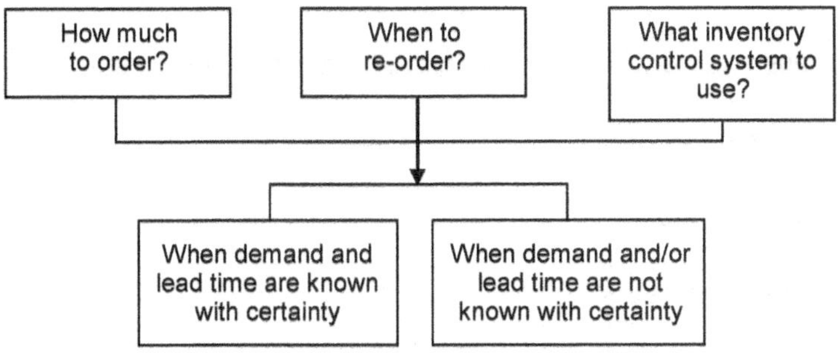

3 ECONOMIC ORDER QUANTITY (EOQ)

Ordering in large quantities reduces the annual costs of ordering. On the other hand, average inventory levels will be higher and so inventory holding costs increase. The economic order quantity is the quantity that minimises the combined costs of ordering and holding inventory.

Definition **Economic order quantity** (EOQ) is the order quantity for an item of inventory that will minimise the combined costs of ordering and holding inventory over a given period of time, say each year.

The economic order quantity for an item of inventory is calculated on the basis of the following assumptions.

- There should be no stockout of the item.
- There is no buffer inventory (buffer stock).
- A new delivery of the inventory item is received from the supplier at the exact time that existing inventory runs out.
- The inventory item is used up at an even and predictable rate over time.
- The delivery lead time from the supplier is predictable and reliable.

There is a formula for calculating the economic order quantity for any item of inventory, given these assumptions, which is:

$$EOQ = \sqrt{\frac{2C_oD}{C_H}}$$ where

C_o is the cost of placing an **order** of the inventory item

C_H is the annual cost of **holding** one unit of the inventory

D is the annual **demand** for the inventory item

Q is the order **quantity**

Note: Holding costs are often based on average inventory held which are estimated as $\frac{\text{Order quantity}}{2}$

Total holding costs are therefore $\frac{\text{EOQ}}{2}$ × Cost of holding one unit.

EXAMPLE

A retailer of soda has an annual demand of 36,750 crates of soda. The crates cost $12 each. Fresh supplies can be obtained immediately, but ordering costs and the cost of carriage inwards are $200 per order. The annual cost of holding one crate in inventory is estimated to be $1.20.

Determine the economic order quantity and total annual inventory costs for the retailer.

$$\text{EOQ} = \sqrt{\frac{2 \times 200 \times 36{,}750}{1.20}}$$

$$= 3{,}500 \text{ crates}$$

$$\text{Total annual costs} = \text{Holding costs} + \text{Re-ordering costs}$$

$$= (\text{Average inventory} \times C_H) + (\text{Number of re-orders pa} \times C_O)$$

$$= \frac{3{,}500 \times \$1.20}{2} + \frac{36{,}750 \times \$200}{3{,}500}$$

$$= \$2{,}100 + \$2{,}100$$

$$= \$4{,}200$$

ACTIVITY 1

Demand for a company's product is about 600,000 units per annum. It costs $3 to keep one unit in inventory for one year. Each time an order is placed, administrative costs of $40 are incurred.

How many units should the company order at a time so as to minimise the costs of ordering and holding inventory?

For a suggested answer, see the 'Answers' section at the end of the book.

4 INVENTORY RE-ORDER LEVEL

The second problem in inventory control concerns the point at which a new order should be placed with a supplier.

The re-order level is the level of inventory at which a fresh order is placed with a supplier.

The lead time is the time gap that arises between an order being placed and its eventual delivery. If the demand and lead time are known with certainty then an exact re-order level may be calculated.

ACTIVITY 2

Return to the original Watton example. Assume that the company adopts the EOQ of 3,500 barrels as its order quantity and that it now takes two weeks for an order to be delivered

Required:

(a) How frequently will the company place an order?

(b) How much inventory will it have on hand when the order is placed?

For a suggested answer, see the 'Answers' section at the end of the book.

In the real world, however, both the supply lead time and the demand for the inventory item during the lead time will vary. To avoid a stockout, the order must be placed so as to leave some buffer inventory (safety stock) if demand and lead time follow the average pattern. The problem is again to decide how to minimise the combined costs of holding higher levels of buffer inventory and the stockout costs if the buffer inventory is low.

You only need to be aware of this problem in general terms, however. For the purpose of your examination, it will be assumed that buffer inventory will be kept at a high enough level to reduce the risk of a stockout to zero. This means that the re-order level must be high enough to cover any foreseeable level of demand for the item of inventory during the lead time period between placing an order and its eventual delivery.

4.1 RE-ORDER LEVEL TO AVOID STOCKOUTS, WITH UNCERTAIN DEMAND AND LEAD TIME

When the demand for an item of inventory is uncertain, because it varies from day to day or week to week, and when the supply lead time is variable, the re-order level that avoids any risk of a stockout during the lead time is:

Re-order level = Maximum supply lead time (in days or weeks) × Maximum daily or weekly demand for the item.

EXAMPLE

A company operates a fixed re-order level of inventory control, and sets the re-order level so as to avoid the risk of stockouts. It is trying to establish the re-order level for a new inventory item, JK6. The daily demand for JK6 is expected to be not less than 60 tonnes and not more than 100 tonnes. The lead time between placing an order and receiving delivery from the supplier will be between one and three days.

What should be the re-order level for JK6?

SOLUTION

Re-order level = 100 tonnes × 3 days = 300 tonnes.

If it is company policy to hold a required level of safety stock (buffer inventory) then the re-order level is calculated in a slightly different way.

Re-order level = Safety stock + (supply lead time × demand)

EXAMPLE

A company is trying to establish the re-order level for a new item of inventory, Product X. The daily demand for this product is 50 units and the lead time between placing an order and receiving delivery from the supplier is 4 days. It is company policy to hold a safety stock level of 10 units.

SOLUTION

Re-order level = Safety stock + (supply lead time × demand)

= 10 + (50 × 4)

= 10 + 200

= 210 units

4.2 CONTROL LEVELS OF INVENTORY

When the so-called fixed re-order level system is used, it is usual to identify two other control levels for each inventory item, in addition to the re-order level. These are the minimum and maximum stock control levels (inventory control levels) for the item.

If the quantity held of an inventory item goes below the minimum control level, or above the maximum control level, a control message should be given to the manager responsible for inventory, for example the stores manager. The message should alert the manager to the fact that the inventory item and its inventory levels should be monitored carefully, and where necessary control measures should be taken. For example, if an item of inventory falls below its minimum control level, action might be taken to check with the supplier when the next delivery of the inventory should be received.

4.3 MINIMUM INVENTORY CONTROL LEVEL

The minimum stock (inventory) control level for an item of inventory is a warning level. If inventory falls to its minimum control level, management should check that a new delivery of the item will be received from the supplier before stockout occurs. Emergency action to replenish might be required.

The **minimum inventory control level** is calculated as:

Re-order level – Average expected demand for the inventory item during the average lead time.

This can be stated as:

Re-order level – (Average demand for the item each day/month × Average length of lead time in days/months)

ACTIVITY 3

Calculate the minimum stock (inventory) control level from the following data:

Re-order level	3,600 units
Average lead time	5 days
Minimum usage	300 units per day
Maximum usage	500 units per day

For a suggested answer, see the 'Answers' section at the end of the book.

4.4 MAXIMUM INVENTORY CONTROL LEVEL

Another useful control level for inventory is the maximum stock (inventory) control level. This is the maximum quantity of an inventory item that should ever be held in store. If actual inventory levels exceed this quantity, something unusual must have happened. Either inventory must have been re-ordered before it reached the re-order level, the quantities consumed in the lead time must have been much lower than usual, or the lead time was shorter than expected.

The **maximum stock (inventory) control level**.is the re-order quantity plus the re-order level minus the minimum quantity of inventory that should ever be consumed during the minimum lead time.

Expressed in a different way, the maximum stock (inventory) control level is therefore:

Re-order quantity plus Re-order level minus (Minimum demand per day/week × Minimum lead time in days/weeks)

EXAMPLE

Z Limited places an order of 500 units, to replenish its inventory of a particular component whenever the inventory balance is reduced to 300 units. The order takes at least four days to be delivered and Z Limited uses at least 50 components each day.

What is the maximum inventory control level?

SOLUTION

The maximum inventory control level is: 500 + 300 – (50 × 4) = 600 units.

ACTIVITY 4

Calculate the re-order level, minimum stock (inventory) control level and maximum stock (inventory) control level from the following data.

Minimum lead time	4 days
Average lead time	5 days
Maximum lead time	7 days
Maximum usage	500 units per day
Minimum usage	300 units per day
Re-order quantity	5,400 units

For a suggested answer, see the 'Answers' section at the end of the book.

5 MATERIALS COSTING AND INVENTORY CONTROL

The previous chapter described the system for costing materials. This chapter has focused on inventory control systems.

The materials costing system is based on stores ledger records, and its purpose is to value inventory, and issues of materials from store. An inventory control system is concerned with monitoring inventory levels, keeping inventory losses to a minimum and minimising the costs of holding and ordering inventory (and avoiding or controlling the costs of any stockouts).

There is a relationship between these two systems, because inventory records need to be accurate. Accuracy is lost whenever errors or unrecorded inventory losses occur, and periodic comparisons of the stores ledger with the physical inventory held should be carried out through stocktakes to ensure that there is consistency between the level of inventory recorded in both systems.

CONCLUSION

Effective inventory control is important, particularly for many manufacturing businesses where raw material costs are high. Purchasing costs, holding costs, ordering costs and stockout costs must all be considered and minimised in total.

KEY TERMS

Buffer stock– level of inventory held for emergencies.

Stockout – running out of inventory.

Stocktake – counting and recording physical quantities of inventory.

Lead time – the time between when an order is placed and the receipt of the inventory.

Economic Order Quantity – the order quantity that minimises ordering and holding costs.

Re-order level – Maximum lead time × Maximum demand.

Minimum inventory control level – Re-order level – (Average demand × Average lead time).

Maximum inventory control level – Re-order quantity + Re-order level – (Minimum demand × Minimum lead time).

Average stockholding – order quantity/2 = EOQ/2.

SELF TEST QUESTIONS

		Paragraph
1	What is a stockout?	2
2	What are the possible costs of a stockout?	2
3	What is buffer stock (inventory)?	2
4	Which combined costs are minimised when an inventory re-order quantity is the EOQ?	3.1
5	What is the formula for the inventory re-order level in a fixed re-order level system?	4.1
6	What is the formula for the minimum inventory control level in a fixed re-order level system?	4.3
7	What is the formula for the maximum inventory control level in a fixed re-order level system?	4.4

EXAM-STYLE QUESTIONS

1 A national chain of tyre fitters holds a popular tyre in inventory for which the following information is available:

Average usage	140 tyres per day
Minimum usage	90 tyres per day
Maximum usage	175 tyres per day
Lead time	10 to 16 days
Re-order quantity	3,000 tyres

Based on the data above, at what level of inventory should a replenishment order be issued?

A 2,240

B 2,800

C 3,000

D 5,740

2 An organisation has the following information on its inventory:

Average usage	1,200 units per day
Minimum usage	750 units per day
Maximum usage	1,600 units per day
Lead time	8 to 12 days
Re-order quantity	28,000 units
Re-order level	19,200 units

Based on the data above, the maximum inventory control level is ______ units

3 A manufacturer buys a liquid for its production process at $8 per litre. There are additional ordering costs and carriage inwards costs of $3,000 per order. The annual cost of holding one litre of the liquid in inventory is estimated to be $0.60. The manufacturer has an annual demand for the liquid of 342,225 litres.

To the nearest litre, what is the economic order quantity for the liquid for the manufacturer?

A 2,426 litres

B 41,366 litres

C 58,500 litres

D 60,000 litres

4 A manufacturer has annual demand for plastic casings of 48,050 units. It costs $0.05 per case in annual holding costs and each order incurs order costs of $500 per order. The manufacturer uses the economic order quantity for inventory control which has been determined at 1,550 units.

To the nearest $, the total annual re-ordering costs are $_____

5 The following are all examples of stockout costs except:

A Loss of revenue from customers

B Loss of bulk purchase discount

C Idle time payments to workers

D Premium paid to supplier for urgent order.

6 A manufacturing organisation uses 5,000 kg of a raw material evenly over a period. The purchase price is $6.50 per kg and the holding cost per period is 10% of purchase price. If the order quantity is 500 kg and a buffer inventory of 100 kg is held, the total holding cost of the raw material in the period is:

A $195

B $227.50

C $325

D $3,250

7 A manufacturer requires a liquid for its production process that has a monthly demand for the liquid of 1,000 litres (which cost at $1.50 per litre). Order costs are $160 per order and the annual cost of holding one litre of the liquid in inventory is estimated to be $0.06.

To the nearest litre, the economic order quantity for the liquid for the manufacturer is ______ litres.

8 Are the following statements true or false?

	True	False
When using re-order level control for inventory the supply lead time is always known		
The economic order quantity assumes that no buffer stock of inventory is held		

For the answers to these questions, see the 'Answers' section at the end of the book.

Chapter 6

ACCOUNTING FOR LABOUR

In this chapter we look at the cost of labour. We begin by looking at the ways in which employees are paid, and the elements of pay in the payroll. We shall then go on to explain the distinctions between direct and indirect labour costs. The procedures for accounting for labour costs will then be described, and finally certain aspects of labour cost control will be explained, such as monitoring labour turnover and productivity. This chapter covers syllabus area B2.

CONTENTS

LEARNING OUTCOMES

At the end of this chapter you should be able to:

- explain, illustrate and evaluate labour remuneration methods
- describe the operation of a payroll accounting system
- distinguish between direct and indirect labour costs
- describe the procedures and documentation required to ensure the correct coding, analysis and recording of direct and indirect labour
- describe and illustrate the accounting for labour costs

- discuss the relationship between the labour costing system and the payroll accounting system
- explain the causes and costs of, and calculate, labour turnover
- describe and illustrate measures of labour efficiency and utilisation (efficiency, capacity utilisation, production volume and idle time ratios).

1 LABOUR REMUNERATION

Most employees are paid a basic wage or salary. They might also earn additional payments, in the form of a bonus or for working overtime. Some employees do not earn a basic wage, but instead are paid according to the amount of output they produce (i.e. they are paid a 'piecework' rate).

You need to understand these basic elements of remuneration, so that you can calculate the cost of labour in an organisation.

1.1 FIXED BASIC SALARIES OR WAGES

A salary is a fixed basic amount of pay, usually payable every month. The amount of the basic salary is fixed for a given period of time.

The cost might be expressed as an annual salary such as $52,000 per year or as a weekly rate such as $1,000 per week.

Employees who are paid a fixed basic salary or wage are required to work a minimum number of hours, and in many organisations, they are not paid extra if they work for longer than this minimum. However, in other organisations, employees who work longer than the minimum number of hours each week or month are entitled to overtime payments.

1.2 PAYMENT FOR EACH HOUR WORKED

Time-rate employees are paid for the actual number of hours of attendance in a period, usually each week. A rate of pay will be set for each hour of attendance.

For employees who are paid for the hours they work, it is obviously extremely important to keep accurate records of the actual number of hours of attendance for each employee.

EXAMPLE

An employee is paid $25 per hour and is expected to work at least a 48-hour week.

What would he be paid for a standard 48-hour week?

SOLUTION

48 hours × $25 = $1,200

ACTIVITY 1

An employee is paid $15.86 per hour and works 31.5 hours in a particular week.

What would be the employee's wage for that week?

For a suggested answer, see the 'Answers' section at the end of the book.

1.3 PIECEWORK

Piecework is also known as payment by results or output-related pay. It is an alternative to time-related pay and fixed basic pay.

Definition **Piecework** is where a fixed amount is paid per unit of output achieved irrespective of the time spent.

EXAMPLE

If the amount paid to an employee is $9 per unit produced and that employee produces 80 units in a week how much should be paid in wages?

SOLUTION

80 units × $9 = $720

As far as an employee is concerned piecework or payment by results means that he can earn whatever he wishes within certain parameters. The harder that he works and the more units that he produces then the higher will be his earnings.

From the employer's point of view, the employees are paid for what they produce, not the hours they work. This can help to control costs.

Piecework is not normally popular with employees. Piecework rates are often low, and it is difficult to earn a reasonable amount of pay without working long hours. In addition, the employee gets no income during holidays or when he or she is unable to work through illness.

There are two other problems associated with payment by results. One is the problem of accurate recording of the actual output produced. The amount claimed to be produced determines the amount of pay and, therefore, is potentially open to abuse unless it can be adequately supervised.

The second problem is that of the maintenance of the quality of the work. If the employee is paid by the amount that is produced then the temptation might be to produce more units but of a lower quality.

Conclusion Basic payment methods for employees will either be time-related or output-related. Time-related methods are either a fixed basic salary or wage for a minimum number of hours per month or week, or a rate per hour worked. Output-related methods of payment are some sort of piecework payment.

1.4 VARIATIONS OF PIECEWORK

Basic piece-rate payments are a set amount for each unit produced e.g. $10 per unit. However, such systems are rare in practice and there are two main variations that could be viewed in a similar way to a bonus.

A **piece-rate with guarantee** operates to give the employee some security if the employer does not provide enough work in a particular period. The way that the system works is that if an employee's earnings for the amount of units produced in the period are lower than the guaranteed amount, then the guaranteed amount is paid instead.

EXAMPLE

Jones is paid $6 for every unit that he produces but he has a guaranteed wage of $60 per eight-hour day. In a particular week he produces the following number of units:

Monday	12 units
Tuesday	14 units
Wednesday	9 units
Thursday	14 units
Friday	8 units

Calculate Jones's wage for this week.

SOLUTION

Total weekly wage

	$
Monday (12 × $6)	72
Tuesday (14 × $6)	84
Wednesday (guarantee)	60
Thursday (14 × $6)	84
Friday (guarantee)	60
	360

ACTIVITY 2

Continuing with the example of Jones above, what would be his weekly wage if the guarantee were for $300 per week rather than $60 per day?

For a suggested answer, see the 'Answers' section at the end of the book.

A **differential piecework system** is where the piece-rate increases as successive targets for a period are achieved and exceeded.

This will tend to encourage higher levels of production and acts as a form of bonus for payment by results for employees who produce more units than the standard level.

ACTIVITY 3

Payment by results rates for an organisation are as follows:

Up to 99 units per week	$1.50 per unit
100 to 119 units per week	$1.75 per unit
120 or more units per week	$2.00 per unit

If an employee produces 102 units in a week how much will he be paid?

For a suggested answer, see the 'Answers' section at the end of the book.

1.5 OVERTIME

If an employee works more than the number of hours set by the organisation as the working week, the additional hours worked are known as overtime. In many organisations employees who work overtime are paid an additional amount per hour for those extra hours that they work.

When the rate per hour for overtime is higher than the basic rate of pay in normal working hours, the additional pay per hour is known as **overtime premium**. For example, suppose that employees are paid a basic rate of $6 per hour, with overtime paid at time and a half, or at 50% above the basic rate, the overtime premium would be $3 per hour.

EXAMPLE

The basic hourly rate of an employee is $7.20. Any overtime is paid at 125% of his normal hourly rate.

What is the amount paid for each hour of overtime, and what is the overtime premium?

SOLUTION

Rate per hour in overtime = $7.20 × 125% = $9.00.

The overtime premium is $7.20 × 25% = $1.80.

In costing, it is important to distinguish, between the basic rate of pay and the overtime premium. This is because it is usual to treat overtime premium as an indirect labour cost, even when the basic rate of pay is a direct labour cost.

The overtime rate is only paid for the hours worked over the basic hours. The basic hours are paid at the basic rate.

ACTIVITY 4

An employee's basic week is 40 hours at a rate of pay of $5 per hour. Overtime is paid at 'time and a half'.

What is the wage cost of this employee if he works for 45 hours in a week?

For a suggested answer, see the 'Answers' section at the end of the book.

Overtime and fixed pay employees

If an employee's pay is a fixed weekly, monthly or annual amount rather than an hourly rate of pay, then any overtime payment will still normally be expressed in terms of a percentage of the basic hourly rate. It is, therefore, necessary to convert the salary into an effective hourly rate based on the standard working week of the organisation.

ACTIVITY 5

An employee is paid an annual salary of $19,500. The standard working week for the organisation is 38 hours per week and the employee is paid for 52 weeks of the year. Any overtime that this employee works is paid at time and a half.

What is the hourly rate for this employee's overtime?

For a suggested answer, see the 'Answers' section at the end of the book.

1.6 BONUSES

Bonuses are payments to employees on top of their basic pay and any overtime payments. They may be paid to employees for a variety of reasons. An individual employee, a department, a division or indeed the entire organisation may have performed particularly well and it is felt by the management that a bonus is due to some or all of the employees.

The basic principle of a bonus payment is that the employee is rewarded for any additional income or savings in cost to the organisation. This may be for example because the employee has managed to save a certain amount of time on the production of a product or a number of products. This time saving will save the organisation money and the amount saved will tend to be split between the organisation and the employee on some agreed basis.

There are many different types of bonus arrangements. However, these different arrangements can be categorised as:

- a collective bonus scheme for all employees. In general a bonus will be paid to employees if the organisation as a whole has performed well in the latest period. Some of the profits from this above average performance will be shared with the employees in the form of a bonus. This is known as a profit-sharing bonus

- a collective bonus scheme for a limited group of employees. In some organisations bonuses may be determined on a departmental or divisional basis. If a particular department or division performs well then the employees in that department or division will receive some sort of bonus

- individual bonus schemes for employees.

Definition A **flat rate bonus** is where all employees are paid the same amount of bonus each regardless of their individual salary.

The principle behind such a payment is that all of the employees have contributed the same amount to earning the bonus no matter what their position in the organisation or their salary level.

EXAMPLE

Suppose that a small business made a profit of $250,000 in the previous quarter and the managing director decided to pay out $20,000 of this as a flat rate bonus to each employee. The business has 50 employees in total including the managing director earning a salary of $68,000 per annum and Chris Roberts, his secretary, who earns $28,000 per annum.

How much would the managing director and Chris Roberts each receive as bonus for the quarter?

SOLUTION

Total bonus		$20,000
Split between 50 employees ($20,000/50)	=	$400 per employee
Managing director's bonus		$400
Chris Roberts's bonus		$400

A percentage bonus scheme is an alternative scheme to a flat rate bonus scheme.

Definition A **percentage bonus** is where the amount paid to each employee as bonus is a set percentage of that employee's annual salary.

The principle behind this method of calculating the bonus payable is to give a larger bonus to those with higher salaries in recognition that they have contributed more to the earning of the bonus than those with a lower salary.

In the above example, if the bonus payable were 1.5% of annual salary, the managing director would receive $1,020 and Chris Roberts would receive $420.

Productivity-related bonuses

A productivity-related bonus is a bonus whereby an employee (or group of employees) are paid extra for completing their work in less than the expected amount of time. In other words, if employees achieve higher-than-expected productivity, they are rewarded.

The principle of a productivity-related bonus or incentive scheme is to encourage the employees affected to achieve additional output in the time they work.

The basis of bonus schemes in these instances is to set a predetermined standard time (or target time) for the performance of a job or production of a given amount of output. If the job is completed in less than the standard time or more than the given output is achieved in the standard time then this will mean additional profit to the employer.

This additional profit will then be split between the employer and the employee in some agreed manner.

EXAMPLE

It is expected that it will take 90 minutes for an employee to make a product.

If the employee makes the product in 60 minutes what is the saving to the employer if the employee's wage rate is $15.00 per hour?

SOLUTION

Time saving = 30 minutes

At a wage rate of $15.00 per hour the cost saving is $7.50.

In a productivity-related bonus scheme, the employee will be rewarded with a share of the cost saving. For example, if the employee receives half of the saving, the bonus would be paid at the rate of $7.50 per hour saved, which in the case of this example would amount to a bonus of $3.75.

Conclusion This employee's efficient work has saved the organisation $7.50. The basis of a bonus scheme for time-rate workers is that a proportion of this $7.50 should be paid to the employee as a bonus. The size of the bonus is for the employer to decide.

ACTIVITY 6

Employee's wage rate	$15 per hour
Time allowed for job	40 minutes
Time taken for job	25 minutes

The company's policy is to calculate the bonus payable to the employee as 35% of the time saved on the job.

What is the bonus on this basis?

For a suggested answer, see the 'Answers' section at the end of the book.

2 ACCOUNTING FOR PAYROLL

Accounting for payroll is a part of the financial accounting system within an organisation. The payroll is prepared every time that employees are paid, which is usually every week or month.

The payroll is a list of each individual employee within the organisation, identifying the employee by name and employment number, and the department or cost centre for which the employee works. For each employee, the payroll is used to calculate:

- the employee's gross pay
- the employer's benefits contribution for the employee.

Gross pay is the employee's total remuneration. The employer's benefits contributions are additional payments of tax the employer must make to the government for the employee. For the organisation, the total cost of labour is the sum of gross pay and employer's benefits contributions, plus any contributions the employer makes to an employees' pension fund.

The payroll is also used to calculate the deductions from each employee's gross pay, for:

- income tax
- the employee's benefits contributions
- any contributions by the employee to a pension scheme
- any other deductions, such as payments for trade union membership.

The gross pay minus all deductions is the employee's net pay, or 'take home' pay, which is the cash payment by the employer to the employee.

The payroll therefore itemises the total labour cost for each employee, the deductions from pay and the net pay. It also shows the total cost of labour and the total amount of deductions, for each department or cost centre and for the organisation as a whole.

3 RELATIONSHIP BETWEEN PAYROLL ACCOUNTING AND LABOUR COSTING

With payroll accounting, the aim is to establish:

- the total amount of wages and salaries payable, deductions from pay and net pay
- the total cost of wages and salaries, for charging as an expense to the statement of profit or loss.

There are two key accounts for recording payroll costs in a financial accounting system:

- a wages and salaries payable account
- a wages and salaries control account.

Illustrative examples of how these accounts are used are shown below. The wages and salaries payable account is used for recording deductions from pay and net pay. The wages and salaries control account is used to establish the total cost of labour for charging to the statement of profit or loss.

Wages and salaries payable account

	$		$
Bank (net pay)	67,000	Wages and salaries control	100,000
Income tax payable	23,000		
Employees' benefit contribution	10,000		
	100,000		100,000

Wages and salaries control account

	$		$
Wages and salaries payable	100,000	Statement of profit or loss	115,000
Employer's benefit contribution	15,000		
	115,000		115,000

With a labour costing system, the total wages and salaries cost (in the above example, $115,000) is analysed to calculate the costs of cost units. The first stage of this analysis is to separate direct labour costs from indirect labour costs, and account for these accordingly.

In a cost accounting system, instead of charging the wages and salaries cost to the statement of profit or loss, the costs are therefore charged to work-in-progress (direct labour) or production overhead, administration overhead or sales and distribution overhead for indirect labour costs.

EXAMPLE

A manufacturing business has total wages and salaries costs in June of $115,000. These total costs consist of:

- direct labour costs $37,000
- indirect production labour $25,000
- administration labour costs $24,000
- sales and distribution labour costs $29,000

These labour costs should be accounted for as follows:

Wages and salaries control account

	$		$
		Work-in-progress	37,000
		Production overhead	25,000
		Administration overhead	24,000
		Sales and distribution overhead	29,000
			115,000

Work-in-progress

	$		$
Wages (direct labour)	37,000		

Production overheads

	$		$
Wages and salaries (indirect production labour)	25,000		

Administration overheads

	$		$
Wages and salaries	24,000		

Sales and distribution overheads

	$		$
Wages and salaries	29,000		

4 DIRECT AND INDIRECT LABOUR COSTS

Employees can be classified as either direct labour or indirect labour. Direct labour means employees who are directly involved in producing goods or services for customers. Indirect labour means employees who are not directly involved in this work. Examples of indirect labour employees in a manufacturing business are:

- employees working in administration or selling and distribution
- employees in departments that support production, but are not directly involved in production, such as staff in production planning, repairs and maintenance and stores
- employees in departments where production work is carried out, but who are not themselves directly involved in production work. These include department supervisors.

In production, direct labour employees are employees in production departments who work directly on making the products or completing the jobs or contracts for customers.

The total wages and salary costs of employees can be traced to individual departments/cost centres. All the labour costs of employees outside direct production departments are indirect labour, and their costs are indirect labour costs.

An aim in cost accounting is to identify direct labour costs and indirect labour costs. These are not the same as the costs of direct labour and indirect labour employees.

- All the costs of indirect labour employees are indirect labour costs.
- However, not all the costs of direct labour employees are treated as direct labour costs. Some of these costs are treated as indirect costs.

Costs of direct labour employees that are usually treated as indirect costs are:

- the costs of idle time
- the costs of overtime premium
- costs of labour time not spent in production, such as the cost of time spent on training courses, and the cost of payments during time off work through illness.

4.1 IDLE TIME

Definition **Idle time** or **down time** is time paid for that is non-productive.

Idle time occurs in most organisations. What is important is that the amount of idle time and the reasons for it are accurately assessed, reported to management for corrective action if necessary and treated correctly in terms of allocation of the cost to products.

The effect of idle time is that for a set number of hours of work, if there is idle time or non-productive time within that period, then less will be produced than expected.

EXAMPLE

Suppose that a workforce of 10 employees is expected to work a 35-hour week each. In the production time available it is expected that 175 units will be produced i.e. each unit requires two hours of labour.

Now suppose that the employees only actually work for 320 of those hours although they will be paid for the full 350 hours.

How many units would be likely to be made in that week? How would the 30 hours that were paid for but not worked be described?

SOLUTION

The anticipated number of units to be produced would be 160 rather than the expected amount of 175. However, the workforce would still be paid for the full 350 hours.

The 30 hours paid for but not worked are an example of idle time.

Recording idle time

The amount of hours that are paid for but are not used for production represent wasted hours for the organisation and warrant close control from management.

To assist control, time booking procedures i.e. timesheets, job cards etc., should permit an analysis of idle time by cause.

Idle time can be classified as avoidable (or controllable) and unavoidable (or uncontrollable). Making this classification is often a matter for discretionary judgement. For example, are the idle time effects of a power cut avoidable? In most situations the answer is probably not, but if a standby generator was available but not used then the idle time would be classified as avoidable.

Avoidable idle time

The main causes of avoidable idle time are:

(a) production disruption: this could be idle time due to machine breakdown, shortage of materials, inefficient scheduling, poor supervision of labour, etc.

(b) policy decisions: examples of this might include run-down of inventory, changes in product specification, retraining schemes, etc.

Idle time as an indirect labour cost

The labour costs of idle time cannot be charged directly to any individual products (or other cost units). Instead, they are treated as an indirect cost and included in production overhead costs.

4.2 OVERTIME

When direct labour works overtime, the basic rate of pay is treated as a direct labour cost. The overtime premium is usually treated as an indirect cost, and included in production overheads, although the premium can sometimes be a direct labour cost.

- If the overtime is at the specific request of a customer (for example, to get a job finished more quickly), the full cost of the overtime work, including the overtime premium, should be treated as a direct labour cost (e.g. as a direct cost of the job).
- In all other circumstances, the overtime premium should be treated as an indirect cost, with only the basic labour cost (i.e. the overtime hours at the basic rate of pay) treated as a direct cost.

EXAMPLE

During a particular month the workers in a factory worked on production for 2,500 hours. Of these 200 hours were hours of overtime of which 50 hours were to cover lost production and 150 were spent on an urgent job at the request of a customer.

The basic wage rate was $15.00 per hour and overtime was paid at the rate of time and a third.

Calculate the total wage cost for the month and show the amount of direct and indirect labour cost.

SOLUTION

Total wage cost(2,300 hours × $15) + (200 hours × $20) $38,500

This can be broken down as follows:

	$
Direct costs	
Basic cost of direct workers (2,500 × $15)	37,500
Overtime premium for urgent job (150 × $5)	750
Total	38,250
Indirect cost	
Overtime premium for lost production (50 × $5)	250
Total	250

4.3 IDENTIFYING DIRECT AND INDIRECT LABOUR COSTS

Within a costing system, the task of identifying the costs of indirect labour employees is quite straightforward. The data in the payroll can be used to identify the cost centre where the employee works, and the full cost of the employee is recorded as an indirect cost of the cost centre.

The task of separating the total costs of direct labour into direct and indirect labour costs is more complicated, because of idle time, overtime premium and other non-productive time. In addition, in order to measure the costs of different products or jobs, it is necessary to establish how much time the employee has spent working on each product or job. To do this, there has to be a system for recording direct labour times, and allocating the time spent to individual products or jobs.

5 DOCUMENTATION OF LABOUR TIME

The most common methods of recording how much time has been spent on particular activities, products or jobs are:

- timesheets
- job sheets
- cost cards.

5.1 TIMESHEETS

Definition A **timesheet** is a record of how a person's time at work has been spent.

The total hours that an employee has worked in a day or week are shown on the employee's clock card but a breakdown of how those hours were spent will be shown on the timesheet.

The employee fills out his or her own timesheet on a daily, weekly or monthly basis depending upon the policies of the organisation.

The employee will enter his name, clock number and department at the top of the timesheet together with details of the work he has been engaged on in the period and the hours spent on that work.

The purpose of a timesheet for salaried employees is simply to allocate their costs to departments or products. No calculations of the amounts payable to the employee are necessary as these are fixed by the employee's salary agreement.

EXAMPLE

In the week commencing 28 March 20X4 Bernard Gill from the maintenance department spent his time as follows:

Monday 28 March	9.30 am – 12.30 pm	Machine X
	1.30 pm – 5.30 pm	Machine X
Tuesday 29 March	9.30 am – 11.00 am	Machine X
	11.00 am – 12.30 pm	Office computer
	1.30 pm – 7.30 pm	Office computer
Wednesday 30 March	Sick leave	
Thursday 31 March	9.30 am – 12.30 pm	Machine L
	1.30 pm – 5.30 pm	Machine L
Friday 1 April	Holiday	

The working day for this organisation is 7 hours per day and any overtime is paid to a salaried employee of Bernard's grade at $20.10 per hour.

Write up Bernard Gill's timesheet for the week commencing 28 March 20X4. His clock card number is 925734.

SOLUTION

TIMESHEET						
Name: Bernard Gill				**Clock Number:** 925734		
Department: Maintenance						
Week commencing: 28 March 20X4						
Date	*Job*	*Start*	*Finish*	*Hours*	*Overtime*	
					Hrs	*$*
28/3	Machine X	9.30	5.30	7.0		
29/3	Machine X	9.30	11.00	1.5		
	Office computer	11.00	7.30	7.5	2	20.10
30/3	Sick leave	9.30	5.30	7.0		
31/3	Machine L	9.30	5.30	7.0		
1/4	Holiday	9.30	5.30	7.0		
Total hours				37.0	2	
Total overtime payment						40.20
Foreman's signature						

5.2 JOB SHEETS

Job sheets take on an even greater importance for employees who are paid on a results or time basis. In these situations the sheet is a record of the products produced and it is also used to calculate the payment due to the employee.

EXAMPLE

Sheila Green is an employee in a garment factory with a clock number of 73645. She is a machinist and she is paid $8.20 for each dress she machines, $10.10 for a pair of trousers and $6.50 for a shirt.

In the week commencing 28 March 20X4 she produces 23 dresses, 14 pairs of trousers and 21 shirts. It took her 28 hours to do this work.

Draft her job sheet for that week.

SOLUTION

JOB SHEET					
Name: Sheila Green				**Clock Number:** 73645	
Department: Factory					
Week commencing: 28 March 20X4					
Product	*Units*	*Code*	*Price*	*Bonus*	*Total*
Dresses	23	DRE	8.20	–	188.60
Trousers	14	TRO	10.10	–	141.40
Shirts	21	SHI	6.50	–	136.50
Gross wages					466.50
Total hours					28
Foreman's signature:					
Date:					

A column is included in the timesheet for any bonus that the employee might earn. There is no overtime column as a payment by results employee does not earn overtime.

5.3 COST CARDS: JOB COSTING

Definition A **job cost card** is a card that records the costs involved in a particular job.

Instead of a record being kept of the work done by each employee, a record can be kept of the work performed on each job by all direct labour employees. This must of course be reconciled to the total amount of work recorded by the employees on their timesheets or clock cards.

ACTIVITY 7

A cake icer works on a number of cakes in a day and each one is costed as a separate job. The rate of pay for cake icing is $15.30 per hour. On 28 March 20X4 the icer worked on the following cakes:

28/3JN	3 hours
28/3KA	5 hours

Prepare job cards for these two jobs showing the amount of labour worked by the cake icer.

For a suggested answer, see the 'Answers' section at the end of the book.

6 LABOUR TURNOVER

Labour costs should be kept under control. There are various reasons why labour costs might be higher or lower than expected. Three such reasons are:

- labour turnover is higher or lower than usual
- labour efficiency or productivity might be better or worse than usual
- idle time might be high or low. Idle time is money spent on labour costs when no work is done. The cost of idle time is therefore a wasted expense.

Definition **Labour turnover** is a measure of the speed at which employees leave an organisation and are replaced.

Labour turnover is often calculated as follows:

$$\frac{\text{Average annual number of leavers who are replaced}}{\text{Average number of employees}} \times 100\%$$

Labour turnover can be monitored over time, to see whether the rate is rising, falling or fairly stable. An organisation might have an idea of what is an acceptable rate of labour turnover, and compare the actual rate against this benchmark.

ACTIVITY 8

On average a company employs 7,000 workers but during the last year 200 of these workers have resigned and have had to be replaced.

What is the labour turnover for the year?

For a suggested answer, see the 'Answers' section at the end of the book.

6.1 COSTS OF LABOUR TURNOVER

Whenever employees leave an organisation, the organisation incurs a cost. The cost of replacing employees ('replacement costs') who have left is not just the obvious costs of advertising the replacement or paying an employment agency, and the costs of time spent interviewing, choosing and taking on the new employee. There are also a number of other less obvious replacement costs such as:

- the costs of training a new employee
- the loss of efficiency whilst new employees are learning the job
- the effect on the morale of the existing workforce when labour turnover is high, leading to a loss of efficiency.

Costs may also be incurred to reduce labour turnover. These costs are known as 'preventative costs' and may include:

- improving employee remuneration or benefits
- improving the working environment
- training existing employees and offering career progression.

ACTIVITY 9

The cost of labour turnover can be classified as preventative or replacement.

Give three examples of each cost.

For a suggested answer, see the 'Answers' section at the end of the book.

6.2 CAUSES OF LABOUR TURNOVER

The employee records should show as clearly as possible the reasons for each employee leaving. If a particular cause is recurrent this should be investigated. However, often employees leaving do not give the full story of why they are leaving, therefore, any statistics gathered from this source should be treated with caution.

In some cases, the loss of employees is unavoidable. For example, employees might retire or move to a different part of the country (or to a different country altogether).

Sometimes, employees leave to take up a job somewhere else that offers more pay, or represents a career move.

Another cause of turnover can be dissatisfaction with the job, unpleasant working conditions, or poor interpersonal relationships with a supervisor or colleagues.

Management should try to identify causes of avoidable labour turnover, and think about whether any measures should be taken to try to reduce the turnover rate.

Conclusion High labour turnover has a high cost to a business that is not necessarily always obvious. Labour turnover should be closely monitored and reduced if possible.

7 LABOUR EFFICIENCY AND UTILISATION

Two other reasons why a workforce might produce more or less output than expected are labour efficiency and labour utilisation.

7.1 EFFICIENT AND INEFFICIENT LABOUR

Definition The labour force of an organisation is described as **efficient** if it produces more than the standard amount of goods in a set period of time.

If the labour force is efficient then it is working faster than anticipated or producing more goods than anticipated in a set period of time.

This might be because the employees are of a higher grade than anticipated or are more experienced or motivated or simply better at their job than the average employee.

Alternatively, it might be due to a better grade of material being used that is easier to work with or an improved design specification that requires fewer labour hours.

Definition The labour force of an organisation is described as **inefficient** if it produces less than the standard amount of goods in a set period of time.

If the labour force is working more slowly than anticipated or producing less units in a set period of time than anticipated then the employees will be said to be inefficient.

This inefficiency might be because of poor morale within the workforce, use of inexperienced or below par employees or workers having an 'off day'.

It could also be due to the use of cheaper or lower grade materials that require more work or a change in the design specification that requires more hours.

7.2 EFFICIENCY RATIO

Labour efficiency or productivity can be measured by means of an **efficiency ratio**. The efficiency ratio compares the time actually taken to do the work and the time that would have been expected to do the work. The expected time to do a piece of work, such as the expected time to make one unit of a product, can be measured in standard hours.

Definition A **standard hour** is the output expected in one hour of production at normal efficiency, i.e. the amount of work than can be produced in one hour under standard conditions

For example, if 2,000 units of an item are produced and the output produced represents 500 hours of work, then the standard hour would be 4 units per hour.

The standard hour is especially useful as a common measure for combining heterogeneous (dissimilar) products so that manufacturing performance for a cost centre (or production unit) as a whole can be assessed. The total expected hours, for example, of a given level of production of all products could be compared to the actual hours taken in order to assess the efficiency of all production. This can be done via the efficiency ratio.

Definition The **efficiency ratio** is a ratio, expressed as a percentage that compares the standard hours of work produced with the actual hours worked. When the output is produced in exactly the time expected, the efficiency ratio is 100%. When output is produced in less than the expected time, the ratio is higher than 100%.

The efficiency ratio is calculated as follows:

$$\frac{\text{Actual output measured in standard hours}}{\text{Actual production hours}} \times 100\%$$

The efficiency ratio may be referred to as the **productivity ratio**.

7.3 CAPACITY UTILISATION RATIO

A capacity utilisation ratio can be used to measure the utilisation of labour. Labour utilisation refers to how much labour time is used, compared to how much available time was expected.

Definition The **capacity utilisation ratio** is expressed as a percentage and compares the actual number of hours actively worked with the budgeted labour hours for the period.

$$\text{Capacity utilisation ratio} = \frac{\text{Actual hours worked}}{\text{Budgeted production hours}} \times 100\%$$

7.4 PRODUCTION/VOLUME RATIO OR ACTIVITY RATIO

Definition The **production/volume ratio** assesses how the overall production level compares to planned levels, and is the product of the efficiency ratio and the capacity ratio.

Over 100% indicates that overall production is above planned levels and below 100% indicates a shortfall compared to plans.

The production/volume ratio is calculated as:

$$\frac{\text{Actual output measured in standard hours}}{\text{Budgeted production hours}} \times 100\%$$

The three ratios calculated above can be summarised diagrammatically as follows:

Production/volume ratio

Equals

Capacity ratio × Efficiency ratio

Conclusion

Ratio	*What it measures*	*A ratio of more than 100% indicates that*
Capacity ratio	utilisation	Labour worked more hours than had originally been budgeted
Efficiency ratio	productivity	Labour have performed their tasks quicker than was expected in a standard hour
Activity ratio	overall production	More volume was produced than was originally budgeted

ACTIVITY 10

The budgeted output for a period is 2,000 units and the budgeted time for the production of these units is 200 hours.

The actual output in the period is 2,300 units and the actual time worked by the labour force is 180 hours.

Calculate the three ratios.

For a suggested answer, see the 'Answers' section at the end of the book.

7.5 IDLE TIME RATIO

The idle time ratio is another useful ratio because it gives an indication of the percentage of working hours that were lost as a result of the labour force being 'idle' during idle time.

Definition The **idle time ratio** shows the percentage of labour hours available that were lost because of idle time.

The idle time ratio is calculated as:

$$\frac{\text{Idle hours}}{\text{Total hours available}} \times 100\%$$

ACTIVITY 11

An organisation's work force were budgeted to work for 40,000 hours during December. The workforce were actually paid for 50,000 hours but only worked for 42,000 hours due to a machine breakdown in the factory.

Use this information to calculate the idle time ratio for the organisation.

For a suggested answer, see the 'Answers' section at the end of the book.

CONCLUSION

This chapter explained the different methods of remunerating employees and how payroll costs and labour costs are recorded. The distinction between direct and indirect labour costs has been explained.

Finally, ratios for monitoring and controlling labour turnover, efficiency and utilisation have been described.

We have now looked at two elements of cost, materials and labour. In the next chapter, we shall look at other expenses.

KEY TERMS

Overtime – time that is paid for, usually at a premium, over and above the basic hours for the period.

Overtime premium – the amount paid for overtime in excess of the basic rate of pay.

Piecework – where a fixed amount is paid per unit of output achieved irrespective of the time spent.

Flat rate bonus – where all employees are paid the same amount of bonus each regardless of their individual salary.

Percentage bonus – where the amount paid to each employee as bonus is a set percentage of that employee's annual salary.

Individual bonus schemes – those that benefit individual workers according to their own results.

Group bonus scheme – where the bonus is based upon the output of the workforce as a whole or a particular group of the workforce. The bonus is then shared between the individual members of the group on some pre-agreed basis.

Timesheet – a record of how a person's time at work has been spent.

Job card – a card that records the costs involved in a particular job.

Idle time or down time – time paid for that is non-productive.

Direct labour cost – the cost of labour that is directly attributable to a cost unit. It consists of the cost of direct labour spent actively working on production, but usually excludes any overtime premium payments.

Indirect labour cost – labour overheads, consisting of all the labour costs of indirect workers plus the indirect labour costs of direct workers.

Labour turnover – the rate at which employees leave the organisation. A labour turnover ratio is measured as the numbers leaving in a period as a percentage of the average total number of employees in the period.

Efficiency ratio – comparison of the expected time for producing output compared with the actual time, expressed as a percentage.

Capacity ratio – comparison of the actual time worked with the budgeted time for the period, expressed as a percentage.

Production/volume ratio – assesses how the overall production level compares to planned levels, and is the product of the efficiency ratio and the capacity ratio.

Idle time ratio – this ratio shows the percentage of working hours available that were lost because of idle time.

SELF TEST QUESTIONS

		Paragraph
1	What is piecework?	1.3
2	What types of bonus scheme are there?	1.6
3	What are timesheets and how are they used?	5.1
4	What are job cost cards?	5.3
5	What is the formula for the labour turnover rate?	6
6	What is the formula for the labour efficiency ratio?	7.2

EXAM-STYLE QUESTIONS

1 A manufacturing firm is very busy and overtime is being worked.

The amount of overtime premium contained in direct wages would normally be classed as:

A part of prime cost

B factory overheads

C direct labour costs

D administrative overheads

2 A contract cleaning firm estimates that it will take 2,520 actual cleaning hours to clean an office block. Unavoidable interruptions and lost time are estimated to take 10% of the operatives' time. If the wage rate is $24 per hour, what is the budgeted labour cost?

A $60,080

B $60,480

C $67,200

D $67,197

3 Which of the following is the correct definition of a piecework payment system?

A A greater amount is paid for each unit of output achieved

B A fixed amount is paid for each unit of output achieved

C A greater total amount is paid if more hours are spent on production

D A fixed amount is paid regardless of time spent on production

4 Gross wages incurred in Department 1 in June were $135,000. The wages analysis shows the following summary breakdown of the gross pay:

	Paid to direct labour	*Paid to indirect labour*
	$	$
Ordinary time	62,965	29,750
Overtime		
Basic pay	13,600	8,750
Premium	3,400	2,190
Shift allowance	6,750	3,495
Sick pay	3,450	650
	$90,165	$44,835

What is the direct wages cost for Department 1 in June?

A $62,965

B $76,565

C $86,715

D $90,165

5 An employee's basic week is 35 hours at a rate of pay of $22 per hour. Overtime is paid at 'time and a half'. During the week the employee worked 42 hours.

What is the wage cost for this employee for the week?

$_____ (*Fill in the missing number to the nearest 1 decimal place*)

6 An organisations' bonus policy is to pay a bonus to employees at 40% of the time saved on production. It has gathered the following information for one of its employees:

Employee's wage rate	$15.00 per hour
Time allowed for job	60 minutes
Time taken for job	50 minutes

Calculate the bonus to be paid to the employee.

A $1.00

B $2.50

C $12.50

D $17.50

7 An organisation uses three different ratios to assess the performance of it labour. Match each ratio with the correct potential use.

Ratio	**Capacity ratio**	**Efficiency ratio**	**Activity ratio**
A measure of productivity			
A measure of overall production			
A measure of utilisation			

Place a tick in the appropriate box

8 An organisation had budgeted for 60,000 units to be produced in February and the budgeted time for the production of these units is 5,000 hours.

The actual output in February was 60,300 units and the actual time worked by the labour force was 6,000 hours.

What is the value of the labour efficiency ratio?

A 84%

B 100%

C 119%

D 120%

9 An organisation had budgeted for 600 units to be produced in a week and the budgeted time for the production of these units is 40 hours.

The actual output in the week was 540 units and the actual time worked by the labour force was 32 hours.

What is the value of the capacity utilisation ratio?

A 64%

B 80%

C 112%

D 125%

10 An organisation had budgeted for 3,000 units to be produced in a period and the budgeted time for the production of these units is 24,000 hours.

The actual output in this period was 3,500 units and the actual time worked by the labour force was 30,000 hours.

What was the labour production/volume ratio for the period?

_____% (fill in the answer to the nearest full percentage)

11 At the start of the year a charity had 312 full time employees. During the year another 41 employees were recruited on top of the 56 employees who had left and had to be replaced.

What was the employee turnover rate for the period?

A 16.8%

B 17.9%

C 15,9%

D 4.8%

For the answers to these questions, see the 'Answers' section at the end of the book.

Chapter 7

ACCOUNTING FOR OTHER EXPENSES

In this chapter we look at the costs of other expenses, apart from materials costs and labour costs. Other expenses include sub-contractors and other invoiced costs. Depreciation charges are also classified as expenses and we cover the main methods of calculating depreciation. This chapter covers syllabus area B3.

CONTENTS

LEARNING OUTCOMES

At the end of this chapter you should be able to:

- describe the nature of expenses by function
- describe the procedures and documentation required to ensure the correct authorisation, coding, analysis and recording of direct and indirect expenses
- describe and calculate capital and revenue expenditure and the relevant accounting treatment
- calculate and explain depreciation charges using straight-line, reducing balance and machine hour and product unit methods
- explain the relationship between the expenses costing system and the expense accounting system.

1 TYPES OF EXPENSE BY FUNCTION

An organisation will incur many different types of expense, other than expenses relating to materials and labour costs. There may be expenses associated with the manufacturing process or the factory, the selling process, general administration or the day-to-day running of the business and the financing of the business.

1.1 MANUFACTURING EXPENSES

Examples of expenses incurred during the manufacturing process include:

- the cost of power necessary for the machinery to be running
- the lighting and heating costs of the factory
- factory rental cost
- payments to external organisations for repair work or factory security operations
- insurance of the machinery
- depreciation of machinery.

1.2 SELLING AND DISTRIBUTION EXPENSES

During the process of selling the goods to the customer the types of expense that might be incurred include:

- advertising costs
- packaging costs
- costs of delivering the goods to the customer: vehicle depreciation and repairs, freight charges
- warehouse rental for storage of goods.

1.3 ADMINISTRATION EXPENSES

The everyday running of the organisation will involve many different expenses including the following types of item:

- rent of office buildings
- insurance of office buildings
- telephone bills
- postage costs
- depreciation of office equipment
- accountancy, legal and auditor's fees.

1.4 FINANCE EXPENSES

The costs of financing an organisation might include the following:

- loan interest
- lease charges if any equipment or buildings are leased rather than purchased.

Note that the cost of the finance department (where the management accounting function is likely to operate) are not part of finance expenses. They would instead be classified as administrative expenses. Finance expenses are costs associated with managing the organisation's finances such as bank loans and overdrafts.

2 DIRECT AND INDIRECT EXPENSES

To a cost accountant there are three types of business expenditure. These are materials, labour and expenses.

Definition **Expenses** are all business costs that are not classified as materials or labour costs.

Definition A **direct expense** is an expense that can be identified in full with a specific cost unit.

Examples of direct expenses

Direct expenses that may be attributed to a particular product or cost unit might include the following:

- running costs of a machine used only for one product
- packaging costs for a product
- royalties payable per product
- subcontractors' fees attributable to a single product or job
- the cost of machinery or equipment hired for a particular job or contract.

It is often difficult to trace an entire expense to a single cost unit, which means that most expenses are treated as indirect costs, and charged to a cost centre as an overhead.

Definition An **indirect expense** is expenditure which cannot be identified with a specific cost unit.

Conclusion The majority of materials and labour costs will be direct costs as they can be specifically attributed to cost units. The majority of expenses, however, will tend to be indirect costs as they will be items of expenditure that relate to a number of different products or cost units.

3 ACCOUNTING FOR EXPENSES AND EXPENSES COSTING

In a financial accounting system, expenses are accounted for by:

- debiting an appropriate expense account; and
- crediting the bank account, payables account or provision for depreciation account.

At the end of an accounting period, the expense account is cleared by:

- crediting the expense account with the total expense for the period; and
- debiting the statement of profit or loss.

In a costing system, expenses are not debited directly to the statement of profit or loss. Instead:

- direct expenses are debited to the work-in-progress account
- indirect expenses are debited to a production overhead, administration overhead or sales and distribution overhead account.

By debiting expenses to work-in-progress or an overhead account, we are able to build up the costs of activities.

Overhead accounts are therefore used to build up the costs of indirect materials, indirect labour and indirect expenses.

The following example might help to illustrate this process.

EXAMPLE

The following costs have been recorded in a period:

Total depreciation	$25,000
Of which production machinery	$15,000
Office equipment	$4,000
Delivery vehicles	$6,000
Factory rental	$16,000
Advertising expenses	$22,000
Subcontractors' costs	$10,000

SOLUTION

The accounting entry for depreciation is to credit the depreciation account and debit the appropriate overhead account. The accounting entry for other expenses is to credit the appropriate expenses account (one aggregate account has been used here but it would be equally correct to use individual accounts for each expense) and debit WIP with direct expenses and the appropriate overhead account with indirect expenses.

Equipment depreciation account

	$		$
		Production overhead	15,000
		Administration overhead	4,000
		Sales and distribution overhead	6,000
			25,000

Expenses

	$		$
Cash or payables			
(Factory rental)	16,000	Production overheads	16,000
(Advertising expenses)	22,000	Sales and distribution overheads	22,000
(Sub-contractors costs)	10,000	Work-in-progress	10,000

Work-in-progress

	$		$
Expenses	10,000		

Production overheads

	$		$
Equipment depreciation	15,000		
Expenses (Factory rental)	16,000		

Administration overheads

	$		$
Equipment depreciation	4,000		

Sales and distribution overheads

	$		$
Equipment depreciation	6,000		
Expenses (Advertising)	22,000		

4 DOCUMENTATION FOR EXPENSES

Most expenses are documented in the form of an **invoice** from a supplier. For example, businesses receive invoices from external contractors, for rent, telephone expenses and electricity charges.

After the invoice has been checked and approved, a copy is sent to the cost accounting department, where the expense is allocated to a cost centre/cost code. (Direct expenses are allocated directly to the cost unit.)

The documentation for **non-current (fixed) asset depreciation** is the **non-current (fixed) asset register**, i.e. a record of the organisation's non-current assets. Each non-current asset can be associated with a particular cost centre, and the depreciation charge can be allocated directly to that cost centre as an overhead expense.

5 CAPITAL AND REVENUE EXPENDITURE

When a business spends money on an item it must be classified as either capital expenditure or revenue expenditure. The importance of the distinction between these two types of expenditure is in their different accounting treatments.

5.1 CAPITAL EXPENDITURE

Definition **Capital expenditure** is expenditure by a business on non-current (fixed) assets.

Definition **Non-current (fixed) assets** are assets of the business that are for long term use in the business.

Therefore when a business buys items of machinery, cars, computers, office furniture or a building these are classified as capital expenditure.

The accounting treatment of capital expenditure is that the cost of the asset is included as a non-current (fixed) asset in the statement of financial position of the business rather than being part of the expenses of the business in the statement of profit or loss.

The cost is written off over the expected useful life of the asset in the form of a periodic **depreciation charge**. Depreciation of non-current assets is an expense for costing purposes and is usually an indirect expense of the cost centre using the asset.

Although depreciation is an expense, it is important to recognise that it does not represent a cash expenditure. Cash is paid when the asset is originally purchased. Recognising depreciation as a non-cash item is important when cost information is presented to management for decision-making purposes (as will be explained in a later chapter).

5.2 REVENUE EXPENDITURE

Definition **Revenue expenditure** is all expenditure other than capital expenditure and represents day-to-day or operating expenses.

Revenue expenditure will therefore include expenditure on materials, wages, power costs, lighting and heating bills, telephone bills, rent, to name but a few.

The accounting treatment of revenue expenditure is that it is treated as an expense in the statement of profit or loss in the period in which the expense is incurred.

Conclusion The importance of the distinction between capital and revenue expenditure is in its accounting treatment. The cost of non-current assets, capital expenditure, is taken straight to the statement of financial position of the business and written off over time in the form of depreciation charges. The cost of all other items of expenditure, revenue expenditure, is taken in full to the statement of profit or loss as an expense for the period.

5.3 REVENUE EXPENDITURE ON NON-CURRENT ASSETS

The purchase cost of non-current assets such as buildings and vehicles should be treated as capital expenditure. But organisations might continue to incur costs on these assets such as paying for maintenance, extending buildings, repairing machines, replacing machine parts etc. Not all of these costs will be treated as capital expenditure.

Capital expenditure should only include the following:

- the initial cost of the asset (this would include any transport costs in bringing it to its current location)
- the cost of upgrading an asset in order to improve the asset in any way that is over and above its previously assessed state. Examples would include:
  - if a retail building is extended in order to accommodate more customers;
  - repairing a derelict building in order to put it back to a usable state;
  - the cost of demolishing a derelict factory to clear space for a new office building.
- the cost of adding something to an asset that was not there before (for example, the cost of adding an extractor fan to a bathroom)

All other expenditure on non-current assets should be treated as revenue expenditure, such as:

- standard repairs to assets that do not enhance their purpose
- the cost of repainting buildings (this would be classed as maintenance)
- the cost of replacing machine parts with similar machine parts in order to maintain a machine
- the cost of relocating a machine within a factory

6 DEPRECIATION

6.1 THE NATURE OF DEPRECIATION

Definition **Depreciation** is the measure of the wearing out, consumption or other reduction in the useful economic life of a non-current asset.

Depreciation is a way of reflecting that when an asset is owned and used in a business there will be a cost to the business of using this asset. This will not just be the cost of running and maintaining the asset but also a cost in terms of using up some of the working life of the asset.

Depreciation is a method of charging some of the initial cost of a non-current asset to the accounts in each period that the asset is used. The reason for doing this is that the asset is being used to benefit the business by making goods or earning revenues, therefore a proportion of the asset's cost should be charged to the business as an expense in order to match with these revenues.

EXAMPLE

A machine is purchased at a cost of $10,000. It is expected to be used for five years in the business to make goods and will have no value at the end of that five year period. The machine will cost $60 each year to insure, $100 to maintain and service and approximately $150 of power to run it for a year.

What are the actual costs to the business associated with this machine, assuming that the annual charge for depreciation is the same amount each year?

SOLUTION

Annual costs

	$
Insurance	60
Maintenance	100
Running costs	150
Depreciation ($10,000/5 years)	2,000

6.2 METHODS OF DEPRECIATION

Depreciation can conveniently be thought of as a method of spreading the cost of an asset (minus any expected residual value at the end of its useful life) over the years in which the asset is expected to be in use.

For example, suppose that a non-current asset costs $30,000 and has an expected useful life of 6 years and a residual value of $5,000 at the end of six years. The total amount of depreciation to charge will be $25,000 ($30,000 – $5,000) over six years. There are different ways in which this can be done. The methods you need to know are:

- straight-line method
- reducing balance method
- machine hours method
- product units method.

6.3 STRAIGHT-LINE METHOD

With the straight-line method of depreciation, the annual charge for depreciation is the same each year. It is calculated as:

$$\frac{\text{Cost less residual value}}{\text{Expected useful life (years)}}$$

When the residual value is zero, the total depreciation charge over the life of the asset will be the original cost of the asset. In such cases, the straight-line rate of depreciation can be expressed as a percentage of the original cost each year.

For example, if an asset has an expected useful life of five years and no residual value, the straight-line depreciation rate could be expressed as 20% of the asset cost.

ACTIVITY 1

Suppose that a vehicle is purchased for $48,000 and is expected to have a resale value of $20,250 in three years' time when the organisation disposes of it.

Calculate the annual depreciation charge for the car on a straight-line basis.

For a suggested answer, see the 'Answers' section at the end of the book.

6.4 REDUCING BALANCE METHOD

The carrying value of a non-current asset is the amount at which the asset is stated in the statement of financial position. This is:

Cost	X
Less Accumulated depreciation charges to date	X
Equals carrying value	X

The reducing balance method of depreciation is where the percentage depreciation rate is applied to the carrying value of the asset in order to calculate the annual depreciation charge.

As a result, the annual depreciation charge becomes smaller each year. It is at its largest in the first year and its smallest in the final year of use.

The reducing balance method is sometimes preferred to the straight-line method for assets such as motor vehicles that lose much of their market value soon after purchase.

EXAMPLE

A lorry is purchased for $50,000 and is to be depreciated at a rate of 20% per annum using the reducing balance method.

Calculate the depreciation charge for the first three years.

SOLUTION

	$
Cost	50,000
Year 1 depreciation charge (20% × 50,000)	10,000
Carrying Value	40,000
Year 2 depreciation charge (20% × 40,000)	8,000
Carrying Value	32,000
Year 3 depreciation charge (20% × 32,000)	6,400
Carrying Value	25,600

ACTIVITY 2

Using the same information as before suppose that a vehicle is purchased for $48,000 and is expected to have a resale value of $20,250 in three years' time when the organisation will dispose of it.

Calculate the depreciation charge for each of the three years if a rate of 25% is applied, using the reducing balance method.

For a suggested answer, see the 'Answers' section at the end of the book.

6.5 MACHINE HOURS METHOD

The machine hours method of depreciation, as the name suggests, is sometimes used for non-current assets such as machinery, where it is considered appropriate to charge depreciation according to the use that has been made of the asset.

Depreciation is charged at a rate per hour for each hour that the asset is actually used in the period.

The rate of depreciation per hour is calculated as:

$$\frac{\text{Cost less residual value}}{\text{Expected total number of hours of use over the life of the asset}}$$

Since the machine hours method of calculating depreciation is based upon the actual usage of the asset rather than the passage of time, it is sometimes considered more appropriate for cost accounting purposes than other depreciation methods.

ACTIVITY 3

A machine has been purchased for $20,000 and has an estimated residual value of zero after the five years that it will be used by the organisation. During those five years it is estimated that the machine will be operational for 5,000 hours. In the first year of operations the machine was used for 1,800 hours.

Using the machine hour's method of calculating depreciation what is the depreciation charge for the first year?

For a suggested answer, see the 'Answers' section at the end of the book.

6.6 PRODUCT UNITS METHOD

The product units method is expressed in the total number of units expected to be produced from an asset. It is typically used when assets have a production capacity over their life which is known. This is common in some machines (for example, a printing machine may only last for so many printed units).

The depreciation is computed in two steps:

1. Compute the 'depreciation per unit' as follows:

   $$\frac{\text{Cost less residual value}}{\text{Expected total number of units that can be produced over the life of the asset}}$$

2. Calculate is the actual depreciation expense, which is recorded on the statement of profit or loss. Depreciation expense equals depreciation per unit multiplied by the number of units produced during the year.

EXAMPLE

A machine costs $60,000 to buy and can produce a total of 12,000 units during its useful economic life, at the end of which it will be sold for $3,000. It is expected to produce 4,000 units this year.

Calculate the depreciation charge for the year.

SOLUTION

The depreciation per unit charge will be ($60,000 – $3,000) divided by 12,000 units = $4.75 per unit. So the charge for the year will be $4.75 × 4,000 units = $19,000.

CONCLUSION

Expenses can be a major cost for organisations which subcontract a high proportion of their work. The same principles apply to analysing and accounting for direct and indirect expenses as for labour and material costs. This enables the total direct costs of a cost unit and the total indirect cost of a cost centre to be identified. The method of attributing indirect costs to cost units to build up a full product cost will be considered in the next chapter.

KEY TERMS

Expenses – all business costs that are not classified as materials or labour costs.

Direct expense – an expense that can be identified in full with a specific cost unit.

Indirect expense – an expense that cannot be identified with a cost unit.

Capital expenditure – expenditure on non-current (fixed) assets.

Non-current (fixed) assets – the assets of the business that are for long term use in the business.

Revenue expenditure – day-to-day expenses or all expenditure other than capital expenditure.

Depreciation – a measure of the wearing out, consumption or other reduction in the useful economic life of a non-current asset.

SELF TEST QUESTIONS

		Paragraph
1	Give three examples of manufacturing expenses.	1.1
2	Define direct expenses.	2
3	Define indirect expenses.	2
4	In which cost ledger account are indirect production expenses recorded?	3
5	What is capital expenditure?	5.1
6	What is the accounting treatment of capital expenditure?	5.1
7	What is revenue expenditure?	5.2
8	Define depreciation.	6.1
9	How is the reducing balance method of depreciation applied?	6.4
10	How is the depreciation rate per hour calculated for the machine rate method of depreciation?	6.5

EXAM-STYLE QUESTIONS

1 All of the following costs relating to a machine in a manufacturing process would be classified as indirect expenses **except:**

A the cost of power to run the machine

B depreciation of the machine

C insurance of the machine

D lubricating oil for the machine.

2 The accounting entry for the subcontractors' fees of freelance artists working on specialist pottery would be:

A	Dr Work-in-progress	Cr Labour control account
B	Dr Work-in-progress	Cr Expenses
C	Dr Work-in-progress	Cr Production overhead control
D	Dr Production overhead control	Cr Expenses

3 A machine has an estimated four-year life and a residual value of $2,500. It originally cost $20,000. The deprecation charge in Year 3, if the reducing balance method at 25% is used, is:

A $2,812.50

B $2,460.94

C $4,375.00

D $3,750.00

4 A new vehicle has an estimated six-year life and nil residual value. Depreciation is currently charged at 20% on a reducing balance method on this type of asset. The company is considering changing to a straight-line method of depreciation. Which of the following statements is correct?

A Depreciation would be higher in the first year if a straight-line method is used.

B The total depreciation charge over the whole life of the asset would be greater using the straight-line method.

C Depreciation would be lower in Year 1 if the straight-line method is used but higher in Year 6, compared to the existing method.

D Depreciation would be lower each year if the straight-line method is used.

For the answers to these questions, see the 'Answers' section at the end of the book.

Chapter 8

ABSORPTION COSTING

In previous chapters, we have seen how costs can be classified as direct material costs, direct labour costs and overhead costs. This chapter explains how the costs of products or services are established using a system of costing known as absorption costing. In absorption costing, the main problem is how to charge a fair share of overhead costs to products or services. This chapter covers syllabus areas C1 and C2(c).

CONTENTS

LEARNING OUTCOMES

At the end of this chapter you should be able to:

- explain the rationale for absorption costing
- describe the nature of production and service cost centres and their significance for production overhead allocation, apportionment and absorption
- describe the process of allocating, apportioning and absorbing production overheads to establish product costs
- apportion overheads to cost centres using appropriate bases
- re-apportion service cost centre overheads to production cost centres using direct and step down methods
- justify, calculate and apply production cost centre overhead absorption rates using labour hour and machine hour methods
- explain the relative merits of actual and pre-determined absorption rates
- describe and illustrate the accounting for production overhead costs, including the analysis and interpretation of over/under absorption
- describe and apply methods of attributing non-production overheads to cost units
- calculate product costs using the absorption costing method
- prepare profit statements using the absorption costing method.

1 PRODUCT COSTS AND SERVICE COSTS

Commercial organisations either sell products or provide services. They need to know what their products or services cost. There are several reasons for wanting to know about product costs and service costs.

- We need to know about costs in order to decide whether the products or services are profitable.
- In some cases, products or services might be priced by adding a profit mark-up on cost.
- In the case of products, closing inventory must be valued at its cost.

We have seen that the costs incurred by an organisation can be categorised as direct or indirect. Unlike direct costs, indirect costs cannot be associated directly with products or services.

Definition **Overheads** is a term for indirect costs.

A key issue with product costing and service costing is deciding what to do about overhead costs.

EXAMPLE

A company makes two products, X and Y. During a given period, the company makes 1,000 units of each product. The direct costs of Product X are $50,000 and the direct costs of Product Y are $80,000. Overhead costs for the period are $150,000.

If we want to establish a cost for Product X and Product Y, the direct costs of each product are easily established. But what about the overheads? Should each product be given a share of the overhead costs? If the overhead costs are to be divided between the two products, on what basis should the total cost be shared?

Definition **Absorption costing** is a method of costing in which the costs of an item (product or service or activity) are built up as the sum of direct costs and a fair share of overhead costs, to obtain a full cost or a fully-absorbed cost.

1.1 PRODUCT COSTS AND ABSORPTION COSTING

When costs are incurred, they can be recorded as:

- direct materials
- direct labour
- (sometimes) direct expenses; or
- overheads.

Overhead costs are charged to a cost centre (or 'responsibility centre'), which might represent:

- production overheads
- administration overheads
- selling and distribution overheads
- general overheads. However, general overheads are shared out between production, administration and selling and distribution overheads.

Fully-absorbed product costs can therefore be built up as follows (with illustrative figures included):

	$
Direct materials	12
Direct labour	8
Direct expenses	2
Total direct costs	22
Production overhead	16
Full production cost	38
Administration overhead	6
Selling and distribution overhead	10
Full cost of sale	54

Notes:

1 In the statement of financial position, closing inventory is valued at its full production cost.

This is consistent with the requirements for financial accounting. In any financial statements that are produced for external users (such as shareholders or the tax authorities), absorption costing must be used. In management accounts, which are only used internally by the business managers, the business can choose any method of stock valuation it wishes.

2 Absorption costing problems are concerned with building up the full production cost and therefore concentrate on production overheads. Non-production overheads may be charged as a period cost against profits or may be added to full production cost using a given percentage.

1.2 SERVICE COSTS AND ABSORPTION COSTING

Fully-absorbed service costs can be built up in the same way. A service business must first of all decide what a unit of service should be. For example:

- for a telecommunications business, a unit of service might be a cost per telephone call per minute or the cost of a communications link

- for a private hospital, a cost might be a cost per patient day

- for an electricity supply business, a unit cost might be a cost per unit of electricity supplied.

Service costs might be established as follows:

	$
Direct materials	2
Direct labour	10
Direct expenses	4
Total direct costs	16
Operating overhead	28
Full operating cost	44
Administration overhead	10
Selling and distribution overhead	16
Full cost of sale	70

1.3 FIXED AND VARIABLE OVERHEADS

Overhead costs might be fixed costs or variable costs. In absorption costing, production overheads, administration overheads and selling and distribution overheads might therefore be separated into their fixed and variable cost components.

In absorption costing for products, the full production cost of a product might therefore consist of direct materials, direct labour, direct expenses, variable production overhead and fixed production overhead.

- **Fixed overheads** remain the same whatever the level of output or activity during a period. It does not vary with changes in output levels or activity, but remains constant.

- **Variable overheads** are amounts of indirect cost that vary with the level of output or activity. As the level of output or activity rises then so does any variable overhead cost.

1.4 REASONS FOR ABSORPTION COSTING

The main reasons for wanting to calculate full costs, as indicated earlier, are mainly to value inventories of manufactured goods, and possibly also to calculate a selling price based on full costs.

Inventory valuation

The costs of making a product include the costs of direct materials, direct labour and direct expenses. In some organisations products are simply valued at this total figure for costing purposes. However the overheads incurred by the production departments are costs that are necessary to make those products. Production overheads, although indirect costs of the cost units, are as much a cost of the product as the direct costs.

Therefore in order to value closing inventory at the full cost of producing each product or cost unit, the cost unit incurred must include a share of the overheads in the product cost. The full cost of producing the product or cost unit is the total direct costs of the product plus its share of indirect production costs.

Pricing at a mark-up over full cost

One reason for costing products at their full cost could be for pricing purposes. If the price of a product is to cover all of the costs of the product plus some margin to give a profit then the full cost must be known in order to apply the profit margin. In the longer term, if absorption costing is used, a business will have a more informed idea of the long term profitability of a product as all production costs and revenues will have been considered.

EXAMPLE

The cost of a unit of Product X is as follows:

	$
Direct materials	1.60
Direct labour	2.20
Direct expenses	0.40
Indirect expenses	0.80

If the organisation's policy is to cover all costs of a product and then make a profit equal to 20% of the total costs, at what price must Product X be sold?

SOLUTION

Total cost of Product X

	$
Direct materials	1.60
Direct labour	2.20
Direct expenses	0.40
Indirect expenses	0.80
	5.00
Profit (20% × $5.00)	1.00
Selling price	6.00

2 TREATMENT OF OVERHEADS IN ABSORPTION COSTING

In absorption costing, products, services or activities are charged with a fair share of indirect costs. There is a three-stage process involved in charging overhead costs to products or services:

- overhead allocation
- overhead apportionment
- overhead absorption, also called overhead recovery.

Each of these stages is explained below. However, in order to appreciate overhead allocation and overhead apportionment, it is first of all necessary to know something about the type of cost centres found in manufacturing organisations.

2.1 COST CENTRES AND ABSORPTION COSTING

A business can decide what its cost centres should be. Generally-speaking, cost centres within a manufacturing organisation are likely to consist of:

- **Production departments**, in which items of product are manufactured. There could be several production departments within any organisation, and production might flow from one department to another and then another. For example, production might flow from a machining department to an assembly department and then a finishing department. Similarly, in textile production, work might flow from a carding department to a spinning department to a weaving department. Each production department might be a separate cost centre. Alternatively, a cost centre might be a single machine or a group of machines under the direction of one supervisor.
- **Service departments** within the production area. These are departments operating within the production function that are not involved directly in the manufacture of products. Instead, they provide service and support to production departments. These can include a stores department, a maintenance and repairs department, a canteen department, and so on.
- **Administration departments** or functions, for administration overheads.

- **Selling and distribution departments** or functions, for selling and distribution costs.

- **General cost items** that cannot be attributed to a single department or work area. Examples are rental costs for a factory building, lighting and heating costs, building security and maintenance costs, and so on.

In the description of absorption costing that follows, administration overheads and selling and distribution overheads are ignored, and the focus of attention is on full production costs. Costs centres will therefore be categorised as production departments, service departments and general costs.

3 OVERHEAD ALLOCATION

Overhead allocation is the first of the three stages in establishing a full cost for a product or service.

Definition **Overhead allocation** is the process of charging a whole item of cost to a cost centre.

ACTIVITY 1

A manufacturing business operates with two production departments, P and Q and a service department S. It manufactures widgets. It incurs the following costs in a given period.

	$
Labour costs in Department S	6,500
Direct labour costs in Department P	4,700
Costs of supervision in Department Q	2,100
Material costs of widgets	10,300
Machine repair costs, Department Q	800
Materials consumed in Department S	1,100
Depreciation of machinery in Department S	700
Indirect materials consumed in Department P	500
Lighting and heating	900
Costs of works canteen	1,500

Allocate these costs as overhead costs to the following cost centres:

- production Department P

- production Department Q

- service Department S

- a cost centre for general costs.

Indicate with reasons why you have not allocated any of the cost items in the list.

For a suggested answer, see the 'Answers' section at the end of the book.

4 APPORTIONMENT OF OVERHEAD COSTS

Once overhead costs have been allocated to cost centres, general overheads must be shared out, or apportioned. This may be to production or service cost centres.

Definition **Overhead apportionment** is the process of sharing out overhead costs on a fair basis.

Apportionment should be on a fair basis, but there are no rules about what 'fair' means.

An organisation should establish, for each item of general cost, what this basis ought to be. For many costs, there are two or more different bases that could be used.

Some examples should help to illustrate the considerations involved.

4.1 EXAMPLES

EXAMPLE 1

A general cost in a manufacturing company is factory rental. Annual rental costs are $80,000. How should this cost be apportioned between production cost centres and service cost centres?

Rental costs are usually apportioned between cost centres on the basis of the floor space taken up by each cost centre. For example, suppose that three cost centres have floor space of 10,000 square metres, 15,000 square metres and 25,000 square metres, and annual rental costs are $80,000. If we apportion rental costs between the cost centres on the basis of their floor space, the apportionment would be as follows:

Annual rental	$80,000
Total floor space (10,000 + 15,000 + 25,000)	50,000 square metres
Apportionment rate ($80,000/50,000)	$1.60/square metre
	$
Apportion to cost centre with 10,000 square metres	16,000
Apportion to cost centre with 15,000 square metres	24,000
Apportion to cost centre with 25,000 square metres	40,000
	80,000

EXAMPLE 2

The costs of heating and lighting might also be apportioned on the basis of floor space. Alternatively, since heating relates to volume rather than floor space, it could be argued that the costs should be apportioned on the volume of space taken up by each cost centre. Yet another view is that electricity costs relate more to the consumption of electrical power by machines, therefore the apportionment of these costs should be on the basis of the number and power of the machines in each cost centre.

A reasonable argument could be made for any of these bases of apportionment.

EXAMPLE 3

Supervisors' costs could be apportioned on either of the following bases:

- the number of employees in each cost centre
- the hours worked by employees in each department (on the grounds that the costs relate more to the number of hours in attendance at work rather than the numbers of employees).

ACTIVITY 2

What would be the most appropriate basis of apportionment of the following overheads?

(a) Oil used for machine lubrication.

(b) Depreciation of machinery.

(c) Petrol for vehicles used by the organisation.

For a suggested answer, see the 'Answers' section at the end of the book.

5 OVERHEAD ANALYSIS SHEET

A record of the overheads allocated and apportioned can be set out on an overhead analysis sheet.

5.1 OVERHEAD ANALYSIS SHEET: OVERHEAD APPORTIONMENT

The purpose of the analysis sheet is to show how the overhead costs are built up for each production and service cost centre.

5.2 WORKED EXAMPLE

The example below illustrates the apportionment of overheads using an overhead analysis sheet.

This example stops at the point where general overheads have been apportioned to production departments and service departments. It does not show how service departments are re-apportioned to the production departments.

Note that this example is longer than any question that could be asked for in an exam. But it should explain all the possible elements that you could be asked to calculate in this area.

EXAMPLE

An organisation has two production departments, A and B, and two service departments, stores and the canteen.

The overhead costs for the organisation in total are as follows:

	$
Rent	32,000
Building maintenance costs	5,000
Machinery insurance	2,400
Machinery depreciation	11,000
Machinery running expenses	6,000
Power	7,000

There are also specific costs that have already been allocated to each cost centre as follows:

	$
Department A	5,000
Department B	4,000
Stores	1,000
Canteen	2,000

The following information about the various cost centres is also available:

	Total	*Dept A*	*Dept B*	*Stores*	*Canteen*
Floor space (sq ft)	30,000	15,000	8,000	5,000	2,000
Power usage	100%	45%	40%	5%	10%
Value of machinery ($000)	250	140	110	–	–
Machinery hours (000)	80	50	30		
Value of equipment ($000)	20	–	–	5	15
Number of employees	40	20	15	3	2
Value of stores requisitions ($000)	150	100	50	–	–

Allocate and apportion the costs to the four departments.

Do not reapportion the service cost centre costs to the production cost centre.

5.3 SOLUTION

OVERHEAD ANALYSIS SHEET	PERIOD ENDING.................				
	TOTAL	**PRODUCTION**		**SERVICE**	
		Dept A	*Dept B*	*Stores*	*Canteen*
	$	$	$	$	$
Overheads allocated directly to cost centres	12,000	5,000	4,000	1,000	2,000
Overheads to be apportioned					
Rent					
Basis: floor space	32,000				
15/30 × $32,000		16,000			
8/30 × $32,000			8,534		
5/30 × $32,000				5,333	
2/30 × $32,000					2,133
Building maintenance					
Basis: floor space	5,000				
15/30 × $5,000		2,500			
8/30 × $5,000			1,333		
5/30 × $5,000				834	
2/30 × $5,000					333
Machinery insurance	2,400				
Basis: machine value					
140/250 × $2,400		1,344			
110/250 × $2,400			1,056	–	–
Machinery depreciation	11,000				
Basis: machine value					
140/250 × $11,000		6,160			
110/250 × $11,000			4,840	–	–
Machinery running expenses	6,000				
Basis: machine hours					
50/80 × $6,000		3,750			
30/80 × $6,000			2,250	–	–
Power	7,000				
Basis: power usage percentages					
$7,000 × 45%		3,150			
$7,000 × 40%			2,800		
$7,000 × 5%				350	
$7,000 × 10%					700
Allocated and apportioned costs	75,400	37,904	24,813	7,517	5,166

6 SERVICE COST CENTRE RE-APPORTIONMENT

The aim of allocating and apportioning production overheads is to establish the total overhead costs for each production cost centre. In order to achieve this, the overhead costs that have been allocated and apportioned to service cost centres within production have to be re-apportioned to the production cost centres.

There are two main methods of service cost centre re-apportionment:

- **Direct method** – this method is used where service cost centres do not provide services for one another.
- **Step-down method** – this method is used where at least one of the service cost centres provides a service to another service cost centre as well as to the production cost centres.

When service cost centre overheads are re-apportioned, the end result is the same. All overhead costs are charged to production departments. However, the amount of overheads charged to each production department will be different. In other words, the direct method and the step-down method will share out the overhead costs in a different way.

6.1 DIRECT METHOD OF RE-APPORTIONMENT

With the direct method of re-apportionment, general overheads which have been apportioned to service cost centres will be re-apportioned to production cost centres only. The order of re-apportionment is irrelevant with this method.

EXAMPLE – Direct method of re-apportionment

Using the information produced in the previous worked example, the allocated and apportioned overhead costs are:

OVERHEAD ANALYSIS SHEET	**PERIOD ENDING................**				
	TOTAL	**PRODUCTION**		**SERVICE**	
		Dept A	*Dept B*	*Stores*	*Canteen*
	$	$	$	$	$
Total overhead	75,400	37,904	24,813	7,517	5,166
	———	———	———	———	———

The apportionment of the stores department costs will be on the basis of the value of requisitions by each production cost centre. The apportionment of the canteen costs should be on the basis of the number of employees in production departments A and B.

It is assumed that the stores cost centre does no work for the canteen and the canteen does no work for the stores cost centre.

Consequently, none of the stores costs should be apportioned to the canteen and none of the canteen costs should be apportioned to stores.

The following data is available:

	Total	*Dept A*	*Dept B*	*Stores*	*Canteen*
Number of employees	40	20	15	3	2
Value of stores requisitions ($000)	150	100	50	–	–

Show how the service cost centre costs should be re-apportioned, and the resulting total overhead costs of each production cost centre.

SOLUTION

OVERHEAD ANALYSIS SHEET **PERIOD ENDING..................**

	TOTAL	**PRODUCTION**		**SERVICE**	
		Dept A	*Dept B*	*Stores*	*Canteen*
	$	$	$	$	$
Allocated/apportioned overhead	75,400	37,904	24,813	7,517	5,166
Apportion stores		5,011	2,506	(7,517)	
Basis: requisitions					
100/150 × $7,517					
50/150 × $7,517					
Apportion canteen		2,952	2,214		(5,166)
Basis: number of employees					
20/35 × $5,166					
15/35 × $5,166					
Total overhead		45,867	29,533		

Conclusion This is the simplest situation, where the service cost centres are isolated from each other. The assumption is implicit that the stores personnel do not use the canteen and that the canteen does not use the stores function. This is a situation where service centres do not service each other.

6.2 STEP-DOWN METHOD OF RE-APPORTIONMENT

With the step-down method, a service cost centre's costs are first re-apportioned to production cost centres and another service cost centre. The second service cost centre's total cost, which now includes a share of the first service cost centre's cost, is re-apportioned to production cost centres. Unlike the direct method, the order of re-apportionment is relevant with the step-down method.

EXAMPLE – Step-down method of re-apportionment

Suppose that, in the previous example, stores cost centre employees use the canteen.

The solution would now change as follows:

SOLUTION

OVERHEAD ANALYSIS SHEET		PERIOD ENDING.................			
	TOTAL	**PRODUCTION**		**SERVICE**	
		Dept A	*Dept B*	*Stores*	*Canteen*
	$	$	$	$	$
Allocated/apportioned overhead	75,400	37,904	24,813	7,517	5,166
Apportion canteen		2,719	2,039	408	(5,166)
Basis: number of employees					
20/38 × $5,166					
15/38 × $5,166					
3/38 × $5,166					
Apportion stores		5,283	2,642	(7,925)	
Basis: requisitions					
100/150 × $7,925					
50/150 × $7,925					
Total overhead		45,906	29,494		

Note: The key to this step-down method of re-apportionment is to start by re-apportioning the overhead costs of the service cost centre that does work for the other service cost centre.

ACTIVITY 3

A manufacturing business has two production cost centres and two service cost centres. The allocated overhead costs and apportioned general overhead costs for each cost centre are as follows.

	$
Production cost centre P1	140,000
Production cost centre P2	200,000
Service cost centre S1	90,000
Service cost centre S2	120,000

Required:

(a) Show how the overheads would be charged to each production cost centre if it is assumed that neither service cost centre does any work for the other. Cost centre S1 does 60% of its work for P1 and 40% of its work for P2. Cost centre S2 does one-third of its work for P1 and two-thirds of its work for P2.

(b) Show how the overheads would be charged to each production cost centre if it is assumed that service cost centre S2 does work for cost centre S1 as well as the two production cost centres, as indicated in the table below.

	Apportionment ratio			
	Cost centre P1	*Cost centre P2*	*Cost centre S1*	*Cost centre S2*
Cost centre S1	60%	40%	–	–
Cost centre S2	25%	50%	25%	–

For a suggested answer, see the 'Answers' section at the end of the book.

7 THE ARBITRARY NATURE OF OVERHEAD APPORTIONMENTS

At the end of the process of allocation and apportionment of production overheads, all overhead costs have been charged to production cost centres.

The process of apportionment attempts to be fair, but the selection of the bases for apportionment is based on judgement and assumption.

- General cost items can often be apportioned on any of two or more different bases, and depending on the basis chosen, the amount of cost charged to each responsibility centre/cost centre will differ.
- Similarly, the basis for apportioning service department costs to production departments can differ, depending on the assumptions made or point of view taken.
- The decision about whether to allow for the work done by service departments for other service departments is also significant. The assumption chosen will affect the amount of overheads charged from the service departments to each production department.

Methods of apportioning overheads should be kept under review, to make sure that they remain valid and sensible.

If a basis of apportionment no longer appears valid, a change in the apportionment basis should be proposed to management, giving the reasons for the proposed change.

8 OVERHEAD ABSORPTION

Allocation and apportionment are the first two stages in the process of charging overhead costs to products or services.

The third stage in the absorption costing process is overhead absorption, also called overhead recovery.

Definition **Overhead absorption** is the process of adding overhead costs to the cost of a product or service, in order to build up a fully-absorbed product cost or service cost.

As a result of overhead absorption, in theory at least, the total amount of overheads incurred should be absorbed into the costs of the products manufactured (or services provided) by the business.

8.1 BASIS OF ABSORPTION

Production overhead costs are absorbed into product costs on a basis selected by the organisation. The absorption basis should be appropriate for the particular products or services. The most common bases of absorption are:

- an absorption rate per unit, but only if the organisation produces a single product or several standard products
- an absorption rate per direct labour hour worked
- an absorption rate per machine hour worked
- an absorption rate based on a percentage of direct labour costs
- an absorption rate based on a percentage of prime cost (a percentage of direct materials, direct labour and direct expense costs).

The only bases for absorption required for your syllabus are direct labour hours and machine hours.

8.2 ABSORPTION RATES

An absorption rate is the rate at which overheads are added to costs.

- If the absorption basis is direct labour hours worked, the absorption rate will be \$Y per direct labour hour. For example, if the absorption rate for production overhead is \$5 per direct labour hour, a job taking 4 direct labour hours will be charged with \$20 of overhead.
- If the absorption basis is machine hours worked, the absorption rate will be \$Z per machine hour. For example, if the absorption rate for production overhead is \$15 per machine hour, a job taking 2 machine hours will be charged with \$30 of overhead.

The absorption rate is calculated as:

$$\frac{\text{Overhead costs}}{\text{Volume of activity (direct labour hours, machine hours)}}$$

Overhead costs for any production department are the allocated and apportioned overheads, assembled by the methods described above.

An organisation might have just one absorption rate for its entire production operations. However, an organisation with more than one production department is likely to have a different absorption rate for each department, so that separately-calculated production overheads are added to product costs for the work done in each department.

The basis of absorption can differ between production departments and the absorption rate can differ between departments.

8.3 ABSORPTION RATES BASED ON THE BUDGET

It might seem logical that overhead absorption rates should be based on the actual overhead costs in a period and the actual volume of activity (direct labour hours or machine hours worked, or units produced).

In practice, this is not the case. Overhead absorption rates are based on budgeted overhead costs and the budgeted volume of activity.

$$\text{Absorption rate} = \frac{\text{Budgeted overhead costs}}{\text{Budgeted volume of activity}}$$

There are several important reasons for using budgeted figures:

1 If we used actual costs we would have to wait until after the end of the period to calculate product costs. This is because actual overhead costs cannot be known until the period has ended and information about actual costs has been gathered and analysed.

2 As full product cost is often used as a basis to set prices, it needs to be known in advance.

3 Overheads, by their nature, are often incurred unevenly throughout the year. For example, heating costs may be higher in the winter, holiday pay may be higher in the summer. By using budgeted costs to calculate an absorption rate, overheads can be spread fairly to all production units throughout the year.

4 The 'average' cost calculated should recover all overhead costs and provides a stable basis to establish prices.

By using absorption rates based on budgeted overhead spending and budgeted activity volume, we can establish absorption rates in advance, and charge overhead costs to products as soon as they are made (and to services as soon as they are performed).

8.4 OVERHEAD ABSORPTION

Once an overhead absorption rate has been calculated, the amount of overhead absorbed can be calculated as follows:

Overhead absorbed = Actual activity level × Budgeted overhead absorption rate

For example, if the budgeted overhead absorption rate of Department M is $8 per machine hour, and the actual machine hours worked in Period 1 were 1,700, the overhead absorbed would be:

Overhead absorbed (Department M) = 1,700 machine hours × $8 = $13,600

The following example shows how the overheads absorbed by three different departments are incorporated into the cost of a job.

EXAMPLE

Job 1234 goes through three production departments. The direct materials cost of the job are $200 and the direct labour costs are:

Department 1	(3 direct labour hours)	$18
Department 2	(1.5 direct labour hours)	$12
Department 3	(6 direct labour hours)	$48

The job takes 3 machine hours in department 2.

The production overhead absorption rates are:

Department 1	$5 per direct labour hour
Department 2	$10 per machine hour
Department 3	$12 per direct labour hour

Calculate the full production cost of Job 1234.

SOLUTION

		$	$
Direct materials			200
Direct labour:			
Department 1		18	
Department 2		12	
Department 3		48	
			78
Production overhead:			
Department 1	(3 direct labour hours at $5 per hour)	15	
Department 2	(3 machine hours at $10 per hour)	30	
Department 3	(6 direct labour hours at $12 per hour)	72	
			117
Full cost of the job			395

ACTIVITY 4

Cuecraft Ltd manufactures pool and snooker cues. It has three production cost centres:

- machining
- finishing
- packing.

The planned overhead for the next budget period has been allocated and apportioned to the cost centres as:

Machining	$65,525
Finishing	$36,667
Packing	$24,367

Budgeted cost centre activity volumes for the same period show:

Machining	7,300 machine hours
Finishing	6,250 direct labour hours
Packing	5,200 direct labour hours

Determine separate overhead absorption (recovery) rates for each cost centre on the following bases:

- Machining – machine hours
- Finishing – direct labour hours
- Packing – direct labour hours.

For a suggested answer, see the 'Answers' section at the end of the book.

ACTIVITY 5

Assume that Cuecraft produces a pool cue 'pot 3' and it takes 4 hours to complete.

The activity takes place in the following cost centres:

Machining	3 hrs
Finishing	0.9 hr
Packing	0.1 hr

Using the overhead absorption rates calculated in Activity 4, show the overhead recovered in a unit of 'pot 3'.

For a suggested answer, see the 'Answers' section at the end of the book.

9 UNDER- AND OVER-ABSORPTION OF OVERHEADS

Overhead absorption rates are based on budgeted overhead costs and the budgeted volume of activity; they are pre-determined.

In practice, for each accounting period, it is often the case that:

- actual overhead expenditure will differ from budgeted overhead expenditure, and
- the actual volume of activity will differ from the budgeted volume of activity.

As a consequence, the amount of overheads charged to product costs will differ from the actual overhead expenditure.

We might charge more overhead costs to production than the amount of overhead expenditure actually incurred. If so, there is over-absorbed or over-recovered overheads.

We might charge less in overhead costs to production than the amount of overhead expenditure actually incurred. If so, there is under-absorbed or under-recovered overheads.

Over-absorbed overhead during a period is treated as an addition to profit, because it is an adjustment to allow for the fact that too much overhead cost has been charged to the items produced in the period. Similarly, under-absorbed overhead during a period is treated as a reduction in profit, because it is an adjustment to allow for the fact that the overhead cost charged to the items produced in the period is less than the actual overhead costs incurred.

EXAMPLE

A company has a single production department. Its budgeted production overheads for 20X4 were $200,000 and its budgeted volume of production was 50,000 direct labour hours. The company has decided to absorb production overheads into product costs on a direct labour hour basis.

During 20X4, actual production overhead expenditure was $195,000 and 54,000 direct labour hours were worked.

The absorption rate is $4 per direct labour hour ($200,000/50,000 hours, based on the budget).

The overheads absorbed into product costs are $4 for each direct labour hour actually worked.

	$
Total production overheads absorbed (54,000 hours × $4)	216,000
Overheads actually incurred	195,000
Over-absorbed overheads	21,000

Here, overheads are over-absorbed because $216,000 in production overhead costs has been charged to the cost of items produced, but actual overhead spending was only $195,000. Production has been charged with too much overhead.

Over-absorbed overhead is taken to the statement of profit or loss as an addition to profit in the period, to compensate for the fact that the recorded costs of production are in excess of actual expenditure.

EXAMPLE

For the year ended 31 December 20X4 the planned overhead for the Machining Cost Centre at Cuecraft Ltd was:

Overhead	$132,000
Volume of activity	15,000 machine hours

In January 20X4 the cost centre incurred $12,000 of overhead and 1,350 machine hours were worked.

Calculate the pre-determined overhead rate per machine hour and the overhead under or over-recovered in the month.

SOLUTION

Absorption rate, based on the budget:

$$\frac{\text{Planned overhead}}{\text{Machine hours}} = \frac{\$132{,}000}{15{,}000 \text{ machine hours}} = \$8.80 \text{ per machine hour}$$

	$
Overhead absorbed	
1,350 machine hours at $8.80	11,880
Overhead incurred	12,000
Under-absorbed overhead	120

Here, the amount of overheads actually charged to production are $11,880, which is less than actual expenditure. We therefore have under absorption of overhead.

Under recovery of overheads is shown as a separate item in the costing statement of profit or loss. Since production has been charged with less overheads than the amount of overheads incurred, under absorption is shown as a cost in the statement of profit or loss, thereby reducing the profit.

ACTIVITY 6

A manufacturing business has two production departments, X and Y, for which the following annual budgeted figures have been prepared.

	Department X	*Department Y*
Budgeted overhead expenditure	$840,000	$720,000
Overhead absorption basis	Machine hours	Direct labour hours
Budgeted activity	40,000 machine hours	60,000 direct labour hours

Actual overhead expenditure and actual activity levels for the year were:

	Department X	*Department Y*
Actual overhead expenditure	$895,000	$735,000
Actual activity	41,500 machine hours	62,400 direct labour hours

Required:

(a) Establish the overhead absorption rates for each department for the year.

(b) Calculate the under- or over-absorbed overhead in each department for the year.

For a suggested answer, see the 'Answers' section at the end of the book.

10 ACCOUNTING FOR PRODUCTION OVERHEADS

If a manufacturing business maintains cost accounts in a cost ledger, overheads are accounted for within the double entry bookkeeping system of the cost ledger.

Three accounts are particularly relevant to accounting for production overheads:

- the **production overhead account.** This account is debited with the actual cost of indirect materials, labour and expenses and credited with overhead absorbed to production. The balance on this account represents over- or under-absorbed overhead and is either written off directly to the statement of profit or loss or is passed to an under/over-absorbed overhead account

- the **work-in-progress account.** This account is debited with production overhead absorbed. The full cost of production is therefore built up on the debit side of this account

- the **under- or over-absorbed overhead account.** This account collects under/over absorption balances from the production overhead account prior to write off to the statement of profit or loss.

The entries in these accounts are as follows:

Production overheads account

Debit side	$	*Credit side*	$
(overheads incurred)		*(overheads absorbed)*	
Stores account	X	Work-in-progress account	X
(indirect materials)		*(overheads absorbed)*	
Wages control account	X		
(indirect labour)			
Various accounts	X		
(indirect expenses)			
[Over-absorbed overhead] *(balancing figure)*	X	[Under-absorbed overhead] *(balancing figure)*	X
	X		X

Work-in-progress account

Debit side	$	*Credit side*	$
(elements of production cost)		*(completed production)*	
Opening inventory, work-in-progress			
Stores account	X	Finished goods account	X
(direct materials)		(completed production)	
Wages control account	X		
(direct labour)			
Production overhead account	X	Closing inventory, work-in-progress	X
(production overhead absorbed)			
	X		X

If under-absorbed

Under-/over-absorbed overhead account

Debit side	$	*Credit side*	$
Production overhead account	X	Statement of profit or loss	X
	—		—
	X		X
	—		—

If over-absorbed

Under-/over-absorbed overhead account

Debit side	$	*Credit side*	$
Statement of profit or loss	X	Production overhead account	X
	—		—
	X		X
	—		—

EXAMPLE

A manufacturing business has a single production department. It uses absorption costing and absorbs production overhead into costs on a direct labour hour basis.

The production overhead budget for the year to 30 June 20X4 was $800,000, and budgeted direct labour hours were 100,000.

During the year to 30 June 20X4, the following costs were incurred:

	$
Direct materials	420,000
Indirect materials	40,000
Direct labour	750,000
Indirect labour	315,000
Indirect expenses	505,000

Opening work-in-progress was $90,000 and closing work-in-progress was $70,000.

The number of labour hours actually worked was 110,000 hours.

Prepare the following accounts in the cost ledger of the business.

- Production overhead account
- Work-in-progress account
- Under-/over-absorbed overhead account.

SOLUTION

Workings

The overhead absorption rate is $8 per direct labour hour ($800,000/100,000 hours).

Production overheads absorbed were $880,000 (110,000 hours × $8 per hour).

Production overheads account

	$		$
Stores account	40,000	Work-in-progress	880,000
Wages control account	315,000		
Indirect expenses	505,000		
Over-absorbed overhead	20,000		
	880,000		880,000

Work-in-progress account

	$		$
Opening inventory	90,000	Finished goods	2,070,000
Stores	*420,000*	*(balancing figure)*	
Wages control	750,000		
Production overhead	880,000	Closing inventory	70,000
	2,140,000		2,140,000

Under/over-absorbed overhead account

	$		$
Statement of profit or loss	20,000	Production overhead account	20,000
	20,000		20,000

11 INVESTIGATING THE CAUSES OF UNDER- OR OVER-ABSORBED OVERHEAD

The intention of absorbing production overhead is to share the costs of the overheads among the various products manufactured or jobs worked on. Ideally, the amount of over-head absorbed should equal the amount of overhead expenditure incurred. In practice, this rarely happens, and there are some under- or over-absorbed overheads. This is because the absorption rate is decided in advance, based on the budgeted overhead expenditure and budgeted volume of activity.

Even so, the amount of under- or over-absorbed overhead should not usually be large, provided the budgeting is realistic and provided that actual results meet budgeted expectations.

If the amount of under- or over-absorbed overhead is large, something could have gone wrong, which should be a matter of some concern to management. Certainly, management should expect to be informed of the reasons why there has been a large amount of under- or over-absorption.

The accountant will be expected to investigate the reasons for the under- or over-absorption, and report his or her findings to management.

There are several reasons why a large amount of under or over absorption of overhead might occur.

- Actual overhead expenditure was much higher than budgeted, possibly due to poor control over overhead spending.
- Actual overhead expenditure was much less than budgeted, possibly due to good control over overhead spending.
- Actual overhead expenditure was much higher or lower than budgeted, due to poor budgeting of overhead expenditure.
- The actual volume of activity was higher or lower than budgeted, for operational reasons that the production manager should be able to explain.
- The actual volume of activity was higher or lower than budgeted, due to poor budgeting of the volume of activity.

12 NON-PRODUCTION OVERHEADS

In a system of absorption costing, it is quite usual for administration overheads and sales and distribution overheads to be treated as period costs and written as a charge to the statement of profit or loss, instead of being added to the cost of cost units.

However, it is also possible to calculate a full cost of sale by absorbing non-production overheads into costs.

- Administration overheads might be absorbed into unit costs as a percentage of full production cost.
- Sales and distribution overheads might be absorbed into unit costs as either a percentage of sales value, or as a percentage of full production cost.

EXAMPLE

Sleepy Limited has budgeted the following sales and costs for next year.

	$
Full production costs	240,000
Administration overheads	60,000
Sales and distribution overheads	80,000
Sales revenue	450,000

Production overheads will be absorbed at the rate of $4 per direct labour hour. Administration overheads will be absorbed as a percentage of full production cost. Sales and distribution overhead will also be absorbed as a percentage of full production cost.

Calculate the fully absorbed cost of sale for a product that has a direct material cost of $240 and a direct labour cost of $160, with labour paid at the rate of $8 per hour.

SOLUTION

Administration overheads will be absorbed at the rate of 25% (60,000/240,000) of full production cost.

Sales and distribution overheads will be absorbed at the rate of 33.33% (80,000/240,000) of full production cost.

The full cost of sale for the product is:

	$
Direct materials	240
Direct labour	160
Production overheads (20 hours × $4)	80
Full production cost	480
Administration overheads (25% × $480)	120
Sales and distribution overheads (33.33% × $480)	160
Full cost of sale	760

13 FIXED, VARIABLE AND SEMI-FIXED OVERHEADS

In the examples above, overheads have been treated as a total cost. An organisation might, however, distinguish between its fixed overheads and variable overheads, and apply a different overhead absorption rate for each.

To do this, it might be necessary in the budget to separate semi-fixed and semi-variable overhead costs into their fixed and variable elements.

This can be done using the high-low method, which we met in Chapter 3.

EXAMPLE

It has been estimated that total production overhead costs are as follows:

	$
At 16,000 direct labour hours of work	86,000
At 19,000 direct labour hours of work	89,750

Required:

(a) Use these estimates to obtain a fixed overhead absorption rate and a variable overhead absorption rate for the budget period, in which the budgeted level of activity is 18,000 direct labour hours. Both the fixed overhead and variable overhead absorption rate should be on a direct labour hour basis.

(b) Suppose that actual results during the period were as follows:

Total overheads incurred	$90,600
Direct labour hours worked	17,400

Calculate the amount of under- or over-absorbed overhead.

SOLUTION

(a)

		$
Total overhead cost of:	19,000 hours	89,750
Total overhead cost of:	16,000 hours	86,000
Variable overhead cost for:	3,000 hours	3,750

The difference must represent variable cost as by definition fixed costs do not change with activity.

Variable overhead cost per hour ($3,750/3,000) $1.25

This is the absorption rate for variable overheads.

	$
As total overhead cost of 19,000 hours is	89,750
And total variable overhead cost of 19,000 hours (× $1.25) is	23,750
Therefore fixed costs must be	66,000

The absorption rate for fixed overhead, given a budget of 18,000 direct labour hours, should therefore be $3.667 per direct labour hour.

(b)

	$
Absorbed overheads:	
Fixed (17,400 hours × $3.67)	63,858
Variable (17,400 × $1.25)	21,750
Total absorbed overheads	85,608
Overheads incurred	90,600
Under-absorbed overhead	4,992

ACTIVITY 7

A manufacturing business uses absorption costing, and establishes separate absorption rates for fixed production overhead and variable production overhead. The absorption rates for next year will be based on 40,000 direct labour hours. Expenditure budgets for fixed and variable costs should be derived from the following estimates of cost:

	$
At 37,000 direct labour hours of work	145,500
At 42,000 direct labour hours of work	153,000

Actual results for the period were:

Direct labour hours worked	41,500 hours
Variable overhead costs incurred	$67,500
Fixed overhead costs incurred	$91,000

Required:

(a) Establish a fixed overhead absorption rate and a variable overhead absorption rate for the year.

(b) Calculate the amount of under- or over-absorbed overhead for both fixed and variable overhead.

(c) Prepare the following accounts for the cost ledger:

- production overhead account
- under-/over-absorbed overhead account.

For a suggested answer, see the 'Answers' section at the end of the book.

ACTIVITY 8

For the year ended 31 December 20X4 the planned overhead for finishing and packing cost centres at Cuecraft Ltd was $74,000 and $49,000 and cost centre activity volumes were planned as 12,750 and 10,500 direct labour hours.

During January 20X4 the following information was available:

	Finishing	*Packing*
Overhead incurred	$6,900	$4,000
Activity		
Direct labour hours	1,100	900

Calculate the pre-determined overhead recovery rates and the overhead under or over-recovered for each cost centre for the month, showing clearly the entries in the overhead control account.

For a suggested answer, see the 'Answers' section at the end of the book.

CONCLUSION

Absorption costing is a very important and complex topic. This chapter explained how to build up a full product cost by including an absorbed amount of overhead. This involved allocation, apportionment and absorption of overhead. You should also be prepared to calculate under or over absorption of overheads and carry out bookkeeping entries in relation to overheads.

KEY TERMS

Overheads – a term for indirect costs.

Absorption costing – a method of costing in which the costs of an item (product or service or activity) are built up as the sum of direct costs and a fair share of overhead costs, to obtain a full cost or a fully-absorbed cost.

Overhead allocation – the process of charging a whole item of cost to a cost centre.

Overhead apportionment – the process of sharing out overhead costs on a fair basis.

Overhead absorption – the process of adding overhead costs to the cost of a product or service, in order to build up a fully-absorbed product cost or service cost.

Under-absorption – overhead absorbed into the product is less than overhead incurred. Under absorption reduces calculated profit.

Over-absorption – overhead absorbed into the product is greater than overhead incurred. Over absorption increases calculated profit.

High-low method – a technique used to separate fixed and variable costs.

SELF TEST QUESTIONS

		Paragraph
1	What are the reasons for using absorption costing?	1.4
2	What are service cost centres?	2.1
3	What bases of apportionment are used for overheads?	4
4	What is the difference between the direct and step-down method of overhead reapportionment?	6
5	What are the particular problems of dealing with service cost centres?	6
6	What are the common methods of absorbing overhead?	8.1
7	Why are absorption rates based on budgeted figures?	8.3
8	What is over and under recovery of overhead?	9
9	What is the accounting entry for production overhead absorbed?	11
10	What are the causes of under- or over-absorbed overhead?	12

EXAM-STYLE QUESTIONS

1 The process of cost apportionment is carried out so that:

A costs may be controlled

B cost units gather overheads as they pass through cost centres

C whole items of cost can be charged to cost centres

D common costs are shared among cost centres.

2 What is cost allocation?

A The charging of discrete identifiable items of cost to cost centres

B The collection of costs attributable to cost centres and cost units using the costing methods, principles and techniques prescribed for a particular business entity

C The process of establishing the costs of cost centres or cost units

D The division of costs amongst two or more cost centres in proportion to the estimated benefit received, using a proxy e.g. square feet

3 A company absorbs overheads on the basis of machine hours which were budgeted at 11,250 with overheads of $258,750. Actual results were 10,980 hours with overheads of $254,692.

Overheads were:

A under absorbed by $2,152

B over absorbed by $4,058

C under absorbed by $4,058

D over absorbed by $2,152.

4 The following budgeted and actual data relate to production activity and overhead costs in Winnie Ltd.

	Budget	*Actual*
Production overhead		
Fixed	$94,000	$102,600
Variable	$57,500	$62,000
Direct labour hours	25,000	26,500

The company uses an absorption costing system and production overheads are absorbed on a direct labour hour basis.

Production overhead during the period was:

A under absorbed by $4,010

B over absorbed by $4,010

C under absorbed by $9,876

D over absorbed by $9,876.

5 An overhead absorption rate is used to:

A share out common costs over benefiting cost centres

B find the total overheads for a cost centre

C charge overheads to products

D control overheads.

6 Floaters plc has the following production and fixed overhead budgets for the coming year:

Production department	*1*	*2*
Fixed overhead	$2,400,000	$4,000,000
Total labour hours	240,000	200,000
Total materials cost	$200,000	$400,000

Department 1 labour is paid $5 per hour and department 2 labour $4 per hour.

The variable production cost of an IC is as follows:

		$
Labour		
Department 1	3 hours	15
Department 2	2 hours	8
Materials		
Department 1: 1kg	@ $4 per kg	4
Department 2: 2 kgs	@ $5 per kg	10
Variable overheads		7
		$44

If fixed overheads are absorbed on the basis of labour hours, the fixed overhead cost per unit of IC is:

A $70

B $72.72

C $102.67

D $148

7 A company has four production departments. The following information is available:

Department	*K*	*L*	*M*	*N*
Fixed costs	$10,000	$5,000	$4,000	$6,000
Labour hours per unit	5	5	4	3

If the company recovers overheads on the basis of labour hours and plans to produce 2,000 units, then the fixed cost per unit is:

A $3.00

B $12.00

C $12.50

D $17.00

8 A firm absorbs overheads on the basis of labour hours. In one period 11,500 hours were worked, actual overheads were $138,000 and there was $23,000 over absorption. The overhead absorption rate per hour was:

A $10

B $12

C $13

D $14

9 What will result if the budgeted level of activity is below the actual volume of activity and actual expenditure on fixed production overheads is the same as budget?

A There will be too much expenditure on fixed production overheads

B There will be too little expenditure on fixed production overheads

C Fixed production overheads will be over-absorbed

D Fixed production overheads will be under-absorbed

10 A company absorbs overheads on the basis of machine hours and had the following data for November:

Budgeted overhead expenditure	$42,000
Actual overhead expenditure	$46,000
Overhead under-absorbed	$1,375
Actual machine hours	7,140

What were the budgeted machine hours for November?

A 7,140 hours

B 7,560 hours

C 6,519 hours

D 6,720 hours

For a suggested answer, see the 'Answers' section at the end of the book.

Chapter 9

MARGINAL COSTING AND ABSORPTION COSTING

In the previous chapter, we looked at how absorption costing can be used to calculate the full cost of a cost unit, and how absorption costing can be used within a cost accounting double entry bookkeeping system. Absorption costing is not the only method of costing to measure costs and profits. An alternative costing method is marginal costing.

This chapter describes marginal costing and compares the marginal costing and absorption costing methods. This chapter covers syllabus area C2.

CONTENTS

LEARNING OUTCOMES

At the end of this chapter you should be able to:

- explain and illustrate the concept of contribution
- prepare profit statements using the marginal costing method
- compare and contrast the use of absorption and marginal costing for period profit reporting and inventory valuation
- reconcile the profits reported by absorption and marginal costing
- explain the usefulness of profit and contribution information respectively.

1 FULL COST AND MARGINAL COST

In **absorption costing** fixed manufacturing overheads are absorbed into cost units. Thus, inventory is valued at total production cost and fixed manufacturing overheads are charged in the statement of profit or loss of the period in which the units are sold.

In **marginal costing**, fixed manufacturing overheads are not absorbed into cost units. Inventory is valued at marginal or variable production cost. All fixed overheads, including fixed manufacturing overheads, are treated as period costs and are charged in the statement of profit or loss of the period in which the overheads are incurred.

EXAMPLE

Company A produces a single product and has the following budget:

Company A Budget per unit

	$
Selling price	10
Direct materials	3
Direct wages	2
Variable production overhead	1

Fixed production overhead is $10,000 per month; production volume is 5,000 units per month.

Calculate the cost per unit to be used for inventory valuation under:

(a) absorption costing

(b) marginal costing.

SOLUTION

(a) Full absorption cost per unit

		$
Direct materials		3
Direct wages		2
Variable production overhead		1
Absorbed fixed production overhead	$\frac{\$10{,}000}{5{,}000 \text{ units}}$	2
Full production cost per unit		$8

(b) Marginal cost per unit

	$
Direct materials	3
Direct wages	2
Variable production overhead	1
Marginal production cost per unit	$6

The **inventory valuation** will be different for marginal and absorption costing. Under absorption costing the inventory value will include variable and fixed production overheads whereas under marginal costing the inventory value will only include variable production overheads.

2 CONTRIBUTION

Contribution is an important concept in marginal costing. It is the difference between sales and the variable cost of sales. This can be written as:

Contribution = Sales – total variable cost of sales

Contribution is short for 'contribution to fixed costs and profits'. The idea is that after deducting the variable costs from sales, the figure remaining is the amount that contributes to fixed costs, and, once fixed costs are covered, to profits.

2.1 CONTRIBUTION AND PROFIT

Marginal costing values goods at variable cost of production (or marginal cost) and contribution can be shown as follows:

Marginal costing

	$
Sales	X
Less: all variable costs	(X)
Contribution	X
Less: fixed production costs	X
Less: all other fixed costs	X
Net profit	X

Profit is contribution less all fixed costs.

Note that there may be variable non-production costs which must also be deducted from sales to arrive at contribution.

In absorption costing profit is effectively calculated in one stage as the cost of sales already includes all overheads.

Absorption costing: profit calculation

	$
Sales	X
Less: absorption cost	(X)
Gross profit	X
Less: non-production costs	(X)
Net profit	X

2.2 WHY IS CONTRIBUTION SIGNIFICANT?

Contribution is an important concept in marginal costing. Changes in the volume of sales, or in sales prices, or in variable costs will all affect profit by altering the total contribution. Marginal costing techniques can be used to help management to assess the likely effect on profits of higher or lower sales volume, or the likely consequences of reducing the sales price of a product in order to increase demand, and so on. The approach to any such analysis should be to calculate the effect on total contribution. The arithmetic is quite straightforward.

EXAMPLE

A company sells a single product for $9. Its variable cost is $4. Fixed costs are currently $70,000 per annum and annual sales are 20,000 units. There is a proposal to make a change to the product design that would increase the variable cost to $4.50, but it would also be possible to increase the selling price to $10 for the re-designed model. It is expected that annual sales at this higher price would be 19,000 units.

How would the redesign of the product affect annual profit?

SOLUTION

Annual profit is increased by $4,500 as a result of the proposal as follows:

	Before		*After*	
		$		$
Sales	(20,000 × $9)	180,000	(19,000 × $10)	190,000
Variable costs	(20,000 × $4)	80,000	(19,000 × $4.50)	85,500
Contribution		100,000		104,500
Fixed costs		70,000		70,000
Profit		30,000		34,500

An alternative presentation of the profit calculation is as follows:

	Before		*After*	
	Per unit ($)	$	Per unit	$
Sales	9		10	
Variable costs	4	4	4.50	
Contribution	5 × 20,000	100,000	5.50 × 19,000	104,500
Fixed costs		70,000		70,000
Profit		30,000		34,500

When calculating the impact of changes to sales price, variable cost and sales volume it is often quicker to calculate unit contribution figures. This approach also focuses on the key information which is important to managers when making a decision.

3 PROFIT STATEMENTS UNDER ABSORPTION AND MARGINAL COSTING

Absorption costing must be used to provide inventory valuations for statutory financial statements. However, either marginal or absorption costing can be useful for internal management reporting. The choice made will affect:

- the way in which the profit information is presented, and
- the level of reported profit, but only if sales volumes do not exactly equal production volumes (so that there is a difference between opening and closing inventory values).

EXAMPLE

This example continues with the earlier example of Company A in Section 1. But the business also has fixed selling costs of $1,500 and variable selling costs of $1 per unit.

Show profit statements for the month if sales are 4,800 units and production is 5,000 units under:

(a) absorption costing

(b) marginal costing.

SOLUTION

(a) Profit statement under absorption costing

	$	$
Sales (4,800 at $10)		48,000
Less:		
Cost of sales		
Opening inventory	–	
Production (5,000 at $8)	40,000	
Less: Closing inventory (200 at $8)	(1,600)	
		(38,400)
Gross profit		9,600
Selling costs:		
Variable		(4,800)
Fixed		(1,500)
Net profit		3,300

(b) Profit statement under marginal costing

	$	$
Sales (4,800 at $10)		48,000
Less:		
Cost of sales		
Opening inventory	–	
Production (5,000 at $6)	30,000	
Less: Closing inventory (200 at $6)	(1,200)	
		(28,800)
Variable selling costs		(4,800)
Contribution		14,400
Less: Fixed product and selling overheads		11,500
Gross profit		$2,900

Note how variable selling costs are deducted in the calculation of contribution in the marginal costing statement.

3.1 EXPLANATION OF THE DIFFERENCE IN PROFIT

The difference in profit between the two costing methods is due to the difference in inventory levels between the beginning and the end of the period. Here, there was an increase from 0 to 200 units during the month. Under absorption costing closing inventory has been valued at $1,600 (i.e. $8 per unit which includes $2 of absorbed fixed overheads). Under marginal costing closing inventory is valued at $1,200 (i.e. at $6 per unit) and all fixed overheads are charged to the statement of profit or loss as a period cost.

If inventory levels are rising or falling, absorption costing will give a different profit figure from marginal costing. If sales equal production, the fixed overheads absorbed into cost of sales under absorption costing will be the same as the period costs charged under marginal costing and thus the profit figure will be the same.

The two profit figures can therefore be reconciled as follows:

	$
Absorption costing profit	3,300
Less: fixed costs included in the increase in inventory (200 × $2)	(400)
Marginal costing profit	2,900

The basic rule

- If inventory levels are rising, absorption costing profit > marginal costing profit.
- If inventory levels are falling absorption costing profit < marginal costing profit.
- If opening and closing inventory levels are the same, the profit will be the same for both absorption and marginal costing.

3.2 UNDER AND OVER ABSORPTION OF FIXED OVERHEADS

Under and over absorption of fixed overheads arises if the actual expenditure and production level are not as estimated in the predetermined overhead absorption rate. Such differences between budgeted and actual expenditure and production cause under or over absorption but have no effect on the different profit figures reported under absorption and marginal costing, which is due to the different inventory valuations. The next example illustrates this.

EXAMPLE

A manufacturing business makes and sells widgets. It has 2,000 units in inventory at the start of the year. Budgeted production and sales for the year are 20,000 units. The variable production cost per unit is $6 and budgeted fixed costs are $80,000. The sales price per unit is $15. Ignore administration and selling and distribution overheads.

During the year, actual production and sales totalled 16,000 units. Unit variable costs and selling prices were as budgeted, and fixed costs were $77,000.

Compare the reported profit for the year with absorption costing and marginal costing.

SOLUTION

Marginal costing

	$
Sales (16,000 × $15)	240,000
(Variable) Production cost of sales (16,000 × $6)	(96,000)
Contribution	144,000
Fixed costs	(77,000)
Profit	67,000

With absorption costing, the absorption rate is ($80,000/20,000) $4 per unit. So production and inventory is valued at $6 + $4 = $10.

Absorption costing

	$	$
Sales		240,000
Production cost of sales (16,000 × $10)		(160,000)
		80,000
Overhead absorbed (16,000 × $4)	64,000	
Overhead incurred	(77,000)	
Under-absorbed overhead		(13,000)
Profit		67,000

Profit is the same whichever costing method is used because there is no difference between opening and closing inventory values.

ACTIVITY 1

A company produces a single unit of product for which the variable production cost is $6 per unit. Fixed production overhead is $10,000 per month and the budgeted production and sales volume is 5,000 units each month. The selling price is $10 per unit. Suppose that, in a particular month, production was in fact 6,000 units with 4,800 units sold and 1,200 units left in closing inventory.

Assume all costs were as budgeted.

Required:

(a) Prepare the profit statement for the month under absorption costing.

(b) Prepare the profit statement for the month under marginal costing.

(c) Prepare a statement to reconcile the two reported profit figures.

For a suggested answer, see the 'Answers' section at the end of the book.

4 ADVANTAGES OF MARGINAL COSTING

Preparation of routine operating statements using marginal costing is considered more informative for the following reasons.

- Marginal costing emphasises variable costs per unit and treats fixed costs in total as period costs, whereas absorption costing includes all production costs in unit costs, including a share of fixed production costs. Marginal costing therefore reflects the behaviour of costs in relation to activity. Since most decision-making problems involve changes to activity, **marginal costing information is more relevant and appropriate for short-run decision-making** than absorption costing.

  It should be noted that, in the long term, as short term inventory fluctuations even out, profits under both absorption and marginal costing will be the same. It is the short term inventory fluctuations which cause the distortions in profits and is why marginal costing is better for short term decision making.

- Profit per unit with absorption costing can be a misleading figure. This is because profitability might be distorted by increases or decreases in inventory levels in the period, which has no relevance for sales.

- Comparison between products using absorption costing can be misleading because of the effect of the arbitrary apportionment of fixed costs. Where two or more products are manufactured in a factory and share all production facilities, the fixed overhead can only be apportioned on an arbitrary basis

EXAMPLE

This example illustrates the misleading effect on profit which absorption costing can have.

A company sells a product for $10, and incurs $4 of variable costs in its manufacture. The fixed costs are $900 per year and are absorbed on the basis of the normal production volume of 250 units per year. The results for the last four years were as follows:

Item	*1st year units*	*2nd year units*	*3rd year units*	*4th year units*	*Total*
Opening inventory	–	200	300	300	–
Production	300	250	200	200	950
	300	450	500	500	950
Closing inventory	200	300	300	200	200
Sales	100	150	200	300	750

Prepare a profit statement under absorption and marginal costing.

SOLUTION

The profit statement under absorption costing would be as follows:

	1st year	*2nd year*	*3rd year*	*4th year*	*Total*
	$	$	$	$	$
Sales value	1,000	1,500	2,000	3,000	7,500
Opening inventory at $7.60	–	1,520	2,280	2,280	–
Variable costs of production at $4	1,200	1,000	800	800	3,800
Fixed costs at 900/250 = $3.60	1,080	900	720	720	3,420
	2,280	3,420	3,800	3,800	7,220
Closing inventory at $7.60	1,520	2,280	2,280	1,520	1,520
Cost of sales	(760)	(1,140)	(1,520)	(2,280)	(5,700)
(Under-)/over-absorption (W)	180	Nil	(180)	(180)	(180)
Gross profit	420	360	300	540	1,620

Working: Calculation of over-/(under)-absorption

Year	*1*	*2*	*3*	*4*	*Total*
	$	$	$	$	$
Absorbed	1,080	900	720	720	3,420
Incurred	900	900	900	900	3,600
	180	0	(180)	(180)	(180)

If marginal costing had been used, the results would have been shown as follows:

Item	*1st year*	*2nd year*	*3rd year*	*4th year*	*Total*
	$	$	$	$	$
Sales	1,000	1,500	2,000	3,000	7,500
Variable cost of sales (at $4)	400	600	800	1,200	3,000
Contribution	600	900	1,200	1,800	4,500
Fixed costs	900	900	900	900	3,600
Gross profit/(loss)	(300)	–	300	900	900

If it is assumed that there are no non-production costs, the marginal costing profit statement indicates clearly that the business must sell at least 150 units per year to break even. At a sales volume of 150 units each unit earns $6 in contribution which covers the total fixed cost of $900. Using absorption costing, it might appear that even at 100 units it was making a healthy profit.

The total profit for the four years is less with marginal costing than with absorption costing because there has been an increase in inventory levels over the four-year period. The closing inventory at the end of the fourth year is valued at $800 ($4 × 200) with marginal costing and $1,520 with absorption costing. With absorption costing, fixed costs of $720 are being carried forward in the closing inventory value, whereas with marginal costing, they have all been charged against profit.

The profit figures shown may be reconciled as follows:

	Year 1	*Year 2*	*Year 3*	*Year 4*	*Total*
Inventory increase/(decrease)	200 units	100 units	0	(100 units)	200 units
	$	$	$	$	$
Profit/(loss) under marginal costing	(300)	Nil	300	900	900
Fixed costs in inventory increase/ (decrease) at $3.60 per unit	720	360	0	(360)	720
Profit with absorption costing	420	360	300	540	1,620

EXAMPLE

The next two examples illustrate the importance of marginal costing as an aid to decision making.

A factory manufactures three components – X, Y and Z – and the budgeted production for the year is 1,000 units, 1,500 units and 2,000 units respectively. Fixed overhead amounts to $6,750 and has been apportioned on the basis of budgeted units: $1,500 to X, $2,250 to Y and $3,000 to Z. Sales and variable costs are as follows:

	Component X	*Component Y*	*Component Z*
Selling price	$4	$6	$5
Variable cost	$1	$4	$4

SOLUTION

The budgeted statement of profit or loss based on the above is as follows:

	Component X		*Component Y*		*Component Z*		*Total*	
Sales units		1,000		1,500		2,000		4,500
	$	$	$	$	$	$	$	$
Sales value		4,000		9,000		10,000		23,000
Variable cost	1,000		6,000		8,000		15,000	
Fixed overhead	1,500		2,250		3,000		6,750	
		2,500		8,250		11,000		21,750
Net profit/(loss)		1,500		750		(1,000)		1,250

There is little information value in comparing products in this way. If the fixed overhead is common to all three products, there is no information value in apportioning it, and the apportionment can be misleading. A better presentation is as follows:

	Component X	*Component Y*	*Component Z*	*Total*
Sales units	1,000	1,500	2,000	4,500
	$	$	$	$
Sales value	4,000	9,000	10,000	23,000
Variable cost	1,000	6,000	8,000	15,000
Contribution	3,000	3,000	2,000	8,000
Fixed overhead				6,750
Net profit				1,250

Analysis may show, however, that certain fixed costs may be associated with a specific product and the statement can be amended to **differentiate specific fixed costs** (under products) **from general fixed costs** (under total).

EXAMPLE

A company that manufactures one product has calculated its cost on a quarterly production budget of 10,000 units. The selling price was $5 per unit. Sales in the four successive quarters of the last year were as follows:

Quarter 1	10,000 units
Quarter 2	9,000 units
Quarter 3	7,000 units
Quarter 4	5,500 units

The level of inventory at the beginning of the year was 1,000 units and the company maintained its inventory of finished products at the same level at the end of each of the four quarters.

Based on its quarterly production budget, the cost per unit was as follows:

Cost per unit

	$
Prime cost	3.50
Production overhead	0.75
Total	4.25

Selling and administration overheads were $3,000 in each quarter.

Fixed production overhead, which has been taken into account in calculating the above figures, was $5,000 per quarter. Selling and administration overhead was treated as fixed, and was charged against sales in the period in which it was incurred.

You are required to present a tabular statement to bring out the effect on net profit of the declining volume of sales over the four quarters given, assuming in respect of fixed production overhead that the company:

(a) absorbs it at the budgeted rate per unit

(b) does not absorb it into the product cost, but charges it against sales in each quarter (i.e. the company uses marginal costing).

SOLUTION

(a) Net profit statement (fixed overhead absorbed)

	1st quarter	*2nd quarter*	*3rd quarter*	*4th quarter*
Sales units	10,000	9,000	7,000	5,500
	$	$	$	$
Sales value ($5 per unit)	50,000	45,000	35,000	27,500
Cost of sales:				
Prime costs ($3.50 per unit)	35,000	31,500	24,500	19,250
Production overhead absorbed ($0.75 per unit)	7,500	6,750	5,250	4,125
Under-absorbed production overhead (Working)	–	500	1,500	2,250
	42,500	38,750	31,250	25,625
Gross profit	7,500	6,250	3,750	1,875
Less: Selling and admin overhead	3,000	3,000	3,000	3,000
Net profit/(loss)	4,500	3,250	750	(1,125)

Working

Fixed production overhead absorption rate =

$$\frac{\text{Fixed production overhead}}{\text{Budgeted production}} = \frac{\$5{,}000}{10{,}000 \text{ units}} = \$0.50 \text{ per unit}$$

The production overhead cost per unit therefore consists of $0.50 of fixed cost and $0.25 of variable cost.

As finished inventory is maintained at 1,000 units, fixed overhead under absorbed in each quarter = $5,000 – (Sales units × $0.50).

	1st quarter	*2nd quarter*	*3rd quarter*	*4th quarter*
	$	$	$	$
Incurred				
Variable	2,500	2,250	1,750	1,375
Fixed	5,000	5,000	5,000	5,000
	7,500	7,250	6,750	6,375
Absorbed (at $0.75)	7,500	6,750	5,250	4,125
Under-absorbed overhead	0	(500)	(1,500)	(2,250)

(b) Net profit statement (fixed overhead charged against period sales)

	1st quarter	*2nd quarter*	*3rd quarter*	*4th quarter*
Sales units	10,000	9,000	7,000	5,500
	$	$	$	$
Sales value	50,000	45,000	35,000	27,500
Less:				
Variable cost of sales				
Prime cost ($3.50 per unit)	35,000	31,500	24,500	19,250
Variable production overhead ($0.25)	2,500	2,250	1,750	1,375
Contribution	12,500	11,250	8,750	6,875
Less:				
Fixed production, selling and admin overhead	8,000	8,000	8,000	8,000
Net profit/(loss)	4,500	3,250	750	(1,125)

5 ADVANTAGES OF ABSORPTION COSTING

In spite of its weaknesses as a system for providing information to management, absorption costing is widely used.

The only difference between using absorption costing and marginal costing as the basis of inventory valuation is the treatment of fixed production costs.

The arguments used in favour of absorption costing are as follows:

- Fixed costs are incurred within the production function, and without those facilities production would not be possible. Consequently such costs can be related to production and should be included in inventory valuation.
- Absorption costing follows the matching concept by carrying forward a proportion of the production cost in the inventory valuation to be matched against the sales value when the items are sold.
- It is necessary to include fixed overhead in inventory values for financial statements; routine cost accounting using absorption costing produces inventory values which include a share of fixed overhead.

- Overhead allotment is the only practicable way of obtaining job costs for estimating prices and profit analysis.
- Analysis of under-/over-absorbed overhead is useful to identify inefficient utilisation of production resources.
- It is quite common to price jobs or contracts by adding a profit margin to the estimated fully-absorbed cost of the work.

The main weaknesses of absorption costing were explained earlier. Absorption costing can provide misleading information to management whenever a decision has to be made.

Marginal costing is consistent with the concept of relevant costs for management decision-making. It is also useful for forward planning, for example in forecasting and budgeting. These applications of marginal costing will be explained more fully in later chapters.

CONCLUSION

This chapter has explained how to prepare profit statements using absorption and marginal costing and how to reconcile any differences in resulting profits. You should also now understand for what purposes an organisation may use absorption costing and marginal costing.

KEY TERMS

Absorption costing – a costing technique that values production and inventory at full production cost.

Marginal costing – a costing technique that values production and inventory at variable production cost. All variable costs are deducted from sales to arrive at contribution and fixed costs are treated as period costs in arriving at profit.

Contribution – sales revenue less variable costs.

SELF TEST QUESTIONS

		Paragraph
1	What is marginal costing?	1
2	What is marginal cost?	1
3	What is the difference between marginal costing and absorption costing?	1
4	What is contribution?	2
5	What is the reason for the difference in profit between marginal costing and absorption costing?	3.1
6	What are the advantages of marginal costing?	4
7	What are the advantages of absorption costing?	5

EXAM-STYLE QUESTIONS

1 In a period closing inventory was 1,400 units, opening inventory was 2,000 units, and the actual production was 11,200 units at a total cost of $4.50 per unit compared to a target cost of $5.00 per unit. When comparing the profits reported using marginal costing with those reported using absorption costing, which of the following statements is correct?

A Absorption costing reports profits $2,700 higher

B Absorption costing reports profits $2,700 lower

C Absorption costing reports profits $3,000 higher

D There is insufficient data to calculate the difference between the reported profits

2 When comparing the profits reported under marginal and absorption costing during a period when the level of inventory has increased:

A absorption costing profits will be higher and closing inventory valuations lower than those under marginal costing

B absorption costing profits will be higher and closing inventory valuations higher than those under marginal costing

C marginal costing profits will be higher and closing inventory valuations lower than those under absorption costing

D marginal costing profits will be lower and closing inventory valuations lower than those under absorption costing.

3 Contribution is:

A sales – total costs

B sales – variable costs

C variable costs of production less labour costs

D none of the above.

4 Identify which of the following statements would be true: fixed production overheads will always be under-absorbed when:

A actual output is lower than budgeted output

B actual overheads incurred are lower than budgeted overheads

C overheads absorbed are lower than those budgeted

D overheads absorbed are lower than those incurred

5 A company uses a standard absorption costing system. The fixed overhead absorption rate is based on labour hours. Extracts from the company's records for last year were as follows:

	Budget	Actual
Overheads ($)	450,000	475,000
Production units	50,000	60,000
Labour hours	900,000	800,000

The ______ (*choose between* over *and* under) absorbed fixed production overheads for the year were $______ (*fill in the value*).

6 Exe Limited makes a single product whose total cost per unit is budgeted to be $45. This includes fixed cost of $8 per unit based on a volume of 10,000 units per period. In a period, sales volume was 9,000 units, and production volume was 11,500 units. The actual profit for the same period, calculated using absorption costing, was $42,000.

If the profit statement were prepared using marginal costing, identify the profit for the period:

A $10,000

B $22,000

C $50,000

D $62,000

7 Which of the following statements is not an advantage of marginal costing?

A Marginal costing is more relevant and appropriate for short-run decision making

B Marginal costing avoids profits being distorted by changes in inventory levels

C Marginal costing follows the matching concept

D Marginal costing avoids arbitrary apportionments of fixed overheads

8 An organisation makes a single product whose total cost per unit is budgeted to be $12. This includes fixed cost of $1.50 per unit based on a volume of 6,000 units per period. In a period, sales volume was 7,000 units, and production volume was 5,000 units. The actual profit for the same period, calculated using absorption costing, was $56,000.

If the profit statement were prepared using marginal costing, identify the profit for the period:

A $53,000

B $56,000

C $59,000

D $63,500

For the answers to these questions, see the 'Answers' section at the end of the book.

Chapter 10

JOB AND BATCH COSTING

In a manufacturing organisation, the cost unit might be a batch of output or a specific job carried out for a customer. In such cases, the appropriate costing system would be a batch costing system or a job costing system respectively. These costing systems are usually associated with absorption costing methodology, and the costs calculated for each batch or each job produced are normally a fully absorbed production cost.

This chapter looks at the characteristics of both batch costing and job costing, which are essentially straightforward applications of absorption costing. This chapter covers syllabus area C3.

CONTENTS

LEARNING OUTCOMES

At the end of this chapter you should be able to:

- identify situations where the use of job or batch costing is appropriate
- calculate unit costs in job and batch costing
- describe the control of costs in job and batch costing
- apply cost plus pricing in job costing.

1 SPECIFIC ORDER COSTING

The purpose of costing is to calculate the cost of each cost unit of an organisation's products. In order to do this the costs of each unit should be gathered together and recorded in the costing system. This is the overall aim, but the methods and system used will differ from organisation to organisation as the type of products and production methods differ between organisations.

There are two main types of costing system:

- **Specific order costing,** where the costs of distinct products or services are collected. Individual cost units are different according to individual customer's requirements. The main examples of specific order costing are job costing and contract costing (which is outside the scope of your syllabus). Batch costing is a form of specific order costing, although costs will be attributed to specific batches rather than specific orders or customers.

- **Continuous costing,** where a series of similar products or services are produced. Costs are collected and averaged over the number of products or services produced to arrive at a cost per unit. The main examples of continuous costing are process costing and service costing which are considered in later chapters.

1.1 COST UNITS

The cost units of different organisations will be of different types and this will tend to necessitate different costing systems. The main types of cost unit are as follows:

- Individual products designed and produced for individual customers. Each individual product is a cost unit. Job costing is used.

- Groups of different products possibly in different styles, sizes or colours produced to be held in inventory until sold. Each of the batches of whatever style, size or colour is a cost unit. Batch costing is used.

- Many units of identical products produced from a single production process. These units will be held in inventory until sold. Each batch from the process is a cost unit. Process costing is used.

2 JOB COSTING

2.1 JOBS

Definition A **job** is an individual product designed and produced as a single order for an individual customer

A job will normally be requested by a customer and that customer's individual requirements and specifications considered. Each individual job is a cost unit. The organisation will then estimate the costs of such a job, add on their required profit margin and quote their price to the customer. If the customer accepts that quote then the job will proceed according to the timetable agreed between customer and supplier.

Each job will tend to be a specific individual order and as such will normally differ in some respects from other jobs that the organisation performs. The costs for each individual job must therefore be determined.

You might be able to think of organisations that perform jobbing work, and charge customers for the jobs they do. Well-known examples include small building and building repair work, car maintenance and repair work, printing, painting and decorating.

2.2 JOB COST CARD

All of the actual costs incurred in a job are eventually recorded on a job cost card. A job cost card can take many forms but is likely at least to include the following information:

JOB COST CARD									
Job number					Customer name:				
Estimate ref:					Quoted estimate:				
Start date:					Delivery date:				
Invoice number:					Invoice amount:				
COSTS:									
Materials					**Labour**				
Date	Code	Qty	Price	$	Date	Grade	Hours	Rate	$
Expenses					**Production overheads**				
Date	Code	Description		$	Hours		OAR		$
				____					____
Cost summary:									
Direct materials									
Direct labour									
Direct expenses									
Production overheads									
Administrative overheads									
Selling and distribution overheads									
Total cost									
Invoice price									

The job cost card may travel with the particular job as it moves around the factory. However it is more likely in practice that the job cost cards will be held centrally by the accounts department and all relevant cost information for that job forwarded to the accounts department.

2.3 DIRECT MATERIALS FOR JOBS

When materials are requisitioned for a job then the issue of the materials will be recorded in the inventory ledger account. They will also be recorded, at their issue price, on the job cost card as they are used as input into that particular job. Materials may be issued at different dates to a particular job but each issue must be recorded on the job cost card.

EXAMPLE

The materials requisitions and issues for Job number 3867 for customer OT Ltd at their issue prices are as follows:

1 June	40 kg Material code T73 at $60 per kg
5 June	60 kg Material code R80 at $5 per kg
9 June	280 metres Material code B45 at $8 per metre

Record these on a job cost card for this job which is due to be delivered on 17 June.

SOLUTION

JOB COST CARD

Job number: 3867					Customer name: OT Ltd				
Estimate ref:					Quoted estimate:				
Start date: 1 June					Delivery date: 17 June				
Invoice number:					Invoice amount:				
COSTS:									
Materials					**Labour**				
Date	Code	Qty	Price	$	Date	Grade	Hours	Rate	$
1 June	T73	40 kg	$60	2,400					
5 June	R80	60 kg	$5	300					
9 June	B45	280m	$8	2,240					
				4,940					
Expenses					**Production overheads**				
Date	Code	Description		$	Hours		OAR		$

Cost summary:

	$
Direct materials	4,940
Direct labour	
Direct expenses	
Production overheads	
Administration overheads	
Selling and distribution overheads	
Total cost	4,940
Invoice price	
Profit/loss	

2.4 DIRECT LABOUR COST FOR JOBS

In an earlier chapter dealing with labour costs the system of recording hours worked in a job costing system was considered.

In summary a job card travels with each individual job and the hours worked by each grade of labour are logged onto this card. The card is then sent to the accounts department and the hours are transferred to the job cost card. The relevant hourly labour rate is then applied to each grade of labour to give a cost for each grade and a total cost for the job.

ACTIVITY 1

The labour records show that the hours worked on Job 3867 were as follows:

1 June	Grade II	43 hours
2 June	Grade II	12 hours
	Grade IV	15 hours
5 June	Grade I	25 hours
	Grade IV	13 hours
9 June	Grade I	15 hours

The hourly rates for each grade of labour are as follows:

	$
Grade I	14.70
Grade II	15.80
Grade III	16.40
Grade IV	17.50

Record the labour costs for Job 3867 on the job cost card.

For a suggested answer, see the 'Answers' section at the end of the book.

2.5 DIRECT EXPENSES

The third category of direct costs are any expenses that can be directly attributed to that particular job. Such expenses will be recorded by the cost accountant when incurred and coded in such a way that it is clear to which job or jobs they relate.

ACTIVITY 2

A specialised piece of machinery has been hired at a cost of $1,200. It is used on job numbers 3859, 3867 and 3874 and has spent approximately the same amount of time being used on each of those jobs. The account code for machine hire is 85.

Record any cost relevant to Job 3867 on the job cost card.

For a suggested answer, see the 'Answers' section at the end of the book.

2.6 PRODUCTION OVERHEADS AND JOB COSTS

In an earlier chapter the apportionment of overheads to cost units was considered and it was determined that the most common method of allocating overheads to specific cost units was on the basis of either the labour hours worked or machine hours worked on that particular cost unit.

This is exactly the same for jobs and so the production overhead will be absorbed into jobs on the basis of the pre-determined overhead absorption rate.

2.7 OTHER OVERHEADS AND JOB COSTS

In order to arrive at the total cost for a particular job any administration, selling and distribution overheads must also be included in the job's cost. Therefore when the job is completed an appropriate proportion of the total administration, selling and distribution overheads will also be included on the job cost card.

ACTIVITY 3

The production overhead absorption rate for this period is $4 per labour hour. The administration overhead to be charged to Job 3867 totals $156 and the selling and distribution overhead for the job is $78.

The job was completed by the due date and the customer was invoiced the agreed price of $9,030 on 17 June (invoice number 26457).

Using this information complete the job cost card for Job 3867.

For a suggested answer, see the 'Answers' section at the end of the book.

2.8 ACCOUNTING FOR JOB COSTS

As well as recording the job costs on the job cost card they must also be recorded in the cost ledger accounts. Each job will have its own job ledger account to which the costs incurred are all debited.

In order to keep track of all of the individual job ledger accounts there will also be a job in progress control account. All of the costs incurred on a job must also be debited to this control account. The job in progress control account fulfils the same role as the work-in-progress control account studied in the previous chapter.

The balance on the job in progress control account at the end of each accounting period should be equal to the total of all of the balances on the individual job ledger accounts.

2.9 JOB COST PER UNIT

Typically, jobs will provide one 'unit' of output and therefore the cost per unit will be the same as the total cost for the job. For example, if an accountant is asked to create a set of financial statements for a client, this 'job' can be treated as one unit of output and the cost per job unit will simply be the total cost of completing the job.

2.10 JOB PRICING

Since each job is different, there will be no set price for each job. A customer often wants to be quoted a price for the job before the work begins, in which case the supplier might:

- estimate a fully-absorbed cost for the job; and
- add a profit mark-up to the cost, to arrive at a price to charge for the work.

In such cases, the organisation has to start by estimating the cost for the job and must decide what the size of the profit mark-up should be. Typically, the profit added on is a standard percentage of the total cost (a profit mark-up) or a standard percentage of sales price (a profit margin). You must be able to work with both mark-ups and margins.

This form of pricing is known as **cost-plus pricing**.

EXAMPLE

A company carries out small building work for domestic customers. A customer has asked the company to quote a price for building an extension at the back of his house. The company's estimator has come up with the following estimated costs:

Direct materials	$2,500
Direct labour	$4,000
Direct expenses	$500
Production overhead	100% of labour cost
Other overheads	20% of total production cost
Profit mark-up	25% of total cost

Required:

(a) Calculate the price to quote for the job.

(b) What would be the price if the profit margin is 20% of sales price?

SOLUTION

(a)

	$
Direct materials	2,500
Direct labour	4,000
Direct expenses	500
Production overhead	4,000
Full production cost	11,000
Other overheads	2,200
Total cost	13,200
Profit mark-up (25%)	3,300
Job price	16,500

(b) Since total cost + Profit mark-up = Sales price, total cost must be 80% of sales price.

So sales price = $\frac{\text{total cost}}{0.8} = \frac{\$13,200}{0.8}$ = $16,500

A profit mark-up of 25% on total cost is the same as a profit margin of 20% of sales price.

Note that there is a difference between a gross profit margin and a net profit margin.

EXAMPLE

A job has production costs of $500. Administration and selling overhead is added at 20% of production cost.

Calculate the selling price of the job if:

(a) the gross profit margin is 30%

(b) the net profit margin is 16%.

SOLUTION

(a) If the gross profit margin is 30%, this means that production costs are 70% of the sales price.

Sales price = Production cost/0.7 = $500/0.7 = $714.29

(b) If the net profit margin is 16%, this means that total costs are 84% of the sales price.

Total cost = $500 + ($500 × 0.2) = $600

Sales price = Total cost/0.84 = 600/0.84 = $714.29

The gross profit margin is higher than the net profit margin to cover non-production overheads.

ACTIVITY 4

A job has production costs of $785. Administration and selling overhead is added at 25% of production cost.

Calculate the selling price if:

(a) the profit mark-up is 20%

(b) the gross profit margin is 30%

(c) the net profit margin is 15%.

For a suggested answer, see the 'Answers' section at the end of the book.

3 BATCH COSTING

The second type of costing system that must be examined is a batch costing system. A batch costing system is likely to be very similar to a job costing system and indeed a batch is in all respects a job.

3.1 BATCH

Definition A **batch** is a group of identical but separately identifiable products that are all made together.

A batch is for example a group of 100 identical products made in a particular production run. For example, a baker may produce loaves of bread in batches.

3.2 BATCH COSTING

Each batch is very similar to a job and in exactly the same way as in job costing the costs of that batch are gathered together on some sort of a batch cost card. These costs will be the materials input into the batch, the labour worked on the batch, any direct expenses of the batch and the batch's share of overheads.

The layout of the batch cost card will be similar to that of a job cost card. This will show the total cost of that particular batch of production.

3.3 COST OF A COST UNIT

Remember that a batch does however differ from a job in that a batch is made up of a number of identical products or cost units. In order to find the cost of each product or cost unit the total cost of the batch must be divided by the number of products in that batch.

EXAMPLE

Batch number 0692 has the following inputs:

15 June Material X 20 kg @ $30 per kg

40 hours of grade II labour @ $16.00 per hour

16 June Material Y 15 kg @ $10 per kg

60 hours of grade III labour at $15.00 per hour

Production overhead is to be absorbed into the cost of each batch on the basis of labour hours at a rate of $0.50 per labour hour.

The number of products produced from batch 0692 was 100.

Calculate the cost of each product from batch 0692.

SOLUTION

Materials cost	$
Material X 20 kg × $30	600
Material Y 15 kg × $10	150
Labour cost	
Grade II 40 hours × $16	640
Grade III 60 hours × $15	900
Production overhead	
100 hours × $0.50	50
	2,340

Cost per cost unit or product

$$\frac{\$2,340}{100\,\text{units}} = \$23.40$$

4 THE CONTROL OF COSTS IN JOB AND BATCH COSTING

One of the purposes of job and batch costing is to arrive at a full cost to which a profit margin can be added to arrive at a price. This price is often quoted to the customer. Special care must be taken to ensure costs are forecast accurately. If costs are higher than expected this excess may not be charged to the customer and therefore profits may be lower than expected. If cost forecasts are too high the price quoted may be uncompetitive and the work lost.

ACTIVITY 5

A builder has produced a quote for some alterations. The price is made up as follows:

		$
Direct materials	100 kg @ $4 per kg	400
Direct labour	5 hours @ $18 per hour	90
	15 hours @ $12 per hour	180
Hire of machine	1 day @ $100 per day	100
Overheads	20 hours @ $8 per hour	160
Total cost		930
	Profit mark-up @ 20%	186
	Price quoted	$1,116

Actual costs for the job were as follows:

Direct materials	120 kg @ $4 per kg
Direct labour	3 hours @ $18 per hour
	20 hours @ $12 per hour
Hire of machine	2 days @ $100 per day

Calculate the actual profit made on the job.

For a suggested answer, see the 'Answers' section at the end of the book

CONCLUSION

Job and batch costing are costing systems used to determine the full cost of a specific job or batch of products or services. A profit mark-up may be added to arrive at a price which can be quoted to the customer. This price is often a fixed price and it is important that costs do not exceed their forecast level otherwise profit levels will be much lower than expected.

KEY TERMS

Job – an individual product designed and produced as a single order for an individual customer.

Batch – a group of identical but separately identifiable products that are all made together.

SELF TEST QUESTIONS

		Paragraph
1	What is job costing?	2.1
2	What does a job cost card look like?	2.2
3	How is labour cost included on a job cost card?	2.4
4	How is production overheads dealt with in job costing?	2.6
5	How do you calculate a profit margin based on sales price?	2.9
6	What is batch costing?	3

EXAM-STYLE QUESTIONS

1 A job requires 2,400 actual labour hours for completion and it is anticipated that there will be 20% idle time. If the wage rate is $10 per hour, what is the budgeted labour cost for the job?

A $19,200

B $24,000

C $28,800

D $30,000

2 The following items may be used in costing jobs in an absorption costing system:

(i) actual manufacturing overheads

(ii) absorbed manufacturing overheads

(iii) actual labour cost.

Which of the above are contained in a typical job cost?

A (i) only

B (i) and (iii) only

C (ii) and (iii) only

D All three of them

3 A small management consultancy has prepared the following information:

Overhead absorption rate per consulting hour	$12.50
Salary cost per consulting hour (senior)	$20.00
Salary cost per consulting hour (junior)	$15.00

The firm adds 40% to total cost to arrive at a selling price.

Assignment number 652 took 86 hours of a senior consultant's time and 220 hours of junior time.

What price should be charged for assignment number 652?

A $5,355

B $7,028

C $8,845

D $12,383

For the answers to these questions, see the 'Answers' section at the end of the book.

Chapter 11

PROCESS COSTING

Some manufacturing businesses manufacture their output in a process operation, or a series of process operations. Process manufacturing has certain distinguishing features. One of these is the loss of materials during processing, for example, due to evaporation or chemical reaction. Another feature of process costing is that once material has been input to a process, it becomes indistinguishable, and there is no easy way of distinguishing between completed output and materials still in process. Special techniques have been developed for costing output from process operations. These are explained in this chapter. This chapter covers syllabus area C4.

CONTENTS

LEARNING OUTCOMES

At the end of this chapter you should be able to:

- identify situations where the use of process costing is appropriate
- explain and illustrate the nature of normal and abnormal losses/gains
- calculate unit costs where losses are separated into normal and abnormal
- prepare process accounts where losses are separated into normal and abnormal
- account for scrap and waste

- distinguish between joint products and by-products
- explain the treatment of joint products and by-products at the point of separation
- apportion joint process costs using net realisable values and weight/volume of output respectively
- discuss the usefulness of product cost/profit data from a joint process
- evaluate the benefit of further processing.

1 FEATURES OF PROCESS COSTING

1.1 INTRODUCTION

Process costing is a method of costing used in industries including brewing, quarrying, chemicals and textiles.

The cost per unit of finished output is calculated by dividing the expected process costs by the expected number of units of output. Process costs consist of direct materials, direct labour and production overheads. When processing goes through several successive processes, the output from one process becomes an input direct material cost to the next process. Total costs therefore build up as the output goes through each successive processing stage.

EXAMPLE

Input to a process is 100 kg of materials. The cost of the direct materials is $200, and the costs of converting these materials into finished output consists of $100 of direct labour and $250 of production overheads. Output from the process was 100 kg of finished product.

The total costs of processing are $550 and the cost per kilogram of output is $5.50 ($550/100kg).

1.2 PROCESS INDUSTRY MANUFACTURING

Process production has certain features that make it different from other types of manufacturing.

- In some production industries, output is manufactured in batches of small value but high quantity e.g. matches, paper clips. In continuous processing production, however, manufacturing operations never stop. Materials are continually being added to the process and output is continually produced e.g. brewing, paint making.
- Usually there are two or more consecutive processes, with output from one process being input to the next process, and finished output only being produced from the final process. For example, suppose there are three consecutive processes, A, B and C. Raw materials might be added to Process A to produce output that is then input to Process B. Further raw materials might be added in Process B, and mixed in with the output from Process A. The output from Process B might then be input to Process C. Output from Process C is the finished product that is sold to customers.

- When processing is continuous, there will be opening inventory in process at the start of any period and closing inventory in process at the end of the period. A problem is to decide what value to put to part-finished inventory in process. Usually, it is necessary to make an estimate of the degree of completion of the closing inventory (which is then part-finished opening inventory at the start of the next period). For example, it might be estimated or measured that closing inventory in a process consists of 100 units of product, which is 100% complete for direct materials but only 50% complete for conversion costs. A value (cost) will then be calculated for the inventory. The problem of measuring and valuing work-in-progress in process costing was covered in Paper MA1. Paper MA2 focuses solely on the accounting for losses and for joint and by-products.

- There could be losses in process. By this we mean that if 100 kg of direct materials are input to a process, the output quantity could be less than 100 kg. Loss could be a natural part of the production process, occurring because of evaporation or chemical change or natural wastage.

- There could be more than one product produced from a common input. For example, an oil refinery may produce petrol, diesel, tar, etc. These products may be significant in their own right or a by-product of the process.

The main problems with process costing are therefore:

- how to treat losses

- how to value inventory and finished output when there is opening and closing inventory of work-in-process. At this stage of your studies, you are only required to know how to value finished output and closing work-in-process when there is no opening work-in-process at the start of the accounting period

- how to cost joint and by-products.

1.3 PROCESS INPUT COSTS

The typical costs of a process are direct materials, direct labour and production overheads absorbed into the cost of the process. In process costing the total of the labour costs and the overhead costs tend to be known as costs of conversion.

Definition **Costs of conversion** are the labour costs of the process plus the overheads of the process.

If you come across the term 'conversion costs', it simply means direct labour cost plus production overhead cost.

2 LOSSES

In many processes, some losses in processing are inevitable. When losses occur, the problem arises as to how they should be accounted for.

Suppose that 100 units of materials are input to a process and the processing costs are $720. Losses in the process are 10 units, and so 90 units are output. What is the cost of the output and how should the loss be accounted for?

In process costing, if losses are a regular and expected aspect of the processing, it is unsatisfactory to make a charge to the statement of profit or loss for losses every time, knowing that the losses are unavoidable. A more sensible approach is therefore to calculate a cost per unit based on the expected output from the process. In this example, if the expected loss from the process is 90 units, the cost of the finished units would be $8 ($720/90 units). The cost of production would therefore be $720 (90 × $8) and the expected loss, or 'normal loss', has no cost.

Thus, the cost per unit of output is calculated after allowing for 'normal loss'. However, a distinction is made between normal loss and unexpected loss or 'abnormal loss'.

Definition **Normal loss** is the expected amount of loss in a process. It is the level of loss or waste that management would expect to incur under normal operating conditions.

Definition **Abnormal loss** is the amount by which actual loss exceeds the expected or normal loss in a process. It can also be defined as the amount by which actual production is less than normal production. Normal production is calculated as the quantity of input units of materials less normal loss.

Normal loss is included in the cost of production and is not charged as an expense in the statement of profit or loss. However, abnormal loss is given a cost, which is charged as an expense to the statement of profit or loss. This is explained further in the following sections.

2.1 NORMAL LOSS

Normal loss is not given a cost.

- If units of normal loss have no scrap value, their value or cost is nil.
- If units of normal loss have a scrap value, the value of this loss is its scrap value, which is set off against the cost of the process. In other words, the cost of finished output is reduced by the scrap value of the normal loss.

EXAMPLE – Normal loss with no scrap value

Input to a process in June consisted of 1,000 units of direct materials costing $4,300. Direct labour costs were $500 and absorbed production overheads were $1,500. Normal loss is 10% of input. Output from the process in the month was 900 units.

Calculate the cost per unit of output, and show how this would be shown in the work-in-process account in the cost ledger.

SOLUTION

Actual loss = 1,000 – 900 units = 100 units.

Normal loss = 10% of 1,000 = 100 units.

All loss is therefore normal loss.

Total production costs were $6,300 ($4,300 + $500 + $1,500).

$$\text{Cost per unit of expected output} = \frac{\$6{,}300}{900 \text{ units}} = \$7 \text{ per unit}$$

Transactions recorded in the process account will be as follows:

Process account

	Units	$		*Units*	$
Direct materials	1,000	4,300	Normal loss	100	–
Direct labour		500	Finished goods	900	6,300
Production overhead absorbed		1,500	(900 units × $7)		
	1,000	6,300		1,000	6,300

Note: In process accounts it is normal to show units of input and output as well as costs.

Normal loss with a scrap value

When normal loss has a scrap value, the value of this loss is set against the costs of production. In the cost accounts, this is done by means of:

Debit Normal loss (or scrap) account

Credit Process account

with the scrap value of the normal loss.

Then:

Debit Bank (or Receivables)

Credit Normal loss (or scrap) account

with the scrap proceeds received

EXAMPLE

Input to a process in June consisted of 1,000 units of direct materials costing $4,300. Direct labour costs were $500 and absorbed production overheads were $1,500. Normal loss is 10% of input. Loss has a scrap value of $0.90 per unit. Output from the process in the month was 900 units.

Calculate the cost per unit of output, and show how this would be shown in the process account in the cost ledger.

SOLUTION

Actual loss = 1,000 – 900 units = 100 units. Normal loss = 10% of 1,000 = 100 units. All loss is therefore normal loss. The normal loss has a value of $90, and will be sold for this amount.

Production costs are $6,300 ($4,300 + $500 + $1,500) less the scrap value of normal loss, $90. Production costs are therefore $6,210.

$$\text{Cost per unit of expected output} = \frac{\$6{,}210}{900 \text{ units}} = \$6.90 \text{ per unit}$$

Transactions recorded in the process account will be as follows:

Process account

	Units	$		Units	$
Direct materials	1,000	4,300	Normal loss	100	90
Direct labour		500	Finished goods	900	6,210
Production overhead absorbed		1,500	(900 units × $6.90)		
	1,000	6,300		1,000	6,300

Normal loss account

	$		$
Process account	90	Bank	90

2.2 ABNORMAL LOSS

Unlike normal loss, abnormal loss is given a cost. The cost of a unit of abnormal loss is the same as a cost of one unit of good output from the process. The cost of abnormal loss is treated as a charge against profit in the period it occurs.

The cost per unit of good output and abnormal loss is the cost of production divided by the expected quantity of output.

In the cost accounts, abnormal loss is accounted for in an abnormal loss account. The double entry transactions are:

Debit Abnormal loss account

Credit Process account

with the cost of the abnormal loss

Then:

Debit Statement of profit or loss

Credit Abnormal loss account

EXAMPLE

Input to a process in November was 2,000 units. Normal loss is 5% of input. Costs of production were:

Direct materials	$3,700
Direct labour	$1,300
Production overhead	$2,600

Actual output during November was 1,780 units.

Calculate the cost per unit of output.

Record these transactions in the cost accounts.

SOLUTION

Expected output = 2,000 units less normal loss of 5% = 2,000 – 100 = 1,900 units.

Actual output = 1,780 units.

Abnormal loss = 1,900 – 1,780 = 120 units.

Total costs of production = $7,600 ($3,700 + $1,300 + $2,600).

$$\text{Cost per unit of expected output} = \frac{\$7,600}{1,900 \text{ units}} = \$4 \text{ per unit}$$

Both good output and abnormal loss are valued at this amount.

These transactions should be recorded in the cost accounts as follows:

Process account

	Units	$		*Units*	$
Direct materials	2,000	3,700	Normal loss	100	–
Direct labour		1,300	Abnormal loss (120 × $4)	120	480
Production overhead		2,600	Finished goods (1,780 × $4)	1,780	7,120
	2,000	7,600		2,000	7,600

Abnormal loss account

	$		$
Process account	480	Statement of profit or loss	480

ACTIVITY 1

Dunmex produces a product in Process A.

The following information relates to the product for week ended 7 January 20X4.

Input 1,900 tonnes, cost $28,804.

Direct labour	$1,050
Process overhead	$1,800

Normal loss is 2% of input.

Output to finished goods was 1,842 tonnes.

Prepare the Process A account together with any other relevant accounts.

For a suggested answer, see the 'Answers' section at the end of the book.

Abnormal loss with a scrap value

When loss has a scrap value, normal loss is accounted for in the way already described.

With abnormal loss, the cost per unit of loss is calculated and recorded in the way also described above. The scrap value of the loss, however, is set off against the amount to be written off to the profit and loss account.

This is done by means of:

Credit	Abnormal loss account
Debit	Normal loss (scrap) account

with the scrap value of the abnormal loss units.

The balance on the abnormal loss account is then written off to the statement of profit or loss.

EXAMPLE

Input to a process in March was 1,000 units. Normal loss is 3% of input. Costs of production were:

Direct materials	$3,705
Direct labour	$600
Production overhead	$3,000

Actual output during November was 950 units. Items lost in process have a scrap value of $1 per unit.

Calculate the cost per unit of output.

Record these transactions in the process account and the abnormal loss account.

SOLUTION

Expected output = 1,000 units less normal loss of 3% = 970 units.

Actual output = 950 units.

Abnormal loss = 970 – 950 = 20 units.

The scrap value of loss is $1 per unit.

The costs of the process, allowing for the scrap value of normal loss, are as follows.

	$
Direct materials	3,705
Direct labour	600
Production overhead	3,000
	7,305
Less: Scrap value of normal loss (30 × $1)	30
	7,275

Cost per unit of expected output = $\frac{\$7,275}{970 \text{ units}}$ = \$7.50 per unit

Both good output and abnormal loss are valued at this amount.

These transactions should be recorded in the cost accounts as follows:

Process account

	Units	$		Units	$
Direct materials	1,000	3,705	Normal loss	30	30
Direct labour		600	Abnormal loss (20 × $7.50)	20	150
Production overhead		3,000	Finished goods (950 × $7.50)	950	7,125
	1,000	7,305		1,000	7,305

Normal loss account

	$		$
Process account	30	Bank	50
Abnormal loss account	20		
	50		50

Abnormal loss account

	$		$
Process account	150	Normal loss account (scrap value of abnormal loss, 20 × $1)	20
		Statement of profit or loss (balance)	130
	150		150

3 ABNORMAL GAIN

When actual losses are less than expected losses, there is abnormal gain.

Definition **Abnormal gain** is the amount by which actual output from a process exceeds the expected output. It is the amount by which actual loss is lower than expected loss.

Abnormal gain can therefore be thought of as the opposite of abnormal loss.

- Abnormal gain is given a value. The value per unit of abnormal gain is calculated in the same way as a cost per unit of abnormal loss would be calculated. It is the cost of production divided by the expected units of output.
- Abnormal gain is recorded in an abnormal gain account.
- The gain is then taken to the statement of profit or loss as an item of profit for the period.

- If loss has any scrap value, the profit should be reduced by the amount of income that would have been earned from the sales of scrap had the loss been normal.

In the cost accounts, abnormal gain is recorded as:

Debit Process account

Credit Abnormal gain account

with the value of the abnormal gain

If loss has a scrap value

Debit Abnormal gain account

Credit Normal loss account

with the scrap value of the abnormal gain. This is income that has not been earned because loss was less than normal.

Then:

Debit Abnormal gain account

Credit Statement of profit or loss

with the balance on the abnormal gain account.

EXAMPLE

Scarborough Chemical manufactures a range of industrial and agricultural chemicals. One such product is 'Scarchem 3X' which passes through a single process.

The following information relates to the process for week ended 30 January 20X5.

Input 5,000 litres of material at $12 per litre.

Normal losses are agreed as 4% of input.

Direct labour $710, process overhead $2,130.

Output is 4,820 litres. Waste units have a scrap value of $1 per litre.

Prepare the process account for the period together with other relevant accounts.

SOLUTION

Expected output = 5,000 litres less normal loss of 4% = 5,000 – 200 = 4,800 litres.

Actual output = 4,820 litres.

Abnormal gain = 4,820 – 4,800 = 20 units.

	$
Direct materials	60,000
Direct labour	710
Production overhead	2,130
	62,840
Less: scrap value of normal loss (200 × $1)	(200)
Production costs	62,640

Cost per unit of expected output = $\frac{\$62,640}{4,800 \text{ units}}$ = \$13.05 per unit

Both good output and abnormal gains are valued at this amount.

Process a/c

	Units	$		Units	$
Direct material	5,000	60,000	Output	4,820	62,901
Direct labour		710	Normal loss	200	200
Process overhead		2,130			
Abnormal gain	20	261			
	5,020	63,101		5,020	63,101

		$
Valuation of output	4,820 litres × $13.05	62,901
Valuation of abnormal gain	20 litres × $13.05	261

Abnormal gain a/c

	Units	$		Units	$
Normal loss (scrap value lost)	20	20	Process a/c	20	261
Statement of profit or loss (balance)		241			
	20	261		20	261

Normal loss a/c

	Units	$		Units	$
Process a/c	200	200	Bank	180	180
			Abnormal gain	20	20
		200			200

Finished goods

	Units	$		Units	$
Process a/c	4,820	62,901			

Because actual loss was only 180 litres, not the normal loss (expected loss) of 200 litres, the amount of cash obtained from selling the scrap was $180. This is provided for by the adjustment between the abnormal gain account and the normal loss account.

ACTIVITY 2

Input to Process X in June was 100,000 kilograms of direct materials, costing $1 per kilogram. Conversion costs for the month were $135,000. Normal loss is 6%, and loss has scrap value of $1 per unit. Actual output in June was 96,000 kilograms.

Required:

(a) Calculate the cost per unit of output in the month.

(b) Write up the process account, the normal loss (scrap) account and the abnormal loss or abnormal gain account for the month.

For a suggested answer, see the 'Answers' section at the end of the book.

4 THE NATURE OF JOINT PRODUCTS AND BY-PRODUCTS

A single process might produce a number of different products. For example a chemical process might involve a number of chemical inputs which give two different chemical liquids as output and a gas.

Quite often, different products produced by a single process might be given further separate processing, before they are ready for sale.

EXAMPLE

A company might produce four items from a process, A, B, C and D. A, B and D are liquids, and C is a gas. Product A is then put through a further process to make Product AA and Product B is put through a different process to make Product BB. Product C is sold in its current form without further processing. Product D has very little value, and is also sold without further processing.

Products A, B, C and D are examples of joint products and a by-product from a single process.

Before we look at the difference between joint products and by-products, you need to understand the meaning of 'separation point'.

Definition **Separation point, or split-off point,** in a process manufacturing operation is the point during manufacture where two or more products are produced from a common process. Items produced at the separation point are either sold in their current form or put through further processing before sale.

Up to the separation point, the processing costs are common to all the products that are subsequently produced. A task in process costing is to share the common process costs up to separation point between the different products.

4.1 JOINT PRODUCTS DEFINED

Definition **Joint products** are separate products that emerge from a single process. Each of these products has a **significant sales value** to the organisation.

The key point about joint products is that they are all relatively significant to the organisation in terms of sales value.

4.2 BY-PRODUCTS DEFINED

Definition A **by-product** is a product that is produced from a process, together with other products, that is of **insignificant sales value**.

A by-product is therefore similar to a joint product in that it is one of a number of products output from a process. However whereas joint products are all saleable products with significant sales value, a by-product will usually have such a small selling price or be produced in such small quantities that its overall sales value to the organisation is insignificant.

Conclusion Joint products and by-products are both one of a number of products produced by a process. The distinguishing feature between the two is whether or not they have a significant sales value. If the sales value of the product is significant it will be a joint product, if not it will be a by-product.

Joint products and by-products are treated differently in cost accounting.

5 COSTING WITH JOINT PRODUCTS

Definition **Joint costs** or **common process costs** are the costs incurred in a process that must be split or apportioned amongst the products produced by the process.

When two or more joint products are produced in a common process, a method is needed for sharing the common costs between the different products. For example, if a process costs $100,000 and produces three joint products, X Y and Z, how should the common costs of $100,000 be shared out between the three products?

The answer is that a suitable basis has to be found for apportioning the costs.

5.1 METHODS OF APPORTIONING JOINT COSTS TO JOINT PRODUCTS: PHYSICAL QUANTITY AND SALES VALUE METHODS

There are two main methods of apportioning pre-separation (joint) costs between joint products:

- split the joint costs in proportion to the physical quantity, volume or weight of each product
- split the joint costs in proportion to their relative sales values.

EXAMPLE

A process produces the following joint products.

Product	*Quantity in kg*	*Selling price per kg*
X	100,000	$1
Y	20,000	$10
Z	80,000	$2.25

The costs incurred in the process prior to the separation point of these three products were $240,000.

Required:

Show how the joint costs would be apportioned to each product on the basis of:

(a) physical quantity, and

(b) relative sales value at the point of separation.

SOLUTION

(a) Physical quantity method

	kg
X	100,000
Y	20,000
Z	80,000
	200,000

Cost per kilogram = Total pre-separation costs/Total quantity produced

= $240,000/200,000 kilograms = $1.20 per kg.

Apportionment of joint costs

	kg	$
X	100,000	120,000
Y	20,000	24,000
Z	80,000	96,000
	200,000	240,000

This method may be appropriate in some processes but it can give peculiar results. For example Product X can only be sold for $100,000 (100,000 kg × $1 per kg) and yet under this method $120,000 of costs have been allocated to it.

Apportioning joint costs on the basis of physical quantities produced is also only possible if the joint products can be measured physically in the same way. It is not appropriate, therefore, where joint products are a mixture of solids, liquids and gases.

(b) Relative sales value method

Sales value at the point of separation

	Output	*Sales value per kg*	*Total sales value*
	kg	$	$
X	100,000	1.00	100,000
Y	20,000	10.00	200,000
Z	80,000	2.25	180,000
	200,000		480,000

Cost per $ of sales = Total pre-separation costs/Total sales value

= $240,000/$480,000 = $0.50 of cost per $1 sale value.

Apportionment of joint costs

	Output	*Total sales value*	*Apportionment of cost*
	kg	$	$
X	100,000	100,000	50,000
Y	20,000	200,000	100,000
Z	80,000	180,000	90,000
	200,000	480,000	240,000

This apportionment of costs gives a completely different picture to that based upon the physical quantities of the products produced.

However, because costs are shared on the basis of sales value, it follows that if all the joint products are sold without further processing, the percentage profit margin will be exactly the same for all of the joint products.

Apportioning costs on the basis of sales value overcomes the problem that the joint products might have different physical characteristics. This method can therefore be used to apportion costs between solids, liquids and gases. However, a drawback to this method is that a joint product might not have a sales value at the point of separation, but might need to be processed further before it can be sold.

To overcome this problem, it might be necessary to apportion costs between joint products on the basis of their eventual sales value minus the further processing costs necessary to get them ready for sale. In other words, the costs might have to be apportioned on the basis of their net realisable value.

5.2 METHODS OF APPORTIONING JOINT COSTS TO JOINT PRODUCTS: NET REALISABLE VALUE METHOD

Definition The **net realisable value** of a joint product is its sales value minus its further processing costs after the point of separation.

A question on this calculation appeared in 2018 exams and the majority of students failed to remember to remove the further processing costs from the sales value.

EXAMPLE

Three joint products are produced from a common process:

Product X: 20,000 kilos

Product Y: 5,000 litres

Product Z: 10,000 litres.

The joint costs of processing up to the point of separation are $166,000.

Product Z can be sold immediately after separation for $15 per litre. Product X needs further processing, at a cost of $8 per kilo, before it is sold for $20 per kilo. Product Y also needs further processing, at a cost of $2 per litre, before it is sold for $7 per litre

Required:

(a) Calculate the cost per unit of each joint product up to the point of separation, if common costs are apportioned between the products on the basis of net realisable value.

(b) Calculate the profit or loss per unit of each joint product.

SOLUTION

Both parts of the problem can be dealt with together.

	Product X	*Product Y*	*Product Z*	*Total*
Units	20,000 kg	5,000 litres	10,000 litres	
	$	$	$	$
Final sales value	400,000	35,000	150,000	
Further processing costs	160,000	10,000	0	
Net realisable value	240,000	25,000	150,000	415,000
Pre-separation costs	96,000	10,000	60,000	166,000
Profit	144,000	15,000	90,000	249,000
Profit per unit	$7.20	$3.00	$9.00	

Apportionment basis = Common costs/Net realisable value

= $166,000/$415,000 = $0.40 of cost per $1 net realisable value.

ACTIVITY 3

A process produces two joint products X and Y. During August the process costs attributed to completed output amounted to $122,500. Information relating to X and Y is as follows:

Product	*Output (tonnes)*	*Sales price* $	*Further processing cost* $
X	3,000	150	30
Y	4,000	50	–

Required:

(a) Calculate the cost attributed to each joint product using:

(i) the weight basis of apportionment

(ii) net realisable value basis of apportionment.

(b) For each basis of apportionment calculate the total profit and profit per unit for each product.

For a suggested answer, see the 'Answers' section at the end of the book.

6 COSTING WITH BY-PRODUCTS

The costing treatment of by-products is different from the costing treatment of joint products. Since by-products have very little sales value, it is pointless to try working out a cost and a profit for units of by-product. By-products are incidental output, not main products.

Either of two accounting treatments is used for a by-product.

(a) **Method 1**. Treat the income from the by-product as incidental income, and add it to sales in the statement of profit or loss.

(b) **Method 2**. Instead of adding the income from by-product sales to total sales income in the statement of profit or loss, deduct the sales value of the by-product from the common processing costs. The pre-separation costs for apportioning between joint products is therefore the actual pre-separation costs minus the sales value of the by-product.

7 THE VALUE OF COST DATA AND PROFIT DATA WITH JOINT PRODUCTS

A cost per unit of joint product and a profit per unit can only be calculated by apportioning pre-separation costs between the products. Pre-separation costs can be a very high proportion (as much as 100%) of the total production cost of a joint product.

It is questionable whether the cost and profit information in such cases has much value as management information. For example:

- If a joint product appears to be making a loss, management cannot decide to stop making the product. In order to carry on making the other joint products that are making a 'profit', the 'loss-making' joint product will have to be made as well.

- Apportioning joint costs is arbitrary. The apportionment basis should be 'fair', but entirely different costs and profits can be calculated for joint products, depending on whether the physical quantity or the net realisable value method of apportionment is used.

- Since cost data and profit data are of questionable meaning and value, it can be argued that where joint products are produced management should monitor total costs and total profits for all of the joint products together, instead of trying to analyse costs and profitability for each product separately.

8 EVALUATING THE BENEFIT OF FURTHER PROCESSING

So far, we have looked at how a cost per unit is calculated for joint products, and the point has been made that unit cost information and product profitability information are of doubtful value.

A completely different costing problem arises when management think about what to do with joint products after the point of separation. A joint product might be in a condition to sell at the point of separation, but can also be processed further to sell for a higher price. In such cases, management have to decide whether to sell the product immediately after the point of separation, or whether to process the product further before selling it.

It is assumed that further processing of products after the point of separation is independent i.e. a decision to process one joint product in no way affects the decision to process further the other joint products.

The pre-separation costs of the common processing of the joint products are irrelevant to the further processing decision. The joint costs are not affected by whether individual products are further processed, and are therefore not relevant to the decision under consideration.

To evaluate processing of the individual products it is necessary to identify the **incremental** costs and **incremental** revenues relating to that further processing, i.e. the **additional** costs and revenue brought about directly as a result of that further processing.

EXAMPLE

The following data relates to Products A and B produced from a joint process:

	Quantity produced	*Sales price at split-off point*	*Further processing costs*	*Sales price after further processing*
	kg	$ per kg		$ per kg
Product A	100	5	$280 plus $2.00 per kg	8.40
Product B	200	2	$160 plus $1.40 per kg	4.50

Common costs prior to the split-off point are $750.

Should each product be sold at the split-off point, or processed further before sale?

SOLUTION

Evaluation of further processing

	Product A		*Product B*	
	$	$	$	$
Sales value after further processing		840		900
Sales value at split off point		500		400
Incremental sales revenue from further processing		340		500
Further processing costs				
Fixed (step cost)	280		160	
Variable	200		280	
		480		440
Gain/(loss) from further processing		(140)		60

On the basis of these figures the recommendation would be:

Product A Sell at split-off point for $5.

Product B Sell for $4.50 after further processing.

This would result in overall profits on this **production** volume of:

	$
Common process ($5 × 100) + ($2 × 200) – $750	150
Further processing of B	60
Profit	210

The recommendation to sell A at the split-off point and B after further processing is based on two assumptions.

(a) All relevant 'effects' of the decision have been included, i.e. quantified.

(b) Production volume achieved is A 100 kg, B 200 kg.

Before a final decision is made these assumptions must be considered.

(a) All effects of decision quantified

The course of action recommended could have other effects not included above, e.g.:

- Products A and B in their final state may be in some way 'complementary' i.e. it may only be possible to sell B for $4.50 if A is also available in a further processed state at a price of $8.40.
- The company may currently be carrying out further processing of A. The decision above could therefore result in having to reduce the workforce employed in this processing. The remaining workforce could, for example, go out on strike, causing a loss of production and sales of A and B. These factors should be carefully assessed before a final decision is made.

(b) Production volume

By looking in more detail at the further processing of A it is possible to see that further processing of 1 kg of A results in an incremental contribution of:

	$
Incremental revenue $(8.40 – 5.00)	3.40
Incremental variable cost	2.00
Incremental contribution	1.40

It is therefore possible to identify the level of activity at which further processing of A becomes worthwhile i.e. the 'break-even volume'.

$$\text{Break-even volume} = \frac{\textit{Incremental fixed costs}}{\textit{Incremental contribution per kg}}$$

$$= \frac{\$280}{\$1.40}$$

$$= 200 \text{ kgs}$$

Hence, if the volume of A in the future is greater than 200 kgs, further processing becomes economically worthwhile.

CONCLUSION

Process costing is a form of absorption costing used in processing industries. One key feature of process costing is that any expected losses are not given any cost or value, except for any scrap value they might have, and costs per unit are calculated on the basis of expected output. If actual output differs from expected output, there is abnormal loss or abnormal gain, which are given a cost/value.

The joint product further processing decision has introduced a new aspect of cost and management accounting, namely the use of relevant cost and revenue information to assist management with decision making. Accounting for decision making is based on the use of relevant costing and marginal costing.

KEY TERMS

Costs of conversion – the labour costs of the process plus the overheads of the process.

Normal loss – expected amounts of loss in a production process. It is the level of loss or waste that management would expect to incur under normal operating conditions.

Abnormal loss – the amount by which actual loss exceeds the expected or normal loss in a process. It can also be defined as the amount by which actual production is less than normal production. Normal production is calculated as the quantity of input units of materials less normal loss.

Abnormal gain – the amount by which actual output from a process exceeds the expected output. It is the amount by which actual loss is lower than expected loss.

Split-off or separation point – before this point, joint products cannot be distinguished. Costs at this point are therefore common and must be apportioned on some basis.

Joint product – a separate product produced from a joint process which has a significant sales value.

By-product – a separate product that is produced incidentally from a joint process and which has an insignificant sales value.

Joint costs – are the costs incurred in a process that must be split or apportioned amongst the products produced by the process. Joint costs are also known as common process costs.

Net realisable value – sales value less any further processing costs.

SELF TEST QUESTIONS

		Paragraph
1	Name four industries where process costing would be used.	1.1
2	Define the term normal loss.	2, 2.1
3	Define the term abnormal loss.	2, 2.2
4	What is the accounting entry for the scrap value of abnormal loss?	2.2
5	Define the term abnormal gain.	3
6	What is the difference between a joint product and a by-product?	4.1, 4.2
7	Name three methods of apportioning pre-separation process costs between joint products.	5.1, 5.2
8	With which of these three methods is the percentage gross profit margin per unit the same for all of the joint products?	5.1
9	What are the two methods normally used to account for by-products?	6

EXAM-STYLE QUESTIONS

Questions 1 and 2 are based on the following data:

Joint products	*Output (kg)*	*Selling price per kg*
X	5,000	$10
Y	10,000	$4
Z	10,000	$3

Joint costs of the process are $100,000.

1 If the joint costs of the process are apportioned to each product on the basis of physical quantity, the profit per unit of Product X is:

A $4

B $6

C $8

D $10

2 If the joint costs of the process are apportioned to each product on the basis of sales value, the total profit of Product Y is:

A $20,000

B $16,667

C $6,667

D $2,000

3 Which of the following statements is correct?

A When joint costs are apportioned on the basis of physical quantity the percentage profit margin is the same for all joint products.

B There will be a higher total profit if joint costs are apportioned on the basis of sales value rather than on the basis of physical quantity.

C By-products are separate products produced from a joint process which have a significant sales value.

D The normal accounting treatment for by-products is to deduct the sales value from common costs.

4 Which one of the following statements is *incorrect*?

A Job costs are collected separately, whereas process costs are averages.

B In job costing the progress of a job can be ascertained from the materials requisition notes and job tickets or time sheets.

C In process costing information is needed about work passing through a process and work remaining in each process.

D In process costing, but not job costing, the cost of normal loss will be incorporated into normal product costs.

5 In a process account, abnormal losses are valued:

A at their scrap value

B at the same cost per unit as good production

C at the cost of raw materials

D at good production cost less scrap value.

6 A chemical process has a normal wastage of 10% of input. In a period, 2,500 kgs of material were input and there was an abnormal loss of 75 kgs.

What quantity of good production was achieved?

A 2,175 kgs

B 2,250 kgs

C 2,325 kgs

D 2,475 kgs

The following information is relevant to Questions 7 and 8.

Mineral Separators Ltd operates a process which produces four unrefined minerals known as W, X, Y and Z. The joint costs for operating the process and output for Period 5 were as below. Process overhead is absorbed by adding 25% of the labour cost.

Joint costs for period 5

	$
Raw material	75,000
Labour	24,000

Inventory levels shown below were on hand at the end of the period, although there was no work-in-progress at that date. The price received per tonne of unrefined mineral sold is shown below and it is confidently expected that these prices will be maintained.

Inventory at the end of period 5

	Tonnes
W	30
X	20
Y	80
Z	5

Output for Period 5

	Tonnes
W	700
X	600
Y	400
Z	100

Price per tonne

	$
W	40
X	90
Y	120
Z	200

7 If joint costs are allocated to products on the basis of sales value, how much would be charged to product X?

A $14,000

B $19,600

C $33,600

D $37,800

8 If weight of output is used as the basis of inventory valuation, the cost value of the closing inventory for product Y would be:

A $292

B $1,167

C $1,750

D $4,667

9 A company processes slurge through two consecutive processes. During Period 12, there was no opening or closing work-in-progress in either process.

Other data for Period 12 were as follows:

Input to Process 1: 2,000 kilograms, material cost $5,000

Normal loss in Process 1: 5% of input

Output to Process 2: 1,850 kilograms

Labour and overhead costs (conversion costs) in Process 1: $4,500.

Added materials in Process 2, cost $1,567

Normal loss in Process 2: 2% of input from Process 1

Output of finished slurge: 1,840 kilograms

Labour and overhead costs (conversion costs) in Process 2: $5,500.

What is the value of output from Process 1:

A $9,000

B $9,750

C $9,250

D $9,500

For the answers to these questions, see the 'Answers' section at the end of the book.

Chapter 12

SERVICE COSTING

In the previous chapters on costing methods, the methods described have been relevant to manufacturing operations. Cost accounting had its origins in manufacturing, but nowadays, many businesses provide services rather than manufacture goods. The principles of costing, both absorption and marginal costing, can be applied to service costing. This chapter looks at the characteristics of service costing. This chapter covers syllabus area C5.

CONTENTS

LEARNING OUTCOMES

At the end of this chapter you should be able to:

- describe the characteristics of service costing
- describe the practical problems relating to the costing of services
- identify situations (cost centres and industries) where the use of service costing is appropriate
- illustrate suitable cost units that may be used for a variety of services
- calculate service unit costs in a variety of situations.

1 WHEN TO USE SERVICE COSTING

Service costing is used when there is no physical product, to obtain a cost for each unit of service provided. Note that inventories of services cannot be held.

When the service can be measured in standard units, costs can be charged to activities and averaged over the units to obtain a cost per cost unit of service. Costing services in this way is appropriate when the service can be expressed in a standardised unit of measurement. For example, an accountant in practice would provide an individual service to each client, but the service could be measured in man-hour units.

Services can be:

- External services to a customer, for which a price is charged. Examples are the provision of telephone and electricity services, consultancy, auditing services by a firm of accountants, hotel services, travel services and so on.

- Internal services within an organisation can be any activity performed by one department for another, such as machine repairs, services of an IT department, payroll activities and so on.

2 SERVICE COSTS AND COST UNITS

2.1 IDENTIFICATION OF COST UNITS

A major problem in service industries is the selection of a suitable unit for measuring the service, i.e. in deciding what service is actually being provided and what measures of performance are most appropriate to the control of costs. Some cost units used in different activities are given below.

Service	*Cost unit*
Electricity generation	Kilowatt hours
Canteens and restaurants	Meals served
Carriers	Miles travelled: ton-miles carried
Hospitals	Patient-days
Passenger transport	Passenger-miles: seat-miles
Accountancy	Accountant-hour (man hour)

Where cost units are in two or more parts such as patient-days or passenger miles these are known as composite cost units.

A service undertaking may use several different units to measure the various kinds of service provided, e.g. a hotel with a restaurant and function rooms might use a different cost unit for each different service:

Service	*Cost unit*
Restaurant	Meals served
Hotel services	Guest-days
Function facilities	Hours rented

When appropriate cost units have been determined for a particular service, provision will need to be made for the collection of the appropriate statistical data. In a transport organisation this may involve the recording of mileages day-by-day for each vehicle in the fleet. For this each driver would be required to complete a log sheet. Information relating to fuel usage per vehicle and loads or weight carried may also be recorded on the log sheet.

2.2 COLLECTION, CLASSIFICATION AND ASCERTAINMENT OF COSTS

Costs will be classified under appropriate headings for the particular service. This will involve the issue of suitable cost codes to be used in the recording and, therefore, the collection of costs.

EXAMPLE

For a transport undertaking the main cost classification may be based on the following activities:

- operating and running the fleet
- repairs and maintenance
- fixed charges
- administration.

Within each of these there would need to be a sub-classification of costs, each with its own code, so that under 'fixed charges', there might appear the following breakdown:

- road fund licences
- insurances
- depreciation
- vehicle testing fees
- others.

In service costing it is often important to classify costs into their fixed and variable elements. Many service applications involve high fixed costs and the higher the number of cost units produced the lower the fixed costs per unit. The variable cost per unit will indicate to management the additional cost involved in the provision of one extra unit of service. In the context of a transport undertaking, fixed and variable costs are often referred to as standing and running costs respectively.

2.3 COST SHEETS

Definition **A cost sheet** is a record of costs for each service provided.

At appropriate intervals (usually weekly or monthly) cost sheets will be prepared by the costing department to provide information about the appropriate service to management. A typical cost sheet for a service would incorporate the following for the current period and the cumulative year to date:

(a) cost information over the appropriate expense or activity headings

(b) cost units statistics

(c) cost per unit calculations using the data in (a) and dividing by the data in (b). Different cost units may be used for different elements of costs and the same cost or group of costs may be related to different cost unit bases to provide additional control information to management. In the transport organisation, for example, the operating and running costs may be expressed in per mile, per vehicle and per day terms

(d) analyses based on the actual cost units.

In service industries, as in industries with physical output, management accountants can provide useful information by calculating the cost required to produce a cost unit.

3 COST ANALYSIS IN SERVICE INDUSTRIES

Cost reports are derived from the cost sheets and other data collected. Usually costs are presented as totals for the period, classified often into fixed and variable costs.

It is impossible to illustrate costing for every type of service, because each service has its own different characteristics and different cost units. The following examples are provided as illustration. You might wish to try calculating a cost per unit of service for each example before you read our solution.

3.1 ILLUSTRATION: POWER SUPPLY INDUSTRY

The following figures relate to two electricity supply companies.

Meter reading, billing and collection costs

	Company A	*Company B*
	$000	$000
Salaries and wages of:		
Meter readers	150	240
Billing and collection staff	300	480
Transport and travelling	30	40
Collection agency charges	–	20
Bad debts	10	10
General charges	100	200
Miscellaneous	10	10
	600	1,000
Units sold (millions)	2,880	9,600
Number of consumers (thousands)	800	1,600
Sales of electricity (millions)	$18	$50
Size of area (square miles)	4,000	4,000

Prepare a comparative cost statement using suitable units of cost. Brief notes should be added, commenting on likely causes for major differences in unit costs so disclosed.

SOLUTION

Electricity Boards A and B Comparative costs – year ending ...

	Company A		*Company B*	
	$000	*% of total*	$000	*% of total*
Salaries and wages:				
Meter reading	150	25.0	240	24.0
Billing and collection	300	50.0	480	48.0
Transport/travelling	30	5.0	40	4.0
Collection agency	–	–	20	2.0
Bad debts	10	1.7	10	1.0
General charges	100	16.6	200	20.0
Miscellaneous	10	1.7	10	1.0
	600	100.0	1,000	100.0

	$	$
Cost per:		
Millions units sold	208	104
Thousand consumers	750	625
$m of sales	33,333	20,000
Square mile area	150	250

Possible reasons for unit cost differences are given below.

- **Area density.** B covers the same size of area but has double the number of consumers, indicating that B is a more urban territory.
- **Industrialisation.** Costs per unit are almost twice as high for A but the pattern is not continued for costs in relation to sales value. B, therefore, probably contains a higher proportion of industrial consumers at cheaper rates.
- **Territory covered.** Comparative costs per square mile deviate from the pattern shown by the other measurement units, confirming that the bulk of costs is incurred in relation to consumers and usage.

3.2 ILLUSTRATION: TRANSPORT OPERATIONS

Remix plc makes ready-mixed cement and operates a small fleet of vehicles which delivers the product to customers within its delivery area.

General data

Maintenance records for the previous five years reveal the following data:

Year	*Mileage of vehicles*	*Maintenance cost*
		$
1	170,000	13,500
2	180,000	14,000
3	165,000	13,250
4	160,000	13,000
5	175,000	13,750

Transport statistics reveal the following data:

Vehicle	*Number of journeys each day*	*Average tonnage carried to customers (tonnes)*	*Average distance to customers (miles)*
1	6	4	10
2	4	4	20
3	2	5	40
4	2	6	30
5	1	6	60

There are five vehicles operating a five-day week, for 50 weeks a year.

Drivers and supervisors are paid for 52 weeks a year.

Inflation can be ignored.

Standard cost data include the following:

Drivers' wages	$550 each per week
Supervisors' wages	$800 per week
Depreciation is on a straight-line basis with no residual value	
Loading equipment	Cost $100,000. Life 5 years
Vehicles	Cost $30,000 each. Life 5 years
Petrol/oil costs	$0.20 per mile
Repairs cost	$0.075 per mile
Vehicle licences cost	$400 pa for each vehicle
Insurance costs	$600 pa for each vehicle
Tyres cost	$4,000 pa in total
Miscellaneous costs	$2,750 pa in total

You are required to calculate a standard rate per tonne/mile of operating the vehicles.

SOLUTION

Calculation of standard rate per tonne/mile.

	$	$
Running costs:		
Maintenance costs (W1)	0.050	
Petrol/oil	0.200	
Repairs cost	0.075	
	0.325	

Total per annum: $0.325 × 170,000 (W2)		55,250
Sundry costs:		
Maintenance costs (W1)	5,000	
Drivers' wages: $550 × 52 × 5	143,000	
Supervisors' wages: $800 × 52	41,600	
Depreciation of loading equipment: $100,000 ÷ 5	20,000	
Depreciation of vehicles: $30,000 × 5 ÷ 5	30,000	
Vehicle licences: $400 × 5	2,000	
Insurance: $600 × 5	3,000	
Tyres	4,000	
Miscellaneous costs	2,750	
		251,350
		306,600

Standard rate per tonne/mile = $\frac{\$306,600}{420,000(W3)}$ = $0.73 per tonne/mile.

Workings

(W1) Maintenance cost, separation of fixed and variable elements using high-low method

	Mileage	*Maintenance* $
High	180,000	14,000
Low	160,000	13,000
Variable cost	20,000	1,000

Variable/running cost per mile	=	$\frac{\$1,000}{20,000}$
	=	$0.05 per mile
Total cost	=	Total fixed cost + Variable cost per mile × Number of miles
$14,000	=	Total fixed cost + ($0.05 × 180,000)
Total fixed cost	=	$(14,000 – 9,000) = $5,000

(W2) Distance travelled

Vehicle		
1	6 × 10 × 2	= 120
2	4 × 20 × 2	= 160
3	2 × 40 × 2	= 160
4	2 × 30 × 2	= 120
5	1 × 60 × 2	= 120
		680

Total distance travelled = 680 miles × 5 days × 50 weeks = 170,000 miles per annum

(W3) Number of tonne/miles

Vehicle		
1	6 × 4 × 10	= 240
2	4 × 4 × 20	= 320
3	2 × 5 × 40	= 400
4	2 × 6 × 30	= 360
5	1 × 6 × 60	= 360
		1,680

Total tonne/miles = 1,680 tonne/miles × 5 days × 50 weeks = 420,000 tonne/miles per annum

4 SERVICE COSTING FOR INTERNAL SERVICES

Internal services may be set up as profit centres rather than cost centres to encourage managers to be efficient and to enable comparison with external suppliers. For example the IT, legal services and building repairs departments could all be operated as profit centres charging internal departments for their services and calculating the notional profit made on their activities.

Costs of internal services can be determined in the same way as for service organisations and may be used to measure the efficiency of departments or compare their costs against costs estimates provided by subcontractors.

CONCLUSION

In this chapter costing principles have been applied to service organisations. You should now be able to explain how and when service costing should be used, and be able to prepare cost statements from cost and related data.

KEY TERMS

Service costing – used when there is no physical product.

Cost sheet – a record of costs for each service provided.

Composite cost units – when cost units are in two or more parts, such as patient-days.

SELF TEST QUESTIONS

		Paragraph
1	Give some examples of cost units appropriate to service industries.	2.1
2	What is the function of a cost sheet?	2.3

EXAM-STYLE QUESTIONS

1 Which of the following is NOT likely to be used by a charitable healthcare provider which provides after-treatment care for cancer patients?

A Cost per patient

B Cost per bed-day

C Bed throughput

D Profit per patient

2 Which of the following statements is untrue?

A Internal services should never use service costing

B Using service costing on internal services can help assess the efficiency of the service

C Service costing is not limited in use to service industries

D External services to customers can be costed using service costing

3 A key performance used in a hotel is average cost per occupied bed. This is calculated as total cost divided by number of beds occupied in the period.

In the month of July the following information was collected by the hotel:

Number of guests in period	6,450
Average length of stay	2 days
Payroll costs for period	$100,000
Items laundered in period	15,000
Cost of cleaning supplies in period	$5,000
Total cost of laundering	$22,500

What was the average cost per occupied bed?

$______. *(Fill in the correct cost per bed to two decimal places)*

4 A hotel uses the following performance measures for the service that it provides to guest. Each measure uses one of the following calculations to determine performance:

Performance measure	Room occupancy	Bed occupancy	Average guest rate
Total revenue divided by number of guests			
Total number of beds occupied as a percentage of beds available.			
Total number of rooms occupied as a percentage of rooms available to let.			

Match each performance measure to the correct calculation (place a tick in the correct box).

5 An organisation has two maintenance service departments – one in the north of the country and one in the south. The departments offer a free repair service for faulty products sold to customers and cost are not recharged internally within the organisation. Repairs are carried out at the customer's home.

In assessing the efficiency of each department, choose from the following list three service cost measures that are likely to be useful to the organisation:

- Cost per item repaired
- Cost per employee
- Profit per item repaired
- Sales per employee
- Cost per square area covered
- Purchase cost of the item repaired

For the answers to these questions, see the 'Answers' section at the end of the book.

Chapter 13

CVP ANALYSIS

In most of the text so far, a variety of costing methods have been described for calculating a cost per unit, from which it is then possible to establish the total costs and the profitability of cost units, such as individual products, jobs or services.

Measuring costs and profits is just one aspect of cost and management accounting. A completely different aspect is the provision of cost information to assist management with decision making.

Accounting for decision making is based on the concept of relevant costs. A starting point for understanding and applying relevant costs is marginal costing. Marginal costing can be used to identify how total costs change as the volume of activity (sales) changes. It can therefore be used to provide management information about costs and profits at different volumes of activity. This is commonly known as cost-volume profit analysis (CVP analysis) or break-even analysis. This chapter covers syllabus area D1.

CONTENTS

LEARNING OUTCOMES

At the end of this chapter you should be able to:

- calculate contribution per unit and the contribution/sales ratio
- explain the concept of break-even and margin of safety
- use contribution per unit and contribution/sales ratio to calculate break-even point and margin of safety
- analyse the effect on break-even point and margin of safety of changes in selling price and costs
- use contribution per unit and contribution/sales ratio to calculate the sales required to achieve a target profit
- interpret break-even and profit/volume charts for a single product or business.

1 COSTS, VOLUMES AND PROFITS

Cost-volume-profit (CVP) analysis is a technique for analysing how costs and profits change with the volume of production and sales. It is also called break-even analysis.

CVP analysis assumes that selling prices and variable costs are constant per unit at all volumes of sales, and that fixed costs remain fixed at all levels of activity.

1.1 UNIT COSTS AND VOLUME

As a business produces and sells more output during a period, its profits will increase. This is partly because sales revenue rises as sales volume goes up. It is also partly because unit costs fall. As the volume of production and sales go up, the fixed cost per unit falls since the same amount of fixed costs are shared between a larger number of units.

EXAMPLE

A business makes and sells a single product. Its variable cost is \$6 and it sells for \$11 per unit. Fixed costs are \$40,000 each month.

We can measure the unit cost and the unit profit at different volumes of output and sales. The table below shows total costs, revenue and profit, and unit costs, revenue and profit, at several levels of sales.

TOTAL
COSTS, REVENUE AND PROFIT

	10,000 units	*15,000 units*	*20,000 units*
	\$	\$	\$
Variable costs	60,000	90,000	120,000
Fixed costs	40,000	40,000	40,000
Total costs	100,000	130,000	160,000
Sales revenue	110,000	165,000	220,000
Profit	10,000	35,000	60,000

UNIT
COSTS, REVENUE AND PROFIT

	10,000 units	*15,000 units*	*20,000 units*
	\$ per unit	\$ per unit	\$ per unit
Variable costs	6.0	6.00	6.0
Fixed costs	4.0	2.67	2.0
Total costs	10.0	8.67	8.0
Sales revenue	11.0	11.00	11.0
Profit	1.0	2.33	3.0

As the sales volume goes up, the cost per unit falls and the profit per unit rises. This is because the fixed cost per unit falls as volume increases, in contrast to unit variable costs and the selling price per unit which are constant at all volumes of sales.

To analyse how profits and costs will change as the volume of sales changes, we can adopt a marginal costing approach. This is to calculate the total contribution at each volume of sales, then deduct fixed costs to obtain the profit figure.

CALCULATION OF PROFIT USING A MARGINAL COSTING APPROACH

	10,000 units		*15,000 units*		*20,000 units*	
	$	$ per unit	$	$ per unit	$	$ per unit
Sales revenue	110,000	11.0	165,000	11.0	220,000	11.0
Variable costs	60,000	6.0	90,000	6.0	120,000	6.0
Contribution	50,000	5.0	75,000	5.0	100,000	5.0
Fixed costs	40,000		40,000		40,000	
Profit	10,000		35,000		60,000	

1.2 THE IMPORTANCE OF CONTRIBUTION IN CVP ANALYSIS

Contribution is a key concept in CVP analysis, because if we assume a constant variable cost per unit and the same selling price at all volumes of output, the contribution per unit is a constant value (and the contribution per $1 of sales is also a constant value).

Definition **Unit contribution** = Selling price per unit – variable costs per unit.

Definition **Total contribution**

= Volume of sales in units × (unit contribution); or

= Total sales revenue – total variable cost; or

= Total sales revenue × contribution/sales ratio

Definition **Contribution/Sales ratio or C/S ratio**

= Contribution per unit/Sales price per unit; or

= Total contribution/Total sales revenue

2 USES OF CVP ANALYSIS

CVP analysis is used widely in preparing financial reports for management. It is a simple technique that can be used to estimate profits and make decisions about the best course of action to take. Applications of CVP analysis include:

- estimating future profits
- calculating the break-even point for sales
- analysing the margin of safety in the budget
- calculating the volume of sales required to achieve a target profit
- deciding on a selling price for a product.

2.1 ESTIMATING FUTURE PROFITS

CVP analysis can be used to estimate future profits.

EXAMPLE

ZC Limited makes and sells a single product. Its budgeted sales for the next year are 40,000 units.

The product sells for $18.

Variable costs of production and sales are:

	$
Direct materials	2.40
Direct labour	5.00
Variable production overhead	0.50
Variable selling overhead	1.25

Fixed expenses are estimated for the year as:

	$
Fixed production overhead	80,000
Administration costs	60,000
Fixed selling costs	90,000
	230,000

Calculate the expected profit for the year.

SOLUTION

Variable cost per unit = $(2.40 + 5.00 + 0.50 + 1.25) = $9.15

Unit contribution = Sales price – Unit variable cost = $18 – $9.15 = $8.85.

	$
Budgeted contribution (40,000 units × $8.85)	354,000
Budgeted fixed costs	230,000
Expected profit	124,000

2.2 BREAK-EVEN ANALYSIS

Break-even is the volume of sales at which the business just 'breaks even', so that it makes neither a loss nor a profit. At break-even point, total costs equal total revenue. Calculating the break-even point can be useful for management because it shows the minimum volume of sales which must be achieved to avoid making a loss in the period.

At break-even point, total contribution is just large enough to cover fixed costs. In other words, at break-even point:

Total contribution = Fixed costs

The break-even point in units of sale can therefore be calculated as:

$$\text{Break-even point in units of sale} = \frac{\text{Fixed costs}}{\text{Contribution per unit}}$$

EXAMPLE

A business makes and sells a single product, which sells for $15 per unit and which has a unit variable cost of $7. Fixed costs are expected to be $500,000 for the next year.

Required:

(a) What is the break-even point in units?

(b) What is the break-even point in sales revenue?

(c) What would be the break-even point if fixed costs went up to $540,000?

(d) What would be the break-even point if fixed costs were $500,000 but unit variable costs went up to $9?

SOLUTION

(a) Unit contribution = $15 – $7 = $8. Fixed costs = $500,000

$$\text{Break-even point} = \frac{\$500{,}000}{\$8 \text{ per unit}} = 62{,}500 \text{ units}$$

(b) 62,500 units at $15 each results in a break-even sales revenue of $937,500. This figure can also be calculated by using another formula:

$$\text{Break-even point in \$ of sale} = \frac{\text{Fixed costs}}{\text{C/S ratio}}$$

In this example the C/S ratio is $8/$15 = 0.5333

The break-even point is therefore $500,000/0.53333 = $937,500

(c) Unit contribution = $8. Fixed costs = $540,000

$$\text{Break-even point} = \frac{\$540{,}000}{\$8 \text{ per unit}} = 67{,}500 \text{ units}$$

(d) Unit contribution = $15 – $9 = $6. Fixed costs = $500,000

$$\text{Break-even point} = \frac{\$500{,}000}{\$6 \text{ per unit}} = 88{,}333 \text{ units}$$

ACTIVITY 1

Fylindales Fabrication produce hinges. The selling price per unit is \$30, raw materials and other direct costs are \$10 per unit and period fixed costs are \$5,000.

Calculate how many hinges must be sold to break-even in a budget period. What is the value of sales revenue at the break-even point?

For a suggested answer, see the 'Answers' section at the end of the book.

2.3 MARGIN OF SAFETY

Actual sales volume may not be the same as budgeted sales volume. Actual sales may fall short of budget or exceed budget. A useful analysis of business risk is to look at what might happen to profit if actual sales volume is less than budgeted.

The difference between the budgeted sales volume and the break-even sales volume is known as the **margin of safety**. It is simply a measurement of how far sales can fall short of budget before the business makes a loss. A large margin of safety indicates a low risk of making a loss, whereas a small margin of safety might indicate a fairly high risk of making a loss. It therefore indicates the vulnerability of a business to a fall in demand.

It is usually expressed as a percentage of budgeted sales.

EXAMPLE

Budgeted sales:	80,000 units
Selling price:	\$8
Variable costs:	\$4 per unit
Fixed costs:	\$200,000 pa

$$\text{Break-even volume} = \frac{200,000}{8-4}$$

$$= 50,000 \text{ units}$$

$$\text{Margin of safety} = (80,000 - 50,000) \text{ units}$$

$$= 30,000 \text{ units or } 37\tfrac{1}{2}\% \text{ of budget}$$

The margin of safety may also be expressed as a percentage of actual sales or of maximum capacity.

In this example, the margin of safety seems quite large, because actual sales would have to be almost 40% less than budget before the business made a loss.

ACTIVITY 2

Your company makes and sells a single product, which has a selling price of $24 per unit. The unit variable cost of sales is $18. Budgeted sales for the year are 140,000 units. Budgeted fixed costs for the year are $800,000.

Required:

(a) Calculate the break-even point in units and $.

(b) Calculate the margin of safety, as a percentage of budgeted sales.

For a suggested answer, see the 'Answers' section at the end of the book.

2.4 TARGET PROFIT

CVP analysis can also be used to calculate the volume of sales that would be required to achieve a target level of profit. To achieve a target profit, the business will have to earn enough contribution to cover all of its fixed costs and then make the required amount of profit.

Target contribution = Fixed costs + Target profit

EXAMPLE

Northcliffe Engineering Ltd has capital employed of $1 million. Its target return on capital employed is 20% per annum.

Northcliffe manufactures a standard product 'N1'.

Selling price of 'N1' = $60 unit

Variable costs per unit = $20

Annual fixed costs = $100,000

What volume of sales is required to achieve the target profit?

SOLUTION

The target profit is 20% of $1 million = $200,000.

	$
Target profit	200,000
Fixed costs	100,000
Target contribution	300,000

Target sales volume

$$= \frac{\text{Target contribution}}{\text{Contribution per unit}}$$

$$= \frac{\$300{,}000}{\$40}$$

= 7,500 units

$$\text{Target sales revenue} = \frac{\text{Target contribution}}{\text{C/S ratio}}$$

C/S ratio = $40 /$60 = 0.666667

Target sales revenue = $300,000/0.666667 = $450,000

Proof:

Sales volume	7,500 units
	$
Sales	450,000
Less: Variable costs	150,000
Contribution	300,000
Fixed costs	100,000
Profit	200,000

ACTIVITY 3

Druid Limited makes and sells a single product, Product W, which has a variable production cost of $10 per unit and a variable selling cost of $4. It sells for $25. Annual fixed production costs are $350,000, annual administration costs are $110,000 and annual fixed selling costs are $240,000.

Calculate the volume of sales required to achieve an annual profit of $400,000.

For a suggested answer, see the 'Answers' section at the end of the book.

2.5 DECIDING ON A SELLING PRICE

CVP analysis can be useful in helping management to compare different courses of action and select the option that will earn the biggest profit. For example, management might be considering two or more different selling prices for a product, and want to select the profit-maximising price.

The profit-maximising price is the contribution-maximising price.

EXAMPLE

A company has developed a new product which has a variable cost of $12. Fixed costs relating to this product are $48,000 each month. Management is trying to decide what the selling price for the product should be. A market research report has suggested that monthly sales demand for the product will depend on the selling price chosen, as follows:

Sales price	$16	$17	$18
Expected monthly sales demand	17,000 units	14,500 units	11,500 units

Identify the selling price at which the expected profit will be maximised.

SOLUTION

	$	$	$
Sales price	16	17	18
Variable cost	12	12	12
Unit contribution	4	5	6
Expected monthly sales demand	17,000	14,500	11,500
	$	$	$
Monthly contribution	68,000	72,500	69,000
Monthly fixed costs	48,000	48,000	48,000
Monthly profit	20,000	24,500	21,000

The profit-maximising selling price is the contribution-maximising selling price i.e. $17.

ACTIVITY 4

Your company is about to launch a new product, ZG, which has a unit variable cost of $8. Management is trying to decide whether to sell the product at $11 per unit or at $12 per unit. At a price of $11, annual sales demand is expected to be 200,000 units. At a price of $12, annual sales demand is expected to be 160,000 units.

Annual fixed costs relating to the product will be $550,000.

Which of the two prices will maximise expected profit?

For a suggested solution, see the 'Answers' section at the end of the book.

3 BREAK-EVEN CHARTS

3.1 THE CONVENTIONAL BREAK-EVEN CHART

CVP analysis can be presented in the form of a diagram or graph, as well as in figures. A graphical presentation of CVP analysis can be made in either:

- a conventional break-even chart; or
- a profit/volume chart.

The conventional break-even chart plots total costs and total revenues at different output levels:

1 The y axis represents costs and revenue.

2 The x axis represents the volume of sales in units or $ of sale.

3 A line is drawn on the graph for sales revenue. This is $0 when sales volume is zero. It rises in a straight line. To draw the revenue line, you therefore need to plot one more point on the graph and join this to the origin of the graph (x = 0, y = 0). For example, if a product has a sales price of $5, you might plot the point x = 100 units, y = $500 on the graph and join this to the origin.

4 A line is drawn for fixed costs. This runs parallel to the x axis and cuts the y axis at the amount of fixed costs.

5 A line is then drawn for total costs. To do this, we must add variable costs to fixed costs. When sales volume is zero, variable costs are $0, so total costs = fixed costs. To draw the total cost line, you therefore need to plot one more point on the graph and join this to the fixed costs at zero sales volume (x = 0, y = fixed costs). For example, if a product has a variable cost of $2, and fixed costs are $250 you might plot the point x = 100 units, y = $450 on the graph (variable costs of $200 plus fixed costs of $250) and join this to the fixed costs at zero sales volume (x = 0, y = fixed costs).

You should learn how to draw a conventional break-even chart. Look at the chart below and see whether you could draw one yourself. You might like to use hypothetical figures. For example, suppose fixed costs were $40,000, the unit selling price is $10 and the unit variable cost is $6: can you draw a break-even chart from this data?

Conventional break-even chart

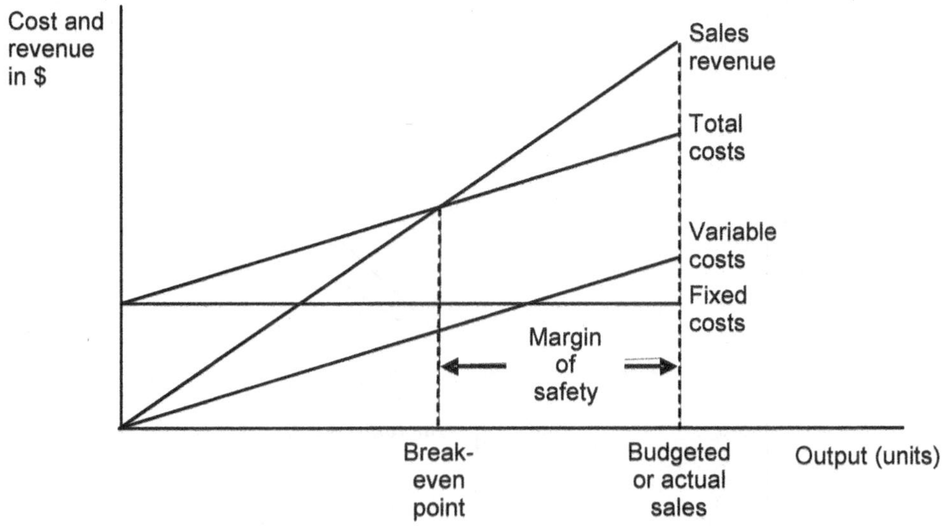

The chart is normally drawn up to the budgeted sales volume.

Break-even point is where total revenues and total costs are the same. At sales volumes below this point there will be a loss. At sales volumes above the break-even point there will be a profit. The amount of profit or loss at any given output can be read off the chart, as the difference between the total revenue and total cost lines.

The margin of safety can also be shown on the chart, as the difference between the budgeted sales volume and break-even sales volume.

EXAMPLE

A company has prepared the following budget.

	$
Total sales	35,400
Variable costs	23,000
Contribution	12400
Fixed costs	5,000
Profit	7,400

Construct a break-even chart from this data and identify the break-even point and margin of safety on the chart.

SOLUTION

1 As we are not given sales in units, the x axis should represent sales revenue in $.

2 To draw the revenue line, join the points x = 0, y = 0 to x = 35,400, y = 35,400.

3 To show fixed costs, draw a line parallel to the x axis at y = $5,000.

4 To show total costs, join the points x = 0, y = 5,000 to x = 35,400, y = 28,000 (variable costs of 23,000 plus fixed costs of 5,000).

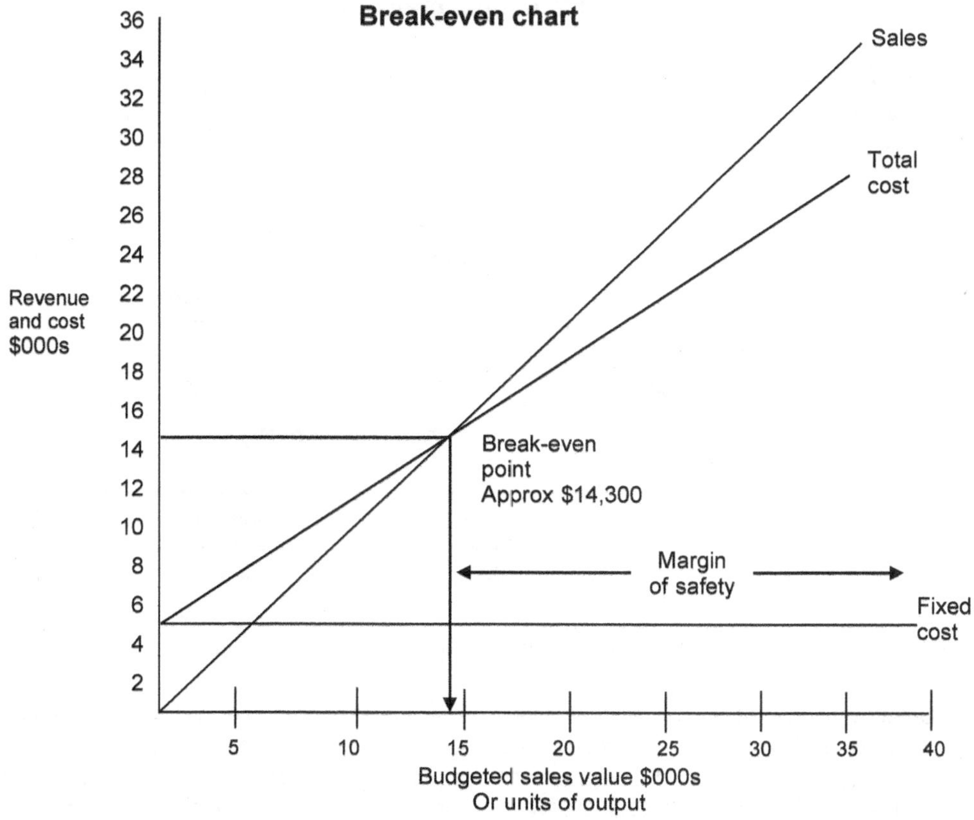

The break-even point is at a level of sales of about $14,300.

The margin of safety is:

$$\frac{(35,400-14,300)}{35,400} \times 100\% = 59.6\%$$

3.2 PROFIT/VOLUME CHART

Break-even charts usually show both costs and revenues over a given range of activity but it is not easy to identify exactly what the loss or profit is at each volume of sales. A graph that simply shows the net profit and loss at any given level of activity is called a **profit/volume chart**.

Given the assumptions of constant selling prices and variable unit costs at all volumes of output, the profit/volume chart shows profit or loss as a straight line.

Profit volume graph

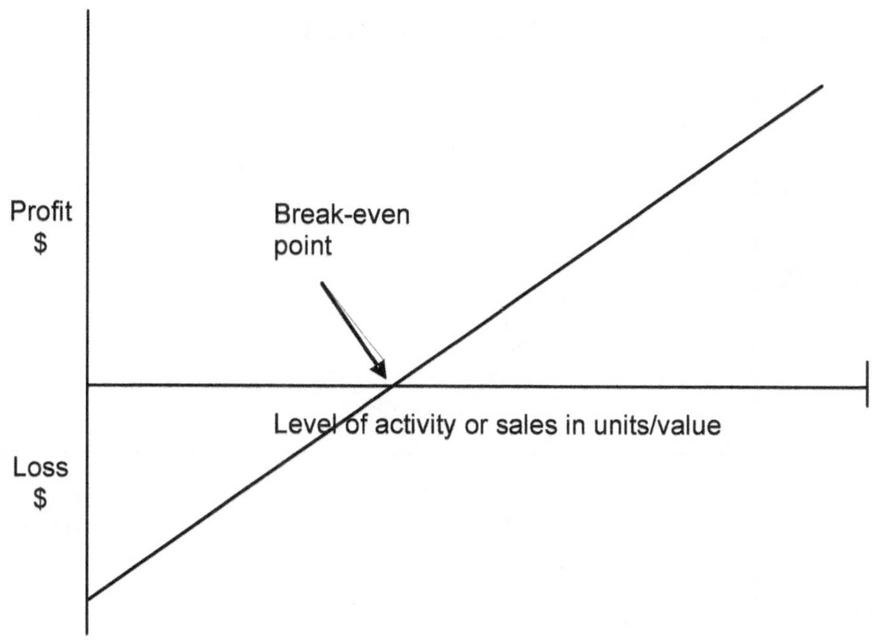

The x axis represents sales volume, in units or $.

The y axis represents loss or profit. The x axis cuts the y axis at break-even point (profit = 0). Losses are plotted below the line and profits above the line.

To draw the chart, only two points need to be plotted on the graph. These can be:

- profit at planned or budgeted sales volume; and
- loss at zero sales volume, which is equal to total fixed costs.

EXAMPLE

Shireoaks Feeds Ltd manufacture a single product 'Shirefeed', an animal food stuff.

The budget for the quarter ended 31 March 20X5 showed:

Production and sales in tonnes	10,000 tonnes
Selling price per tonne	$75
Variable costs per tonne	$40
Fixed costs for the period	$150,000

The break-even point in units for the quarter is:

$$\frac{\text{Fixed costs}}{\text{Contribution per unit}}$$

$$= \frac{\$150{,}000}{\$75 - \$40}$$

= 4,286 tonnes

Margin of safety is 57.14% (10,000 – 4,286/10,000)

This information can be plotted on a profit/volume chart, as follows.

Profit/volume chart

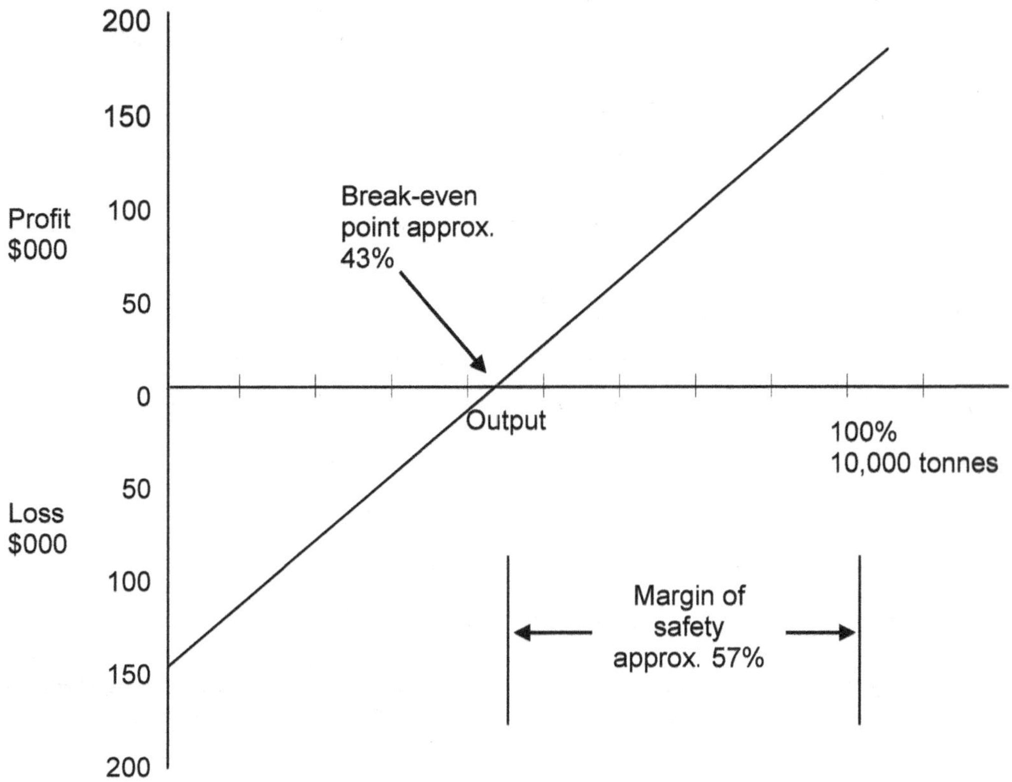

Shireoaks Feeds Ltd

Operating statement for quarter ended 31 March

Units	10,000
	$
Sales	750,000
Less variable costs	400,000
Contribution	350,000
Fixed costs	150,000
Profit	$200,000

From the above chart the amount of net profit or loss can be read off for any given level of sales activity.

The points to note in the construction of a profit/volume chart are:

(a) The horizontal axis represents sales (in units or sales value, as appropriate). This is the same as for a break-even chart.

(b) The vertical axis shows net profit above the horizontal sales axis and net loss below.

(c) When sales are zero, the net loss equals the fixed costs and one extreme of the 'profit/volume' line is determined – therefore this is one point on the graph or chart.

(d) If variable cost **per unit** and fixed costs **in total** are both constant throughout the relevant range of activity under consideration, the profit/volume chart is depicted by a straight line (as illustrated above). Therefore, to draw that line it is only necessary to know the profit (or loss) at one level of sales. The 'profit/volume' line is then drawn between this point and that determined in (c) and extended as necessary.

ACTIVITY 5

The budget for the year for Shireoaks Feeds Ltd was:

Output and sales	50,000 tonnes
Selling price per tonne	$75
Variable cost per tonne	$40
Fixed costs	$650,000

Required:

(a) Calculate the break-even point in units and the margin of safety.

(b) Calculate the break-even point in sales value.

(c) Draw a break-even chart (clearly showing the margin of safety).

For a suggested answer, see the 'Answers' section at the end of the book.

4 CVP ANALYSIS AND COST BEHAVIOUR ANALYSIS

4.1 COST ESTIMATION

CVP analysis is based on marginal costing principles. Its greatest value as a technique is for estimating and providing information for decision making. The value of CVP analysis depends on making reliable estimates of variable costs and fixed costs. Where some costs are semi-fixed and semi-variable, these should be divided into a variable cost element and a fixed cost element.

One technique for separating semi-fixed and semi-variable costs into their fixed and variable components is the high-low method, which was explained in Chapter 3.

EXAMPLE

A company sells a single product at a price of $15 per unit. It has not worked out what its variable costs and fixed costs are, but the following reliable estimates of total costs have been produced.

At sales volume of 24,000 units, total costs = $320,000.

At sales volume of 36,000 units, total costs = $380,000.

Required:

(a) Calculate the break-even point in sales.

(b) Calculate the margin of safety if budgeted sales are 27,000 units.

(c) Calculate the volume of sales required to achieve a target profit of $100,000.

SOLUTION

The first step is to calculate a variable cost per unit using the high-low method.

	$
Total costs of 36,000 units	380,000
Total costs of 24,000 units	320,000
Therefore variable costs of 12,000 units	60,000

Variable cost per unit = $60,000/12,000 = $5 per unit.

We can now calculate fixed costs, in either of the ways shown below.

	36,000 units	*24,000 units*
	$	$
Total costs	380,000	320,000
Variable costs at $5 per unit	180,000	120,000
Therefore fixed costs	200,000	200,000

Contribution per unit = Sales price – Variable cost = $15 – $5 = $10.

Break-even point = $200,000/$10 per unit = 20,000 units.

Margin of safety = 27,000 – 20,000 = 7,000 units. As a percentage of budgeted sales, this is 25.9%.

To achieve a **target profit** of $100,000, total contribution must be $300,000 ($200,000 fixed costs + $100,000 profit). Required sales = $300,000/$10 contribution per unit = 30,000 units.

ACTIVITY 6

A company makes and sells widgets. The sales price is $10 per unit. The company does not know what its variable costs and fixed costs are, but the following estimates of total cost have been produced.

At sales volume of 55,000 units, total costs = $607,500

At sales volume of 70,000 units, total costs = $675,000.

Required:

(a) Calculate the break-even point in sales.

(b) Calculate the margin of safety if budgeted sales are 68,000 units.

(c) Calculate the volume of sales required to achieve a target profit of $40,000. Comment on whether you think this target profit is achievable.

For a suggested answer, see the Answers section at the end of the book.

4.2 CHANGES IN COSTS AND REVENUES

As costs and revenues change the break-even point and margin of safety will also change. Generally, as the selling price of a product increases then, assuming that costs do not change, the break-even point will fall and the margin of safety will increase. Conversely, as costs rise, assuming that the selling price remains the same, then the break-even point will rise and the margin of safety will fall.

The following example aims to illustrate this point.

EXAMPLE

A company plans to sell 10,000 units at \$40 per unit. It has a variable cost of \$10 and fixed costs of \$90,000. Its existing break-even point and margin of safety are therefore:

Break-even point	= \$90,000\\$(40 – 10) =	3,000 units
Margin of safety	= 10,000 – 3,000	7,000 units (70%)

Consider separately the impact of the following:

(i) A \$10 rise in selling price

(ii) Fixed costs double

(iii) A 40% increase in variable costs

SOLUTION

(i) Rise in selling price

Break-even point	= \$90,000\\$(50 – 10) =	2,250 units
Margin of safety	= 10,000 – 2,250	7,750 units (78%)

(ii) Rise in fixed costs

Break-even point	= \$180,000\\$(40 – 10) =	6,000 units
Margin of safety	= 10,000 – 6,000	3,000 units (35%)

It can be seen from this solution that the break-even point and margin of safety change in indirect proportion to fixed costs.

(iii) Rise in variable costs

Break-even point	= \$90,000\\$(40 – 14) =	3,462 units
Margin of safety	= 10,000 – 3,462	6,538 units (65%)

CONCLUSION

CVP analysis is a useful technique for analysing the impact on profits of changes in costs, paying particular attention to the different behaviour of fixed and variable costs. There are limitations in its use as it assumes fixed cost, unit variable cost and unit revenue remain constant over the whole range of output. It is also only appropriate in a single product organisation or, for a multi-product company, the ratio of product sales must be constant (this analysis is outside of the scope of your syllabus).

Note: In exam questions you will not be asked to draw diagrams, but you may have to interpret one that has been provided for you.

KEY TERMS

Break-even point (in units) – fixed costs/contribution per unit.

Break-even point (in $) – fixed costs/contribution to sales ratio.

Margin of safety – the difference between budgeted sales and break-even sales, usually expressed as a percentage of the budget.

SELF TEST QUESTIONS

		Paragraph
1	Define contribution.	1.2
2	Define the contribution/sales ratio.	1.2
3	How is the break-even point in units calculated?	2.2
4	How is the break-even point in sales revenue calculated?	2.2
5	What is the margin of safety?	2.3
6	How do we calculate the volume of sales required to achieve a target level of profit?	2.4

EXAM-STYLE QUESTIONS

Questions 1, 2 and 3 are based on the following data:

Shoe shop

The following details relate to a shop which currently sells 25,000 pairs of shoes annually.

Selling price per pair of shoes	$40
Purchase cost per pair of shoes	$25

Total annual fixed costs

	$
Salaries	100,000
Advertising	40,000
Other fixed expenses	100,000

1 What is the contribution per pair of shoes?

A $15

B $30

C $7.50

D $18

2 What is the break-even number of pairs of shoes?

A 14,000

B 16,000

C 28,000

D 32,000

3 What is the margin of safety in units?

A 0

B 8,000

C 9,000

D Cannot be calculated from the data provided

Questions 4, 5 and 6 are based on the following data:

Sales units	52,000
Sales revenue	312,000
Variable costs	124,800
Fixed costs	130,000

4 What sales revenue is required to earn a profit of $75,000?

A $216,667

B $341,667

C $343,200

D $366,667

5 How many sales units are required to earn a profit of $82,000?

A 58,889

B 65,462

C 73,902

D 90,200

6 What is the margin of safety?

A 13.2%

B 23.8%

C 30.6%

D 44.0%

For the answers to these questions, see the 'Answers' section at the end of the book.

Chapter 14

DECISION MAKING

Managers use cost and profit information to help them make decisions. For short-term decisions, marginal costing information is the most useful. In particular, marginal costing concepts help managers to identify how profits will be maximised when there is a shortage of a key resource (a 'limiting factor'). For all decision making, only relevant costs and revenues should be used for analysis. This chapter looks at a number of applications of accounting for decision making and explains the concept of relevant costs. This chapter covers syllabus area D2.

CONTENTS

LEARNING OUTCOMES

At the end of this chapter you should be able to:

- explain the importance of the limiting factor concept
- identify the limiting factor in given situations
- formulate and determine the optimal production solution when there is a single resource constraint
- solve make/buy-in problems when there is a single resource constraint
- explain the concept of relevant costs
- apply the concept of relevant costs in business decisions.

1 DECISION MAKING AND RELEVANT COST INFORMATION

Managers often use financial information to help them make decisions. Typically, a manager will want to know whether profits will be increased if a particular course of action is taken, or which of two alternative courses of action will earn more profit.

Absorption costing information is of limited value for decision making, and can even be misleading. This is because absorption costing includes absorbed overhead but fixed overheads often do not change as a result of a decision.

For decision making, it is necessary to identify the costs and revenues that will be affected as a result of taking one course of action rather than another. The costs that would be affected by a decision are known as relevant costs.

A managerial decision is a choice between alternative options, possibly including the option of doing nothing. The choice is likely to have cost implications, in the sense that the amount of some costs will differ depending upon which option is selected. Such costs are described as relevant to the decision: the manager must consider what will happen to these costs as a result of his decision. On the other hand, there may be costs which will remain the same no matter which option is selected; such costs are not relevant to the decision. A similar argument applies to relevant and non-relevant revenues.

Since relevant costs and revenues are those which are different, the term effectively means costs and revenues which change as a result of the decision. Since it is not possible to change the past (because it has already happened), then relevant costs and revenues must be future costs and revenues. Past costs are usually referred to as sunk costs, and can never be relevant to a decision.

1.1 RELEVANT COSTS

Definition A **relevant cost** is a future incremental cash flow which arises as a direct result of a decision.

The definition highlights several important features of a relevant cost.

1 A relevant cost is an incremental cost. This means that it will change as a direct consequence of the decision. Thus relevant costs are often calculated as any change in contribution plus any change in specific fixed costs.

2 A relevant cost is a future cost. This means that any costs that have been incurred in the past (sunk costs) cannot be relevant to a decision.

3 A relevant cost is a cash flow. Any 'costs' that are not cash flow items are not relevant. These include:

- non-cash charges such as depreciation of fixed assets (non-current assets)
- notional costs such as notional interest charges
- absorbed fixed overheads. Cash overheads incurred are relevant if they change as a result of the decision and are future cash flows, but absorbed overheads are a notional accounting cost. Absorbed fixed overheads are not avoided as a result of a decision but will have to be reallocated elsewhere.

A relevant cost is one that will arise as a direct consequence of the decision being taken. If a cost is a future cash flow that will be incurred anyway, regardless of the decision that is taken, it is not relevant to the decision and so should be ignored. As a general rule, it is assumed that variable costs are relevant costs and fixed costs are unchanged regardless of a decision and so are irrelevant. However, in many decision situations, the effect of a decision could be to alter the variable cost per unit or to result in a step rise or fall in total fixed costs. These changes, provided that they affect future cash flows, are relevant costs.

1.2 SUNK COSTS

Definition A **sunk cost** is a cost that has already been incurred or committed, and so cannot be relevant for decision making.

For example, suppose that a company is wondering whether to sell a new product as part of its summer season range. It has spent $10,000 on market research, which has shown that if the product is sold for $10 per unit (variable cost of sale = $8 per unit), the company will sell 4,000 units.

The money spent on market research is a sunk cost and irrelevant to the decision. The question for the company's management is: Should we make a product for a variable cost of $8 in order to sell 4,000 units at $10 each. Contribution and profit would increase by $8,000.

1.3 AVOIDABLE AND UNAVOIDABLE COSTS

If a cost can be avoided, it is a relevant cost, because a decision can be taken that will prevent the cost from occurring. If a cost is unavoidable, it cannot be relevant to a decision, because it will be incurred anyway.

1.4 CASH FLOW COSTS

Cash flow costs are those arising in cash terms as a consequence of the decision. Such costs can never include past costs or costs arising from past transactions. Costs such as depreciation based on the cost of an asset already acquired can never be relevant, nor can committed costs, e.g. future lease payments in respect of an asset already leased. Nor will reallocations of total costs ever be relevant to the decision. Only costs which change in total because of the decision are relevant costs.

1.5 THE RELEVANCE OF VARIABLE COSTS AND FIXED COSTS

Variable costs are costs that change in total in proportion to changes in the level of activity. Therefore whenever the decision involves increases or decreases in activity it is almost certain that variable costs will be affected and therefore will be relevant to the decision.

On the other hand fixed costs are constant regardless of the level of activity. Unless the decision causes fixed costs to be increased or decreased (in which case the fixed cost would rise or fall as a step cost), fixed costs are irrelevant to a decision, and should therefore be ignored.

Where unit variable costs are constant and total fixed costs are also constant, the relevant costs for a decision are simply marginal costs, and CVP analysis can be used for relevant cost analysis.

1.6 OPPORTUNITY COSTS

Definition **Opportunity cost** is the value of the benefit forgone from the next best alternative course of action.

Relevant costs may involve incurring a cost or losing a revenue which could be obtained from an alternative course of action. Opportunity cost can only arise when resources are limited or only one option can be selected. Otherwise an organisation will select all profitable options.

EXAMPLE

A company has been asked by a customer to carry out a job for which materials would have to be purchased, costing $600, and which would incur other additional expenses of $200. The labour time required to do the job would be 50 hours, and labour is paid $8 per hour. If the company does the job, the labour to do the work would have to be switched from other operations that earn a contribution of $5 per labour hour. Overhead costs are absorbed at the rate of $10 per direct labour hour. The customer is willing to pay $1,800 for the job.

Should the company accept the job?

SOLUTION

Here, there is an opportunity cost of using the labour to do the job, costing $5 per labour hour. The labour cost of $8 per hour is also a relevant cost, even though the employees will be paid anyway. This is because the contribution of $5 per hour is calculated on the assumption that direct labour is a variable cost. The alternative work therefore earns a contribution of $5 per hour after covering labour costs of $8 per hour.

Absorbed production overhead is not a relevant cost, because it represents an allocation of overhead that doesn't change as a result of the decision. The only relevant overhead costs would be any change in actual overhead spending. For example, any variable overhead costs would be a relevant cost. In this example, there is no suggestion that the overhead costs are variable costs.

The relevant information is as follows.

	$
Relevant costs	
Direct materials	600
Other expenses	200
Direct labour (50 hours × $8)	400
Opportunity cost (50 hours × $5)	250
Total relevant costs	1,450
Price for the job	1,800
Incremental profit	350

If the company wishes to maximise its profits, it should agree to take on the job for $1,800.

1.7 SUMMARY

The basic principles of relevant costing for decision making have now been set out, and we shall now look at a variety of situations in which the concept of relevant costs should be applied.

2 LIMITING FACTORS AND LIMITING FACTOR DECISIONS

Often the only factor stopping a business from increasing its profits is sales demand. However, situations sometimes arise when a resource is in short supply, and a business cannot make enough units to meet sales demand.

A resource in short supply is called a limiting factor, because it sets a limit on what can be achieved by an organisation.

Definition A **scarce resource** is an item in short supply. In the context of decision making in business, it is a resource in short supply, as a consequence of which the organisation is limited in its ability to provide and sell more of products or services. Such scarce resources are called **limiting factors**.

Typically, a scarce resource could be:

- a limit to the availability of a key item of raw materials or a key component
- a limit to the availability of a key type of labour, such as skilled or qualified labour
- a limit to the available machine time. For example, if a business has just two machines for producing a range of products, the available machine time will be limited to the number of hours in which the two machines can be operated each week or month.

When a business has a limiting factor, a decision must be taken about how the available resources should be used. If the business makes and sells more than one product, and all the products make use of the scarce resource, the decision involves allocating the available resources to the production of one or more of the products, up to the point where all the scarce resources are used up.

Marginal costing principles can be used to identify how a scarce resource should be used to maximise profits. However, in order to do this, a business must first of all recognise that there is a limiting factor.

2.1 IDENTIFYING A SCARCE RESOURCE

To identify a scarce resource, it is necessary to:

- obtain estimates of sales demand for each of the products (or services) sold by the business
- obtain estimates of the quantities of resources needed to make the units to meet the sales demand
- from these estimates, calculate how many units of each resource will be needed
- for each resource, compare the amount needed with the amount available
- if the amount needed exceeds the amount available, the resource is in short supply and so is a limiting factor.

EXAMPLE

A manufacturer makes two products, X and Y. One unit of Product X requires 5 kg of materials and 2 hours of labour. One unit of Product Y requires 4 kg of the same material and 3 hours of the same labour. There are only 2,000 hours labour available each week and the maximum amount of material available each week is 3,000 kg. Potential sales demand each week is 300 units of Product X and 450 units of Product Y.

Identify whether materials or labour is a limiting factor.

SOLUTION

	Materials	*Labour*
	kg	*hours*
Required for 300 units of Product X	1,500	600
Required for 450 units of Product Y	1,800	1,350
Total required	3,300	1,950
Amount available	3,000	2,000
Surplus/(shortfall)	(300)	50

So material is a limiting factor.

2.2 LIMITING FACTOR DECISIONS: IDENTIFYING THE MOST PROFITABLE USE OF A SCARCE RESOURCE

When a business has a limiting factor, its total sales volume is restricted by its availability.

- If the business makes and sells just one product, all it can do is to make and sell as many units of the product that it can with the scarce resource available. This will maximise total contribution.

- If the business makes and sells two or more products and each product makes use of the scarce resource, profits will be maximised by making the product which has the highest contribution per unit of limiting factor.

ACTIVITY 1

A business makes two products, X and Y. Both products use the same machine and a common raw material, supplies of which are limited to 200 machine hours and $500 per week respectively. Individual product details are as follows:

	Product X	*Product Y*
Machine hours/unit	5	2.5
Cost of materials/unit	$10	$5
Contribution/unit	$20	$15

Required:

(a) Identify the limiting factor.

(b) Recommend which product the business should make and sell (assuming that demand is unlimited).

For a suggested answer, see the 'Answers' section at the end of the book

2.3 LIMITING FACTORS AND SALES DEMAND CONSTRAINTS

Maximum sales demand

In the above activity, the sales demand for the products was unlimited. Once the contribution per unit of the limiting factor has been determined, the product earning the highest contribution per unit of limiting factor should be made until the scarce resource is fully utilised. The other products will not be made and sold at all, if the aim is to maximise total contribution and total profit.

In many situations, however, there is a maximum level of sales demand for each product. In these situations, there is no point in making more units of a product than it can sell. The problem is then to decide which products to make and sell, given the limiting factor and the limitations of sales demand. To solve such problems, a ranking approach is used. The products (or services) of the business are ranked in order of their contribution per unit of limiting factor.

The approach, if there are two or more products all using a scarce resource, is as follows:

1 Identify the scarce resource.

2 Calculate contribution per unit of product.

3 Calculate the units of the scarce resource used by each product.

4 Calculate the contribution per unit of scarce resource.

5 Rank products according to the contribution earned per unit of scarce resource (with the highest being ranked first).

6 Allocate the scarce resource according to the ranking.

This approach is best explained by means of an example.

EXAMPLE

A manufacturer makes two products which both use the same types of material and grade of labour, but in different quantities as shown by the table below:

	Product A	*Product B*
Labour hours/unit	0.4	0.8
Material kg/unit	5	2
Demand (units)	500	250
Sales price per unit	$30	$36

During each week the maximum number of labour hours available is 360 and the quantity of material available is limited to 3,000 kg. The labour rate is $25 per hour and material costs $2 per kg.

Advise the manufacturer how many of each product it should make.

SOLUTION

Step 1 Identify the scarce resource.

Maximum labour required is (500 × 0.4) + (250 × 0.8) = 400 hours. There are only 360 available so labour is a limiting factor.

Maximum material required is (500 × 5) + (250 × 2) = 3,000 kg. Material is not a scarce resource.

Note: You will never have to deal with a situation with more than one scarce resource, so you only need to find the one that is scarce.

Step 2 Calculate the contribution per unit of product.

	Product A	*Product B*
	$	$
Sales price	30	36
Less: Labour cost	(10)	(20)
Material cost	(10)	(4)
Contribution	10	12

Step 3 Calculate the contribution per unit of scarce resource.

	Product A	*Product B*
Contribution per unit	$10	$12
Labour hours (scarce resource)	0.4	0.8
Contribution per labour hour	$25	$15

Step 4 Rank products 1st 2nd

Step 5 Allocate the scarce resource according to ranking.

First, make Product A. The maximum demand of 500 uses 200 labour hours.

This leaves 160 hours to use on Product B so 200 units can be made.

The production plan is to make 500 units of Product A and 200 units of Product B.

This earns a total contribution of (500 × $10) + (200 × $12) = $7,400.

ACTIVITY 2

A company makes three products: A, B and C. All three products use the same type of labour which is limited to 1,500 hours per month. Individual product details are as follows:

Product	*A*	*B*	*C*
Contribution/unit	$25	$40	$35
Labour hours/unit	5	6	8
Maximum demand	100	200	400

Advise the company as to the quantities of each product it should make.

For a suggested answer, see the 'Answers' section at the end of the book.

3 MAKE-OR-BUY DECISIONS

There are two situations where a make-or-buy decision might arise.

- A business currently manufactures its own products or components, and an external supplier offers to make them instead. The choice is therefore whether to make the items 'in-house' or whether to buy them externally. A make-or-buy decision of this type could be described as an 'outsourcing decision'.
- A business has a limiting factor preventing it from making and selling more than a limited volume of products. For example, a business might have a shortage of labour. One or more external suppliers might offer to supply some of the products to make up the shortage. In such a situation, the business might have to decide not only whether it is worthwhile buying extra units of product from outside, but which products should be purchased so as to maximise profitability.

3.1 OUTSOURCING DECISIONS

When a business is considering whether or not to buy items externally rather than make them internally, the relevant financial information is a comparison of the costs of making and buying. If the items are purchased externally, it is likely that some fixed cost expenditures will be saved. Any fall in cash fixed costs would be relevant to the decision.

EXAMPLE

A company manufactures an assembly used in the production of one of its product lines. The department in which the assembly is produced incurs annual fixed costs of $24,000. The variable costs of production are $2.55 per unit. The assembly could be bought outside at a cost of $2.65 per unit.

The current annual requirement is for 80,000 assemblies per year. Should the company continue to manufacture the assembly, or should it be purchased from the outside suppliers?

SOLUTION

A decision to purchase outside would cost the company $(2.65 – 2.55) = 10p per unit, which for 80,000 assemblies would amount to $8,000 each year. Thus, the fixed costs of $24,000 should be analysed to determine if more than $8,000 would actually be saved if production of the assembly were discontinued.

Other considerations affecting the decision

Management would need to consider other factors before reaching a make-or-buy decision. Some would be quantifiable and some not:

- **Continuity and control of supply.** Can the external supplier be relied upon to meet the requirements in terms of quantity, quality, delivery dates and price stability?
- **Alternative use of resources.** Can the resources used to make this article be transferred to another activity which will save costs or increase revenues?
- **Social/legal.** Will the decision affect contractual or ethical obligations to employees or business connections?

3.2 MAKE-OR-BUY AND LIMITING FACTORS

If a business cannot fulfil orders because it has used up all available capacity, it may be forced to purchase from outside in the short term (unless it is cheaper to refuse sales). In the longer term management may look to other alternatives, such as capital expenditure.

It may be, however, that a variety of components is produced from common resources and management would try to arrange manufacture or purchase to use its available capacity most profitably. In such a situation the limiting factor concept makes it easier to formulate the optimum plans; priority for purchase would be indicated by **ranking components in relation to the excess purchasing cost per unit of limiting factor.**

EXAMPLE

Fidgets manufactures three components used in its finished product. The component workshop is currently unable to meet the demand for components and the possibility of subcontracting part of the requirement is being investigated on the basis of the following data.

	Component A	*Component B*	*Component C*
	$	$	$
Variable costs of production	3.00	4.00	7.00
Outside purchase price	2.50	6.00	13.00
Excess cost per unit	(0.50)	2.00	6.00
Machine hours per unit	1	0.5	2
Labour hours per unit	2	2	4

Required:

(a) Decide which component should be bought from external suppliers if the company has no limiting factors.

(b) Decide which component should be bought from external suppliers if production is limited to 4,000 machine hours per week.

SOLUTION

(a) Component A should always be bought from an outside company, regardless of any limiting factors, as its variable cost of production is higher than the external purchase price.

(b) **If machine hours are limited to 4,000 hours**:

	Component B	*Component C*
Excess cost	$2	$6
Machine hours per unit	0.5	2
Excess cost per machine hour	$4	$3

Component C has the lowest excess cost per limiting factor and should, therefore, be bought from an outside company.

The decision can be proven (although you would not have to do this in an examination) by looking at the total excess cost of purchase for each component:

Proof:

	Component B	*Component C*
Units produced in 4,000 machine hours	8,000	2,000
	$	$
Production costs	32,000	14,000
Purchase costs	48,000	26,000
Excess cost of purchase	16,000	12,000

This illustrates that Component B is much more expensive to buy in and should therefore be prioritised for production – the same answer as that provided by our quick determination of the excess cost per machine hour which will always tell us which product to PRODUCE (i.e. the one with the highest excess cost per machine hour).

ACTIVITY 3

Using the information from the previous example, decide which component should be bought from external suppliers if production is limited to 4,000 labour hours per week.

For a suggested answer, see the 'Answers' section at the end of the book.

4 OTHER TYPES OF DECISION

Relevant costs should be applied to any type of decision. Here are some more examples.

4.1 DECISIONS ABOUT VOLUME AND COST STRUCTURE CHANGES

Management will require information to evaluate proposals aimed at increasing profit by changing operating strategy. The cost accountant will need to show clearly the effect of the proposals on profit by pin-pointing the changes in costs and revenues and by quantifying the margin of error which will cause the proposal to be non-viable.

EXAMPLE

A business produces and sells one product and its forecast for the next financial year is as follows:

	$000	$000
Sales 100,000 units at $8		800
Variable costs:		
Material	300	
Labour	200	
		500
Contribution ($3 per unit)		300
Fixed costs		150
Net profit		150

As an attempt to increase net profit, the business is proposing to launch an advertising campaign costing $14,000. This will increase the sales to 150,000 units, although the price will have to be reduced to $7.

Determine the impact on profit of the new business proposal and the extra sales that would need to be generated in order to make the proposal worthwhile

SOLUTION

The proposal will increase the sales revenue but the increase in costs will be greater:

	$000
Sales 150,000 × $7	1,050
Variable costs	750
	300
Fixed costs plus advertising	164
Net profit	136

The proposal is therefore of no value and sales must be increased in order to maintain net profit:

Reduced profit at 150,000 units	$14,000
Contribution per unit	$2
Therefore additional volume required	7,000 units

ACTIVITY 4

Using the information from the previous example, determine the extra sales that would need to be generated from a separate proposal to produce in-house some components that are currently bought-in from external suppliers. This proposal will reduce material costs by 20% but will increase fixed costs by $72,000.

This proposal should be considered separately from the original proposal to invest in an advertising campaign

For a suggested answer, see the 'Answers' section at the end of the book.

4.2 SPECIAL CONTRACT PRICING

A business which produces to customer's orders may be working to full capacity. Any additional orders must be considered on the basis of the following questions:

- What price must be quoted to make the contract profitable?
- Can other orders be fulfilled if this contract is accepted?

In such a situation the limiting factor needs to be recognised so that the contract price quoted will at least maintain the existing rate of contribution per unit of limiting factor.

EXAMPLE

Oddjobs manufactures special purpose gauges to customers' specifications. The highly-skilled labour force is always working to full capacity and the budget for the next year is as follows:

	$	$
Sales		40,000
Direct materials	4,000	
Direct wages 800 hours at $20	16,000	
Fixed overhead	10,000	
		30,000
Profit		10,000

An enquiry is received from XY for a gauge which would use $60 of direct materials and 20 labour hours.

What is the minimum price to quote to XY?

SOLUTION

The contribution made by Oddjobs is $20,000 (either take sales less the variable costs, or take the profit and add back the fixed costs).

The limiting factor is 800 labour hours.

A decision should be take account of the potential lost budgeted contribution per hour = $20,000 ÷ 800 hours = $25 per hour. The minimum price is therefore:

	$
Materials	60
Wages 20 hours at $20	400
	460
Add*:* Contribution 20 hours at $25	500
Contract price	960

At the above price the contract will maintain the budgeted contribution (check by calculating the effect of devoting the whole 800 hours to XY).

Note, however, that the lost contribution of $25 per hour is the average contribution per hour made by all of Oddjobs contracts. It is likely that some jobs will be making more than $25 per hour and some less. It may be that the XY contract could be provided at the expense of some of the lower earning contracts and a lower price could be offered to XY. Oddjobs would need to perform an investigation in order to determine whether or not this is possible.

4.3 UTILISATION OF SPARE CAPACITY

Where production is below capacity, opportunities may arise for sales at a specially reduced price, for example, export orders or manufacturing under another brand name. Such opportunities are worthwhile if the answer to two key questions is 'Yes':

- Is spare capacity available?
- Does additional revenue (units × price) exceed additional costs (units × relevant variable cost, plus any incremental fixed cost expenditure)?

However, the evaluation should also consider the following questions:

- Is there an alternative more profitable way of utilising spare capacity (e.g. sales promotion, making an alternative product)?
- Will fixed costs be unchanged if the order is accepted?
- Will accepting one order at below normal selling price lead other customers to ask for price cuts?

The longer the time period in question, the more important are these other factors.

EXAMPLE

At a production level of 8,000 units per month, which is 80% of capacity, the budget of Export Traders is as follows:

	Per unit	*8,000 units*
	$	$
Sales	5.00	40,000
Variable costs:		
Direct labour	1.00	8,000
Raw materials	1.50	12,000
Variable overheads	0.50	4,000
	3.00	24,000
Fixed costs	1.50	12,000
Total	4.50	36,000
Budgeted profit	0.50	4,000

An opportunity arises to export 1,000 units per month at a price of $4 per unit.

Should the contract be accepted?

SOLUTION

Is spare capacity available? Answer: Yes

The relevant cost or benefit is therefore calculated as follows:

		$
Additional revenue	1,000 × $4	4,000
Additional costs	1,000 × $3	3,000
Increased profitability		1,000

Therefore, the contract should be accepted.

Note that fixed costs are not relevant to the decision and are therefore ignored.

4.4 CLOSURE OF A BUSINESS SEGMENT

Part of a business may appear to be unprofitable. The segment may, for example, be a product, a department or a channel of distribution. In making a financial decision on potential closures, the cost accountant should consider:

- loss of contribution from the segment
- savings in specific fixed costs from closure
- penalties, e.g. redundancy, compensation to customers
- alternative use for resources released

As well as considering financial factors in evaluating the closure of a business segment, the cost accountant should also consider non-financial effects such as the impact on other business units, the reaction of the company's customers, the impact on employee motivation etc.

EXAMPLE

Harolds fashion store comprises three departments – Men's wear, Ladies' Wear and Unisex. The store budget is as follows:

	Men's	*Ladies'*	*Unisex*	*Total*
	$	$	$	$
Sales	40,000	60,000	20,000	120,000
Direct cost of sales	20,000	36,000	15,000	71,000
Department costs	5,000	10,000	3,000	18,000
Apportioned store costs	5,000	5,000	5,000	15,000
Profit/(loss)	10,000	9,000	(3,000)	16,000

Apportioned store costs are a fixed cost (including items such as store rent, management salaries etc.). It is suggested that Unisex be closed as it is currently making a loss.

Would this be acceptable from a financial perspective?

SOLUTION

This decision is likely to cost the money in terms of an overall downturn in financial performance. The company would lose contribution from the Unisex department of $2,000 – that is, sales of $20,000 less direct costs of $15,000 and departmental costs of $3,000. The apportioned store costs would still be incurred (and the amount would be transferred to the other departments) and therefore these costs are not relevant to the decision.

5 IDENTIFYING RELEVANT COSTS

In most of the examples shown so far, the relevant costs have consisted of variable costs, incremental fixed costs and opportunity costs of scarce resources. There are, however, situations where identifying relevant costs is a bit more complex.

5.1 THE RELEVANT COSTS OF MATERIALS

In any decision situation the cost of materials relevant to a particular decision is their opportunity cost. This can be represented by a decision tree.

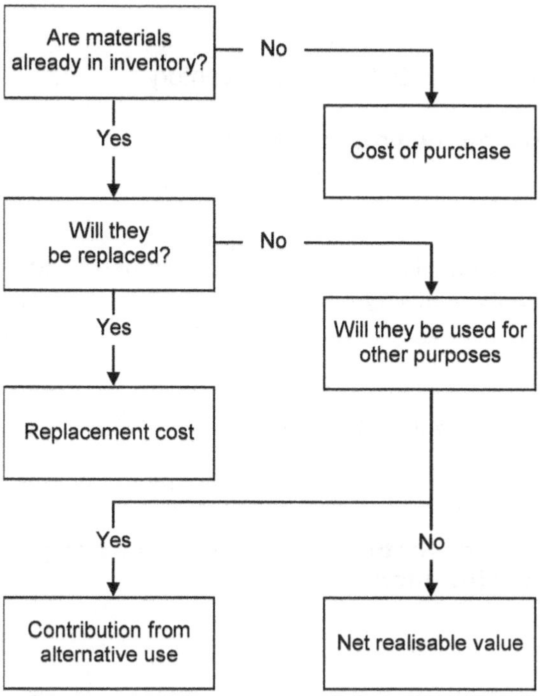

This decision tree can be used to identify the appropriate cost to use for materials. It can be summarised as follows:

- If the materials will be replaced if they are used, their relevant cost is the cost of replacing them. This is their current purchase price.
- If the materials will not be replaced if they are used, they could still have an opportunity cost. This is because they might be disposed of (e.g. for scrap) or they might have an alternative use that would earn some additional profit. The opportunity cost of the materials would then be the higher of their disposal value (net realisable value) or the value they would earn in their alternative use.

5.2 EXAMPLES

EXAMPLE 1

A new contract requires the use of 50 tons of metal ZX 81. This metal is used regularly on all of the firm's projects. There are 100 tons of ZX 81 held in inventory at the moment, which were bought for $200 per ton. The current purchase price is $210 per ton, and the metal could be disposed of for net scrap proceeds of $150 per ton.

With what cost should the new contract be charged for the ZX 81?

SOLUTION

The use of the material already held in inventory for the new contract means that more ZX 81 must be bought for normal workings. The cost to the organisation is therefore the money spent on purchase, no matter whether existing inventory or new inventory is used on the contract. Assuming that the additional purchases are made in the near future, the relevant cost to the organisation is current purchase price, i.e.:

50 tons × $210 = $10,500

Note that the original purchase price is a sunk cost and is never relevant.

EXAMPLE 2

Suppose the organisation has no use for the ZX 81 held in inventory.

What is the relevant cost of using it on the new contract?

SOLUTION

Now the only alternative use for the material is to sell it for scrap. To use 50 tons on the contract is to give up the opportunity of selling it for:

50 × $150 = $7,500

The contract should therefore be charged with this amount.

EXAMPLE 3

Suppose that there is no alternative use for the ZX 81 other than a scrap sale, but that there is only 25 tons held in inventory.

SOLUTION

The relevant cost of 25 tons is $150 per ton. The organisation must then purchase a further 25 tons, and assuming this is in the near future, it will cost $210 per ton.

The contract must be charged with:

	$
25 tons at $150	3,750
25 tons at $210	5,250
	9,000

ACTIVITY 5

Zara has 50kg of material P currently held in inventory which was bought five years ago for $70. It is no longer used but could be sold for $3 per kg.

Zara is currently pricing a job which could use 40 kg of Material P.

What is the relevant cost of P which should be included in the price?

For a suggested answer, see the 'Answers' section at the end of the book.

5.3 THE RELEVANT COST OF LABOUR

A similar problem exists in determining the relevant costs of labour. In this case the key question is whether spare capacity exists:

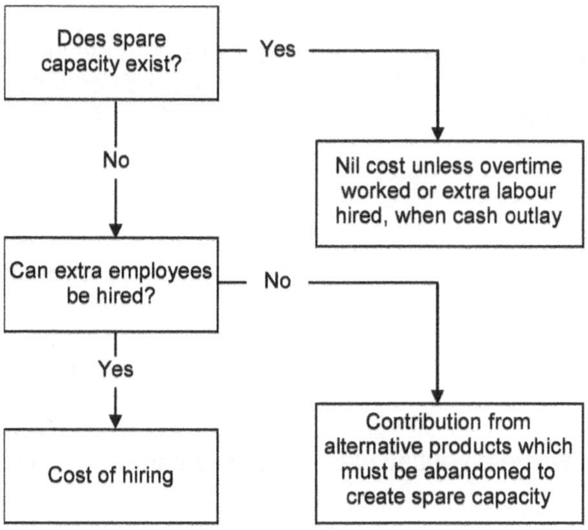

Again this can be used to identify the relevant opportunity cost.

EXAMPLE

A business uses skilled labour costing $40 per hour, which generates a contribution, after deducting these labour costs, of $30 per hour. Skilled labour is scarce.

A new project is now being considered which requires 5,000 hours of skilled labour. Skilled labour used on the new project must be transferred from normal working.

What is the relevant cost of using the skilled labour on the project?

SOLUTION

The contribution cash flow lost if the labour is transferred from normal working is;

	$
Contribution per hour lost from normal working	30
Add back: labour cost per hour which is not saved	40
Cash lost per labour hour as a result of the labour transfer	70
The contract should be charged with 5,000 × $70	$350,000

ACTIVITY 6

Consider how the answer to the previous example would change if there is a surplus of skilled labour already employed (and paid) by the business and sufficient to cope with the new project. The presently idle men are being paid full wages.

For a suggested answer, see the 'Answers' section at the end of the book.

CONCLUSION

This chapter has shown examples of the different kinds of decision which must be made in order to maximise short-term profitability. Other decisions are made for the longer term and involve capital expenditure. These are explained in the next chapter.

Relevant costs for decisions have been identified and the techniques used to evaluate decision options illustrated. Sometimes, identifying relevant costs can be a bit complicated and you are strongly advised to work on the practice questions at the end of this chapter.

KEY TERMS

Relevant cost – a future cash flow arising as a direct consequence of a decision. Relevant costs should be used to provide cost information for decision making.

Sunk cost – a cost that has already been incurred or committed, and so cannot be relevant for decision making.

Notional cost – a cash that does not involve an outlay of cash, and so cannot be relevant for decision making.

Opportunity cost – a benefit forgone by taking one course of action instead of the next most profitable alternative.

Scarce resource – an item in short supply. In the context of decision making in business, it is a resource in short supply, as a consequence of which the organisation is limited in its ability to provide and sell more of its products or services. Such scarce resources are called **limiting factors**. A limiting factor has an opportunity cost.

SELF TEST QUESTIONS

		Paragraph
1	Define a relevant cost.	1.1
2	What is a sunk cost?	1.2
3	Explain the relevance of variable costs to decision making.	1.5
4	Explain the relevance of fixed costs to decision making.	1.5
5	What is an opportunity cost?	1.6
6	How can a limiting factor be identified?	2.1
7	Draw a decision tree to show how to determine the relevant cost of materials.	5.1
8	Draw a decision tree to show how to determine the relevant cost of labour.	5.2

EXAM-STYLE QUESTIONS

1 Which of the following statements is NOT true?

A Relevant costs change according to the decision

B Relevant costs are always future costs

C Fixed costs can never be relevant costs

D Relevant costs are those specific to a decision

2 A cost where no actual cash expenditure is incurred is better known as:

A avoidable cost

B non-valued cost

C historical cost

D notional cost

3 The cost of an asset acquired three months ago is a good example of:

A sunk cost

B relevant cost

C notional cost

D avoidable cost

The following information is relevant for Questions 4, 5 and 6:

R Ltd makes three products which use the same type of materials but in different quantities, as shown by the table below:

Product	*P*	*Q*	*R*
Material/unit	3 kg	4 kg	5 kg
Contribution/unit	$10	$12	$20
Maximum demand per month (units)	100	150	300

The available materials are limited to 1,680 kg per month.

4 The rank in which the products should be made in order to maximise contribution is:

A P, Q, R

B P, R, Q

C R, Q, P

D R, P, Q

5 The number of units of product P that should be manufactured are:

A 40

B 60

C 80

D 100

6 How much contribution is made from the optimal production plan?

A $6,000

B $6,600

C $7,000

D $7,600

The following information is relevant for Questions 7 and 8:

A company is preparing a quote for some printing work which requires two types of labour. Some weekend working would be required to complete the printing, and the following illustrates the necessary total hours required and standard costs for the labour:

Direct labour		$
Skilled	250 hours at $4.00	1,000
Unskilled	100 hours at $3.50	350

The following notes are relevant to the standard costs above:

1 Skilled direct labour is in short supply, and to accommodate the printing work, 50% of the time required would be worked at weekends for which a premium of 25% above the normal hourly rate is paid. The normal hourly rate is $4.00 per hour.

2 Unskilled labour is presently under-utilised, and at present 200 hours per week are recorded as idle time. If the printing work is carried out at a weekend, 25 unskilled hours would have to occur at this time, but the employees concerned would be given two hours' time off (for which they would be paid) in lieu of each hour worked.

7 What cost should be included in the quote for skilled labour?

A $0

B $1,000

C $1,125

D $1,250

8 What cost should be included in the quote for unskilled labour?

A $0

B $350

C $525

D $700

9 A project requires 60 kg of material.

All of the material is currently held in inventory and the material is used elsewhere in the business. Excess material can be sold on the open market at $8 per kg. If used in the project it will have to be adapted slightly at a cost of $1 per kg.

The material could be acquired (without the need for any adaptations) from a supplier for $10 per kg.

What is the cost of using it in the project?

A $60

B $480

C $540

D $600

10 A company requires 5,000 hours of unskilled labour on a large new product. Skilled labour employees are paid a fixed salary of $20,000 each and this project will require 20 of these staff.

The unskilled labour will be able to complete 40% of the work alongside their existing workload, but the remaining work will be carried out during weekends, when staff will be entitled to an overtime premium of 25% of their normal hourly rate of $10 per hour.

The total relevant cost of skilled labour to be included in the project decision is $_______.

For the answers to these questions, see the 'Answers' section at the end of the book.

Chapter 15

DISCOUNTED CASH FLOW AND CAPITAL EXPENDITURE APPRAISAL

Relevant costs are used to evaluate both short-term and long-term decisions. Long-term decisions usually concern whether or not to invest in capital expenditure. For most capital expenditure projects, there is an initial expenditure of cash to acquire non-current assets, and the cash returns from the investment are obtained over a period of several years. This chapter looks at how capital expenditure decisions should be appraised, using discounted cash flow, to allow for the 'time value' of money invested. This chapter covers syllabus area D3.

CONTENTS

LEARNING OUTCOMES

At the end of this chapter you should be able to:

- explain and illustrate the difference between simple and compound interest, and between nominal and effective interest rates
- explain and illustrate compounding and discounting
- explain the distinction between cash flow and profit and the relevance of cash flow to capital investment appraisal
- explain and illustrate the net present value (NPV) and internal rate of return (IRR) methods of discounted cash flow
- calculate present value using annuity and perpetuity formulae
- calculate payback (discounted and non-discounted)
- interpret the results of NPV, IRR and payback calculations of investment viability.

1 INVESTMENT APPRAISAL

1.1 CAPITAL INVESTMENT

Most businesses have to spend money from time to time on new non-current assets. Spending on non-current assets is capital expenditure. There are various reasons why capital expenditure might be either necessary or desirable, and these can be categorised into the following types.

(a) **Maintenance** – This is spending on new non-current assets (sometimes called fixed assets) to replace worn-out assets or obsolete assets, or spending on existing non-current assets to improve safety and security features.

(b) **Profitability** – This is spending on non-current assets to improve the profitability of the existing business, to achieve cost savings, quality improvement, improved productivity, and so on.

(c) **Expansion** – This is spending to expand the business, to make new products, open new outlets, invest in research and development, etc.

(d) **Indirect** – This is spending on non-current assets that will not have a direct impact on the business operations or its profits. It includes spending on office buildings, or welfare facilities, etc. Capital spending of this nature is necessary, but a business should try to make sure that it gets good value for money from its spending.

In contrast to revenue expenditure, which is normally continual spending but in fairly small amounts, capital expenditure is irregular and often involves large amounts of spending. Because of the large amounts of money involved, it is usual for decisions about capital expenditure to be taken at a senior level within an organisation.

1.2 THE FEATURES OF CAPITAL EXPENDITURE APPRAISAL

Before any capital expenditure is authorised, the proposed spending (or 'capital project') should be evaluated. Management should be satisfied that the spending will be beneficial.

- If the purpose of a capital project is to improve profits, we need to be convinced that the expected profits are big enough to justify the spending. Will the investment provide a reasonable return?

- If the capital expenditure is for an essential purpose, such as to replace a worn-out machine or to acquire a new office building, we need to be convinced that the spending decision is the best option available, and that there are no cheaper or more effective spending options.

When a capital project is proposed, the costs and benefits of the project should be evaluated over its foreseeable life. This is usually the expected useful life of the non-current asset to be purchased, which will be several years. This means that estimates of future costs and benefits call for long-term forecasting.

A 'typical' capital project involves an immediate purchase of a non-current asset. The asset is then used for a number of years, during which it is used to increase sales revenue or to achieve savings in operating costs. There will also be running costs for the asset. At the end of the asset's commercially useful life, it might have a 'residual value'. For example, it might be sold for scrap or in a second-hand market. (Items such as motor vehicles and printing machines often have a significant residual value.)

A problem with long-term forecasting of revenues, savings and costs is that forecasts can be inaccurate. However, although it is extremely difficult to produce reliable forecasts, every effort should be made to make them as reliable as possible.

- A business should try to avoid spending money on non-current assets on the basis of wildly optimistic and unrealistic forecasts.

- The assumptions on which the forecasts are based should be stated clearly. If the assumptions are clear, the forecasts can be assessed for reasonableness by the individuals who are asked to authorise the spending.

1.3 METHODS OF CAPITAL EXPENDITURE APPRAISAL

When forecasts of costs and benefits have been made for a capital project, the estimates must be analysed to establish whether the project should go ahead. Should the business spend money now in order to earn returns over a number of years into the future?

Capital investment appraisal is an analysis of the expected financial returns from a capital project over its expected life.

There are several methods of carrying out a capital expenditure appraisal. The methods that will be described in this chapter are:

- payback

- net present value method of discounted cash flow

- internal rate of return method of discounted cash flow

- discounted payback.

A common feature of all four methods is that they analyse the expected *cash flows* from the capital project, not the effects of the project on reported accounting profits.

Before describing the four techniques in detail, it will be helpful to look at the 'cash flow' nature of capital investment appraisal.

2 INVESTMENT APPRAISAL AND CASH FLOWS

2.1 ACCOUNTING PROFITS AND CASH FLOWS

An investment involves the outlay of money 'now' in the expectation of getting more money back in the future. In capital investment appraisal, it is more appropriate to evaluate future cash flows – the money actually spent, saved and received – rather than accounting profits. Accounting profits, prepared on an accruals basis, do not properly reflect investment returns.

Suppose for example that a business is considering whether to buy a new machine for $80,000 that is expected to increase profits before depreciation each year by $30,000 for four years. At the end of Year 4, the asset will be worthless.

The business should assess whether the expected financial return from the machine is sufficiently high to justify buying it.

(a) If we looked at the accounting returns from this investment, we might decide that annual depreciation should be $20,000 each year ($80,000/4 years). Annual profits would then be $10,000. We could then assess the project on the basis that it will add $10,000 each year to profit for the next four years. But depreciation is a notional cost and is not a relevant cash flow.

(b) If we looked at the investment cash flows, the analysis is different. Here we would say that to invest in the project, the business would spend $80,000 now and would expect a cash return of $30,000 each year for the next four years.

Capital investment appraisal should be based on cash flows, because these are relevant costs for decision making. Capital spending involves spending cash and getting cash back in return, over time.

2.2 CASH FLOWS AND RELEVANT COSTS

The only cash flows that should be taken into consideration in capital investment appraisal are:

- cash flows that will happen in the future, and
- cash flows that will arise only if the capital project goes ahead.

These cash flows are direct revenues from the project and relevant costs. Relevant costs are future costs that will be incurred or saved as a direct consequence of undertaking the investment.

- Costs that have already been incurred are not relevant to a current decision. For example, suppose a company makes a non-returnable deposit as a down-payment for an item of equipment, and then re-considers whether it wants the equipment after all. The money has already been spent and cannot be recovered and so is not relevant to the current decision about obtaining the equipment.

- Costs that will be incurred anyway, whether or not a capital project goes ahead, cannot be relevant to a decision about investing in the project. Absorbed fixed costs are an example of 'committed costs'. For the purpose of investment appraisal, a project should not be charged with an amount for a share of fixed costs that will be incurred anyway.

- Non-cash items of cost can never be relevant to investment appraisal. In particular, the depreciation charges on a fixed (non-current) asset are not relevant costs for analysis because depreciation is not a cash expenditure.

ACTIVITY 1

A company is evaluating a proposed expenditure on an item of equipment that would cost $160,000. A technical feasibility study has been carried out by consultants, at a cost of $15,000, into benefits from investing in the equipment. It has been estimated that the equipment would have a life of four years, and annual profits would be $8,000. Profits are after deducting annual depreciation of $40,000 and an annual charge of $25,000 for a share of fixed costs that will be incurred anyway.

What are the cash flows for this project that should be evaluated?

For a suggested answer, see the 'Answers' section at the end of the book.

3 PAYBACK METHOD OF APPRAISAL

3.1 INTRODUCTION

Definition **Payback** is the amount of time it is expected to take for the cash inflows from a capital investment project to equal the cash outflows.

It is the time that a project will take to pay back the money spent on it. It is based on expected cash flows from the project, not accounting profits.

The payback method of appraisal is used in one of two ways.

- A business might establish a rule for capital spending that no project should be undertaken unless it is expected to pay back within a given length of time. For example, a rule might be established that capital expenditure should not be undertaken unless payback is expected within, say, five years.

- When two alternative capital projects are being compared, and the decision is to undertake one or the other but not both, preference might be given to the project that is expected to pay back sooner.

Payback is commonly used as an initial screening method, and projects that meet the payback requirement are then evaluated using another investment appraisal method.

3.2 CALCULATING PAYBACK: CONSTANT ANNUAL CASH FLOWS

If the expected cash inflows from a project are an equal annual amount, the payback period is calculated simply as:

$$\text{Payback period} = \frac{\text{Initial payment}}{\text{Annual cash inflow}}$$

It is normally assumed that cash flows each year occur at an even rate throughout the year.

EXAMPLE

An expenditure of $2 million is expected to generate cash inflows of $500,000 each year for the next seven years.

What is the payback period for the project?

SOLUTION

$$\text{Payback} = \frac{\$2,000,000}{\$500,000} = \mathbf{4\ years}$$

The payback method provides a rough measure of the liquidity of a project, in other words how much annual cash flow it earns. It is not a measure of the profitability of a project over its life. In the example above, the fact that the project pays back within four years ignores the total amount of cash flows it will provide over seven years. A project costing $2 million and earning cash flows of $500,000 for just five years would have exactly the same payback period, even though it would not be as profitable.

A payback period might not be an exact number of years.

EXAMPLE

A project will involve spending $1.8 million now. Annual cash flows from the project would be $350,000.

What is the expected payback period?

SOLUTION

$$\text{Payback} = \frac{\$1,800,000}{\$350,000} = 5.1429 \text{ years}$$

This can be stated in any of the following ways.

- Payback will be in 5.1 years.
- Payback will be in just over 5 years (or between 5 and 6 years).
- Payback will be in 5 years 2 months.

Payback in years and months is calculated by multiplying the decimal fraction of a year by 12 months. In this example, 0.1429 years = 1.7 months (0.1429 × 12 months), which is rounded to 2 months.

ACTIVITY 2

An investment would cost $2.3 million and annual cash inflows from the project are expected to be $600,000.

Calculate the expected payback period in years and months.

State an assumption on which this estimate is based.

For a suggested answer, see the 'Answers' section at the end of the book.

3.3 CALCULATING PAYBACK: UNEVEN ANNUAL CASH FLOWS

Annual cash flows from a project are unlikely to be a constant annual amount, but are likely to vary from year to year.

Payback is calculated by finding out when the cumulative cash inflows from the project will pay back the money spent. Cumulative cash flows should be worked out by adding each year's cash flows, on a cumulative basis, to net cash flow to date for the project.

The simplest way of calculating payback is probably to set out the figures in a table.

An example will be used to illustrate how the table should be constructed.

EXAMPLE

A project is expected to have the following cash flows.

Year	*Cash flow*
	$000
0	(2,000)
1	500
2	500
3	400
4	600
5	300
6	200

What is the expected payback period?

SOLUTION

Figures in brackets are negative cash flows. In the table below a column is added for cumulative cash flows for the project to date. Figures in brackets are negative cash flows.

Each year's cumulative figure is simply the cumulative figure at the start of the year plus the figure for the current year. The cumulative figure each year is therefore the expected position as at the end of that year.

Year	*Cash flow*	*Cumulative cash flow*
	$000	$000
0	(2,000)	(2,000)
1	500	(1,500)
2	500	(1,000)
3	400	(600)
4	600	0
5	300	300
6	200	500

The payback period is exactly four years.

Payback is not always an exact number of years.

EXAMPLE

A project has the following cash flows.

Year	*Cash flow*
	$000
0	(1,900)
1	300
2	500
3	600
4	800
5	500

The payback period is calculated as follows.

Year	*Cash flow*	*Cumulative cash flow*
	$000	$000
0	(1,900)	(1,900)
1	300	(1,600)
2	500	(1,100)
3	600	(500)
4	800	300
5	500	800

Payback is between the end of Year 3 and the end of Year 4 – in other words during Year 4.

If we assume a constant rate of cash flow through the year, we could estimate that payback will be three years, plus (500/800) of Year 4. This is because the cumulative cash flow is minus 500 at the star of the year and the Year 4 cash flow would be 800.

We could therefore estimate that payback would be after 3.625 years or 3 years 8 months.

ACTIVITY 3

Calculate the payback period in years and months for the following project.

Year	*Cash flow*
	$000
0	(3,100)
1	1,000
2	900
3	800
4	500
5	500

For a suggested answer, see the 'Answers' section at the end of the book.

3.4 MERITS OF PAYBACK METHOD AS AN INVESTMENT APPRAISAL TECHNIQUE

The payback method of investment appraisal has some advantages.

(a) Simplicity

As a concept, it is easily understood and is easily calculated.

(b) Rapidly changing technology

If new plant is likely to be scrapped in a short period because of obsolescence, a quick payback is essential.

(c) Improving investment conditions

When investment conditions are expected to improve in the near future, attention is directed to those projects which will release funds soonest, to take advantage of the improving climate.

(d) Payback favours projects with a quick return

It is often argued that these are to be preferred for three reasons:

(i) Rapid project payback leads to rapid company growth – but in fact such a policy will lead to many profitable investment opportunities being overlooked because their payback period does not happen to be particularly swift.

(ii) Rapid payback minimises risk (the logic being that the shorter the payback period, the less there is that can go wrong). Not all risks are related to time, but payback is able to provide a useful means of assessing time risks (and only time risk). It is likely that earlier cash flows can be estimated with greater certainty.

(iii) Rapid payback maximises liquidity – but liquidity problems are best dealt with separately, through cash forecasting.

3.5 WEAKNESSES OF PAYBACK METHOD

(a) Project returns may be ignored

Cash flows arising after the payback period are totally ignored. Payback ignores profitability and concentrates on cash flows and liquidity.

(b) Timing ignored

Cash flows are effectively categorised as pre-payback or post-payback – but no more accurate measure is made. In particular, the time value of money is ignored.

(c) Lack of objectivity

There is no objective measure (target) as to what length of time should be set as the minimum payback period. Investment decisions are therefore subjective.

Conclusion Payback is best seen as an initial screening tool – for example a business might set a rule that no project with a payback of more than five years is to be considered.

It is an appropriate measure for relatively straightforward projects e.g. those which involve an initial outlay followed by constant long-term receipts.

However in spite of its weaknesses and limitations the payback period is a useful initial screening method of investment appraisal. It is normally used in conjunction with another method of capital investment appraisal, such as the NPV or IRR methods of discounted cash flow analysis.

4 TIME VALUE OF MONEY

Money is invested to earn a profit. For example, if an item of equipment costs $80,000 and would earn cash profits (profits ignoring depreciation) of $20,000 each year for four years, it would not be worth buying. This is because the total profit over four years ($80,000) would only just cover its cost.

Capital investments must make enough profits to justify their costs. In addition, the size of the profits or return must be large enough to make the investment worthwhile. In the example above, if the equipment costing $80,000 made total returns of $82,000 over four years, the total return on the investment would be $2,000, or an average of $500 per year. This would be a very low return on an investment of $80,000. More money could be earned putting the $80,000 on deposit with a bank to earn interest.

If a capital investment is to be justified, it needs to earn at least a minimum amount of profit, so that the return compensates the investor for both the amount invested and also for the *length* of time before the profits are made. For example, if a company could invest $80,000 now to earn revenue of $82,000 in one week's time, a profit of $2,000 in seven days would be a very good return. However, if it takes four years to earn the money, the return would be very low.

Money has a time value. By this we mean that it can be invested to earn interest or profits, so it is better to have $1 now than in one year's time. This is because $1 now can be invested for the next year to earn a return, whereas $1 in one year's time cannot. Another way of looking at the time value of money is to say that $1 in six years' time is worth less than $1 now. Similarly, $1 in five years' time is worth less than $1 now, but is worth more than $1 after six years.

Discounted Cash Flow (DCF) is a capital expenditure appraisal technique that takes into account the time value of money.

In order to understand DCF, you need to be familiar with how interest is earned on investments. The syllabus requires you to know about both simple interest and compound interest, although DCF is based on compound interest arithmetic.

5 INTEREST

A sum of money invested or borrowed is known as the **principal**.

When money is invested it earns interest. Similarly when money is borrowed, interest is payable.

Interest on an investment can be calculated as either simple interest or compound interest.

5.1 SIMPLE INTEREST

With **simple interest**, the interest is payable or recoverable each year but it is not added to the principal. For example, the interest payable (or receivable) on $100 at 15% p.a. for 1, 2 and 3 years will be $15, $30 and $45 respectively.

The usual notation is:

P	=	Principal
r	=	Interest rate % pa
n	=	Time in years
I	=	Interest in $

EXAMPLE

A man invests $160 on 1 January each year. On 31 December simple interest is credited at 12% but this interest is put in a separate account and does not itself earn any interest. Find the total amount standing to his credit on 31 December following his fifth payment of $160.

Year (1 Jan)	*Investment ($)*		*Interest (31 December)*	
1		160	$\frac{12}{100} \times 160 =$	$19.20
2	160 + 160 =	320	$\frac{12}{100} \times 320 =$	$38.40
3	160 + 320 =	480	$\frac{12}{100} \times 480 =$	$57.60
4	160 + 480 =	640	$\frac{12}{100} \times 640 =$	$76.80
5	160 + 640 =	800	$\frac{12}{100} \times 800 =$	$96.00
Total				$288.00

Total investment amount at 31 December, Year 5

= $(800 + 288) (principal plus simple interest)

= $1,088.

5.2 COMPOUND INTEREST

With compound interest, the interest earned is added to the principal before interest is calculated for the next year.

EXAMPLE

$1,000 is invested for four years and interest of 10% is earned each year.

What is the value of the investment at the end of Year 4?

SOLUTION

Principal ($)	*Interest* ($)	*Total amount* ($)
1,000	$\frac{10}{100} \times 1{,}000 = 100$	1,000 + 100 = 1,110
1,100	$\frac{10}{100} \times 1{,}100 = 110$	1,100 + 110 = 1,210
1,210	$\frac{10}{100} \times 1{,}210 = 121$	1,210 + 121 = 1,331
1,331	$\frac{10}{100} \times 1{,}331 = 133.1$	1,331 + 133.1 = 1,464.1

An alternative way of writing this is shown in the following table.

Year	*Principal* ($)		*Total amount* ($)
1	1,000	$1{,}000\,(1 + 0.1) =$	1,100
2	$1{,}000\,(1 + 0.1)$	$1{,}000\,(1 + 0.1)(1 + 0.1) = 1{,}000\,(1 + 0.1)^2 =$	1,210
3	$1{,}000\,(1 + 0.1)^2$	$1{,}000\,(1 + 0.1)^2(1 + 0.1) = 1{,}000\,(1 + 0.1)^3 =$	1,331
4	$1{,}000\,(1 + 0.1)^3$	$1{,}000\,(1 + 0.1)^3(1 + 0.1) = 1{,}000\,(1 + 0.1)^4 =$	1,464.1

So the amount (S) at the end of the *n*th year is given by:

$S = P(1 + r)^n$

where r is the annual interest rate expressed as a proportion or decimal.

(For example 12% is expressed as 0.12 and 4.5% is expressed as 0.045.)

Compound interest is generally given on all savings accounts.

Try to learn this formula.

5.3 NOMINAL AND EFFECTIVE INTEREST RATES

The compounding examples considered so far have all added interest on an annual basis. In reality interest may be paid or charged on a daily, weekly, monthly, quarterly or half yearly basis. The equivalent annual rate of interest, when interest is compounded at intervals other than yearly, is known as the effective annual rate of interest. The annual interest rate quoted before compounding is called the nominal rate of interest.

The effective rate of interest can be calculated using the formula:

$$(1+r)^n - 1$$

where r is the rate of interest for the time period, expressed as a decimal

n is the number of times interest is added in one year.

For example, if interest is added quarterly, then it is added four times in one year and n = 4. If interest is added half yearly, then interest is added twice in one year and n = 2. You will notice that if interest is added annually then the effective rate of interest calculated using the formula is equivalent to the nominal rate of interest.

EXAMPLE

A bank offers savers three accounts

Account 1 – Nominal interest of 10% is added quarterly

Account 2 – Nominal interest of 11% is added half yearly

Account 3 – Nominal interest of 12% is added annually

Which account should savers choose?

SOLUTION

The effective rate of interest should be calculated to enable a comparison of accounts to be made.

Account 1

The nominal rate of interest is 10% per annum. Therefore 2.5% is added each quarter. Compounding this four times gives an effective annual rate of:

$$(1+0.025)^4 \quad 1 = 10.4\%$$

Account 2

The nominal rate of interest is 11% per annum. Therefore 5.5% is added each half year. Compounding this twice gives an effective annual rate of:

$$(1+0.055)^2 \quad 1 = 11.3\%$$

Account 3

As interest is added annually the effective annual rate is the nominal rate of interest i.e. 12%.

Savers should choose Account 3 as this offers the highest effective annual rate of interest.

6 DISCOUNTED CASH FLOW (DCF)

Discounted cash flow, or DCF, is an investment appraisal technique that takes into account both the timing of cash flows and also the total cash flows over a project's life.

- As with the payback method, DCF analysis is based on future cash flows, not accounting profits or losses.
- The timing of cash flows is taken into account by discounting them to a 'present value'. The effect of discounting is to give a higher value to each $1 of cash flows that occur earlier and a lower value to each $1 of cash flows occurring later in the project's life. $1 earned after one year will be worth more than $1 earned after two years, which in turn will be worth more than $1 earned after five years, and so on. Cash flows that occur in different years are re-stated on a common basis, at their present value.

6.1 COMPOUNDING AND DISCOUNTING

To understand discounting, it is helpful to start by looking at the relationship between compounding and discounting.

Discounting is compounding in reverse. It starts with a future amount of cash and converts it into a **present value**.

Definition A **present value** is the amount that would need to be invested now to earn the future cash flow, if the money is invested at the 'cost of capital'.

For example, if a business expects to earn a (compound) rate of return of 10% on its investments, how much would it need to invest now to build up an investment of:

(a) $110,000 after 1 year

(b) $121,000 after 2 years

(c) $133,100 after 3 years?

The answer is $100,000 in each case, and we can calculate it by discounting. The discounting formula to calculate the present value of a future sum of money (S) at the end of n years is:

$$PV = S \frac{1}{1+r^n}$$

This is just a rearrangement of the compound interest formula.

(a) After 1 year, $\$110,000 \times \frac{1}{1.10} = \$100,000$

(b) After 2 years, $\$121,000 \times \frac{1}{1.10^2} = \$100,000$

(c) After 3 years, $\$133,100 \times \frac{1}{1.10^3} = \$100,000$

Both cash inflows and cash payments can be discounted to a present value. By discounting all payments and receipts from a capital investment to a present value, they can be compared on a like-for-like basis.

ACTIVITY 4

Required:

(a) How much would you need to invest now to earn $2,000 after four years at a compound interest rate of 8% a year?

(b) What is the present value of $5,000 receivable at the end of Year 3 at a cost of capital of 7% per annum?

For a suggested answer, see the 'Answers' section at the end of the book.

6.2 DISCOUNT FACTORS AND DISCOUNT TABLES

A present value for a future cash flow is calculated by multiplying the future cash flow by a factor:

$$\frac{1}{1+r^{n}}$$

Check that you know how to do this on your calculator.

For example:

$$\frac{1}{1.10} = 0.909$$

$$\frac{1}{1.10^{2}} = 0.826$$

$$\frac{1}{1.10^{3}} = 0.751$$

However, there are tables that give you a list of these 'discount factors' without you having to do the calculation yourself.

To calculate a present value for a future cash flow, you simply multiply the future cash flow by the appropriate discount factor. (Discount tables are included in the introductory pages to this text, but the relevant factors are also included in some of the examples and activities that follow.)

Any cash flows that take place 'now' (at the start of the project) take place in Year 0. The discount factor for Year 0 is 1.0, regardless of what the cost of capital is. Cash flows 'now' therefore do not need to be discounted to a present value equivalent, because they are already at present value.

ACTIVITY 5

The cash flows for a project have been estimated as follows:

Year	$
0	(25,000)
1	6,000
2	10,000
3	8,000
4	7,000

The cost of capital is 6%. Discount factors at a cost of capital of 6% are:

Year	*Discount factor at 6%*
1	0.943
2	0.890
3	0.840
4	0.792

Convert these cash flows to a present value.

Add up the total of the present values for each of the years.

For a suggested answer, see the 'Answers' section at the end of the book.

6.3 THE COST OF CAPITAL

The cost of capital has used by a business in DCF analysis is the cost of funds for the business. It is therefore the minimum return that the business should make from its own investments, to earn the cash flows out of which it can pay interest or profits to its own providers of funds.

For the purpose of this course, the cost of capital will be given.

7 NET PRESENT VALUE METHOD (NPV)

The **net present value** or **NPV** method of DCF analysis involves calculating a net present value for a proposed investment project. The NPV is the value obtained by discounting all of the cash outflows and inflows for the investment project at the cost of capital, and adding them up. Cash outflows are negative and inflows are positive values. The sum of the present value of all of the cash flows from the project is the 'net' present value amount.

The NPV is the sum of the present value (PV) of all of the cash inflows from a project minus the PV of all of the cash outflows.

- **If the NPV is positive**, it means that the cash inflows from a capital investment will yield a return in excess of the cost of capital. The project should therefore be accepted on a financial basis.

- **If the NPV is negative**, it means that the cash inflows from a capital investment will yield a return below the cost of capital. The project should therefore be rejected on a financial basis.

- **If the NPV is exactly zero**, the cash inflows from a capital investment will yield a return exactly equal to the cost of capital. The project is therefore just acceptable on a financial basis.

EXAMPLE

Rug Limited is considering a capital investment in new equipment. The estimated cash flows are as follows.

Year	*Cash flow*
	$
0	(240,000)
1	80,000
2	120,000
3	70,000
4	40,000
5	20,000

The company's cost of capital is 9%.

Calculate the NPV of the project to assess whether it should be undertaken.

The following are discount factors for a 9% cost of capital.

Year	*Discount factor at 9%*
1	0.917
2	0.842
3	0.772
4	0.708
5	0.650

SOLUTION

Year	*Cash flow*	*Discount factor at 9%*	*Present value*
	$		$
0	(240,000)	1.000	(240,000)
1	80,000	0.917	73,360
2	120,000	0.842	101,040
3	70,000	0.772	54,040
4	40,000	0.708	28,320
5	20,000	0.650	13,000
Net present value			+ 29,760

The PV of cash inflows exceeds the PV of cash outflows by $29,760, which means that the project will earn a DCF return in excess of 9%. It should therefore be undertaken.

ACTIVITY 6

Fylingdales Fabrication is considering investing in a new delivery vehicle which will make savings over the current out-sourced service.

The cost of the vehicle is $35,000 and it will have a five-year life.

The savings it will make over the period are:

Cash flow:

Year	$
1	8,000
2	9,000
3	12,000
4	9,500
5	9,000

The firm currently has a return of 12% and this is considered to be its cost of capital.

Discount factors at 12%.

Year	
1	0.893
2	0.797
3	0.712
4	0.636
5	0.567

Required:

(a) Calculate the NPV of the investment.

(b) On the basis of the NPV you have calculated, recommend whether or not the investment should go ahead.

For a suggested answer, see the 'Answers' section at the end of the book.

7.1 ASSUMPTIONS IN DCF ABOUT THE TIMING OF CASH FLOWS

In DCF, certain assumptions are made about the timing of cash flows in each year of a project.

- A cash outlay at the beginning of an investment project ('now') occurs in Year 0.
- A cash flow that occurs **during the course of a year** is assumed to occur all at once at the end of the year. For example, profits of $30,000 in Year 3 would be assumed to occur at the end of Year 3.
- If a cash flow occurs **at the beginning of a year**, it is assumed that the cash flow happens at the end of the previous year. For example, a cash outlay of $10,000 at the beginning of Year 2 would be treated as a cash flow in Year 1, occurring at the end of Year 1.

8 ANNUITIES AND PERPETUITIES

8.1 ANNUITIES

An annuity is a constant annual cash flow over a number of years. For example, if there is a cash flow of $3,000 from Year 1 to Year 5, this is an annuity.

EXAMPLE

Find the present value of $500 payable for each of three years given a discount rate of 10%. Each sum is due to be paid annually in arrears.

SOLUTION

The PV can be found from three separate calculations of the present value of each annual cash flow.

$$PV = \left[\$500 \times \frac{1}{(1.10)}\right] + \left[\$500 \times \frac{1}{(1.10)^2}\right] + \left[\$500 \times \frac{1}{(1.10)^3}\right]$$

$$= \$454 + \$413 + \$376 = \$1,243$$

However, it might be worth looking again at the expression for the present value and restating it as follows:

$$PV = \$500 \times \left[\frac{1}{(1.10)} + \frac{1}{(1.10)^2} + \frac{1}{(1.10)^3}\right]$$

$$= \$500 \times 2.48685 = \$1,243$$

Annuities formula

For this last expression a formula can be produced (which could be proved although there is no need to do so) for the present value of an annuity. Applying this to the example:

$$PV = A \times \frac{1}{r}\left(1 - \frac{1}{(1+r)^n}\right)$$

where A is the annual cash flow receivable in **arrears**.

$$PV = \$500 \times \frac{1}{0.10}\left(1 - \frac{1}{(1.10)^3}\right)$$

$$= \$500 \times \frac{1}{0.10}(1 - 0.7513148)$$

$$= \$500 \times 2.48685$$

$$= \$1,243$$

Annuities tables

The annuities formula is fairly daunting for non-mathematicians, and it is much more convenient to calculate the present value of an annuity using either a financial calculator, or using discount tables for annuities.

Annuities tables are also called cumulative present value tables. A copy is included in the introductory pages to this text.

To calculate a present value of an annuity, you multiply the annual cash flow by the appropriate annuity factor. The annuity factor is the cumulative present value of $1 per annum for every year from Year 1 up to the year shown in the left hand column of the tables. There is a different set of cumulative discount factors for each cost of capital.

So, to establish the present value of $500 a year for Years 1 to 3, you multiply $500 by the cumulative factor in the annuity tables shown in the 10% column and the Year 3 row. This is 2.487.

The PV of $500 for 3 years at a cost of capital of 10% is therefore $500 × 2.487 = $1,243.

ACTIVITY 7

Lindsay Ltd wishes to make a capital investment of $1.5m but is unsure whether to invest in one of two machines each costing that amount. The net cash inflows from the two projects are shown below.

Time	*1*	*2*	*3*
Dennis plc machine ($000)	900	600	500
Thompson plc machine ($000)	700	700	700

Find the present value of the two patterns of cash flows at the company's required rate of return of 10% and thus decide which of the two identically priced machines (if either) should be acquired.

(Assume all cash flows occur annually in arrears on the anniversary of the initial investment.)

For a suggested answer, see the 'Answers' section at the end of the book.

ACTIVITY 8

A company is considering the purchase of an item of equipment costing $60,000. It would have a five-year life. The equipment would be expected to generate net cash flows of $18,000 each year for the first four years and $6,000 in the fifth year. After the end of Year 5 it would be disposed of for $5,000.

The company's cost of capital is 7%.

Calculate the NPV of this investment and indicate whether or not it would be financially viable.

For a suggested answer, see the 'Answers' section at the end of the book.

8.2 PERPETUITIES

Sometimes it is necessary to calculate the present values of annuities which are expected to continue for an indefinitely long period of time, known as 'perpetuities'.

Definition A **perpetuity** is a constant annual cash flow that will continue 'forever'.

The present value of a perpetuity is quite easy to calculate.

The present value of an annuity, A, receivable in arrears in perpetuity given a discount rate, r, is given as follows:

$$\text{PV perpetuity} = \frac{A}{r} \left(= \frac{\text{Annual cash flow}}{\text{Discount rate (as a decimal)}} \right)$$

EXAMPLE

The present value of \$5,000 receivable annually in arrears at a discount rate of 8% is:

$$\frac{\$5{,}000}{0.08} = \$62{,}500$$

ACTIVITY 9

An investment company is considering whether to purchase an investment that would earn an income of \$25,000 each year in perpetuity. The company would want a return of at least 8% on this investment.

What is the maximum price it should be prepared to pay for the investment?

For a suggested answer, see the 'Answers' section at the end of the book.

9 INTERNAL RATE OF RETURN METHOD (IRR)

Using the NPV method of discounted cash flow, present values are calculated by discounting cash flows at a given cost of capital, and the difference between the PV of costs and the PV of benefits is the NPV. In contrast, the **internal rate of return (IRR)** method of DCF analysis involves calculating the exact DCF rate of return that the project is expected to achieve. This is the discount rate at which the NPV is zero.

If the expected rate of return (known as the internal rate of return or IRR, and also as the DCF yield) is higher than a target rate of return, the project is financially worth undertaking.

Calculating the IRR of a project can be done with a programmed calculator. Otherwise, it has to be estimated using a rather laborious technique called the interpolation method. The interpolation method produces an estimate of the IRR, although it is not arithmetically exact.

The steps in this method are as follows:

Step 1 Calculate two net present values for the project at two different discount rates. You should decide which discount rates to use. However, you want to find discount rates for which the NPV is close to 0, because the IRR will be a value close to them. Ideally, you should use one discount rate where the NPV is positive and the other where the NPV is negative, although this is not essential.

Step 2 Having found two costs of capital where the NPV is close to 0, we can then estimate the cost of capital at which the NPV is 0. In other words, we can estimate the IRR. This estimating technique is illustrated in the example below.

EXAMPLE

A company is trying to decide whether to buy a machine for $13,500. The machine will create annual cash savings as follows:

Year	$
1	5,000
2	8,000
3	3,000

Calculate the project's IRR.

SOLUTION

Step 1 The first step is to calculate the NPV of the project at two different discount rates. Ideally the NPV should be positive at one cost of capital and negative at the other.

So what costs of capital should we try?

One way of making a guess is to look at the cash returns from the project over its life. These are $16,000 over the three years. After deducting the capital expenditure of $13,500, this gives us a net return of $2,500, or an average of $833 each year of the project. $833 is about 6% of the capital outlay. The IRR is actually likely to be a bit higher than this, so we could start by trying 7%, 8% or 9%.

Here, 8% is used.

Year	*Cash flow*	*Discount factor at 8%*	*PV*
	$		$
0	(13,500)	1.000	(13,500)
1	5,000	0.926	4,630
2	8,000	0.857	6,856
3	3,000	0.794	2,382
			+ 368

The NPV is positive at 8%, so the IRR is higher than this. We need to find the NPV at a higher discount rate. Let's try 11%.

Year	*Cash flow*	*Discount factor at 11%*	*PV*
	$		$
0	(13,500)	1.000	(13,500)
1	5,000	0.901	4,505
2	8,000	0.812	6,496
3	3,000	0.731	2,193
			(306)

The NPV is negative at 11%, so the IRR lies somewhere between 8% and 11%.

Step 2 The next step is to use the two NPV figures we have calculated to estimate the IRR.

We know that the NPV is + $368 at 8% and that it is – $306 at 11%.

Between 8% and 11%, the NPV therefore falls by 674 (368 + 306).

If we assume that the decline in NPV occurs in a straight line, we can estimate that the IRR must be:

$$8\% + \left[\frac{368}{674} \times (11-8)\%\right]$$

= 8% + 1.6% = 9.6%.

An estimated IRR is therefore 9.6%.

Note that your estimate will depend on the discount rate chosen for the NPVs. A small variation either side of the suggested answer can be expected.

9.1 ESTIMATING THE IRR USING A GRAPH

The NPVs calculated in the above example could be plotted on a graph and joined by a straight line. The line cuts the x axis where the NPV = 0 i.e. at the IRR.

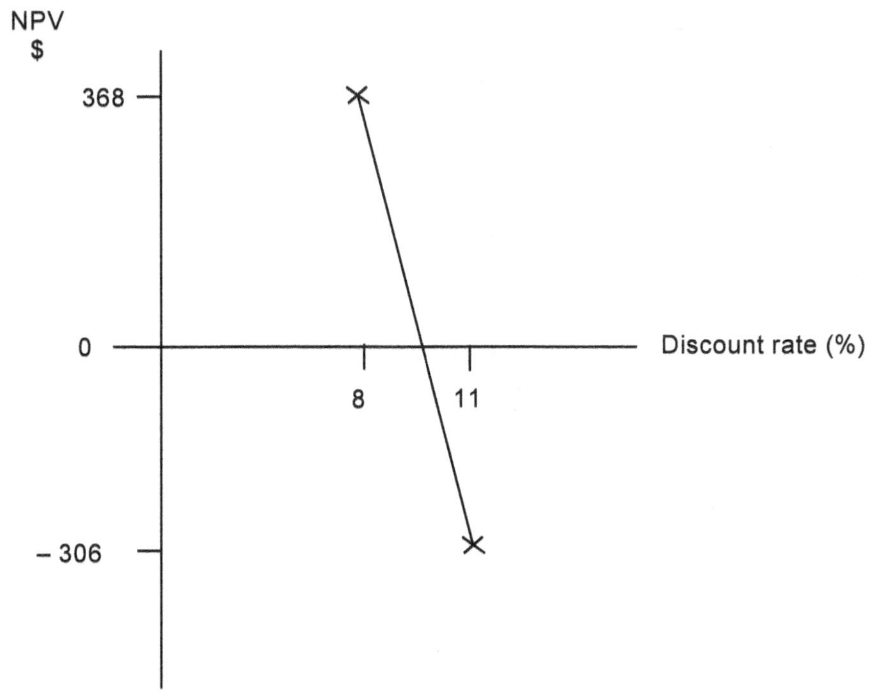

In this example the IRR is between 9 and 10%. In an exam question you might be given a diagram and asked to approximate the IRR. If, say, using the above graph the options were 5%, 10%, 15% or 20%, you would be expected to choose 10% as the closest approximation of the IRR.

The diagram provides an example of interpolation, where a value is estimated which lies within the range of values. If two positive (or negative) NPV values were used to form the relationship and the line extended until it met NPV = 0, this would be extrapolation.

Note: In reality the relationship between NPV and IRR is not linear and the graphical method only gives an approximation to the true IRR. The closer the NPV values are to 0, the better will be the estimate.

9.2 FORMULA FOR CALCULATING IRR

You might find the following formula for calculating the IRR useful.

If the NPV at A% is positive, + \$P

and if the NPV at B% is negative, – \$N

then

$$IRR = A\% \left[\frac{P}{(P+N)} \times (B-A)\% \right]$$

Ignore the minus sign for the negative NPV. For example, if P = + 60 and N = – 50, then P + N = 110.

EXAMPLE

A business undertakes high-risk investments and requires a minimum expected rate of return of 17% on its investments. A proposed capital investment has the following expected cash flows.

Year	$
0	(50,000)
1	18,000
2	25,000
3	20,000
4	10,000

Required:

(a) Calculate the NPV of the project if the cost of capital is 15%.

(b) Calculate the NPV of the project if the cost of capital is 20%.

(c) Use the NPVs you have calculated to estimate the IRR of the project.

(d) Recommend, on financial grounds alone, whether this project should go ahead.

Discount factors:

Year	*Discount factor at*	
	15%	*20%*
1	0.870	0.833
2	0.756	0.694
3	0.658	0.579
4	0.572	0.482

SOLUTION

(a) and (b)

Year	*Cash flow*	*Discount factor at 15%*	*Present value at 15%*	*Discount factor at 20%*	*Present value at 20%*
	$		$		$
0	(50,000)	1.000	(50,000)	1.000	(50,000)
1	18,000	0.870	15,660	0.833	14,994
2	25,000	0.756	18,900	0.694	17,350
3	20,000	0.658	13,160	0.579	11,580
4	10,000	0.572	5,720	0.482	4,820
NPV			+ 3,440		(1,256)

(c) The IRR is above 15% but below 20%.

Using the interpolation method:

The NPV is + 3,440 at 15%.

The NPV is – 1,256 at 20%.

The NPV falls by 4,696 between 15% and 20%.

The estimated IRR is therefore:

$$IRR = 15\% + \left[\frac{3,440}{4,696} \times (20-15)\%\right]$$

$$= 15\% + 3.7\%$$

$$= 18.7\%$$

(d) Recommendation

The project is expected to earn a DCF return in excess of the target rate of 17%, so on financial grounds it is a worthwhile investment.

ACTIVITY 10

A company is considering the purchase of a machine for $100,000. Buying the machine would save the company running costs of $25,000 each year for five years. At the end of this time, the machine could be sold off for $12,000. The company has a cost of capital of 9%.

Required:

(a) Calculate the NPV of the project at the company's cost of capital of 9%.

(b) Calculate the NPV of the project at a cost of capital of 12%.

(c) Use the two NPV figures you have calculated to estimate the IRR of the project.

For a suggested answer, see the 'answers' section at the end of the book.

10 DISCOUNTED PAYBACK METHOD

The discounted payback method of capital investment appraisal is similar to the payback method, except that the payback period is measured with present values of cash flows.

With the simple payback method, the time value of money is ignored. In theory, a project might be acceptable according to the payback method when it has a negative NPV or an IRR lower than the cost of capital.

With discounted payback, the payback period is the time when the project NPV reaches 0. A project can only be acceptable applying a discounted payback rule if it has an NPV of 0 or higher.

Discounted payback is used in the same way as simple payback. An organisation can apply a rule that an investment should not be undertaken unless it achieves discounted payback within a given period of time, say within four years.

10.1 CALCULATING THE DISCOUNTED PAYBACK PERIOD

To calculate the discounted payback period for an investment, you can add an extra column to your table for calculating the NPV. In the column, you can enter the cumulative NPV to date. Discounted payback occurs during the year when the cumulative NPV turns from being negative to being positive.

EXAMPLE

An investment in a new business activity would cost $90,000. The project would have a life of six years, and the estimated cash flows each year would be as follows:

Year	*Cash flow*
	$
1	30,000
2	35,000
3	40,000
4	35,000
5	25,000
6	15,000

The cost of capital is 11%.

The company will not invest in a project unless it has a discounted payback period of four years or less.

Required:

(a) Calculate the approximate discounted payback period, to the nearest month.

(b) On the basis of the information given should the project be undertaken?

SOLUTION

Note: The project's NPV is calculated in the table below, although this is not required for the solution. The cumulative NPV column is filled in up to the point where the NPV turns from being negative to being positive.

Year	*Cash flow*	*Discount factor at 11%*	*Present value of cash flow*	*Cumulative NPV*
	$		$	$
0	(90,000)	1.000	(90,000)	(90,000)
1	30,000	0.901	27,030	(62,970)
2	35,000	0.812	28,420	(34,550)
3	40,000	0.731	29,240	(5,310)
4	35,000	0.659	23,065	17,755
5	25,000	0.593	14,825	
6	15,000	0.535	8,025	
NPV			+ 40,605	

Discounted payback occurs during Year 4.

An approximate estimate of the discounted payback to the nearest month is:

$$3 \text{ years} + \left[\frac{5{,}310}{(5{,}310 + 17{,}755)} \times 12 \text{ months}\right]$$

= 3 years + 2.76 months, say 3 years 3 months. So the project would be acceptable.

11 USING NPV, IRR AND PAYBACK

This chapter has explained several techniques for analysing the financial viability of capital investments. They can be used to provide information to management about whether, on the basis of the financial information available, an investment appears to be worthwhile.

The 'decision rules' applied for each technique are:

- **Simple payback**. Ignoring discounting, the net cash flows from an investment must pay back the original capital outlay within a given period of time. If the investment is not expected to do this, it should not be undertaken.

- **Net present value**. The expected cash flows relating to an investment are discounted at the organisation's cost of capital, and the NPV is the sum of the present values of the investment over its expected life. The project is viable if its NPV is positive ($0 or higher).

- **Internal rate of return**. The IRR is that discount rate at which the NPV is zero. The investment is financially viable if the IRR is higher than the organisation's cost of capital.

- **Discounted payback**. The expected cash flows relating to an investment are discounted at the organisation's cost of capital, and the discounted payback period is the length of time before the cumulative NPV reaches $0. The cumulative NPV must reach $0 within a given period of time. If the investment is not expected to do this, it should not be undertaken.

The preferred method of capital investment appraisal is the NPV method, although the IRR method might be used instead. An organisation is unlikely to use both methods.

Either the simple payback method or the discounted payback method are unlikely to be used on their own. Instead, they are likely to be used, if at all, in addition to NPV or IRR.

It is important to recognise that all of these methods of appraisal use the expected cash flows from a capital investment. These are the relevant costs and revenues from the investment. For decision-making purposes, relevant costs and cash flows should always be used, not figures for accounting profits.

CONCLUSION

Cost and management accounting is a broad subject area, but this text has introduced you to two of its elements: measuring the cost of cost units and providing financial information to assist with management decision making.

You will come across other aspects, notably budgeting and budgetary control, and performance measurement, later in your studies.

KEY TERMS

Payback – the amount of time it is expected to take for the cash inflows from a capital investment project to equal the cash outflows.

Nominal rate of interest – the annual money rate of interest.

Effective rate of interest – the equivalent annual rate of interest when interest is compounded at intervals other than yearly.

Present value – the amount that would need to be invested now to earn the future cash flow, if the money is invested at the 'cost of capital'.

Net present value – the net value of the expected cash flows from an investment, if all the expected cash flows are measured in present values.

Annuity – a constant annual cash flow.

Perpetuity – a constant annual cash flow that will continue 'forever'.

Internal rate of return – the cost of capital at which an investment has an NPV of 0.

Discounted payback – the amount of time it is expected to take for the cumulative NPV of an investment to reach 0.

SELF TEST QUESTIONS

		Paragraph
1	What is the payback period for a project?	3.1
2	What are the merits and disadvantages of using the payback method?	3.4, 3.5
3	What is the time value of money?	4
4	What is the difference between simple interest and compound interest?	5.1, 5.2
5	What is the future value at the end of Year n of an amount P, invested now at an annual compound rate of interest of r (where r is expressed as a decimal)?	5.2
6	What is the formula for calculating the discount factor for year n when the cost of capital (expressed as a proportion) is r?	6.1
7	What is meant by the NPV of a capital investment project?	7
8	What assumptions are used in DCF about the timing of cash flows?	7.1
9	What is an annuity?	8.1
10	What are annuity tables?	8.1
11	What is the present value of an annual cash flow in perpetuity?	8.2
12	What is the IRR of an investment project?	9
13	What formula should be used to estimate an IRR using the interpolation method?	9.2
14	What is the discounted payback period of a capital investment project?	10
15	How are NPV, IRR and payback each used to assess the financial viability of a capital expenditure project?	11

EXAM-STYLE QUESTIONS

1 The cumulative expected NPV of a project is – $6,200 at the end of Year 2 and + $1,100 at the end of Year 3. Assuming that cash flows each year occur at an even rate throughout the year, what is the expected discounted payback period, to the nearest month?

A 2 years 2 months

B 2 years 8 months

C 2 years 10 months

D 3 years 10 months

2 The NPV of a project would be – $53,000 at a discount rate of 14% and + $17,000 at a discount rate of 10%. Using these figures, what is the approximate IRR?

A 10.8%

B 11.0%

C 11.3%

D 13.0%

3 A capital expenditure project would have a negative cash flow in Year 0, followed by positive net cash flows in every other year. Its NPV is + $20,000.

Which of the following statements is correct?

A The discounted payback period is longer than the simple payback period, and the IRR is higher than the company's cost of capital.

B The discounted payback period is shorter than the simple payback period, and the IRR is higher than the company's cost of capital.

C The discounted payback period is longer than the simple payback period, and the IRR is lower than the company's cost of capital.

D The discounted payback period is shorter than the simple payback period, and the IRR is lower than the company's cost of capital.

4 What would be the interest earned (compound) on an investment of $15,000 for three years at an annual interest rate of 6%?

A $1,072

B $1,200

C $2,700

D $2,865

5 X Company takes on a five-year lease of a building for which it pays $27,200 as a lump sum payment. X Company then sub-lets the building for five years at a fixed annual rent, with the rent payable annually in arrears.

What is the annual rental charge, if the rent is set at a level that will earn a DCF yield of 17% for X Company?

Cumulative discount factor at 17%, years 1 – 4 = 2.743

Cumulative discount factor at 17%, years 1 – 5 = 3.199

A $5,440

B $8,502

C $9,916

D $87,013

6 A project has an initial outflow followed by a series of positive inflows. The A project has project has positive NPVs at a cost of capital of 12% and 18%. Which of the following statements will be true of the project's IRR?

A The project's IRR will be lower than 12%

B The project's IRR will be between 12% and 18%

C The project's IRR will be higher than 18%

D The projects IRR exactly 18%

7 A project has an initial outflow followed by a series of positive inflows. The A project has project has a positive NPV at a cost of capital of 14% and a zero NPV at a cost of capital of 22%. Which of the following statements will be true of the project's IRR?

A The project's IRR will be lower than 14%

B The project's IRR will be between 14% and 22%

C The project's IRR will be higher than 22%

D The projects IRR exactly 22%

8 A company is considering an investment of $400,000 in new machinery. The machinery is expected to yield incremental profits over the next five years as follows:

Year	*Profit ($)*
1	175,000
2	225,000
3	340,000
4	165,000
5	125,000

Thereafter, no incremental profits are expected and the machinery will be sold. It is company policy to depreciate machinery on a straight line basis over the life of the asset. The machinery is expected to have a value of $50,000 at the end of year 5.

What is the payback period of the investment in this machinery to the nearest 0.01 years?

A 1.48 years

B 1.53 years

C 2.00 years

D 2.25 years

9 An investment company is considering the purchase of a commercial building at a cost of $0.85m. The property would be rented immediately to tenants at an annual rent of $80,000 payable in arrears in perpetuity.

What is the net present value of the investment assuming that the investment company's cost of capital is 8% per annum?

A $68,000

B $70,000

C $150,000

D $230,000

For the answers to these questions, see the 'Answers' section at the end of the book.

Chapter 16

THE NATURE OF CASH AND CASH FLOWS

Businesses exist to make profit, but they cannot survive without cash. This chapter explains the nature of cash receipts and payments in a business, and considers the importance of cash flow and liquidity. Cash flow is compared with profitability. The elements of cash management are explained, and the relationship between cash management and credit control is introduced. This chapter covers syllabus area E1.

CONTENTS

LEARNING OUTCOMES

At the end of this chapter you should be able to:

- Define cash and cash flow
- Outline the various sources of cash receipts and payments (including regular/exceptional revenue/capital receipts and payments, and drawings)
- Describe the relationship between cash flow accounting and accounting for income and expenditure
- Distinguish between the cash flow pattern of different types of organisations
- Explain the importance of cash flow management and its impact on liquidity and company survival. (**Note:** Calculation of ratios is not required.)

1 THE NATURE OF CASH AND CASH FLOWS

1.1 RELEVANT DEFINITIONS

The first requirement in this syllabus is for you to be able to define cash, cash flows and funds.

Cash can be defined as money, in the form of notes and coins. It is the most liquid of assets and represents the lifeblood for growth and investment. Cash includes:

- coins and notes
- current accounts and short-term deposits
- bank overdrafts and short-term loans
- foreign currency and deposits that can be quickly converted to your currency.

It does **not** include:

- long-term deposits
- long-term borrowing
- money owed by customers
- inventory (inventories).

It is important not to confuse cash with profit. Profit is the difference between the total amount a business earns and all of its costs, usually assessed over a year or other trading period. A business may be able to forecast a good profit for the year, yet still face times when it is strapped for cash.

Cash flow is a term for receipts and payments of cash. Cash flow shows the money **flowing into** a business from sales, interest payments received, and any borrowings and the amount of money **flowing out** of a business through paying for wages, rent, interest owing, paying back loans, buying raw materials, tax and so on.

Cash flow can be described as a cycle: a business uses cash to acquire resources. The resources are put to work and goods and services produced. These are then sold to customers, the business then collects and deposits the cash from the sales and so the cycle repeats.

Net cash flow is the difference between the cash received in a period and the cash paid out in the same period

On any single day, or in any week or month, cash receipts can exceed cash payments, in which case the cash flow is positive. Equally, cash payments can exceed cash receipts, and the cash flow is negative. Over time, a business should expect cash receipts to exceed cash payments, or at least that cash payments should not exceed cash receipts.

Funds can be defined as any arrangement that enables goods or services to be bought. It therefore usually means money (i.e. cash or bank balances) or credit (i.e. lending or borrowing). Every transaction that a business makes can be interpreted in terms of a source of funds and use of funds, which must be equal in total.

Managing cash in a business is basically similar to the management of cash by an individual. An individual might receive cash every month in the form of a salary and pay out money on a variety of expenses, such as food and drink, travel, rent and so on. Some spending is likely to be on credit (using a credit card, perhaps), just as businesses take credit for most of their purchases, but credit card bills have to be paid eventually. Individuals have to make sure that they have enough cash coming in each month to make all the payments that have to be made. An individual might have a bank overdraft facility, but the bank will not let the overdraft exceed the agreed limit.

Businesses have the same concerns. They can buy on credit, but suppliers eventually have to be paid. They can borrow and negotiate an overdraft facility, but there are limits to borrowing. Consequently, cash has to be managed, to make sure that there is always enough money to keep the business going

1.2 WORKING CAPITAL CYCLE

The working capital cycle, in its simplest form, revolves around the company's trading cycle. The process involves purchasing inventory (inventories), converting it to cash or accounts receivable via sales, collecting those accounts receivable, and paying suppliers who extended trade credit.

The working capital cycle is the period of time required for an organisation to receive invested funds back in the form of cash. The working capital cycle is the length of time between the company's outlay on raw materials, wages and other expenditures and the inflow of cash from the sale of goods.

The working capital cycle reflects a firm's investment in working capital as it moves through the production process towards sales. The investment in working capital gradually increases, first being only in raw materials, but then in labour and overheads as production progresses. This investment must be maintained throughout the production process, the holding period for finished goods and up to the final collection of cash from trade receivables. However, the net investment can be reduced by taking trade credit from suppliers.

Calculation of the working capital cycle

For a manufacturing business, the working capital cycle is calculated as:

Raw materials holding period	X
Less: payables' payment period	(X)
WIP holding period	X
Finished goods holding period	X
Receivables' collection period	X
Working capital cycle	X

The cycle may be measured in days, weeks or months and it is advisable, when answering an exam question, to use the measure used in the question.

For a wholesale or retail business, there will be no raw materials or WIP holding periods, and the cycle simplifies to:

Inventory holding period	X
Less: payables' payment period	(X)
Receivables' collection period	X
Working capital cycle	X

EXAMPLE

A company has provided the following information:

Receivables collection period	56 days
Raw material inventory holding period	21 days
Production period (WIP)	14 days
Suppliers' payment period	42 days
Finished goods holding period	28 days

Calculate the length of the working capital cycle

SOLUTION

	Days
Raw materials inventory holding period	21
Less: suppliers' payment period	(42)
WIP holding period	14
Finished goods holding period	28
Receivables' collection period	56
Working capital cycle (days)	77

The cycle could then be compared to previous years, targets or industry averages in order to determine whether the organisation has working capital problems. Working capital problems will almost inevitably results in cash flow problems. Using information for comparison is explored in a later chapter.

2 THE SOURCES AND APPLICATIONS OF FINANCE

2.1 SOURCES AND USES OF CASH

Sources and uses of cash cover three activities in an enterprise:

1 **Operating activities** are activities that create revenue or expense in the entity's major line of business. The largest cash inflow from operations is the collection of cash from customers. Operating activities that create cash outflows include payments to suppliers, payments to employees, interest payments, payment of income taxes and other operating cash payments.

2 **Investing activities** include lending money and collecting on those loans, buying and selling productive assets that are expected to generate revenues over long periods, and buying and selling securities not classified as cash equivalents. Cash inflows generated by investing activities include sales of long-lived assets such as property, plant and equipment, sales of debt or equity instruments and the collection of loans.

3 **Financing activities** include borrowing and repaying money from payables (payables), obtaining resources from owners and providing both a return on their investment and a return of their investment. The return on investment is provided in the form of dividends.

Sources of cash	Uses of cash
Obtaining finance: • Increase in long-term debt • Increase in equity • Increase in current liabilities Selling assets • Decrease in current assets • Decrease in fixed assets (non-current assets)	Paying payables or inventories holders: • Decrease in long-term debt • Decrease in equity • Decrease in current liabilities Buying assets • Increase in current assets • Increase in fixed assets (non-current assets)

Fixed assets (which are also known as non-current assets), as you know, are assets that are used by the business on a continuing basis. Current assets are items which are either cash already or which the business intends to turn into cash. Current liabilities are debts that the business has to pay in the near future – which we take to mean debts due for payment within the next year.

Working capital is the net difference between current assets and current liabilities. This is the only money in the business, which is not either tied up in non-current assets or needed for paying payables.

2.2 MAIN TYPES OF CASH RECEIPTS AND PAYMENTS

The cash receipts for a business come from a variety of sources, and there are various reasons for making cash payments. Cash receipts and payments can be categorised into the following types:

- revenue receipts and payments
- capital receipts and payments
- drawings/dividends and disbursements
- exceptional receipts and payments.

All of these types of cash receipt and payment affect the cash flows of a business, and cash management involves making sure that the total amount of cash received from these sources is always enough to make all the necessary cash payments.

Revenue receipts and payments are cash receipts and payments arising from the normal course of business. Revenue receipts are cash receipts from:

- cash sales, and
- payments by trade receivables.

Revenue payments are payments in the normal course of business, and include payments:

- to trade payables
- to employees for salaries and wages (and to the tax authorities for income tax deductions)
- for business expenses such as office rental payments, telephone bills, payments out of petty cash, and so on.

Capital receipts are receipts of long-term funds or cash from the sale of non-current assets or long-term investments. The owners of a business put new capital into the business in the form of new cash. For example, the shareholders in a company might agree to put more cash into the business by subscribing for a new issue of shares. Similarly, a sole trader might decide to put some extra money into the business by transferring cash from his personal bank account to his business bank account.

Capital payments are payments for capital expenditure, such as the purchase of new non-current assets (equipment, motor vehicles and so on).

Occasionally, a business might raise new cash by obtaining a long-term loan. A loan from a bank is a liability, but long-term (non-current) liabilities can be thought of as a 'capital receipt'. Similarly, the repayment of a loan might be thought of as a 'capital payment'.

Drawings/dividends

When a business makes profits, it usually pays out some of those profits to its owners.

- Payments out of profits to a sole trader or partners in a partnership are known as drawings.
- Payments out of profits to the shareholders of a company are known as dividends. Dividends are not normally paid more than twice per year.

Businesses can pay drawings or dividends whenever they want to.

Exceptional receipts and payments

The foregoing are all relatively routine transactions. They are known and they can be planned for. There is always the possibility that there will be a significant movement because of an unusual or 'exceptional' transaction that does not fall into any of the categories described above. An example would be the costs of closing down part of a business.

2.3 CASH FLOW PATTERNS IN DIFFERENT BUSINESSES

The 'dynamics' or patterns of revenue receipts and payments varies greatly between different types of business. Many businesses have regular expenditure patterns, such as constant monthly salary costs and regular monthly accommodation costs. However, patterns of cash receipts vary enormously, as the following examples might suggest.

- A retail business with a chain of shops or stores buys goods for resale, often obtaining credit of 30 to 60 days from suppliers. It might hope to re-sell many of the items fairly quickly, typically for cash. As we have already noted, many retail businesses are therefore able to receive cash from selling their goods even before they have had to pay their suppliers. Cash receipts are also daily, or at least every day that the shops are open.

- A hat manufacturer has a seasonal business, with most sales in the spring and early summer. Its sales are likely to be on credit to retailers and other distributors, on 30 to 60 days' credit. It produces hats continually throughout the year, so has fairly constant monthly cash expenditures.

- A large contracting business might have to spend a lot of cash in bidding to win a large construction contract. Some companies, for example, have spent several years in bidding for government contracts to build schools, hospitals or roads. If they win a new contract, they are likely to have to spend heavily on hiring labour and buying or renting equipment. Cash receipts from the customer are likely to be in the form of progress payments, which are usually occasional large amounts.

- A training college or university is likely to receive most of its income at the start of its courses, mainly at the beginning of the academic year. Its costs and cash expenditures occur over the duration of the course. It should therefore expect a large cash surplus at the start of the academic year, which then gradually reduces as the year progresses.

You might be aware of other businesses with different cash flow patterns to these.

Seasonality

Another factor to consider in the pattern of cash flow in a business is the impact of seasonality. The timing of receipts and payments may be affected by particularly low or high 'seasons' in a business. For example, a company who sells toys to children, may find that there are greater sales in the final few months of the calendar year than there are on the first few months of the year. Therefore, at the end of the calendar year, cash and receivables are likely to be high and inventories low. Whereas, a few months later receivables are likely to be much lower and inventory levels beginning to rise. It means that large cash surpluses could be available at the start of each year that slowly get reduced as the year goes on and inventory is built up in preparation for the year end's busy period.

3 CASH FLOW AND PROFIT

For a business to survive, over the longer term it has to be profitable. In the short term, however, cash flow is more important than profit. If a business cannot make an essential payment, it could be faced with insolvency and payables could take action to recover the money owing to them. In the short term:

- a business can make a loss but still have enough cash to survive, receiving more cash than it pays
- a business can be profitable but run out of cash, spending more cash than it receives.

In the short term, profits and cash flow are different. There are several reasons for this.

- Some items of cash spending and cash receipt do not affect profits at all. In particular capital receipts and capital payments do not affect profits. A business could earn a profit but spend large sums of money on capital expenditure, so that it makes a profit but has a negative cash flow.
- Profits are calculated after deducting depreciation charges on non-current assets. Depreciation is a notional charge, and does not affect cash flow at all. It is an accounting device for spreading the cost of a non-current asset over its useful life.
- Cash flow is affected by the need to invest in operational working capital. Operational working capital is defined as the working capital a business needs to carry on its day-to-day business operations. It consists of its inventory (inventories) plus its trade receivables minus its trade payables.

Investing in working capital affects cash flow, and when the total amount of working capital of a business changes, the profits earned in the period will differ from the operational cash flows. It might not seem obvious why this should be the case.

- **Inventory (inventories).** A business buys raw materials or supplies and uses these to manufacture goods or provide services. Materials and supplies are bought before goods can be produced or services can be provided, which means that a business has to pay for its inventory before it earns anything from sales.
- **Receivables (receivables).** When businesses sell goods or services on credit, they make a profit when the sale occurs, but they do not get any cash receipts until the customer pays. A business therefore incurs the costs of making a sale, and spends cash in advance of receiving the cash income.
- **Payables (payables).** On the other hand, if a business buys goods and services on credit, it benefits by not having to pay for them until sometime after they have been received.

We can compare the gross profit from trading with the operating cash flows from trading in a company that buys and resells goods.

The statement of profit or loss reports the total value of sales and the cost of goods sold in a year and shows:

Sales revenue – Cost of sales = Profit

However, if goods are sold on credit the cash receipts will differ from the value of sales, as receivables will pay after the year-end. The cost of goods sold will also differ as some goods are purchased on credit and some may remain in inventory at the year-end.

The operational cash flow is reported as cash in (Sales + Opening receivables – Closing receivables) – Cash out (Purchases + Opening payables – Closing payables).

ACTIVITY 1

Calculate the operational cash inflow from sales resulting from these trading figures:

Sales revenue	$240,000
Receivables at start of year	$18,000
Receivables at end of year	$28,800

For a suggested answer, see the 'Answers' section at the end of the book.

3.1 CASH FLOW AND BUSINESS SURVIVAL

In the short run, a loss-making business can survive, provided that it has enough cash or access to new borrowings. A profitable business might not survive if it has negative cash flows, unless it has enough cash in the bank to cover the deficit or unless it has access to new borrowings. In the past, there have been many examples of apparently successful businesses collapsing because they ran out of cash.

3.2 LIQUIDITY

Liquid assets consist of both cash and items that could or will be converted into cash within a short time, with little or no loss. They include some investments, for example:

- deposits with banks or building societies where a minimum notice period for withdrawal is required
- investments in government securities, which in the UK are called gilt-edged inventories (or 'gilts').

Other liquid assets are trade receivables and, possibly, inventory.

- Trade receivables should be expected to pay what they owe within a fairly short time, so receivables are often considered a liquid asset for a business.
- In some businesses, such as retailing, inventory will be used or re-sold within a short time, to create sales for the business and cash income. Inventory is less liquid than receivables.

A business has liquidity if it has access to enough liquid assets to meet its essential payment obligations when they fall due. This means that a business is extremely liquid if it has a large amount of cash, plus investments in gilts and funds in notice accounts with a building society, plus a large amount of trade receivables and inventory.

Liquidity is also boosted if a business has an unused overdraft facility, so that it could go into overdraft with its bank if it needed to.

A business that has good liquidity is unlikely to have serious cash flow problems. For all businesses, it is important to make revenue payments when they fall due. Trade payables and employees should all be paid on time. When a liquid business has to make a cash payment, it should be able to obtain the money from somewhere to do it. Normally, the cash to pay suppliers and employees comes from the cash received from trade receivables.

The liquidity of a business, particularly its operational activities, is therefore related to its working capital, and in particular its inventory, receivables and short-term payables.

ACTIVITY 2

What separates cash from profits?

Explain why lots of sales might not mean lots of cash.

For a suggested answer, see the 'Answers' section at the end of the book.

4 CASH ACCOUNTING AND ACCRUALS ACCOUNTING

For accounting purposes, in preparing an statement of profit or loss there are two possible systems that can be used:

- Cash accounting
- Accruals accounting

These systems will provide different profit figures for the basis based on different assumptions about how revenues and costs are recorded in the statement of profit or loss.

In a system of accruals accounting, revenues and costs are reported in the period where the sale occurs, even if the cash flows for the sale and costs of sale occur in different periods, whereas a system of cash accounting records cash payments and cash receipts as they occur within an accounting period.

4.1 CASH ACCOUNTING

Cash accounting is an accounting method where receipts are recorded during the period they are received, and the expenses in the period in which they are actually paid. Basically, when the cash is received for a sale, it is recorded in the accounting books as a sale. It's focus is on determining the operational cash flow for the year.

However, cash accounting is not generally accepted as good accounting practice because businesses enter into transactions that are legally enforceable prior to the exchange of cash, but the use of cash accounting does not reflect any transactions which have taken place but are not yet paid for.

Although cash accounting is not used for measuring profitability, cash flow management is a vital aspect of business. Businesses should:

- forecast what their cash flows are likely to be in the future, so that they can take measures to ensure that they will have enough cash/liquidity. Cash flow forecasts might be prepared as cash budgets

- monitor actual cash flows, to make sure that these are in line with expectation (for example, by comparing them with the cash budget) and that the business still has enough cash to meet its requirements.

4.2 ACCRUALS ACCOUNTING

Accruals accounting applies the accruals concept to transactions. Its focus is on calculating the accounting profit for the year.

Definition The **accruals concept** in accounting has been defined as follows. 'Revenues and costs are accrued (that is, recognised as they are earned or incurred, not as money is received or paid), matched with one another so far as their relationship can be established or justifiably assumed, and dealt with in the statement of profit or loss of the period to which they relate.'

Revenues are included in the period in which the sale takes place rather than when cash is received. It is therefore appropriate to 'match' the costs or expenses incurred in generating this income in the same period.

For example, a business has received $50,000 in cash sales during the year. It has spent $40,000 in cash on expenses. It has receivables owing $10,000 at 30 June. It owes suppliers $7,000 for goods and services received. On a cash accounting basis, the net profit of the business would be $10,000 (i.e. $50,000 less $40,000). On an accruals accounting basis, the net profit would be $13,000 (i.e. $50,000 + $10,000 – $40,000 – $7,000).

Accruals accounting is recognised by law, and businesses are required to use it to measure their profitability for the purpose of **external** financial reporting.

The accruals concept is extended to the expenses in the statement of profit or loss and this can mean taking account of what are referred to as accruals and prepayments.

Accruals – it may be that an expense has been incurred within an accounting period, for which an invoice may or may not have been received. Such charges must be matched to the accounting period to which they relate and therefore an estimate of the cost (an accrual) must be made and included as an accounting adjustment in the accounts for that period.

Prepayment – it may be that an expense has been incurred within an accounting period that related to future period(s). As with accruals, these costs are not necessarily related to sales and cannot be matched with sales. Such charges must also be matched to the period to which they relate and therefore the proportion of the charges that relate to future periods (a prepayment) must be calculated and included as an adjustment in the accounts for that period.

For example, let's say that a business has received rent bills for the year totalling $20,000 but has only paid $16,000. In accruals accounting, the $16,000 paid would be included as an expense in the statement of profit or loss, but there would also be an accrual adjustment that increased this expense by $4,000 in order to show a total rent charge for the year in the statement of profit or loss of $20,000.

4.3 THE IMPACT OF USING ACCRUALS ACCOUNTING

The impact of accruals accounting is that the profit figure given in a company's statement of profit or loss can be very different to the change in cash for the year. It may actually disguise potential cash flow problems. Section 3 has already examined this issue and the problems that it might create for businesses.

For this reason, many businesses will prepare a cash flow statement alongside their statement of profit or loss so that users of the external accounts get a better picture of the company's cash position and its changes over the year.

CONCLUSION

This chapter provided an introduction to cash and credit management. We also discussed the types of cash flow and their different patterns. Some cash flows will be regular, but others will be less frequent, or unpredictable, and these can be a major influence on an enterprise's cash position.

Cash management is absolutely crucial to the smooth running of the company, and possibly even to its survival. A key to successful cash management is accurate cash forecasting and cash budgeting. This is described in the next chapter.

KEY TERMS

Cash flow – receipts and payments of cash.

Revenue receipts – cash receipts from cash sales and payments by credit customers.

Revenue payments – payments for operating expenses incurred in the normal course of business (payments to suppliers, employees and so on).

Capital receipts – receipts of cash as new long-term finance or from the sale of non-current assets or long-term investments.

Capital payments – cash payments for the purchase of non-current (fixed) assets and other long-term investments.

Liquid assets – cash and other assets that can be cashed easily (short-term investments) or will turn into cash fairly soon (e.g. receivables).

Liquidity – liquid assets and access to new sources of short-term finance (e.g. overdraft facility).

SELF-TEST QUESTIONS

		Paragraph
1	Define cash flow.	1.1
2	What are the main types of cash flow for a business?	2.2
3	State some of the reasons why the profit in a period is different from the net cash flow.	3
4	What are liquid assets?	3.2
5	Define liquidity.	3.2
6	Explain 'cash accounting'.	4
7	Explain 'accruals accounting'.	4.1

EXAM STYLE QUESTIONS

1 Which of the following businesses is likely to have the longest working capital cycle?

A A large supermarket chain

B A band organising a gig in a nightclub in one week's time

C A college selling courses and materials to government funded students

D A company manufacturing ships

2 Select from the following list the items that relate to an organisation obtaining finance:

- Increases in long-term debt
- Increasing trade receivables
- Increases in equity
- Purchasing inventory
- Increasing current liabilities

3 Which of the following items would adversely affect a company's profit but not affect its cash flow?

A A tax charge

B Interest paid on a bank loan

C Depreciation of a non-current asset

D Repayment of a loan

4 Which of the following items would adversely affect a company's cash flow but not affect its profit?

A Purchase of inventory on credit

B Payment to a supplier for goods supplied on credit

C The writing off of an amount owed by a customer that refuses to pay

D Payment of a directors' bonus in cash

5 Which of the following items would be classed as a revenue receipt by a business?

A The sale of unnecessary inventory at below its initial cost

B An investment of funds from the shareholders

C Receipt of a loan repayment from a lendee

D The sale of a non-current assets

6 A company has provided the following information:

Receivables collection period	2 months
Raw material inventory holding period	1 months
Production period (WIP)	1 months
Suppliers' payment period	1 months
Finished goods holding period	2 months

What was the length of the working capital cycle?

____ months

For the answers to these questions, see the 'Answers' section at the end of the book.

Chapter 17

CASH MANAGEMENT, INVESTING AND FINANCE

A business should manage its cash balances and ensure that it has adequate liquidity. In this chapter we consider how companies can optimise their cash positions by using a specialised treasury department. If the firm has surplus cash for its day-to-day needs, it should perhaps think about investing it. This means understanding the nature of the money markets, and the various opportunities that exist for investing the cash for the short term. On the other hand, when the firm is experiencing a deficit it needs to consider how bank finance might alleviate this position. This chapter covers syllabus areas E2 and E4.

CONTENTS

LEARNING OUTCOMES

At the end of this chapter you should be able to:

- Outline the basic treasury functions
- Describe cash handling procedures
- Outline guidelines and legislation in relation to the management of cash balances in public sector organisations
- Describe how trends in the economic and financial environment can affect management of cash balances

- Explain how surplus cash and cash deficit may arise
- Explain the following types of short term investments and the associated risks/returns
  - bank deposits
  - money- market deposits
  - certificates of deposit
  - government stock
  - local authority stock
- Explain different ways of raising finance from a bank and the basic terms and conditions associated with each financing

1 TREASURY MANAGEMENT

Treasury management covers activities concerned with **managing the liquidity of a business**, the importance of which to the survival and growth of a business cannot be over-emphasised

The term 'treasurer', and therefore 'treasury department', is an old one that has been resurrected in a modern context. It essentially covers the following activities:

- banking and exchange
- cash and currency management (including foreign currency)
- investment in short-term assets
- raising finance.

Although the treasury function is not usually responsible for credit control and collecting debts, it should work closely with the credit control function.

1.1 WHY HAVE A TREASURY DEPARTMENT?

The functions carried out by the treasurer have always existed, but have been absorbed historically within other finance functions. A number of reasons may be identified for the modern development of separate treasury departments:

- Size and internationalisation of companies. These factors add to both the scale and the complexity of the treasury functions.
- Size and internationalisation of currency, debt and security markets. These make the operations of raising finance, handling transactions in multiple currencies and investing much more complex. They also present opportunities for greater gains.
- Sophistication of business practice. This process has been aided by modern communications, and as a result the treasurer is expected to take advantage of opportunities for making profits or minimising costs, which did not exist a few years ago.

For these reasons, most large international corporations have moved towards setting up a separate treasury department.

1.2 TREASURY RESPONSIBILITIES

Treasury departments are not large, since they are not involved in the detailed recording of transactions. The treasurer will typically be responsible for cash management, overseeing bank relationships, including bank borrowing (short and long term), liquidity management, foreign exchange, risk management, corporate finance, and the management of pension assets.

He or she will generally:

- report to the finance director (financial manager), with a specific emphasis on borrowing and cash and currency management
- have a direct input into the finance director's management of debt capacity, debt and equity structure, resource allocation, equity strategy and currency strategy
- be involved in investment appraisal, and the finance director will often consult the treasurer in matters relating to the review of acquisitions and divestments, dividend policy and defence from takeover.

2 PROCEDURES, AUTHORISATION AND SECURITY

2.1 AUTHORISATION LIMITS FOR INVESTING

Cash management is a day-to-day concern, and decisions about whether to invest surplus cash have to be taken quickly. Similarly, it might be necessary to decide quickly to cash in existing investments in order to raise cash to meet an unexpected cash shortage.

Decisions about investing and cashing in investments therefore cannot be taken easily by senior management, and the task is likely to be delegated to an authorised individual. This individual is likely to be someone in the accounts section or, in larger companies, in the treasury section.

However, this individual should be given a limit to the total amount he or she can invest without approval by senior management, and to the amount that he or she can invest in a particular form of security. For example, a company might allow a designated individual in the accounts department to invest surplus cash of up to $250,000, but set limits so that no more than $100,000 should be invested in Certificates of Deposit and no more than $100,000 in government securities.

If the cash available for investment goes above an individual's authorised limit, he or she must notify the appropriate person (e.g. a supervisor) and ask for instructions.

2.2 INVESTMENT GUIDELINES

Organisations might have guidelines for their cash managers about how any surplus cash should be invested. For example, a company might have a rule that all surplus cash should be held in bank deposit accounts and available for immediate withdrawal without notice. Alternatively, a company might have a stated policy of investing surplus cash in short-dated gilts.

In public sector organisations, investment guidelines are likely to be very strict. This is because any surplus cash is 'public money', and a public organisation should not be exposed to the risk of large investment losses. Such organisations are therefore likely to specify how any surplus cash should be used.

The following investment guidelines applied in a UK local borough council have been published on the Internet. They provide a useful example of what the nature of investment guidelines can be.

1 **Maturity and liquidity parameters**

Minimum of 50% of the investment portfolio should have a maturity of one year or less.

The maximum average maturity of the total portfolio should be three years.

All investments with over three months to maturity must be in negotiable instruments (i.e. investments that can be sold if required).

The maturity of any one investment in the portfolio must not exceed 10 years.

2 All investments must be in sterling-denominated instruments.

3 All investments must be made through banks or building societies that are on an approved list.

4 The amount invested through/with any individual bank or building society must not exceed 25% of the total value of the investment portfolio.

5 Investments must have a credit rating of no less than a certain grade. (The minimum credit rating is specified, and the authority requires all investments to have a high 'investment grade' credit rating.

6 The total value of gilts and corporate bonds in the portfolio must not exceed 50% of the value of the portfolio.

7 The maximum that can be invested with any individual borrower, with the exception of the UK government, is 10% of the value of the portfolio.

8 The investment guidelines end with a list of the types of securities that can be purchased for the portfolio. They include government securities (Treasury bills and gilts), local authority bills and bonds, bank bills, sterling CDs, commercial paper and corporate bonds.

Local authorities regularly invest short-term because they raise a large part of their taxes early in the year, and hold the money until it is needed for spending.

2.3 LEGAL RESTRICTIONS ON LOCAL AUTHORITIES

Various rules affect the ways that public sector organisations can handle cash and invest any surplus funds they have.

- Section 43 of the Local Government and Housing Act 1989 empowers councils to borrow money.

- Under Section 111 of the Local Government Act 1972, local authorities also have the power to lend surplus funds to facilitate the discharge of their functions.

- The Local Government Act 2003, and subsequent regulations, introduced a new 'prudential' framework that governs the capital financing and treasury management arrangements of local authorities. This framework replaced the previous rules whereby local authorities could only borrow to finance capital expenditure if given approval by the Government through the credit approval system.

  The implicit policy objective of the current regime is to encourage authorities to place their funds in forms of deposit that are relatively safe and quickly accessible. The underlying idea is that authorities should normally keep only the funds needed in the reasonably near future for their expenditure programmes and that in the meantime they should not take undue risks with the public money they hold in trust.

  The regulations do not prohibit any forms of investment. However, non-approved investments must be charged in-year when made and, when realised, up to 75% of the proceeds have to be set aside as provision for credit liabilities (PCL). This is a powerful incentive to use only the listed options, which are:

  - UK clearing banks and wholly owned subsidiaries where the repayment is guaranteed by a parent bank with the appropriate ratings

  - building societies

  - non-UK deposit taking banks:

    (i) local authorities

    (ii) gilts

    (iii) Euro-Sterling bonds permitted by the Regulations

    (iv) Public Works Loans Board/Government.

  - In accordance with the Code of Practice for Treasury Management in the Public Services and recent guidance from the Office of the Deputy Prime Minister (ODPM), the annual Treasury Management and Investment Strategy has to be approved by the full Council.

2.4 CASH HANDLING PROCEDURES

Management is responsible for ensuring that cash, cheques, credit and debit card receipts are safeguarded against loss or theft, promptly deposited into the enterprise's bank account, and accurately recorded in the accounts. To fulfil this responsibility each unit receiving cash and equivalent should develop appropriate procedures that reflect the unit's size, complexity and method of operation.

There are four critical areas:

1 Accountability

2 Segregation of duties

3 Physical security

4 Reconciliation.

Accountability – this requires the person to have the authority to carry out the task. Any person who has delegated a task to someone remains accountable for ensuring the task is properly performed. Tasks can be delegated to someone only if that individual:

- possesses the appropriate knowledge and technical skill
- is actively involved in the task being performed.

Segregation of duties – the essence of the segregation of duties is that no one is to be put in a position in which they are able to both commit and conceal an error or fraud. Staff duties should be developed so that cash receipt and initial recording is assigned to one individual and reconciling duties are assigned to another. Cash handling work must be subject to daily review. Functions that need to be separated include:

- record keeping – creating and maintaining department records
- authorisation – review and approval of transactions
- asset custody – access to and/or control of physical assets, i.e. cash, cheques
- reconciliation – assurance that transactions are properly recorded.

These functions are *separated* when a different employee performs each of these four major functions. Often these duties are performed by different levels of personnel.

Physical security is assurance that the safety of people and assets (specifically cash) is maintained and controlled. It is effective when:

- assets are properly stored
- shortages/excesses are reported
- keys are secured
- cash counting is not visible
- safe combinations are changed
- background checks on personnel are performed.

Equipment and forms used should be appropriate for the amount of cash handled by the department and the number of individuals handling the cash. This applies to equipment used for both recording cash transactions and safeguarding cash (safes and lock boxes).

Reconciliation requires assurance that transactions are properly documented and approved and competent and knowledgeable individuals are involved. A reconciliation is performed to verify the processing and recording of transactions.

Documentation

Another important area is documentation. Current documentation of procedures should be maintained, regularly reviewed and updated. This should include a description of the responsibilities of staff and supervisors; operating instructions for equipment used in the cash handling process; and clear rules about who should have the authority to perform certain actions. For example, there should be rules about:

(i) Opening new bank accounts. Who is authorised to open a new account, and who should be the authorised signatories for the account? Who is authorised to specify what payments should be made into the account?

(ii) Borrowing. Who is authorised to negotiate new borrowing arrangements with banks, and up to what borrowing limits?

(iii) Who is authorised to invest surplus cash, and up to what investment limits?

(iv) Holding cash in the office. Who has the keys for the safe? Who has the duplicate keys for the safe?

(v) Existing bank accounts. Who are the authorised signatories? Are two signatories needed for payments above a certain amount?

(vi) Authorising payments. Who authorises purchase invoices and who decides when payments should be made?

3 SURPLUS FUNDS

3.1 WHAT IS MEANT BY SURPLUS FUNDS?

So far, cash management has been described in the context of ensuring that a business has sufficient cash and funding for its needs. Another aspect of cash management/treasury management is making use of cash surpluses that might arise from time to time.

Surplus funds comprise liquid balances held by a business, which are neither needed to finance current business operations nor held permanently for short-term investment.

Surplus funds can fall into two categories:

1 Long-term surpluses. Permanent cash surpluses and long-term cash surpluses are rare. These are cash surpluses that a business has no foreseeable use for. When they arise, the business is likely to repay liabilities or pay out the money to its owners in the form of dividends or drawings.

2 Short-term surpluses that need to be invested temporarily (perhaps in short-term securities or deposit accounts) until they are required.

The availability of surplus cash is temporary, awaiting employment either in existing operations or in new investment opportunities (whether already identified or not). The 'temporary' period can be of any duration from one day to the indefinite future date at which the new investment opportunity may be identified and seized. The business will need its cash at some future time in the not-too-distant future, but for a short time, perhaps several months, the business has more cash than it needs.

Cash surpluses should be used, and should not be left in a current bank account earning no interest. The cash might be transferred to a deposit account that does pay interest, or it might be invested in 'financial securities' such as government bonds (in the UK, gilt-edged securities or gilts). When cash surpluses are large, the interest income from investing the money can be quite large, adding to cash flow and profit.

3.2 HOW SURPLUS FUNDS MAY ARISE

Short-term surplus funds arise due to timing differences between the receipt of revenue and payment of expenditures i.e., a temporary surplus of cash inflows over cash outflows. This can be due to:

- unexpectedly large amounts of cash that have been generated from operations; this could be higher income from sales due to an increase in sales revenue
- lower costs maybe because of improved productivity or a cost-cutting exercise
- improvements in working capital management
- sales of non-current assets
- seasonal factors – surpluses generated in good months are used to cover shortfalls later.

4 INVESTING CASH SURPLUSES

When a business forecasts that it will have surplus funds, it should consider how to make the most profitable use of the cash surplus, without risking the liquidity of the business.

If a cash surplus is expected to be permanent, this means that it has no use for the cash and so there is no reason to keep it. The most appropriate decision is probably to pay the money back to the business owners.

If a cash surplus is expected to be temporary, the business should use the surplus to obtain additional income, but without exposing itself to unacceptable risk of losses.

The amount of surplus cash to invest, and the length of time for investing it, should be guided by the cash budget or cash forecast. The main points to remember are that:

- cash in a current bank account earns no interest and so should be kept to a minimum
- but at the same time, a business must have adequate liquidity, and it might therefore be prudent to keep some cash in the current account to meet unforeseen demands for payment.

5 TYPES OF INVESTMENT

A wide (and expanding) number of short-term investment opportunities are available offering various degrees of liquidity, risk and return. They include:

Deposits

These are available for various maturity dates and offer varying returns. Interest rates are normally variable. Examples:

- **Money market deposits** for periods of overnight upwards to six months or, occasionally, a year. Usually a minimum of $10,000 is required.
- **Bank deposits** are similar to personal deposit accounts, with seven days' notice required for withdrawal. Interest penalties are usually levied for faster withdrawal.
- **Local authority deposits** with various maturities available; often the stocks are negotiable.
- **Sterling certificates of deposit** are certificates issued by a bank when funds are deposited. The certificates may be sold to a third party, being fully negotiable instruments, and this makes the deposits highly marketable.

Loan stocks and equities

- **Loan stocks** are issued by governments (UK and foreign) and companies. Maturities, risks and returns vary. Many of these are explored in more detail in section 6.
- **Equities** are probably the riskiest short-term investment opportunities for the following reasons:
  - Dividends are not mandatory. A company can choose not to pay dividends if it wishes (for example it may hold cash back to fund new projects, or it may have had a difficult year and be unable to pay a dividend). The investment therefore not pay any return in a period. This is different from deposit accounts or loan stocks where there is a legal requirement to meet interest payments.
  - The capital value of the equities can vary wildly and are affected by uncontrollable factors such as changes in interest rates, economic cycles, market confidence and company performance. This further adds to the risk of equities.
  - There is also no guarantee with equities that all of the capital will be returned. The only way to realise the capital is to either find a buyer for the equity or to liquidate the company. Some equity shares may not be listed on a recognised stock market and therefore it will be hard to convert them to cash when the treasurer wants to sell them. If on the other hand the company is liquidated a company must repay any debts before it returns money to equity holders and often there is no money left for equity holders and the investor loses their capital invested.

  Equities are, therefore, not popular with most corporate treasurers. If chosen, they are best used in the context of a well-diversified portfolio.

5.1 RETAIL BANK AND BUILDING SOCIETY ACCOUNTS

Traditionally, retail banks provide banking services to individuals and small businesses dealing in large volumes of low value transactions. This is in contrast to wholesale banking which deals with large value transactions, generally in small volumes.

All of the high street banks and building societies offer different types of interest-earning accounts. For example:

A **deposit account** is an account for holding cash for a longer term. Banks pay interest on the money held in a deposit account. These accounts can be divided into:

- **Instant access accounts** that obviously allow instant access to your cash.
- **Notice accounts**, where savings earn a better rate of interest if you agree to lock them away for some time. The trade-off is that you cannot get at your money immediately. With notice accounts, you can only get your cash by giving notice of your intention to withdraw it. For example, with a 90-day notice account you would have to wait three months to get your money. You pay a penalty to access it earlier.
- **High interest accounts** are preferable when larger sums are available to invest (minimum $500). These usually give instant access to funds as well as a higher rate of interest.

Other types of investment with banks include:

Money market deposits offer real flexibility for larger amounts of money. For example, with $50,000 or more, fixed-term, fixed-rate deposits can be arranged for periods from overnight to five years.

Option deposits are arrangements for predetermined periods of investment, ranging from two to seven years. Interest rates are generally linked to base rates, giving a guaranteed return in real terms but restricted access to funds is the price paid for higher guaranteed interest rates. Investors would have to be sure of their cash position for that period before considering investing in an option deposit account.

Specialist bonds – all with different objectives – for those with at least $5,000 to invest.

An important feature of the banking system in the UK is that it is financially stable. Investment in a bank or building society deposit account offers high security with relatively low returns. In the event of default, investors are protected by statutory compensation schemes that will refund any funds lost, but only up to specified limits. The income received depends on the type of account and in some circumstances payment of interest can be made without deduction of tax. The risk factor on deposit accounts is very low although the real return (i.e. the return in excess of inflation) is also likely to be low. Deposit accounts are useful for short-term investment or as a readily accessible emergency fund.

6 MARKETABLE SECURITIES

Marketable securities are those that can be traded between investors. They represent stocks and bonds that are easily sold. Some are traded on highly developed and regulated markets while others can be traded between individual investors with brokers acting as middlemen. A marketable security has a readily determined fair market value and can be converted into cash at any time.

They can be classified into:

Money market securities which are short-term debt instruments sold by governments, financial institutions and corporations. The important characteristic of these securities is that they have maturities when issued of one year or less. The minimum size of transactions is typically large, usually exceeding $50,000. Money market securities tend to be highly liquid and safe assets. These investments include certificates of deposit, gilts, bills of exchange and treasury bills.

Capital market securities which have long maturities. These securities include instruments having maturities greater than one year and those having no designated maturity at all e.g. equities and preferred shares. They include fixed income securities, e.g. bonds, that promise a payment schedule with specific dates for the payment of interest and the repayment of principal. Any failure to conform to the payment schedule puts the security into default with all remaining payments. The holders of the securities can put the defaulter into bankruptcy. However, if an investor sells a bond before maturity the price that will be received is uncertain.

Indirect investments which can be undertaken by purchasing the shares of an investment company, which sells shares in itself to raise funds to purchase a portfolio of securities. The motivation for doing this is that the pooling of funds allows advantage to be taken of diversification and of savings in transactions costs. Many investment companies operate in line with a stated policy objective, for example on the type of securities that will be purchased and the nature of the fund management.

6.1 CERTIFICATES OF DEPOSIT

When banks accept deposits from customers, they are usually prepared to pay a higher interest rate for fixed long-term deposits than for deposits where the customer might withdraw the money at short notice. For example, suppose that an investor has $1 million to invest for three months. A bank might offer to pay 4% on a deposit if the customer has the right to withdraw the money at any time. However, if the investor agrees to keep the money on deposit for the full three months, the bank might be willing to pay 4.25%.

The investor would presumably prefer to invest at 4.25%, but only if he knew that he would not want any of the money during the fixed three-month deposit period.

Certificates of Deposit offer a way round this problem – they are marketable securities.

Definition A **Certificate of Deposit (CD)** is a financial instrument issued by a bank, certifying that the holder has the right to a fixed-term deposit of funds earning a specified interest rate. A CD is negotiable, which means that it can be sold by its original holder to another investor at any time before the end of the deposit period.

EXAMPLE

An investor agrees to deposit $1 million with a bank for a fixed three-month period to earn interest at 4.25%. This means that at the end of the deposit period, the deposit with interest will be about $1,010,625. The bank issues a CD to the investor, certifying his entitlement to the deposit plus interest after three months.

If the investor holds the CD to maturity, he will be able to withdraw the $1,010,625.

However, if the investor wants cash earlier, he can sell the CD in the money market. There is a market for trading in 'second-hand' CDs. The sale value of a CD will depend on how much a buyer is willing to pay to obtain the right to the deposit plus interest at maturity.

In this example, if the investor decided to sell the CD after two months, the sale value would depend on what a buyer would be willing to pay to receive the right to $1,010,625 in one month's time, when the deposit period ends. A buyer will offer a price that gives a suitable return on his investment.

For example, a buyer might offer $1,006,600 for the CD. If the CD is sold for this amount after two months (and so with one month to maturity):

The buyer of the return will receive $1,010,625 in one month's time, for an investment of $1,006,600. This gives a return of just over $4,000 in one month.

The original investor has made a return of $6,600 on the deposit of $1,000,000 in two months.

Investing in CDs

Banks and building societies issue CDs. The amount of the deposit and the date of repayment will be stated on the certificate. The deposit amount will usually be at least $100,000 and the repayment date will be anything from one week to five years.

Repayment is obtained by presenting the CD to the issuer on the designated date.

Advantages and disadvantages

Since CDs are negotiable, the holder can sell them at any time. This makes them far more liquid than a money-market time deposit, with the same bank.

CDs usually offer an attractive rate of interest when compared to deposit accounts and a low credit risk (as long as a reputable bank is used). They are useful for investing funds in the short term since they can be sold at any time on the secondary market.

An investor could ask the bank to make an early repayment, but there are normally penalty charges for doing this. If a high level of liquidity is not required, however, an investor may prefer to place money on a time deposit which, being less liquid, will usually pay a higher level of interest.

6.2 GILT-EDGED SECURITIES (GILTS)

These are marketable British Government securities. The government issues them to finance its spending, but also uses them to control the money supply. Most gilts have a face value of $100 at which the government promises to buy the gilt back on a specific date in the future.

Gilts usually have fixed interest rates, although there are also various index-linked gilts. Where they are the index-linked type, both the interest and the redemption value are linked to inflation, ensuring that a decent real return is gained.

For example, here are just a few gilts currently in issue:

Treasury Stock 5% 2012

Treasury Stock 6% 2028

3½% War Loan

For investment purposes, gilts are categorised according to how long it will be before they reach their redemption date. The main categories are:

- short-dated: these have up to 5 years remaining to maturity
- medium-dated: these have between 5 and 15 years remaining to maturity
- long-dated: these have over 15 years remaining to maturity
- perpetuals: there are some issues of gilts, such as 3.5% War Loans, that will never be redeemed, unless the government chooses to redeem them.

Advantages and disadvantages

Gilts are generally seen as being one of the lowest risk investments. Generally governments will repay their debts. Gilts are transferable on the secondary market in multiples of a cent, but if they are bought from new, the minimum investment is $1,000. There is no maximum investment limit. They are easy to transfer and nowadays the title can even be passed electronically. Gilts are a good choice of investment for risk-averse investors.

Gilts are also traded on the stock market. Their price can go up or down, depending on what people think will happen to interest rates. When interest rates are expected to fall, the price of the gilt rises, and when interest rates are expected to rise, the gilt price falls. Using gilts in this way makes them a more risky investment, but still relatively safe when compared with other types of investments.

The recent worldwide recession highlighted that on some occasions governments may not be able to meet their liabilities. Countries such as Greece defaulted on their debts because they didn't have the money to repay them. So gilts are not entirely risk free.

Gilt yields

Gilt yields are measured and reported in three ways.

- **Coupon yield.** The coupon yield is the fixed rate of interest, expressed as a percentage of nominal value. So 7% Treasury Stock 2021 would have a coupon yield of 7%, regardless of its market price.

- **Interest yield.** The interest yield on gilts is the annual interest receivable, expressed as a percentage of the market price. For example, if 7% Treasury Stock 2001 has a market price of 103.80, the interest yield is 6.7% (100% × 7/103.80).

- **Redemption yield.** The interest yield measures the interest return on gilts, but ignores any capital gain or loss on investment when the gilts are eventually redeemed. Redemption yield is the interest yield plus or minus an amount to reflect the difference between the market price of the gilt and its eventual redemption value.

The current interest yield and redemption yield on each issue of gilts is reported continually to investors in the gilts market and daily in the financial press. The redemption yield is more significant for investors.

EXAMPLE

An issue of 9% Treasury Stock has a market value of $105.80, and it is redeemable at par in two years' time.

The interest yield on the stock is 8.5% (100% × 9/105.80). However, an investor buying a quantity of the stock now at 105.80 and holding it until maturity will only receive $100 for every $105.80 of investment. Although the investor will receive an interest yield of 8.5% per annum, there will be a capital loss of $5.80 for each $105.80 invested. Since the stock has two years remaining to maturity this represents an average loss of $2.90 each year, which is 2.7% of the investment value.

As a rough approximation, the redemption yield on the stock is 5.8% (8.5% – 2.7%).

ACTIVITY 1

An issue of 4% Treasury Stock has a current market price of $94.00. The stock has exactly three years to redemption, when it will be redeemed at par.

Required:

(a) Calculate the current interest yield on the stock.

(b) Calculate an approximate redemption yield.

For a suggested answer, see the 'Answers' section at the end of the book.

6.3 LOCAL AUTHORITY STOCK

Definition **Local authority stock** is issued by local government authorities ('local councils') with the ultimate backing of the government.

Local authority debt instruments are issued with a period to maturity ranging from as little as two days to 10 or 15 years. Local authority bonds are longer-dated stock, and most new issues have a maturity of one to four years. The most popular local authority bonds are called 'yearlings' which have a maturity of one year and six days. Local authority bills are shorter-dated stock, which are issued to meet short-term liquidity problems.

Local authority bonds pay a fixed coupon rate of interest, and interest is paid every six months. The minimum investment is $1,000. Investors can subscribe to a new issue and purchase bills or bonds from the local authority, or they can buy and sell bonds on the stock exchange.

Advantages and disadvantages

Local authority stock is similar to gilts but the yield to investors on local authority debt instruments is usually slightly higher than the yield currently available on gilt-edged stock or Treasury bills.

The credit risk is low, but any issue of local authority bills or bonds is only as secure as the local authority issuing them. The market for local authority bills and bonds is much smaller than for central government stock, which is another reason why yields are a bit higher. Local authority stock is also slightly less liquid than gilts and therefore investors may take longer to convert them back into stock.

Conclusion Local authority securities offer slightly higher yields than government stock because the market is less liquid and the security of a local authority is not regarded quite so highly as that of central government.

6.4 THE DISCOUNT MARKET

A business with a short-term cash surplus can arrange through its bank to invest in the discount market, by purchasing either Treasury bills or bills of exchange (preferably bank bills, for which the credit risk is much lower). Since Treasury bills are an undertaking to pay by the central government, the risk to an investor is even lower than for bank bills. Treasury bills and government bonds (gilts) are commonly described as 'risk-free investments'.

An investor in bills needs to consider the risks and returns involved. There are two risks for an investor in bills.

- **Credit risk.** This is the risk that the bill will not be paid at maturity. As explained above, this risk is non-existent with Treasury bills and should be low for bank bills. It can be high for trade bills.
- **The risk of a change in interest rates**. This risk does not exist for any investor who buys a bill and then holds it to maturity. Interest rate risk only exists for investors who buy bills with the intention of re-selling them before maturity. The risk arises because if market rates of interest go up, the market value of bills will fall. (Equally, if market rates of interest fall, the market value of bills will rise.)

EXAMPLE

An investor buys a 91-day bank bill with a face value of $1 million in the discount market for $987,500. Although the calculations are not shown, the bill will give the investor a return of 5% per annum if he holds the bill to maturity and takes the $1 million payment.

However, suppose that the investor sells the bill seven days later, when interest rates in the discount market have risen to 6%. The sale value of the bill would be about $986,000 (workings not shown) and the investor would have made a loss on his investment.

The market value of a bill goes down when interest rates rise, because when interest rates go up, investors want a bigger return. To get a bigger return, they will buy bills at a bigger discount to face value, in other words, bill prices will fall.

ACTIVITY 2

Your company has $5 million to invest for 50 days. You are interested in investing the money in bills, but you want to do so at a low risk.

Advise your manager what might be a suitable way of investing in bills to obtain a fairly low-risk return.

For a suggested answer, see the 'Answers' section at the end of the book.

6.5 RISK AND RETURN

As a general rule, money market investments should offer a higher yield to investors than ordinary bank deposits, as compensation for the higher risk. Whenever a business is planning to invest surplus cash, it should look at the interest rates currently obtainable.

EXAMPLE

The interest yields on a range of investments are currently as follows:

Investment	*Current yield*
Short-dated gilts	4.73%
Bank bills (1 month)	4.5625%
Bank bills (3 months)	4.5%
Treasury bills (3 months)	4.4375%
CDs	4.625%
Bank deposit	4.30%

Your company has $10 million to invest for three months. How should it invest the money?

SOLUTION

It is essential to understand that unless there are clear guidelines and policies within the organisation about how surplus cash should or should not be invested, the choice between different investments is a matter of judgement and preference.

In this example:

- The lowest yield would be obtained by putting the money into a bank deposit account for three months, but it should be possible to secure a fixed interest rate for the three-month period, and there is no risk that the money held on deposit will lose value.
- Short-dated gilts offer the highest yield, but to cash in the investment, the gilts will have to be sold in the market, and there is a risk of a fall in market value due to an increase in interest rates over the next three months. If an increase in interest rates is not expected, gilts could be the favoured investment option.
- Of the money market investments, CDs offer a higher yield than three-month bank bills or three-month Treasury bills. All these investments can be held until maturity in three months' time, which means that there is no interest rate risk unless the business has to sell off its investments unexpectedly before the end of the three-month period.

- The yield on one-month bank bills is higher than the yield on three-month bills. However, it is not yet clear what interest rates will be available on investments at the end of one month, when the bills mature and are redeemed. The business will need to invest for a further two months, and there is a risk that interest rates could fall over the next month.

Whatever investment decision is taken, the choice of investments should be made for clear and logical reasons.

7 FINANCING

7.1 MEANING AND CAUSES OF A CASH DEFICIT

A cash deficit arises when there is an excess of expenditures over revenues during a certain period. There are many reasons why this may occur, including the following:

- **Poor trading performance.** It could be that receipts are lower than expected due to poor sales, which may have been caused by poor marketing or an uncontrollable downturn in the market, for example.

- **Poor control.** It may be that the business has lost control of payments, perhaps making poor purchasing decisions or spending too much on overheads such as wages.

- **Poor planning.** It may be that the company has poorly timed a capital investment so that, for example, a machine has been purchased when there is not enough of a surplus to finance it.

- **Poor working capital management.** Working capital management concerns the efficiency with which the business collects money from receivables, pays payables and manages inventory balances. So if, for example, the company is lax at collecting money from customers then the delay in receipts can cause a deficit.

- **Unexpected expenditure.** Some expenditure may arise that wasn't planned for such as urgent repairs or staff recruitment costs.

When a company experiences a deficit position it needs to raise finance, often from a bank, in order to cover that deficit.

8 RAISING BANK FINANCE

Credit is the capacity to borrow. It is the right to incur debt for goods and/or services and repay the debt over some specified future time period. Credit provision to a company means that the business is allowed the use of a productive good while it is being paid for.

The process of using borrowed, leased or 'joint venture' resources from someone else is sometimes called leverage. Using the leverage provided by someone else's capital helps the user business go farther than it otherwise would. For instance, a company that puts up $1,000 and borrows an additional $4,000 is using 80% leverage. The objective is to increase total net income and the return on a company's own equity capital.

8.1 BANK LOANS

Bank loans are a very flexible form of finance. Banks will consider applications for loans for virtually any term, from a few months to several years. Bank loans to businesses are rarely for more than seven years, unlike loans to individuals which can be for anything up to 25 years in the case of a mortgage for the purchase of a home.

Interest on a bank loan can be fixed for the duration of the loan, particularly if the loan is short-term. However, for longer-term loans, the interest is usually at a variable rate or 'floating rate'. Variable rate interest means that the interest payable is linked to a reference interest rate, which is either the bank's base rate or a market benchmark rate. For example, a business might pay 2% above base rate on a loan, or 1.5% above market benchmark rate, and so on. At regular intervals throughout the term of the loan, the interest rate is adjusted if the reference interest rate has changed since the previous review date.

EXAMPLE

BVC borrows $30,000 from its bank for three years. Interest is charged at 1.5% above the bank's base rate. The starting date for the loan is 1 April Year 1, and interest is charged every six months. The interest rate will be reviewed every six months, on 1 October Year 1, 1 April Year 2 and so on. On 1 April Year 1, the bank's base rate is 5%.

When the loan is provided, the bank will open a loan account for BVC, showing that BVC owes $30,000. (The borrowed money might be paid into BVC's current account, but the loan account shows how much BVC owes the bank.)

For the first six months of the loan period, BVC will pay interest at 6.5% on the $30,000. The interest will be charged to BVC's loan account, and under the terms of the loan agreement, BVC will be required to:

- pay the interest, probably from its current account, and
- possibly also repay some of the loan principal, depending on the repayment terms in the loan agreement.

After six months, the interest rate will be reviewed. If the bank's base rate has gone up since 1 April from 5% to, say, 5.5%, the interest on the loan for the next six months will be at the rate of 7%.

(**Note:** Interest rates are always quoted at an annual rate. So interest at 7% for six months will actually be $3.50 for each $100 borrowed.)

With a variable rate loan, the interest rate therefore goes up and down over the term of the loan depending on changes in the bank's base rate or a benchmark rate. There are a number of benchmark rates that may be used such as the SOFR (Secured Overnight Financing Rate) for loans denominated in dollars, or the Sterling Overnight Index Average (SONIA) used in the UK. These benchmark rates reflect the actual cost of borrowing and depositing for the market as a whole over a short-term basis and will vary daily.

8.2 TYPES OF BANK LOAN

There are various ways of classifying loans:

- *payment terms,* e.g. instalment versus single payment
- *period-of-payment terms,* e.g. short-term versus intermediate-term or long-term
- *in the manner of its security terms,* e.g. secured versus unsecured
- *in interest payment terms,* e.g. simple interest versus add-on, versus discount, versus balloon.

On the basis of the above classification, there are twelve common types of loans, namely: short-term loans, intermediate-term loans, long-term loans, unsecured loans, secured loans, instalment loans, single payment ('bullet') loans, simple-interest loans, add-on interest loans, discount or front-end loans, balloon loans and amortised loans.

- Short-term loans are credit that is usually paid back in one year or less. They are usually used in financing the purchase of operating inputs, wages for hired labour, machinery and equipment, and/or family living expenses. Usually lenders expect short-term loans to be repaid after their purposes have been served, e.g. after the expected production output has been sold.

  Included under short-term loans are loans for operating production inputs, which are assumed to be self-liquidating. In other words, although the inputs are used up in the production, the added returns from their use will repay the money borrowed to purchase the inputs, plus interest.

- Intermediate-term (IT) loans are credit extended for several years, usually one to five years. This type of credit is normally used for purchases of buildings, equipment and other production inputs that require longer than one year to generate sufficient returns to repay the loan.

- Long-term loans are those loans for which repayment exceeds five to seven years and may extend to 40 years. This type of credit is usually extended on assets (such as land) which have a long productive life in the business. Some land improvement programmes like land levelling, reforestation, land clearing and drainage-way construction are usually financed with long-term credit.

- Unsecured loans are credit given out by lenders on no other basis than a promise by the borrower to repay. The borrower does not have to put up collateral and the lender relies on credit reputation. Unsecured loans usually carry a higher interest rate than secured loans and may be difficult or impossible to arrange for businesses with a poor credit record.

- Secured loans are those loans that involve a pledge of some or all of a business's assets. The lender requires security as protection for its depositors against the risks involved in the use planned for the borrowed funds. The borrower may be able to bargain for better terms by putting up collateral, which is a way of backing one's promise to repay.

- Instalment loans are those loans in which the borrower or credit customer repays a set amount each period (week, month, year) until the borrowed amount is cleared. Instalment credit is similar to charge account credit, but usually involves a formal legal contract for a predetermined period with specific payments. With this plan, the borrower usually knows precisely how much will be paid and when.

- Simple interest loans are those loans in which interest is paid on the unpaid loan balance. Thus, the borrower is required to pay interest only on the actual amount of money outstanding and only for the actual time the money is used (e.g. 30 days, 90 days, 4 months and 2 days, 12 years and 1 month).

- Add-on interest loans are credit in which the borrower pays interest on the full amount of the loan for the entire loan period. Interest is charged on the face amount of the loan at the time it is made and then 'added on'. The resulting sum of the principal and interest is then divided equally by the number of payments to be made. The company is thus paying interest on the face value of the note although it has use of only a part of the initial balance once principal payments begin. This type of loan is sometimes called the 'flat rate' loan and usually results in an interest rate higher than the one specified.

- Discount or front-end loans are loans in which the interest is calculated and then subtracted from the principal first. For example, a $5,000 discount loan at 10% for one year would result in the borrower only receiving $4,500 to start with, and the $5,000 debt would be paid back, as specified, by the end of a year.

  On a discount loan, the lender discounts or deducts the interest in advance. Thus, the effective interest rates on discount loans are usually much higher than (in fact, more than double) the specified interest rates.

- Bullet loans are those loans in which the borrower pays no principal until the amount is due. Because the company must eventually pay the debt in full, it is important to have the self-discipline and professional integrity to set aside money to be able to do so. This type of loan is sometimes called the 'lump sum' or 'single payment' loan, and is generally repaid in less than a year.

- Balloon loans are loans that normally require mainly interest payments each period with only a small amount of principle repaid each period. This is then followed by a larger repayment at the end of the loan period. They are sometimes referred to as the 'last payment due', and have a concept that is the same as the bullet loan, but the due date for repaying principal may be five years or more in the future rather than the customary 90 days or 6 months for the bullet loan. In some cases a principal payment is made each time interest is paid, but because the principal payments do not amortise (fully pay off) the loan, a large sum is due at the loan maturity date.

- Amortised loans are a partial payment plan where part of the loan principal and interest on the unpaid principal are repaid each year. The standard plan of amortisation, used in many intermediate and long-term loans, calls for equal payments each period, with a larger proportion of each succeeding payment representing principal and a small amount representing interest.

  The constant annual payment feature of the amortised loan is similar to the 'add on' loan described above, but involves less interest because it is paid only on the outstanding loan balance, as with simple interest.

ACTIVITY 3

Distinguish between a bullet loan and a balloon loan.

For a suggested answer, see the 'Answers' section at the end of the book.

8.3 OVERDRAFTS

A bank loan is for a given period of time and for a given amount (the 'loan principal'). When a bank makes a loan to a customer, it opens a loan account, and the loan is eventually paid back when the balance on the loan account is reduced to 0.

With a bank overdraft, a bank allows a customer to pay more out of his current account than there is cash in the account. An overdraft is therefore a form of borrowing through the current account. The bank sets a limit to the size of the overdraft, and the customer can be overdrawn on the account up to the agreed limit. The size of the overdraft continually changes, with payments into and out of the account reducing and increasing the balance.

Interest on an overdraft is usually charged at a daily rate on the overdraft balance, and the rate is variable (usually subject to change whenever the bank alters its base rate). Overdrafts are repayable on demand. Unlike for private individuals, businesses pay an arrangement fee on an overdraft. This is in addition to the overdraft interest and is charged for setting up the overdraft facility.

There are two types of overdraft facility (overdraft arrangement):

- committed
- uncommitted.

With a committed facility, the bank agrees to allow the customer to be overdrawn up to the agreed limit, at any time during an agreed period of time. For example, a bank might allow a business to be overdrawn by up to $100,000 at any time for the next two years after the agreement is made.

With an uncommitted facility, the bank agrees to allow the customer to be overdrawn up to an agreed limit, but reserves the right to reduce the overdraft limit, or withdraw the overdraft facility completely, at any time and without notice. The customer therefore relies on the goodwill and support of the bank for any overdraft that it has.

A committed facility is more expensive to arrange, but an uncommitted facility exposes a business to the risk that the bank can demand repayment at any time, and effectively make the business insolvent.

8.4 LOAN TERMS AND CONDITIONS

The terms and conditions of a loan agreement or an overdraft agreement can vary considerably. Every agreement should specify:

- the term of the agreement
- the amount of the loan (the 'loan principal') or overdraft limit
- the interest rate payable, which is usually a variable rate and expressed as a margin above base rate or benchmark rate
- the frequency of interest payments.

For a loan, the agreement will specify whether the loan principal is to be repaid gradually over the term of the loan, or whether there will be no principal repayments until the end of the loan period.

Secured and unsecured loans

Loans and overdrafts can be either secured or unsecured. Borrowing is secured when the bank takes security for the money it lends. For companies that borrow, security is provided in the form of a charge over its assets. A charge can be either a fixed charge or a floating charge.

With a fixed charge, the borrower provides security in the form of a specified asset. If the borrower subsequently defaults and fails to make a scheduled interest payment or a scheduled repayment of loan principal, the lender can take the secured asset. This can then be sold to raise the money to pay off the loan. A fixed charge can be taken over an item of equipment or property. Until the loan is repaid in full, the borrower cannot sell off the secured asset, which must remain available to the lender as security for the loan.

With a floating charge, the borrower provides security in the form of assets such as its inventory and receivables. The bank allows the borrower to continue to trade, using up its inventory and buying new inventory, and using the money received from receivables but creating new receivables from new sales. However, if the borrower defaults, and fails to make a scheduled payment on the loan, the bank can call in its security. The floating charge will 'crystallise', and the bank will acquire the rights over the categories of assets that are subject to the floating charge that the business owns at that time. For example, if a bank has a floating charge over a borrower's receivables, if the borrower defaults and the bank calls on its security, the floating charge over the receivables will crystallise, and the bank will obtain the right to the money currently due from the receivables of the business.

The main difference between a fixed and floating charge is that a fixed charge relates to a specific asset, which the borrower cannot sell off or use until the loan is repaid. In contrast, a business can use assets subject to a floating charge. Even when there is a floating charge over receivables, the business can use the money from its receivables in whatever way that it wants, and does not have to use the money to pay interest or repay principal on the loan. Assets subject to a floating charge are therefore under the full control of the borrower unless and until the security is exercised and the floating charge crystallises.

With some loan agreements, a bank will take a fixed and floating charge from a company. The fixed charge might be a charge on a property owned by the company and the floating charge might be a charge on the 'undertaking' – in other words, all the other assets of the business.

For non-corporate borrowers, banks might take security in a form other than a charge, which will operate in a way similar to a fixed charge.

A bank might also ask for a personal guarantee from the business owner. For example, the owner of a business wanting to arrange a loan or overdraft facility might be required to provide a personal guarantee, whereby if the business defaults on its loan payment obligations, the bank can seek to recover the money from the individual's personal assets, such as his or her home.

Loans and overdrafts might be unsecured. When borrowing is unsecured, the bank relies on the borrower to pay the interest and repay the loan principal. If the borrower defaults, the bank does not have any security to call on, and cannot claim any assets of the business that it can sell off to raise money to repay the loan. Instead, the bank can take action through the courts to put the business into liquidation but would be one of the unsecured payables of the business in the 'winding up' of the business.

Other terms and conditions ('covenants')

A loan or overdraft agreement will also have other terms and conditions called covenants. Most of these relate to undertakings given by the borrower to the bank.

For example, if a loan is unsecured, the borrower might be required to give an undertaking that he will not subsequently take out any secured loans from any other lender.

The borrower might give an undertaking to provide the bank with regular information about its financial position, such as a statement of profit or loss every six months or a regular cash budget or cash forecast.

A borrower might also give undertakings to keep its financial position acceptable to the bank. For example, the borrower might undertake that its current assets (inventory, receivables and cash) will always be at least twice the amount of its current liabilities (short-term payables). Any such financial ratios in a loan agreement will be continually monitored by the bank.

If the borrower breaches any of the covenants on a loan, he will be in default, and the bank will have a right to call in the loan and exercise any security that it has.

Default

A borrower is in default if he breaches any condition of the loan. Typically, default occurs when the borrower is late with an interest payment.

Under the terms of a loan agreement, a breach of condition gives the bank the right to call in the loan immediately, and if the loan is secured the bank can sell off the secured asset or assets and use the proceeds to repay the loan. In practice, banks are often reluctant to take this action immediately. Instead, a bank will seek to discuss the problem with the borrower, and consider whether a solution can be found. Often, if the borrower is having short-term cash flow difficulties, the bank will be prepared to reschedule the loan repayments and give the borrower more time to pay.

Whenever a business thinks that it might be unable to make a scheduled payment on a loan, it should notify the bank immediately. If the borrower is open and honest with the bank, the bank will normally be prepared to discuss a solution.

In contrast, if a business exceeds its overdraft limit without notifying the bank, the bank's reaction is likely to be hostile. The bank could well insist on reducing the overdraft limit even if that effectively means putting the business into liquidation.

ACTIVITY 4

A business wants to buy a new production machine for $600,000.

Which type of bank finance might be most suitable for this type of purchase?

For a suggested answer, see the 'Answers' section at the end of the book.

9 EXTERNAL INFLUENCES ON CASH BALANCES

Cash balances will be affected by internal controls, business performance, planning etc. as detailed in sections 3 and 7 of this chapter. But they will also be affected by the uncontrollable, external environmental and financial environment. Some examples of this might be:

- In time of economic downturn (a recession) consumers are less willing to spend and this will have an adverse impact on a business' cash inflows. It may also become harder to collect from receivables, further adversely affecting the cash inflows.

- On the other hand, in times of economic booms the opposite may be true and cash balances may rise.

- Other environmental influences such as inflation and exchange rates can also impact on cash balances. For example, when the domestic currency is strong consumers may choose to buy overseas, to the detriment of domestic firms.

- There may also be trends in the financial environment. There will be times when banks, for example, may be less willing to lend (as has happened in recent years in most developed countries). This will mean that managers will need to manage cash better as they will not be able to rely as easily on external finance to solve their problems.

- At other times there may be government policies or incentives to encourage bank lending and therefore businesses may find it easier to borrow cash at these times.

- Interest rates in the economy will also have an influence on these decisions, as businesses would prefer to borrow when interest rates are low and invest when interest rates are high.

- Markets also follow trends. A 'bull' market refers to a time when security prices are rising and therefore market securities become more attractive. In a 'bear' market the opposite is true.

Treasury managers therefore need to consider the external economic and financial environment as well at their internal business performance and policies when managing cash.

CONCLUSION

Companies have a variety of opportunities for using their surplus funds, but when deciding on how they should invest, their choice will be determined by four considerations – risk, liquidity, maturity and return.

This chapter has looked at the nature of the money markets and the gilts market and the use of these markets by businesses, largely as an opportunity for short-term investment of surplus cash.

A business must have enough liquidity to survive, and careful cash management should help to ensure that liquidity remains sufficient. At times of deficit bank finance can be used in the short-term to alleviate the problems.

A treasury department can insure that the business is aware of surpluses and deficits and manages its cash accordingly. This management should happen within the wider economic environment.

KEY TERMS

Deposit account – interest-earning bank account, used for holding surplus funds. There is no risk of capital loss with money in a deposit account.

Bill of exchange – a 'You Owe Me', drawn by a payable on another person (the drawee). In the case of a bill payable at a future date (a 'term bill'), the drawee accepts the bill by signing it, thereby acknowledging his obligation to pay the debt at the specified future date.

Bank bill – a bill of exchange drawn on a bank. A bill accepted by a bank is usually regarded as a lower credit risk than a bill accepted by a non-bank company.

Treasury bill – an IOU issued by the government, promising to pay a fixed sum of money after a given period of time (usually 91 days after issue).

Discount market – a market for selling and buying bills of exchange and Treasury bills. Bills are bought and sold in this market at a discount to face value, the discount reflecting the interest rate return that the buyer of the bill obtains if he holds the bill to maturity.

Certificate of deposit (CD) – a negotiable instrument issued by a bank, giving its holder the right to a sum of money (with interest) in a bank deposit account, at a specified future date.

Gilts – gilt-edged securities. Long-term debt securities (bonds) issued by the UK government. Gilts are used extensively as both long-term and short-term investments, and there is a large and liquid secondary market for buying and selling gilts.

SELF-TEST QUESTIONS

		Paragraph
1	How might cash surpluses arise?	3.2
2	What is a notice account?	5.1
3	Explain what a short-dated gilt is.	6.2
4	What are the two risks for an investor in bills?	6.4
5	Outline two advantages of overdrafts.	8.3
6	What is the essence of the segregation of duties?	2.4

EXAM STYLE QUESTIONS

1 Which of the following is not a critical area in the handling of cash?

A Profitability

B Segregation of duties

C Physical security

D Reconciliation.

2 Which department in a company is likely to be responsible for the payment of factory labour wages?

A Production department

B Personnel department

C Finance department

D Treasury department

3 Which of the following is a source of equity investment?

A Money market deposit

B Buying shares in another company

C Paying dividends

D Issue shares to new shareholders

4 The annual interest receivable, expressed as a percentage of market price, is known as:

A Coupon yield

B Interest yield

C Redemption yield

D Investment yield

5 8% Treasury stock is currently valued at $88 and is redeemable in one year's time. What is the redemption yield?

A 6%

B 8%

C 10%

D 12%

For the answers to these questions, see the 'Answers' section at the end of the book.

Chapter 18

CASH BUDGETS

Cash budgets are a very important tool used by managers to ensure that they do not run out of cash. This chapter discusses the purpose of cash budgets and explains how they should be constructed. This chapter covers syllabus area E3.

CONTENTS

LEARNING OUTCOMES

At the end of this chapter you should be able to:

- Explain the objectives of a cash budget
- Explain and illustrate statistical techniques used in cash forecasting including moving averages and allowance for inflation
- Prepare a cash budget/forecast
- Explain and illustrate how a cash budget can be used as a mechanism for monitoring and control

1 OBJECTIVES OF A CASH BUDGET AND TYPES OF CASH BUDGET

1.1 CASH BUDGETS AND CASH FORECASTS

Definition A **cash budget** (or cash flow budget) is a detailed forecast of cash inflows and outflows for a future time period, incorporating revenue and capital items and other cash flow items.

Some businesses prepare cash budgets on a month-by-month basis over a longer budget period. For example, a business might include a cash budget in its annual budget, and the cash budget might be for each month over the one-year budget period.

Some businesses prepare cash budgets or cash flow forecasts much more frequently, because it is essential to forecast and plan cash flows in detail on a week-by-week, or even a day-by-day basis.

A cash budget is a management plan for the most important factor of a company's viability – its cash position. A company's cash position determines how suppliers will be paid, how a banker will respond to a loan request, how fast a company can grow, as well as directly influencing dividends, increases to owner's equity and profitability.

1.2 OBJECTIVES OF A CASH BUDGET

Cash budgets have two main objectives.

1 A cash budget is used to estimate or plan future cash shortages/surpluses and allow time to make plans for dealing with them. If the forecast is for a large cash surplus, management can plan in advance what it intends to do with the money. If the forecast is for a cash deficit, management can make arrangements in advance to have access to additional funds, for example an overdraft facility. Alternatively, it can devise ways of trying to improve cash flows, so that the cash position will be better than forecast.

2 A cash budget can be used as a reference point for monitoring actual cash flows. Actual cash flows can be compared with budgeted cash flows. This comparison can help to identify weaknesses in cash management, such as inadequate procedures for collecting money from receivables. It can also help to review forecasts of cash flows, and decide whether the business will still have enough cash or whether new sources of borrowing will be necessary.

1.3 ESTIMATING FUTURE CASH FLOWS

To be useful for management, cash budgets must be reasonably reliable. This means that they have to be based on realistic assumptions. Cash budgets depend on estimates or assumptions about:

- budgeted sales and costs of sales
- assumptions about lagged receipts and payments, for example how long will it take for receivables to pay what they owe, and how much credit will be taken from payables.

1.4 TYPES OF CASH BUDGET

There are two types of cash budget:

(a) **Receipts and payments budget.** This is a forecast of cash receipts and payments based on predictions of sales and cost of sales and the timings of the cash flows relating to these items.

(b) **Statement of financial position forecast.** This is a forecast derived from predictions of future statement of financial positions. Predictions are made of all items excepting cash, which is then derived as a balancing figure.

Receipts and payments budgets are much more detailed than statement of financial position forecasts and it is these budgets that will be examined.

2 FORMAT OF A CASH BUDGET

Cash flow based forecasts (receipts and payments) are forecasts of the timing and amount of cash receipts and payments, net cash flows and changes in cash balances. A cash budget (or cash flow budget) covers a planning period, and is sub-divided into shorter individual time periods, which could be quarters, months, weeks or even days. For each individual time period, the budget shows:

- the opening cash balance at the start of the time period (which is just the closing balance brought forward from the previous period)
- the expected cash receipts, itemised and in total
- the expected cash payments, itemised and in total
- the net cash flow for the period, which is the difference between total cash receipts and total cash payments
- the closing cash balance, which is calculated from the opening balance and the net cash flow for the period.

A typical receipts and payments cash budget format is as follows, with illustrative figures included. We have limited most of the examples in this chapter to four months for the sake of clarity – but in the real world these could last for any period of time. In an exam question, however, you will likely to have to find figures for only one month of the budget.

EXAMPLE – Cash budget

Cash receipts

	January	*February*	*March*	*April*
Cash receipts	$	$	$	$
Cash from receivables	54,000	63,000	58,000	54,000
Cash sales	3,000	4,000	2,000	1,000
Cash from sale of non-current assets	–	1,000	–	500
Total receipts	57,000	68,000	60,000	55,500

Cash payments				
Payments to suppliers	24,000	29,000	24,000	27,000
Payments of wages and salaries	26,000	28,000	26,000	28,000
Payments for non-current asset purchases	4,000	14,000	–	3,000
Payment of dividend	–	5,000	–	–
Total payments	54,000	76,000	50,000	58,000
Net cash flow	3,000	(8,000)	10,000	(2,500)
Opening cash balance	6,000	9,000	1,000	11,000
Closing cash balance	9,000	1,000	11,000	8,500

It is important to include all expected items of cash receipt and cash payment, including exceptional payments and receipts.

2.1 LAGGED RECEIPTS AND PAYMENTS

A receipts and payments budget is often based on a statement of profit or loss forecast. The starting point is therefore to estimate sales and the cost of sales for the period. To forecast the cash flows from sales and costs of sales, we must then allow for the fact that receipts from credit sales occur sometime after the sale has taken place, and payments to suppliers take place sometime after the purchase. In other words, receipts and payments lag behind the sale and cost of sale.

The task in preparing a receipts and payments cash budget is largely to forecast when the cash receipts and cash payments will take place, given forecasts for:

- sales and purchases, and
- assumptions about the length of the time lag between (a) sale and receipt and (b) purchase and payment.

3 PREPARING A CASH BUDGET

To prepare a cash budget based on receipts and payments, you need to take each item of cash receipt and cash payment in turn, and work out the expected cash flow in each time period. The most complex calculations are normally those for receipts from sales and payments to suppliers.

3.1 RECEIPTS FROM SALES

A business might have some cash sales, but most businesses sell mainly on credit. To prepare a cash budget, assumptions have to be made about:

- when customers will pay
- the level of bad (irrecoverable) debts.

For example, it might be estimated that for credit sales, 50% of customers will pay in the month following sale, 30% two months after sale, 15% three months after sale and bad (irrecoverable) debts will be 5% of credit sales.

You can then take sales for each time period in turn, and estimate when the money will actually be received as cash.

EXAMPLE

A business has estimated that 10% of its sales will be cash sales, and the remainder credit sales. It is also estimated that 50% of credit customers will pay in the month following sale, 30% two months after sale, 15% three months after sale and bad (irrecoverable) debts will be 5% of credit sales.

Total sales figures are as follows:

Month	$
October	80,000
November	60,000
December	40,000
January	50,000
February	60,000
March	90,000

Prepare a month-by-month budget of cash receipts from sales for the months January to March.

SOLUTION

Credit customers take up to three months to pay so, in the first month of the budget period, January, the business should expect some cash receipts for credit sales three months earlier, in October. It might be useful to prepare a table for workings, as follows:

Sales month	*Total sales*	*Cash receipts January*	*Cash receipts February*	*Cash receipts March*
	$	$	$	$
October	80,000	10,800	–	–
November	60,000	16,200	8,100	–
December	40,000	18,000	10,800	5,400
January	50,000	5,000	22,500	13,500
February	60,000	–	6,000	27,000
March	90,000	–	–	9,000
Total receipts		50,000	47,400	54,900

For example, October sales were $80,000 and 90% of these ($72,000) were credit sales. Of these 15% are expected to pay three months later in January, so the cash receipts in January from October sales are expected to be $10,800 (15% of $72,000).

Similarly, November sales were $60,000 in total and of these $54,000 were credit sales. Of the credit sales, 30% will pay two months later in January and 15% three months later in February.

January sales are expected to total $50,000, of which $5,000 will be cash sales and $45,000 credit sales. Of the credit sales, there should be receipts from 50% ($22,500) in February and 30% ($13,500) in March.

Make sure that you can see how all the figures in this workings table have been calculated.

In this table receipts from cash sales and receipts from credit sales are combined into a single figure for receipts from sales for the month. The receipts from cash sales and receipts from credit sales could be calculated separately if required.

ACTIVITY 1

A business is preparing a cash budget for the period July to September. Sales are as follows:

Month	*Cash sales*	*Credit sales*
	$	$
April (actual)	4,500	60,000
May (actual)	3,700	64,000
June (actual)	2,100	50,000
July (budget)	4,500	60,000
August (budget)	4,500	65,000
September (budget)	5,000	75,000

It is estimated that 60% of credit customers will pay in the month following sale, 30% two months after sale and 10% three months after sale. No bad (irrecoverable) debts are expected.

Required:

Prepare a month-by-month cash receipts budget, showing:

- receipts from cash sales
- receipts from credit sales
- total receipts.

For a suggested answer, see the 'Answers' section at the end of the book.

3.2 PAYMENTS TO SUPPLIERS AND FOR WAGES AND SALARIES

Budgeted payments to suppliers for purchases can be calculated in a similar way to calculating budgeted sales receipts. You need figures for:

- purchases in each time period, analysed between credit purchases and (if any) cash purchases
- estimates for the amount of credit taken from suppliers (for example, one month or two months).

Payments for materials purchases

An added complication with payments for material purchases could be that in order to calculate purchase quantities in each time period, you must first calculate the quantities used and then allow for any planned increase or decrease in inventory levels in the period to work out purchase quantities.

EXAMPLE

A manufacturing business makes and sells widgets. Each widget requires two units of raw materials, which cost $3 each. Production and sales quantities of widgets each month are as follows:

Month	*Sales and production units*
December (actual)	50,000
January (budget)	55,000
February (budget)	60,000
March (budget)	65,000

In the past, the business has maintained its inventory of raw materials at 100,000 units. However, it plans to increase raw material inventory to 110,000 units at the end of January and 120,000 units at the end of February. The business takes one month's credit from its suppliers.

Calculate the budgeted payments to suppliers each month for raw material purchases.

SOLUTION

When raw materials inventory levels are increased, the quantities purchased will exceed the quantities consumed in the period. Purchase quantities and the cost of purchases are therefore as follows. Figures for December are shown because December purchases will be paid for in January, which is in the budget period.

		Purchases of raw materials for production and for increase in inventory levels			
	Units of widgets produced	*December*	*January*	*February*	*March*
December	50,000	100,000			
January	55,000		110,000		
February	60,000			120,000	
March	65,000				130,000
Increase in inventory		–	10,000	10,000	–
Total purchase quantities		100,000	120,000	130,000	130,000
Purchase cost (at $3 per unit)		$300,000	$360,000	$390,000	$390,000

Having established the purchases each month, we can go on to budget the amount of cash payments to suppliers each month. Here, the business will take one month's credit.

	January	*February*	*March*
	$	$	$
Payments to suppliers	300,000	360,000	390,000

At the end of March, there will be unpaid purchase from suppliers of $390,000 for raw materials, and these suppliers will be paid in April.

Payments of wages and salaries

Wages and salaries are usually paid in arrears, at the end of the week or month. This means, however, that employees who are paid a monthly salary will receive their money at the end of the month to which the salary cost relates. It is therefore usual to assume that salaries are paid for in the same month as they are incurred.

A similar assumption is often made for wages. However, each organisation can establish its own assumptions for cash budgeting, and you should apply whatever assumptions are required.

Payments for overheads expenses

You might be required to calculate the budgeted cash payments for overheads expenses. Overheads expenses might be variable or fixed.

Total variable overhead costs vary with the volume of production or sales.

Fixed overheads are a fixed amount for the period. Unless there is any information to the contrary, you should assume that fixed overhead costs are an equal amount every time period. However, this might not be the case and you should check carefully the information available.

Most overhead costs are expenses that are paid in cash, and the business might take credit from its suppliers of overhead cost items. However, depreciation is an overhead expense, but is not a cash flow item. If there are any depreciation charges in total overhead costs, these must be deducted to calculate a 'cash expenses' figure for overheads.

EXAMPLE

A manufacturing company makes product WSX, for which the variable overhead cost is $2 per unit. Fixed costs are budgeted at $450,000 for the year, of which $130,000 are depreciation charges. The remaining fixed costs are incurred at a constant rate every month, with the exception of factory rental costs, which are $80,000 each year, payable 50% in December and 50% in June.

With the exception of rental costs, 10% of overhead expenses are paid for in the month they occur and the remaining 90% are paid in the following month.

The budgeted production quantities of product WSX are:

	Units
September	40,000
October	60,000
November	50,000
December	30,000

Prepare a month-by-month cash budget for overhead payments in the period October – December.

SOLUTION

Workings: fixed overheads	$
Annual fixed overheads	450,000
Deduct depreciation	130,000
Cash expenses	320,000
Deduct annual factory rental	80,000
Regular monthly cash expenses for the year	240,000
Regular cash expenses each month	20,000

These expenses will be paid for as follows: $2,000 in the month incurred and $18,000 in the following month. However, total cash spending on these regular fixed cost items will be $20,000 in every month. An additional $40,000 is paid in June and December, for rent.

Workings: Variable overheads

	Units	*Variable overhead costs*		*Payment in*	
			October	*November*	*December*
		$	$	$	$
September	40,000	80,000	72,000	–	–
October	60,000	120,000	12,000	108,000	–
November	50,000	100,000	–	10,000	90,000
December	30,000	60,000	–	–	6,000
Total payments			84,000	118,000	96,000

An overhead cash payments budget can now be prepared.

	October	*November*	*December*
	$	$	$
Variable overheads	84,000	118,000	96,000
Fixed overheads	20,000	20,000	60,000
Total payments	104,000	138,000	156,000

ACTIVITY 2

You are given the following budgeted information about an organisation.

	Jan	*Feb*	*March*
Opening inventory in units	100	150	120
Closing inventory in units	150	120	180
Sales in units	400	450	420

The cost of materials is $2 per unit and 40% of purchases are for cash whilst 60% are on credit and are paid two months after the purchase.

Calculate the budgeted purchases payments for March.

For a suggested answer, see the 'Answers' section at the end of the book.

3.3 OTHER RECEIPTS AND PAYMENTS

For most cash budgets, the most time-consuming tasks are calculating the budgeted cash receipts from sales and the cash payments for operating costs. Once you have done this, you should then obtain forecasts for other receipts and payments, such as:

- payments for non-current asset purchases
- receipts from non-current asset disposals
- payments of income tax (corporation tax in the UK)
- payments of dividends (or drawings, in the case of a sole trader business or a partnership)
- interest, for example, a business might have a bank loan on which it has to pay interest.

These should be included in the cash budget, using the format shown earlier.

ACTIVITY 3

The following data and estimates are available for ABC for June, July and August:

	June	*July*	*August*
	$	$	$
Sales	45,000	50,000	60,000
Wages	12,000	13,000	14,500
Overheads	8,500	9,500	9,000

The following information is available regarding direct materials:

	June	*July*	*August*	*September*
	$	$	$	$
Opening inventory	5,000	3,500	6,000	4,000
Material usage	8,000	9,000	10,000	

Notes:

1 10% of sales are for cash, the balance is received the following month. The amount received in June for May's sales is $29,500.

2 Wages are paid in the month they are incurred.

3 Overheads include $1,500 per month for depreciation. Overheads are settled the month following. $6,500 is to be paid in June for May's overheads.

4 Purchases of direct materials are paid for in the month purchased.

5 The opening cash balance in June is $11,750.

6 A tax bill of $25,000 is to be paid in July.

Required:

(a) Calculate the amount of direct material purchases in EACH of the months of June, July and August.

(b) Prepare a cash budget for June, July and August.

For a suggested answer, see the 'Answers' section at the end of the book.

4 FORECASTING IN CASH BUDGETS

Some businesses may experience some seasonality across a year. For example, a business selling skiing holidays may have higher cash receipts in the winter than in the summer. For these types of businesses it will be important to build in these seasonal variations in cash receipts and/or payments into the cash forecast. One technique for doing this is to use time series analysis.

4.1 TIME SERIES AND MOVING AVERAGES

Time series analysis examines past data to establish two elements from the data:

- an underlying **trend** (or pattern) in cash receipts or payments (for example it might be found to be increasing month on month or year on year)
- **seasonal variations** in the data that identify peaks and troughs in year.

To identify the trend a moving averages technique is used.

EXAMPLE

Consider the following quarterly sales (in $000) for a business that experiences some seasonality:

Year	*Q1*	*Q2*	*Q3*	*Q4*
20X2	85	62	66	108
20X3	90	66	71	125
20X4	97	68	75	142

From observation we can see a trend in the data – each year has a quarter-on-quarter increase from the previous year. We can also see evidence of the seasonality, with quarters 1 and 4 being peak periods and quarters 2 and 3 being quieter periods. We can use a moving average technique to quantify the trend and associated seasonal variations.

Let's determine the trend. If we take the observations for all quarters in 20X3, add them up (giving 352) and then divide by 4, we arrive at 88. This figure may be taken as being on the trend line as at the end of quarter 2, 20X3, since the averaging gives a 'de-seasonalised' figure. That exercise can be repeated for subsequent quarters (averaging the observations for the two previous and two subsequent quarters) and this gives a series of de-seasonalised trend figures as follows:

Year	*Quarter*	*Trend*
20X3	2	88.00
20X3	3	89.75 (i.e. (66 + 71 + 125 + 97)/4)
20X3	4	90.25 (i.e. (71 + 125 + 97 + 68)/4)
20X4	1	91.25 (i.e. (125 + 97 + 68 + 75)/4)

These figures show us the gradual increase (or trend) in average sales over the period of the data. We can then add another column to our table to determine the seasonal variations in the data. This will be the difference between the actual sales and the underlying average trend, as follows:

Year	*Quarter*	*Trend*	*Seasonal variation*
20X3	2	88.00	–22.00 (i.e. 66.00 – 88.00)
20X3	3	89.75	–18.75 (i.e. 71.00 – 89.75)
20X3	4	90.25	+34.75 (i.e. 125.00 – 90.25)
20X4	1	91.25	+5.75 (i.e. 97.00 – 91.25)

We can see that, for example, Quarter 4 is $34,750 above average (or trend). Note that this is the simplest possible example. In particular, we are basing our analysis on only one set of observations (the 4 quarters that we are examining). In practice, one would prefer to calculate the seasonal variations on the basis of the average of two or three sets of observations. Thus we would, for example, calculate the quarter 1 seasonal variation for each of the three years and take an average of these values. The averaging process has the effect of 'ironing out' the impact of random variations over the past periods. The seasonal variations can be averaged over longer periods so that the more past data we have the more accurate this number becomes.

Once we have the information for the trend and the seasonal variation we can use this to forecast sales for the future. Let's say that we forecast the trend for 20X5 to look as follows:

Year	*Quarter*	*Trend*
20X5	1	98.25
20X5	2	99.75
20X5	3	101.25
20X5	4	102.25

We can then adjust this for the seasonal variations that we expect to happen in order to determine forecast sales for the year, as follows:

Year	*Quarter*	*Trend*	*Seasonal variation*	*Forecast sales*
20X5	1	98.25	+5.75	104.00
20X5	2	99.75	–22.00	77.75
20X5	3	101.25	–18.75	82.50
20X5	4	102.25	+34.75	137.00

We can therefore see the importance of identifying and incorporating seasonal variations into our forecasts. Once we have forecast the sales and built in the seasonal effects, this is likely to have a knock on impact on other data in our forecasts such as purchases and maybe even wage payments (if, for example, extra staff are hired during peak periods).

Where the forecast trend might come from is discussed later.

4.2 MOVING AND CENTRED AVERAGES

In the previous example we computed the average of the first 4 time periods and placed it next to quarter 2. However, because there are an even number of time periods considered in this calculation (i.e. we looked at four quarters) this really should have been place in the middle position between quarters 2 and 3 as follows:

Year	*Quarter*	*Moving average*
20X3	1	
20X3	2	
		88.00
20X3	3	
20X3	4	

So that the 88.00 is the mid-point between quarters 1 and 4 and appears between quarters 2 and 3. This would also apply to all subsequent averages:

Year	*Quarter*	*Moving average*
20X3	2	
		88.00
20X3	3	
		89.75
20X3	4	
		90.25
20X4	1	
		91.25

Technically, the moving average would fall at quarters 2.5, 3.5, etc. which means that we can't really compare the quarter 2 or 3 actuals against these as they do not fully line up with each quarter.

To avoid this problem we smooth the moving averages by calculating a centred average. This centred average is the average value for the point between two moving averages. So, for example, the first centred average is 88.875 (i.e. [88.00 + 89.75]/2) and we could now match up the centred average to appropriate periods:

Year	*Quarter*	*Moving average*	*Centred average (the trend)*	
20X3	2			
		88.00		
20X3	3		88.875	
		89.75		
20X3	4		90.00	i.e.(89.75 + 90.25)/2
		90.25		
20X4	1		90.75	i.e.(90.25 + 91.25)/2
		91.25		

We can see that the centred average matches up exactly with individual quarters. It is therefore this centred average that is used as the trend and which will be used to calculate the seasonal variation. This is a more accurate calculation that is necessary when there is an even number of periods considered in a year. This would improve the accuracy of our original calculation and is the approach that should be used in the examination.

4.3 THE MULTIPLICATIVE MODEL

The method of time series that we have illustrated so far is known as the additive model – we calculate the forecast by taking the trend and adding on the seasonal variation. There is an alternative known as the multiplicative model. This model is used when the seasonal variation is not calculated as an absolute number but instead as a percentage against the trend. For example, an organisation selling ice cream may know that sales are 50% higher in quarter 2 than the average trend for the year.

In order to determine the forecast we therefore take the trend and multiply by the seasonal variation. The model is calculated in much the same way as in the additive model but the results will be illustrated differently.

EXAMPLE

A hotel in a major holiday result has determined that its sales are seasonal and has calculated the following trend and seasonal variation based on its most recent set of results:

Year	*Quarter*	*Actual sales ($m)*	*Moving average*	*Seasonal variation*
20X1	1	64	60	1.07
20X1	2	79	70	1.13
20X1	3	70	80	0.87
20X1	4	84	90	0.93

In this scenario the seasonal variation, say, for quarter 2 tells us that sales in that quarter are typically 113% of the normal trend. In quarter 4 they are normally 93% of the trend.

We could build that into our forecasts. If the forecast trend for quarter 4 in 20X2 is 130, then we can estimate that actual sales in that quarter will be $121m (i.e. 130 × 93%).

4.4 FORECASTING TRENDS

In order to make the predictions in the forecast for next year we needed both the expected trend and the seasonal variation. We have illustrated how the seasonal variation can be determined from past behaviour but it will also be important that the organisation can forecast its trend.

There are a number of ways in which it might achieve this:

- it may use market forecasts of expected growth and build these into the expected growth in its trend (although this assumes that the organisation will grow at the same rate as the market)

- mathematical techniques such as linear regression (often compiled on a spreadsheet) can be used to develop an expected linear growth in the trend (although this assumes that the past behaviour will provide an accurate estimate of the expected change in future behaviour). **Note:** Calculations on this technique would not be required in an examination.

- the high-low method (explored in earlier chapters) could be used to forecast the change (though this would suffer from similar problems to the linear regression model, in that it assumes that the trend is linear and will continue to rise at the same rate in the future).

4.5 CHECKING THE REASONABLENESS OF FORECASTS

There are two important methods of checking the reasonableness of cash forecasts.

- Individuals who are in a good position to **verify the accuracy of forecasts or estimates** should be consulted. These individuals should also be in a position to identify any exceptional items of cash receipt or payment that the person preparing the budget is unaware of.

- The **assumptions in the budget should be checked for reasonableness**. For example, if the sales budget provides for a 10% increase in sales but the cash budget provides for a reduction in cash, the reasons for this apparent inconsistency should be checked.

5 FORECASTING WITH INFLATION

5.1 INFLATION AND INDEX NUMBERS

Inflation is the process whereby the price of commodities steadily rises over time. The result of inflation is that a given sum of money will buy fewer and fewer goods over time, i.e. money has less and less purchasing power. In periods of severe inflation, price rises take place at an increasing rate. This makes it very difficult for governments, businesses and individuals to plan ahead. Inflation reduces the value of money so that savings in particular become less attractive, and people on fixed incomes such as pensioners find that their purchasing power is reduced. Whilst a high rate of inflation is undesirable, regular and predictable price rises over a period of time are seen as positive since they encourage economic growth.

Inflation often makes information difficult to interpret. If data simply shows, for example, the cost of raw materials used, it may be difficult to assess changes in quantities used when the prices of the raw materials are subject to inflation. If management wishes to interpret changes in quantities of materials used, they must first adjust the expenditure figures for price changes.

An **index number** shows the rate of change of a variable from one specified time to another. A price index measures the change in the money value of a group of items over a period of time. In the UK, the inflation rate is calculated from the prices of a range of different goods and services selected to represent average spending patterns. The different items in the 'basket' of goods and services are given different weights, so that things we spend more on, such as housing, motoring and food, are given more importance. The best known is probably the retail price index (RPI), which measures changes in the prices of goods and services supplied to retail customers. This index is often thought of as a 'cost of living' index.

Inflation is usually measured as a percentage increase in the RPI. If the rate of inflation is 10% a year, for example, $50,000 worth of purchases last year will, on average, cost $55,000 this year. At the same inflation rate, those purchases will cost $60,500 next year, and their cost will double after only seven years.

5.2 THE IMPACT OF INFLATION ON CASH FLOW AND PROFITS

As we have already noted, inflation can be defined as a general increase in prices. This can also be described as a general decline in the real value of money. The main impact on an organisation's forecasts is that they can become out of date very quickly.

When inflation is very high the value of financial assets e.g. debt declines. Organisations will try to collect their debts quickly so that the cash can be reinvested. By delaying payments to suppliers, the underlying value of the debt can be reduced.

In periods of increasing inflation lenders will require an increasing return i.e. interest rates may be very high, so in the short term a treasurer will invest surplus cash on short-term deposit.

Index numbers are used to predict future cash inflows and outflows, estimating the future price index and giving management a better idea of the amount of sales in cash or the likely size of cash payments. They can also be used in forecasting borrowing limits, which might be fixed in monetary terms. Different indices can be used for items, such as capital goods or various types of revenue, which may be subject to differing rates of inflation.

6 CASH BUDGETS AS A MECHANISM FOR MONITORING AND CONTROL

6.1 CONSULTING STAFF ABOUT FUTURE CASH FLOWS

Cash budgets are prepared by accountants, but operational managers are responsible for earning income and for spending. When a cash budget is drafted, appropriate individuals (operational managers) should be consulted, to check:

- that they agree with the assumptions in the cash budget about income and expenditure, and receipts and payments
- whether there are any other exceptional items of receipt or payment that have been overlooked and so are missing from the draft cash budget.

As a general approach to reviewing cash budgets, you should think about:

- whether there is a noticeable trend in sales, and whether this seems reasonable
- whether the trend in variable costs is consistent with the trend in sales
- whether there are any changes in payment patterns, in receipts from customers or payments to suppliers
- whether all items of cash receipt and payment have been considered, including capital expenditures and any exceptional items
- whether inflation in costs and any planned sales price increases have been taken into account.

These points might seem sensible and straightforward. Attempt the following activity to check that you understand them.

6.2 MONITORING ACTUAL CASH FLOWS

One of the objectives of a cash budget is to provide a basis or reference point against which actual cash flows can be monitored. Comparing actual cash flows with the budget can help with:

- identifying whether cash flows are much better or worse than expected
- predicting what cash flows are now likely to be in the future, and in particular whether the business will have enough cash (or liquidity) to survive
- the reasons for any significant differences between actual and budgeted cash flows.

The forecast might differ from the actual due to poor forecasting techniques or to unpredictable events or developments such as the loss of a major customer, changes in interest rates or inflation, which can affect costs and revenues differently.

Monitoring against the cash flow forecast can take place over different timescales, depending upon:

- the nature of the business
- the scale of the cash flowing into and out of the business
- whether forecast assumptions require additional funding.

Just as cash flows can highlight shortfalls in funding within a business, so too can they highlight whether surplus funds are being generated. This would allow the business to invest those surplus funds to its benefit.

The benefit from preparing timely cash flow forecasts is that you have early indications of both good and not so good events. This allows you to take early action to avoid possible problems and to maximise returns on cash generated within the business.

Possible decisions that could be taken to deal with forecast short-term cash deficits include:

- additional short-term borrowing
- negotiating a higher overdraft limit with the bank
- the sale of short-term investments, if the company has any
- using different forms of financing to reduce cash flows in the short term, such as leasing instead of buying outright
- changing the amount of discretionary cash flows, deferring expenditures or bringing forward revenues. For example:
  - reducing the dividend to shareholders
  - postponing nonessential
  - capital expenditure
  - bringing forward the planned disposal of non-current assets
  - reducing inventory levels
  - shortening the operating cycle by reducing the time taken to collect receivables, perhaps by offering a discount
  - shortening the operating cycle by delaying payment to payables.

If the forecast shows cash surpluses, these will be dealt with according to their size and duration. Management should consider a policy for how surplus cash should be invested so as to achieve a return on the money, but without investing in items where the risk of a fall in value is considered too high. The interest or other return earned can be used to improve the overall cash position. Care must be taken to ensure these investments can be realised as needed, to fund forecast deficits.

Where long-term cash surpluses are forecast, management might consider other possible uses of the surpluses, such as paying a higher dividend or repaying loans and other debts.

6.3 CASH FLOW CONTROL REPORTS

Regular reporting of actual budgeted cash flows compared with budgeted cash flows should be carried out on a daily, weekly or monthly basis, depending on the size of the business and the frequency and value of its cash receipts and payments.

In common with all management reports, the purpose of a cash flow report is to provide a basis for management decision making. For this reason the report needs to be addressed to the manager who can control the cash flows.

Cash receipts

There are normally two main types of cash receipt to monitor: receipts from customers and investment income (e.g. interest).

Cash receipts from customers depend on:

- the volume and value of sales, and
- the time taken by customers to pay.

It is important to identify the cause of any difference in cash flow between budget and actual because the control action required will differ in each case.

If budgeted and actual cash receipts differ because budgeted and actual sales volumes are different, it should be remembered that the difference in volume should affect expenditures and cash payments too. The implications for cash flow should therefore be considered in terms of net cash flows – in other words the difference in cash receipts less the difference in cash payments.

If budgeted and actual cash receipts differ because customers are taking more or less time to pay what they owe, action should be taken either to amend the budget or to take measures to speed up customer payments.

Cash payments

Payments can be divided into three categories:

- payments of a routine, recurring nature which are unrelated to activity level (e.g. rent, senior management salaries)
- payments of a routine nature which are related to activity level (e.g. payments to suppliers for purchases/expenses, wage payments, payments to sales staff of sales commissions)
- payments of a non-recurring nature (e.g. taxation, dividends, major capital expenditures).

Some payments will be committed and uncontrollable. Others might be reduced or deferred to improve cash flow.

Revising the cash budget or preparing a new cash forecast

It is important that comparisons of actual cash flows should be against meaningful targets. From time to time it may therefore be necessary to revise the cash budget or prepare a new cash flow forecast. This should take account of the cash flows that have actually occurred and what future cash flows are now expected to be, in the light of revised estimates and management measures to deal with some of the problems.

CONCLUSION

Cash budgets are important because they help a business to plan its cash flows, and manage the risk. Constructing a cash budget is a fairly straightforward exercise, although it can involve a large amount of number crunching. You should try to gain as much practice as you can in preparing cash budgets, particularly receipts and payments budgets.

Cash flow is vital to the survival of a business, and the cash budget and cash flow reports are important sources of information for monitoring and managing the cash position.

Sensitivity analysis or 'what if' investigations allow you to alter assumptions and figures and see what happens. The ability to ask 'what if' questions using a spreadsheet is of considerable benefit to managers. This is mainly because they can analyse the effect of changes in any of the variables in a very short time, without any elaborate recalculations.

KEY TERMS

Cash budget – a detailed forecast of cash inflows and outflows for a future time period, incorporating revenue and capital items and other cash flow items.

Cash flow forecast – used to describe the preparation of future cash flow estimates.

Cash budget – a forecast that is adopted as a formal plan or target.

Lagged receipts and payments – receipts from credit sales occur sometime after the sale has taken place, and payments to suppliers take place sometime after the purchase.

SELF-TEST QUESTIONS

		Paragraph
1	What are the main cash receipts itemised in the cash budget?	2
2	What are lagged receipts?	2.1
3	Cash flow reports are used to monitor actual cash flows. How often should they be produced?	6.3

EXAM STYLE QUESTIONS

The following information relates to Questions 1, 2 and 3.

Chase, a distributor, is preparing a cash budget for the three months to 30 June 20X5. The following information could be relevant.

(a) Sales are expected to be $70,000 each month in January to March. 20% of total sales are paid for in the month of sale, 50% in the following month and 30% in the month after that.

(b) Receivables at the end of December were $80,000. Of these, $60,000 are expected to pay in January and 2% will be bad (irrecoverable) debts. The remainder will pay in February.

(c) The gross profit is 25%.

(d) Purchases are made two months before the month of sale, and 30 days' credit is taken from suppliers.

1 What are the sales receipts for the month of January?

A $14,000

B $70,000

C $74,000

D $80,000

2 What are the sales receipts for the month of February?

A $14,000

B $18,400

C $35,000

D $67,400

3 What is the payment to payables for the month of February?

A $10,500

B $52,500

C $55,500

D $60,000

4 A company is preparing a cash budget for the first six months of the year.

Administration and distribution expenses are expected to be $8,500 each month. Of these $500 each month consists of depreciation charges and $2,000 comprise rental charges. The rental charges are paid half-yearly with the period ended 30 June due in June. The expenses also include $1,000 each month for the rental of a delivery van. The remaining expenses are paid for at an even rate each month.

How much should be included for the administration and distribution payment for the month of January?

A $5,000

B $6,000

C $8,000

D $8,500

5 A company is preparing a cash budget for the first six months of the year.

Fixed overhead costs are estimated at $75,000 per annum and are expected to be incurred in equal amounts each month. 60% of the fixed overhead costs will be paid in the month in which they are incurred and 30% in the following month. The balance represents depreciation of non-current (fixed) assets.

How much should be included for fixed overhead payment for month 2?

A $0

B $3,750

C $5,625

D $6,250

The following information relates to Questions 6 and 7.

A new company is preparing its first ever budget for its first three months of trading based on the following assumptions:

Sales

The forecast sales for the first four months are as follows:

Month	*Number of components*
1	1,500
2	1,750
3	2,000
4	2,100

The selling price has been set at $10 per component in the first four months.

Sales receipts

Time of payment	% of customers
Month of sale	20*
One month later	45
Two months later	25
Three months later	5

The balance represents anticipated bad debts.

*A 2% discount is given to customers for payment received in the month of sale.

Production

There will be no opening inventory of finished goods in Month 1 but after that it will be policy for the closing inventory to be equal to 20% of the following month's forecast sales.

Direct materials will cost $1.90 per component. 100% of the materials required for production will be purchased in the month of production. No inventory of materials will be held. Direct materials will be paid for in the month following purchase.

6 What are the sales receipts for month 2?

- **A** $6,750
- **B** $10,180
- **C** $10,250
- **D** $17,500

7 How many units will be produced in month 1?

- **A** 1,850 units
- **B** 1,750 units
- **C** 1,500 units
- **D** 5,000 units

8 A time series analysis to business uses to forecast future sales based on quarterly sales from the last four years. Which of the following will most accurately represent the trend in sales used to calculate the seasonal variation?

- **A** Actual sales per quarter
- **B** Moving average sales per quarter
- **C** Centred average sales per quarter
- **D** Seasonal sales per quarter

For the answers to these questions, see the 'Answers' section at the end of the book.

Chapter 19

INFORMATION FOR COMPARISON

The syllabus so far has concerned itself with creating and gathering information. In the most recent chapters we have looked at preparing budgets and making plans for keeping the business under control and ensuring its progress towards the business goals. It will then be important for an organisation to compare actual performance to budgeted performance to determine whether these plans are being achieved and if the business is performing better or worse than expected. In this chapter we will look at making comparisons between actual results and budgeted plans to determine what are known as 'variances'. We begin by examining the types of comparison that may be made (and why), and then move on to the key comparisons that an accountant might make when considering the financial performance of the business. The chapter covers syllabus areas A4.

CONTENTS

LEARNING OUTCOMES

On completion of this chapter the student should be able to:

- explain the purpose of making comparisons.
- identify relevant bases for comparison: previous period data, corresponding period data, forecast/budget data.
- explain the forecasting/budgeting process and the concept of feed forward and feedback control.
- explain and illustrate the concept of flexible budgets.
- calculate variances between actual and historical/forecast data which may or may not be adjusted for volume change.
- identify whether variances are favourable or adverse.
- identify possible causes of variances.
- explain the concept of exception reporting.
- explain factors affecting the decision whether to investigate variances.

1 PURPOSE OF MAKING COMPARISONS

The purpose of management information is to help management:

- make decisions about the future of the business and about the day-to-day running of the business
- plan the strategy of the business and its operations
- control the operations, costs and income of the business.

Without comparisons management will not know whether it is achieving its targets, whether it is improving, how it compares with this time last year and how it compares with its competitors. Comparisons and their analysis are one of the ways in which management can identify whether control action is needed.

2 COMPARISONS FREQUENTLY USED

2.1 PREVIOUS PERIODS

In some cases you will be required to compare current costs and income to the same costs and income from previous periods in order to determine any significant differences. Comparisons with the results for previous periods will help to identify any trends in the company's costs and income.

The previous period's costs and income will have been summarised in management cost reports and you need to be able to find these reports in your organisation's filing system.

2.2 CORRESPONDING PERIODS

Although comparison with previous periods can help to identify trends it can be misleading if the company's activity is subject to seasonal fluctuations. Think about a company in the UK that sells ice creams.

The following results show the sales revenue generated during the latest two quarters.

	$000
July to September 20X5	98
October to December 20X5	29

This comparison shows an apparently alarming reduction in sales between the two quarters. However the sales of ice cream in this situation will be subject to seasonal fluctuation therefore this comparison is not particularly effective. Either the effect of the seasonal variation should be removed from the data, or a comparison should be made with a corresponding period to obtain more useful information. A comparison with the results for the corresponding periods in the preceding year might be as follows:

	20X4	*20X5*	*%*
	$000	$000	*increase*
July to September	75	98	31
October to December	22	29	32

Now managers can see that there has been a significant increase in sales revenue when a comparison is made between corresponding periods.

2.3 FORECAST DATA

Current forecasts might be compared with the budgeted results for the forthcoming period in a system of **feed forward control** (explained again later). If the comparison shows that the future expected results are different from the budgeted outcome then managers may take action now to bring expected results more into line with the budget.

2.4 BUDGET DATA

You may also be required to compare current costs and income to the amounts that were budgeted for this period. Again you will need to be able to find the relevant budgets in the organisation's filing system.

In making a budgetary control comparison it will be important to take account of the possible impact of activity levels. If activity levels fluctuate and a significant proportion of costs are variable then it will be necessary to use a system of flexible budgets, as we saw in the last chapter.

2.5 STANDARD COSTS

Finally you may have to compare costs for this period with the standard costs that have been set in order to determine if there are any variances. You will therefore need to know where to find the relevant standard cost information.

2.6 CURRENT PERIOD COSTS

In most cases you will be comparing current costs and income. These figures will have to be extracted from the relevant cost and income ledger accounts.

3 THE BUDGETING PROCESS

One of the most common types of comparison is against budgeted results. In order to understand budgets there are two elements that must be understood before using budgets in comparisons:

- the reason that budgets are prepared (the budgetary control process), and
- the meaning of a flexible (or flexed) budget.

3.1 THE BUDGETARY CONTROL PROCESS

Essentially the budgetary control process consists of two distinct elements:

(i) **Planning**

This involves the setting of the various budgets for the appropriate future period. Managers at various levels in an organisation should be involved in the budgetary planning stage for their area of responsibility. The budgets for the different divisions of an organisation need to be coordinated to ensure that they are all complementary and in line with overall company objectives and policies – feedback is essential.

(ii) **Control**

Once the budgets have been set and agreed for the future period, the formal element of budgetary control is ready to start. This control involves comparing the plan in the form of the original budget with the actual results achieved for the period under consideration. Any significant differences between the budgeted and the actual results should be reported to appropriate management so that action can be taken if necessary. Again, appropriate feedback is an essential component of the budgeting control process.

Feedback control is action taken by a manager in response to recorded differences between the budget and actual performance. The action may be taken to correct deviations or to revise the budget if appropriate.

If current forecasts show that the future expected results are different from the budgeted outcome then managers may take action now to bring expected results more into line with the budget. This type of corrective action, taken in advance to prevent or reduce expected deviations from budgeted performance, is called **feed forward control**.

3.2 FLEXIBLE BUDGETS

The simple budgeting process described above is the preparation of a fixed budget. A fixed budget assumes a level of costs and revenues for a specific level of activity. This might be appropriate in the short term or if a large amount of the costs are fixed in nature.

If the nature of the costs is predominantly variable then quite small changes in the level of activity could destroy any meaningful comparison between the budgeted and actual costs. It would be difficult therefore to determine whether or not the business was operating efficiently.

EXAMPLE

Consider a decorating department run by the local council for its housing stock.

A fixed budget might look like this:

	June 20X3
	$
Labour	40,000
Materials	8,000
Other costs	2,000
	50,000

Expected number of houses to decorate: 20

If the actual result for the month was:

	June 20X3
	$
Labour	39,000
Materials	9,000
Other costs	2,200
	50,200

Number of houses decorated: 21

Is this better or worse than budgeted? The department has incurred higher costs than expected but has decorated more houses than budgeted. At first sight this looks good.

However it would be useful to give a target budget based on the level of activity achieved. To do this we need to know which costs are fixed and which are variable. We would expect the budget cost allowance for variable costs to increase since more houses were decorated than expected in the original fixed budget.

Continuing this example, suppose that the budgeted fixed costs were identified as follows:

Other costs	$200
Labour costs	$30,000

All other costs are variable in proportion to the number of houses decorated.

In this case the target budget cost allowance would be prepared as follows:

	June 20X3 *Variable costs per house*
	$
Labour $((40,000 – 30,000)/20)	500
Materials $8,000/20	400
Other costs $((2,000 – 200)/20)	90
	990

and therefore the target budget for 21 houses would be:

	Variable cost	*Fixed cost*	*Flexed Budget June 20X3*	*Actual cost*	*Variance**
	$	$	$	$	$
Labour	10,500	30,000	40,500	39,000	1,500 F
Materials	8,400	–	8,400	9,000	600 A
Other costs	1,890	200	2,090	2,200	110 A
	20,790	30,200	50,990	50,200	790 F

*F = favourable, (A) = adverse

So the flexed budget has taken the original (fixed) budget and adjusted it to the actual level of activity (21 houses). It is this flexed budget that is then used for comparison with the actual cost. For example, the revised (flexed) budget for labour cost is now $40,500 whereas the actual cost is $39,000. This results in what is called **a variance** – the actual cost varies from the flexed budget by $1,500. Because the actual cost is lower than the flexed budget it means that the variance is in the business' favour (i.e. the businesses costs are $1,500 less than expected) and this is reflected in the table with a letter F. If the actual cost had been higher than the flexed budget this would have harmed the business' profit and be known as an adverse variance (reflected in the table with a letter A).

The department has therefore performed even better when the actual results are compared with a realistic budget for 21 houses. The overall variance is $790 Favourable – actual costs were $790 less than would have been expected based on the budgeted cost.

This type of target budget is a flexible budget where the focus of the budget is in terms of the activity variables achieved, i.e. in the case above for 21 houses.

This approach can be used for a business or a department where the variable element of the costs is proportionately high and where the units produced are not necessarily in the control of the manager for whom the budget is prepared.

For this paper, it is assumed that costs are either:

- fixed
- proportionately variable.

Proportionately variable costs, such as direct labour and direct material costs, vary with the level (volume) of activity as follows:

EXAMPLE – Flexed budgets

10,000 units of product A are budgeted to be produced at a cost of $50,000 for direct materials and $30,000 for direct labour. The actual production level was only 8,000 units.

Flexed direct material budget = 8,000/10,000 × $50,000 = $40,000

Flexed direct labour budget = 8,000/10,000 × $30,000 = $24,000

Since the material and labour costs are 'proportionately variable', the change in activity level results in the same change in budgeted direct costs.

4 CURRENT AND PREVIOUS PERIOD

Let's now consider making more comparisons of data, including the budgeted data that we have just considered.

The first example of a comparison of information that will be considered is a comparison of the current period's costs to the costs of the previous period.

EXAMPLE

You have been asked to prepare a comparison of the wage cost for each cost centre for the month of May and the month of June. The gross wages account from the costing ledger is given for both May and June. In May 22,500 units were produced but in June only 18,000. Sales were the same quantity in both May and June.

May

Gross wages cost control account

Dr	$		$ Cr
Cost ledger control account	51,000	WIP control account	31,500
		Sales cost centre	7,500
		Administration cost centre	12,000
	51,000		51,000

June

Gross wages cost control account

Dr	$		$ Cr
Cost ledger control account	46,300	WIP control account	26,500
		Sales cost centre	8,200
		Administration cost centre	11,600
	46,300		46,300

You also discover from the payroll records that one weekly paid employee was on holiday for two weeks in June with no holiday pay. The gross pay of this employee is $250 per week. This employee was working in the administration cost centre.

Prepare a schedule showing any significant differences in the wage costs for each cost centre for May and June.

SOLUTION

	May	*May (Flexed)*	*June*	*Differences F/(A)*
Activity level	22,500 units		18,000 units	
Production labour	$31,500			
($31,500 × 18,000/22,500)		$25,200	$26,500	$1,300 (A)
Sales labour	$7,500	–	$8,200	$700 (A)
Administration labour	$12,000	$11,500	$11,600	$100 (A)

Tutorial note: The sales labour cost is not flexed for comparison purposes because the sales level was the same in May and June. The administration labour cost is assumed to be fixed in relation to the level of activity, but for a valid comparison the May cost of $12,000 is 'flexed' or adjusted by removing the $500 of cost of the employee who was on unpaid holiday leave in June.

5 CURRENT PERIOD AND BUDGET

Now we will look at a comparison of actual current costs with the figures that were budgeted for the current period.

EXAMPLE

Shown below is last month's expense costs and activity, both budget and actual, for department 7 in a manufacturing company:

	Month's budget	*Month's actual*
Production (units)	8,000	8,400
	$	$
Fixed expenses:		
Rent	6,750	6,400
Maintenance	3,250	3,315
	10,000	9,715
Variable expenses:		
Power	17,600	20,140
/Machine repairs	6,000	5,960
Packaging	4,400	4,480
Total expenses	$38,000	$40,295

Draw up a schedule highlighting any variances both in the totals for fixed and variable expenses and for each category of expense within the totals.

SOLUTION

	Budget	*Flexed budget*	*Actual*	*Variance F/(A)**
	$	$	$	$
Fixed expenses:				
Rent	6,750	6,750	6,400	350 F
Maintenance	3,250	3,250	3,315	65 (A)
	10,000	10,000	9,715	285 F
Variable expenses:				
Power	17,600	18,480	20,140	1,660 (A)
Machine repairs	6,000	6,300	5,960	340 F
Packaging	4,400	4,620	4,480	140 F
	28,000	29,400	30,580	1,180 (A)

*F = favourable, (A) = adverse

Tutorial note: Fixed expenses are not flexed as they would not be expected to change despite the fact that actual production is 400 units more than budgeted production.

Variable expenses have been flexed to reflect that the activity level was 8,400 units rather than the budgeted figure of 8,000 units.

Power $17,600 × 8,400/8,000 = $18,480

Machine repairs $6,000 × 8,400/8,000 = $6,300

Packaging $4,400 × 8,400/8,000 = $4,620

6 SALES COMPARISONS

So far in this chapter we have only considered the comparison of costs to previous periods and budgeted figures. The same type of comparison can be made for sales income.

EXAMPLE

The sales figures for your organisation's two products, X and Y, are given below for May and June.

	May		*June*	
	Product X	*Product Y*	*Product X*	*Product Y*
Units	2,000	3,500	2,400	3,300
Price per unit	$5.40	$3.80	$5.00	$4.10

Prepare a schedule showing changes in units and total income from sales between May and June.

SOLUTION

		May	*June*	*Difference F/(A)**
Product X	units	2,000	2,400	400 F
	value	$10,800	$12,000	$1,200 F
Product Y	units	3,500	3,300	200 (A)
	value	$13,300	$13,530	$230 F
Total	value	$24,100	$25,530	$1,430 F

* F = favourable; (A) = adverse

7 EXCEPTION REPORTING

7.1 INTRODUCTION

Managers need useful information in order to make decisions, to plan and to control a business. You will have seen from your studies so far and from the work for this paper that companies produce significant amounts of data and information. If all of the information was passed to management in a raw form it would be difficult for them to determine what was important for them to assimilate and act on in order to make appropriate decisions, to plan or to control the business.

Exception reporting is the principle of highlighting for management attention only those variances which exceed a certain limit. The limit might be expressed in terms of an absolute amount or as a percentage.

For example, variances on individual overhead cost items might only be highlighted when an adverse variance exceeds, say 5% of the standard cost and a favourable variance exceeds, say, 10% of the standard cost.

EXAMPLE – Exception reporting

The following extract shows the budget and actual overhead costs recorded for a company for the latest period.

The company's reporting policy is to produce an exception report detailing those overhead cost variances which, when compared to the budgeted cost, are more than 5% adverse or 10% favourable.

	Actual	*Budget*	*Variance*	*Variance*
	$	$	$	%*
Rent	23,800	22,100	1,700 (A)	7.7% (A)
Electricity	18,200	18,700	500 F	2.7% F
Catering	9,860	10,150	290 F	2.9% F
Advertising	12,300	15,100	2,800 F	18.5% F

(A) denotes an adverse variance; F denotes a favourable variance

* Example calculation (1,700/22,100) × 100% = 7.7%

SOLUTION

An exception report prepared according to the company's reporting policy would look like this.

Exception report: overhead variances for latest period

	Actual	*Budget*	*Variance*	*Variance*
	$	$	$	%*
Rent	23,800	22,100	1,700 (A)	7.7% (A)
Advertising	12,300	15,100	2,800 F	18.5% F

Management attention is therefore directed to areas where control action might be necessary. Managers are not overwhelmed with information about areas of the business that are operating according to budget and where control action is not necessary.

Note that favourable variances are not necessarily good news for the company. In this example there is a significant shortfall on advertising expenditure compared with the budget. The manager responsible for advertising should be made aware of this because the difference might have a detrimental effect on the company. Less spending on advertising in future periods might lead to lower sales volumes and therefore lower profits.

8 COST VARIANCES

8.1 INTRODUCTION

Cost variances occur for the following reasons:

- changes in the volume of activity
- changes in the prices paid for direct resources (such as material and labour) and changes in the efficiency with which these resources are used/employed.

8.2 FLEXED BUDGETS

In order to calculate variances, you need to be able to produce flexed budgets. We looked at flexible budgets in an earlier chapter. Flexible budgets allow flexed budgets to be prepared at different activity levels. In order to prepare flexed budgets, it is essential to have an understanding of the way in which the budgeted costs behave.

8.3 CALCULATING COST VARIANCES

In the following sections we shall be looking at the main types of cost variance that you need to be able to calculate: materials and labour cost variances. You might find it useful to refer to the 'rules' shown below as you work through the following sections:

- Total direct cost variance = Original budgeted direct cost – Actual direct cost incurred
- Activity (volume) cost variance = Original budgeted direct cost – Flexed direct cost budget
- Variance due to other changes = Flexed direct cost budget – Actual direct cost incurred

9 COST VARIANCES – MATERIALS

9.1 INTRODUCTION

One of the main types of cost variance is the total materials cost variance. The total materials cost variance can be analysed as follows:

- variances due to the change in the volume of activity (materials volume variances)
- variances due to changes in the prices paid for materials and/or the efficiency with which the materials are used.

9.2 CALCULATION OF MATERIALS VARIANCES

The calculation of materials variances is best explained by means of an example.

EXAMPLE – Calculation of material cost variances

The budget for period 6 shows a budgeted production level of 3,000 units for a total budgeted material cost of $12,000.

The actual output was 2,800 units for an actual material cost of $11,890.

Total material cost variance

The total material cost variance is the difference between the original budgeted direct material cost and the actual cost of the materials.

Budgeted material cost per unit = $12,000/3,000 = $4 per unit

Total material cost variance = $12,000 – $11,890 = $110 favourable

The variance is favourable because less was spent on materials than originally budgeted.

The total material cost variance can be broken down into a materials activity (volume) variance and a variance due to changes in the purchase price and/or the efficiency of usage.

Materials activity (volume) variance

The flexed budget for the revised direct material cost based on actual production is:

$$\frac{2{,}800\text{ units}}{3{,}000\text{ units}} \times \$12{,}000 = \$11{,}200$$

The activity (volume) variance is the difference between the original (fixed) budget and the flexed budget i.e. $12,000 – $11,200 = $800 favourable. The variance is favourable because less units were produced compared to the original budget. This means that less direct material costs were incurred.

Variance due to changes in purchase price and/or efficiency of usage

This variance is calculated by comparing the flexed budget to the actual costs incurred = $11,200 – $11,890 = $690 adverse.

Summary

	$
Materials activity (volume) variance	800 favourable
Variance due to other changes	690 adverse
Total materials cost variance	110 favourable

9.3 POSSIBLE REASONS FOR MATERIALS VARIANCES

Possible reasons for materials variances include the following:

- an unexpected change to a new supplier of the material who may be cheaper or more expensive
- an unexpected quantity discount offered or removed by the current supplier of the material
- use of lower or higher quality and, therefore, cheaper or more expensive grade of material than budgeted for
- a change to the design or quality of the product since the budget was set which requires more or less material
- more or less wastage of materials than anticipated

- use of a higher or lower grade of material resulting in less or more being required
- using staff who are better or worse and therefore waste less or more materials
- changing to new machinery that wastes less or more materials.

ACTIVITY 1

In the recent past an organisation has always paid $5 per litre for a particular material. This is the budgeted price. The most recent invoice shows that the supplier has chosen to give a 2% discount due to the large quantities of the material purchased.

Will the total material cost variance be favourable or adverse?

For a suggested answer, see the 'Answers' section at the end of the book.

ACTIVITY 2

The latest purchase of a particular material shows that the price has increased from the previous price of $4.00 per metre to $4.25 per metre. The budgeted cost is based upon a budgeted price of $4.00 per metre.

Will the total material cost variance be favourable or adverse?

For a suggested answer, see the 'Answers' section at the end of the book.

ACTIVITY 3

A chemical company requires a particular liquid chemical for input into one of its products. The technical specification on which the budgeted usage is based states that 10 millilitres of this chemical is required for each batch of the product.

However, since the specification was drawn up the company policy has changed in that a lower grade of this liquid chemical is now used. This means, however, that in order to have the same effect on a batch of the product 15 millilitres must be used.

Will this change in company policy give rise to an adverse or favourable total material cost variance?

For a suggested answer, see the 'Answers' section at the end of the book.

ACTIVITY 4

The following is the materials cost extract from the budget cost card for a unit of 'Chemex'.

'CHEMEX'	
	$
Material AC25	7.20

The budgeted costs were based upon the expectation of 1,000 units being produced in the period but in fact only 940 were produced. The actual cost of material AC25 bought and used was $6,240.

Calculate the following variances for the 'Chemex' production:

(a) materials activity (volume) variance

(b) variance due to changes in the purchase price of the material and/or the efficiency of the usage of the material

(c) materials total variance.

For a suggested answer, see the 'Answers' section at the end of the book.

10 COST VARIANCES – LABOUR

10.1 CALCULATION OF LABOUR COST VARIANCES

The labour cost variances are very similar to the materials cost variances that we looked at in the previous section. As with materials, the total labour variance can be broken down to show how much of the variance is due to changes in the volume of activity and how much is due to changes in the rate paid and/or efficiency of workers.

EXAMPLE – Calculation of labour cost variances

Last month a company budgeted to make 4,200 units of a product at a cost of $33,600. Last month 4,000 units were manufactured and the total labour cost was $34,000.

Total labour cost variance

The total labour cost variance is the difference between the original budgeted labour cost and the actual cost of labour:

Total labour cost variance = $33,600 – $34,000 = $400 adverse

Labour activity (volume) variance

This is the difference between the original fixed budget and the flexed budget.

The flexed budget calculates the revised labour cost based on the actual volume of production.

Flexed labour budget = 4,000 units × $33,600/4,200 units = $32,000

Labour activity variance = $33,600 – $32,000 = $1,600 favourable

The variance is favourable because less units were produced than originally budgeted.

Variance due to changes in rate paid and/or efficiency of workers

This variance is calculated by comparing the flexed budget to the actual costs incurred = $32,000 – $34,000 = $2,000 adverse

Summary

	$
Labour activity (volume) variance	1,600 favourable
Variance due to other changes	2,000 adverse
Total labour variance	400 adverse

ACTIVITY 5

The budget for product B includes the following information about direct labour:

	$
	30.00

During January 100 units of product B were produced. The total wage payment for the period for those direct workers involved with product B was $3,660.

Calculate the total direct labour cost variance.

For a suggested answer, see the 'Answers' section at the end of the book.

10.2 REASONS FOR LABOUR COST VARIANCES

Reasons for labour cost variances include the following:

- When the wage rate paid per hour worked is different to the budgeted wage rate.
- When the actual hours taken to produce a given output are different from the budgeted hours allowed for the actual production.
- When fewer hours have been worked than the budget for the actual production or a lower hourly rate was paid than the budgeted rate.
- When more hours have been worked than the budget for the actual production or a higher hourly rate was paid.
- If a cheaper grade of labour is used on a product than the budgeted grade.
- If pay increases expected in the original budget were not as large as forecast.
- If there is an unexpected increase in wages due to, for example, a negotiated or national pay award.
- When a more expensive or more skilled grade of labour than expected is used.

ACTIVITY 6

The wage rate for a particular grade of labour has been $12.80 per hour for the last six months and was expected to remain at this level for some months to come. However, due to a threat of strike action by the employees the management decided to give a pay rate increase to all workers of 2.5%.

The budgeted rate of labour included for this grade is $12.80 per hour.

What type of total labour cost variance will this increase cause?

For a suggested answer, see the 'Answers' section at the end of the book.

ACTIVITY 7

When the budgeted labour for the production of one unit of 'Micro' was set it was expected that Grade II labour would be used and that production of one unit would take five minutes.

Due to unavoidable circumstances a less skilled grade of labour, Grade V, has had to be used and this has increased the time taken to produce a unit to six minutes.

What type of total labour cost variance would this cause?

For a suggested answer, see the 'Answers' section at the end of the book.

11 REVENUE VARIANCES

11.1 INTRODUCTION

The purpose of calculating revenue (sales) variances is to show their effect on profit when reconciling budget and actual profit. There are two causes of sales variances:

- a difference in the level (volume) of sales
- a difference in the selling price.

The activity (sales) volume variance shows the effect on profit of selling a different volume from that budgeted.

The selling price variance shows the effect on profit of selling at a different price from that budgeted.

11.2 CALCULATION OF REVENUE VARIANCES

The calculation of revenue variances is best explained by means of an example.

EXAMPLE – Calculation of revenue variances

A company has budgeted sales of 10,000 units per month at $15.00 per unit. Last month it actually sold 11,000 units for $159,500.

Total sales variance

Budgeted sales revenue for the month was $150,000, which means that there is a total sales variance of $150,000 – $159,500 = $9,500 (favourable). The total sales variance is therefore the difference between the budgeted sales revenue and the actual sales revenue.

The total sales variance can be broken down into a sales (activity) volume variance and a selling price variance.

Sales activity (volume) variance

The flexed budget for actual sales calculates a revised budgeted revenue of 11,000 × $15 = $165,000. Therefore, sales activity (volume) variance = $165,000 – $150,000 = $15,000. The variance is favourable because more units were sold than originally budgeted.

Selling price variance

The actual selling price per unit was $159,500/11,000 = $14.50 per unit. This means that the selling price was $0.50 per unit less than budgeted. Multiplying this by the actual quantity sold, the sales price variance = 11,000 × $0.50 = $5,500 (adverse). The variance is adverse because the selling price per unit was less than budgeted.

Summary	$
Sales activity (volume) variance	15,000 favourable
Selling price variance	5,500 adverse
Total sales variance	9,500 favourable

11.3 POSSIBLE REASONS FOR SALES VARIANCES

Possible reasons for sales variances include the following:

- charging a higher price (favourable selling price variance) or lower price (adverse selling price variance) than budgeted per unit
- increasing advertising expenditure to boost sales (favourable sales activity (volume) variance)
- increased activity from competitors resulting in customers going elsewhere (adverse sales activity (volume) variance).

ACTIVITY 8

The selling price budgeted for sales of 10,000 units (per month) of product X was $8 per unit. Last month 8,000 units were sold for $68,000.

Calculate the following revenue variances:

(a) sales activity (volume) variance

(b) selling price variance

(c) total sales variance.

For a suggested answer, see the 'Answers' section at the end of the book.

12 CAUSES OF VARIANCES

12.1 INTRODUCTION

It is not enough to calculate and report variances; they must also be explained to senior management.

The original explanation of how each variance arose must come from the line manager responsible for that particular cost.

The explanations for each individual cost variance will then be brought together by the management accountant when producing a variance or exception report for senior management. It may be seen at this stage that one particular occurrence affects a number of different costs in different ways and can explain a number of different variances.

12.2 GENERAL REASONS FOR VARIANCES

One management accounting author suggested four general causes for variances:

- bad budgeting
- bad measurement or recording
- random factors
- operational factors.

We have already looked at the operational factors that cause variances in some detail when we looked at materials and labour cost variances.

12.3 INTERDEPENDENCE OF VARIANCES

It is possible that one occurrence or event might be the cause of more than one variance. This is known as the interdependence of variances.

EXAMPLE – Improving productivity

If the workforce attempts to improve its productivity then this could have an effect on both labour cost variances and materials cost variances.

An improvement in productivity should lead to a favourable labour cost variance. However, if the improvement in productivity has come about by rushed work and more waste being created then there could also be an adverse materials cost variance.

EXAMPLE – Overhead variances interrelated with direct cost variances

If a supplier of raw materials offers an organisation a quantity discount and this is accepted then this will lead to a favourable materials cost variance because prices will be lower than expected. However, if the quantity that must be purchased is such that additional warehouse space must be rented, then this might also cause an adverse overhead variance.

Conclusion Variances can be caused by bad budgeting, bad recording, random factors or operational factors. The cause of one variance may well give rise to another variance. Therefore, it is important that variances should be considered as a whole rather than separately.

13 DECIDING WHETHER TO INVESTIGATE VARIANCES

Once variances have been calculated and presented to management a decision will need to be made as to whether each variance should be investigated. It would probably not be worthwhile investigating every variance and the organisation will need to establish criteria which can be used to assess whether a particular variance should be investigated.

Factors which may be considered include the following:

The likelihood of the variance being controllable when the cause is identified. Certain variances may be caused by uncontrollable factors such as a general increase in the price of an essential raw material.

The cost of an investigation and the savings arising if the variance is corrected. A costly investigation might outweigh the benefits.

The size of the variance. We have seen that variances may arise due to random causes and how exception reporting might be used to highlight those variances which may be worthy of investigation.

Possible interrelationships between variances. A detailed investigation into the cause of a particular variance may be unnecessary because it has arisen as a direct result of another variance.

The trend in variances. Although an individual variance may be small it may be steadily increasing. It might be worthwhile investigating its cause now, instead of waiting until the variance becomes significant in the future.

CONCLUSION

Management compare data to produce useful information for planning, control and decision-making purposes. Comparisons are often made with previous years, budget data, forecast data and standard costs

These comparisons often lead to a variance between what was planned and/or expected and what actually happened. The calculation of variances is a useful control tool for management. By considering the size and trend of variances management can decide whether to investigate the causes of significant variances and therefore be in a position to take action to bring performance in line with plans.

KEY TERMS

Exception reporting – the principle of highlighting for management attention only those variances which exceed a certain limit.

Total direct cost variance = Original budgeted direct cost – Actual direct cost incurred

Activity (volume) cost variance = Original budgeted direct cost – Flexed direct cost budget

Cost variances due to other changes = Flexed direct cost budget – Actual direct cost incurred

Interdependence – one occurrence causes several variances.

SELF TEST QUESTIONS

		Paragraph
1	Against which data might current period data be compared?	2
2	What is meant by exception reporting?	7
3	How is a total direct cost variance calculated?	8.3
4	How is an activity (volume) cost variance calculated?	8.3
5	The variance calculated by comparing the flexed direct cost budget and the actual direct cost budget is due to changes in what?	8.3
6	What are the two causes of sales variances?	11.3
7	State four general reasons for variances.	12.2
8	Explain why variances might be interdependent.	12.3
9	State the factors to be considered when deciding whether to investigate a variance.	13

EXAM-STYLE QUESTIONS

1 A favourable direct labour cost variance has been reported for the latest period. Which of the following factors would NOT have contributed to this variance?

A Employees worked at a faster rate than had been expected in the budget

B The original budgeted labour rate per hour was set too low

C Higher quality material was used which was easier to process

D New and more efficient working practices were instigated which had not been included in the budget

2 The following information relates to a company for the last period:

	Budget	*Actual*
Production units	700	720
Material cost	$2,625	$2,628

The total material cost variance is:

A $3 Adverse

B $3 Favourable

C $20 Favourable

D $72 Favourable

3 A favourable material cost variance could have been caused by all except which of the following:

A an unexpected bulk discount given for the material purchased

B inexperienced labour causing higher usage of material

C a new machine which is more efficient in cutting material

D a change in product design

4 Action taken to correct deviations or to revise the budget if appropriate is an example of **feedback/feed forward** control *(select the correct term)*

5 An organisation created a budget for January showing a budgeted production level of 8,000 units for a total budgeted material cost of $48,000.

The actual output was 9,000 units for an actual material cost of $53,100.

Calculate the materials activity (volume) variance for January.

A $5,100 Favourable

B $5,100 Adverse

C $6,000 Favourable

D $6,000 Adverse

6 An organisation had an original total cost budget as follows:

	$
Budgeted variable costs	150,000
Budgeted	80,000
Total sales variance	230,000

Actual production output was twice as high as originally planned. The flexed total cost budget for the period would be $_____ (insert the correct amount to the nearest $)

7 Which of the following is likely to cause an adverse labour activity (volume) variance?

A An increase in the labour wage rate

B The use of a lower grade of labour

C Labour finishing jobs more quickly

D Fewer units produced than were expected

8 A company has budgeted sales of 1,000 units per month at $2000 per unit. Last month it actually sold 800 units for $1,680,000.

The selling price for the period is $______ (fill in the answer to the nearest $) and it would be _______ (choose between adverse/favourable)

9 Which of the following is not normally considered when determining whether or not to investigate a variance?

A Whether the variance is adverse or favourable

B The size of the variance

C The cost of investigation

D The trend in the variance

For suggested answers, see the 'Answers' section at the end of the book.

Chapter 20

REPORTING MANAGEMENT INFORMATION

This chapter starts with the various principles and rules concerned with presenting information. It focuses on the advantages of charts and graphs as visual aids, and draws attention to the use of IT packages in presenting information to management. It then goes on to cover how management information is communicated and how confidential information should be handled. The chapter covers syllabus area A5.

CONTENTS

LEARNING OUTCOMES

On completion of this chapter the student should be able to:

- identify suitable formats for the presentation of management information according to purpose
- describe methods of analysing, presenting and communicating information
- identify suitable formats for communicating management information according to purpose and organisational guidelines including: informal business reports, letter and email or memo
- identify the general principles of distributing reports (e.g. procedures, timing, recipients) including the reporting of confidential information
- interpret information presented in management reports.

1 REPORTS

Accountants are used to dealing with figures, but they must also learn to express themselves clearly in words. Accountants are (or should be) well prepared for the degree of precision and organisation required in report writing, but may need practice to improve their written style.

Reports may be prepared routinely, as a part of the regular reporting system within the company. These routine reports will contain standard information that is often produced at set times.

An **ad hoc report** is prepared only once or occasionally. It will not have a set content and the content will vary according to the requirements of the recipient. An ad hoc report may be prepared, for example, if a manager is making a one-off decision that requires more detail on a particular aspect of the business than is available from the routine reporting system.

1.1 FORMAT

The following guidelines for report writing should be observed:

(a) Reporting objectives

Every report has several objectives. Typically they will define the problem, consider alternatives and make a reasoned recommendation for a specific alternative.

(b) Recipient

The writer should consider the position of the recipient and design the report accordingly. Some recipients will require detailed calculations; others will have little time to study a lengthy report and should therefore be given one of minimum length consistent with providing the required information.

(c) Heading

Each report should be headed to show who it is from and who it is being sent to, the subject and the date.

(d) Paragraph point system – each paragraph should make a point; each point should have a paragraph

This simple rule should always be observed. Important points may be underlined.

(e) Jargon and technical terms

The use of jargon should be avoided at all times. If it is necessary to use technical terms, these should be fully explained, as should any techniques with which the recipient may be unfamiliar e.g. marginal costing, flexible budgets, etc.

(f) Conclusion

A report should always reach a conclusion. This should be clearly stated at the end of the report, and justified. It is not enough simply to state all the alternatives and then to recommend one of them without supportive reasoning.

(g) Figures

All detailed figures and calculations should be relegated to appendices; only the main results appearing in the body of the report. Remember that comparative figures will often be useful.

1.2 WORD-PROCESSED DOCUMENTS

All of the above documents would usually be produced using word processing software. Memos and short reports should follow your company style. An example report and memo follow.

REPORT

To: Managing Director

From: Candidate dy

Date: Dec X3

Subject: Evaluation of a new product X

We have evaluated the new product X in terms of its impact on profitability. On the basis of the information provided, the product should generate profit of $28,600 p.a. and should be carried out.

It would be helpful to know:

1 Whether the introduction of X will affect sales of existing products.

2 Further details on costs throughout the product lifecycle.

INTERNAL MEMO

To: **Bobby Forster, Accounts Assistant**

From: **General Manager**

Date: **28 October 20X3**

Subject: **Budgeted production costs for 20X4**

As you know we have begun our budgetary planning exercise for 20X4.

I understand that you have been working on the analysis of budgeted production costs.

Could you please pull together all the information you have gathered and carry out the allocation and apportionment exercise for production overhead costs for 20X4.

Thanks. Then we will have the necessary information that we need to calculate the predetermined overhead absorption rates for 20X4.

1.3 REPORTS AND THE PRESENTATION OF INFORMATION

Reports may be produced in a number of forms ranging from periodic printed reports, through to a senior executive producing an individual report on an executive information system. Typical reports produced in a medium-sized manufacturing company might include the following:

Type of activity	*Typical reports*
Production and material control	Forward loading plans for production cycles Machine capacity forecast Departmental operating statements Inventory and work-in-progress reports Wastage report Labour utilisation report
Marketing, including distribution	Market surveys Order reports by product and geographical area Discount trends Transport and warehouse cost statements Salesperson performance Product service and support costs
Personnel	Numbers employed by category Overtime hours Sickness, absence, lateness Training requirements Career development plans Recruitment policy Job descriptions
Financial and management accounting	Annual statutory accounts Budgets and forecasts Sales and contribution analyses Cash management and working capital evaluation Capital project appraisal Standard cost and variance analysis reports Returns to government departments, e.g. returns for Sales Tax (VAT returns in the UK)

1.4 THE NATURE OF INTERNAL REPORTING

Management accounting (and cost accounting) differs from financial accounting because:

- the financial accounts provide the data for preparing financial statements for external users, such as a company's shareholders or the government (tax authorities)
- management accounting/cost accounting reports are prepared exclusively for internal use by management.

Internally-produced information can be provided to managers:

- in as much or as little detail as management require
- relating to whatever items management need information about
- in whatever format is preferred (for example, there are no regulations about how management accounting statements should be formatted and presented)
- as frequently or infrequently as management require.

1.5 WRITING REPORTS

You might be required to prepare a short report for presentation to a manager. There are a number of general principles to apply when writing a report.

Conciseness

The report itself should be concise, avoiding unnecessary length and unnecessary detail. Managers like to see the essential features of a report quickly, and to do this, they need short reports that they can read quickly.

Any detailed statements and tables should form appendices to the main report rather than being included in the main body of the report. If such statements are numerous they should be clearly numbered in appendices for ease of reference. The main conclusions and recommendations, if any, should be summarised and highlighted separately in the report.

Structure

The report should be broken down into logical sections with a heading for each section. These should be numbered for easy reference, particularly if the report is quite lengthy.

Style

Short sentences expressed in simple and clear language are preferable to long and elaborate sentences. The aim is to communicate quickly and unambiguously, not to entertain. Opinion must be clearly separated from facts.

Presentation

The report should have a descriptive title. It should also indicate who the report is being addressed to, who has written it and the date of the report. Any terms of reference should be included at the beginning of the report.

Using graphics to improve presentation

Modern software packages make it easy to create graphs, charts, diagrams and other graphic elements from numerical data. These can enhance the appearance of a report as well as improving clarity and impact. For example, a report discussing sales trends over the last few accounting periods could be illustrated by any or all of the following visual aids:

- a table
- a pictogram
- a bar chart analysing sales by product category
- a line graph showing the ups and downs of sales levels over the period
- a pie chart analysing sales by geographical destination.

2 PRESENTATION OF DATA

The two main methods of presenting data are to present it in the form of a table or some form of diagrammatic presentation.

Data is tabulated to present a clearer picture of the message the data is trying to convey. In some cases, an even clearer picture is given if diagrammatic or pictorial representation of the data is made.

2.1 TABLES AND DIAGRAMS

The choice as to whether a table or a diagram is the most appropriate method to illustrate data will depend upon three main factors:

- the nature and complexity of the data itself
- the audience that the data is designed for
- the method of delivery of the data.

2.2 NATURE OF THE DATA

A diagram is often most suitable if only a few specific points about a set of data are to be made. A diagram can make these points or relationships very clear. However if a large number of relationships or points are to be made by a set of data, then a table is more appropriate.

For example if the breakdown of sales into the four products that an organisation produces is required then this might well be shown clearly in a diagram. However if the purpose of the data was to indicate the detailed makeup of the profit or loss on each of the four types of product then a table would probably be more useful.

2.3 NATURE OF THE AUDIENCE

When determining the method of presenting data it is important to consider exactly who the data is being prepared for. For example in some circumstances the data might be prepared for a board of a company or alternatively the purpose might be to inform the workforce of the company as a whole.

It is difficult to generalise about this area but some individuals might find diagrammatic data more easily to understand than tabulated data. Equally the level of detail of data required at board level might be higher than that required to inform the workforce of the relevant information.

2.4 METHOD OF DELIVERY

The method of eventual delivery of the data will often affect the choice of the most appropriate form of presentation.

For example if the data is to be presented in the form of a written report to management which the management team will have time to study and digest then tabulated data might be most appropriate. However if the data is to be presented as part of an oral presentation then a diagram might be most useful in order to highlight the most important points quickly and clearly.

3 TABLES

Very often raw data is in a form that is not easy to understand or form a clear opinion on. The purpose of writing any type of report is to present the necessary information clearly. Tabulation is a common method of achieving this aim of clarity.

In order to do this, the layout that is chosen for the table is obviously of great importance. A table typically consists of an ordered arrangement of rows and columns.

	20X4 ($k)	**20X3 ($k)**	**20X2 ($k)**
Revenue	1,803	1,085	923
Costs	1,032	618	479
Gross profit	771	467	444
Gross profit %	**42.8%**	**43.0%**	**48.1%**

Advantages

- Tables can cope with presenting large quantities of data together. When data is presented as a narrative if is often spread across various parts of a report and can distract from the key messages. A table will pull the information together into one location and can be as large as necessary.
- Figures can be easily located (tables, when designed properly) are easy to navigate. Column and row headings should allow report users to quickly navigate to the data that they need. For example, in the above table a user could quickly tell that Gross profit in 20X3 was $467,000.
- Comparisons can be made. On a row-by-row basis or column-by-column basis a manager can see changes in data by different category. For example, in the table above a manager could easily compare sales over each year.
- Patterns can be highlighted. So a manager using the above table, for example, could easily see that revenue is increasing each year.
- Tables can provide exact and more accurate data than can be achieved with graphs and diagrams.
- Tables are widely used and readily understood

Disadvantages

- Tables can contain too much data at times so that they become cumbersome and difficult to understand.
- Analysis and relationships often require separate work for the user of the table. For example, new calculations might be need to compare sales growth rates over time.
- The most significant are often difficult to find in tables as all the data is presented – even data that may be less relevant to the user.
- Tables can be disconcerting for those report users who might prefer a more visual style of presentation and are less inclined to understand statistics and numbers.

4 DIAGRAMMATIC REPRESENTATION OF DATA

Charts, diagrams and graphs are more popular ways of displaying data simply. Such visual representation of facts plays an important part in everyday life since diagrams can be seen daily in newspapers, advertisements and on television.

There are various methods of representing data diagrammatically. These include:

- bar charts – simple, component and multiple
- pie charts
- scatter graphs
- single and double line graphs
- area charts.

4.1 BAR AND COLUMN CHARTS

Bar and column charts are effectively the same idea, with the bars and columns representing data points and the **height** of the column or length of the bar representing a value. In bar charts, the width of the bar is always the same.

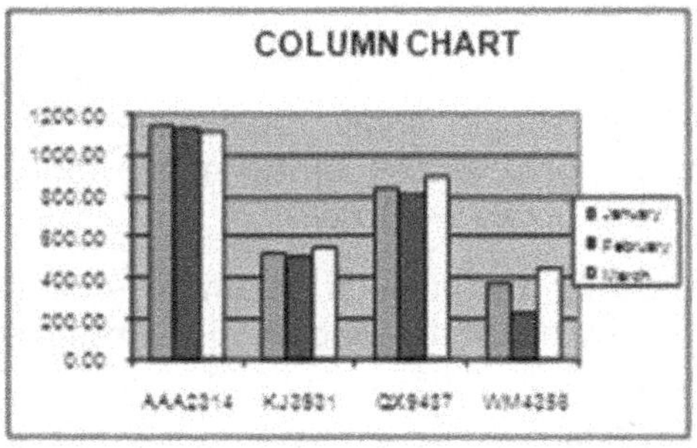

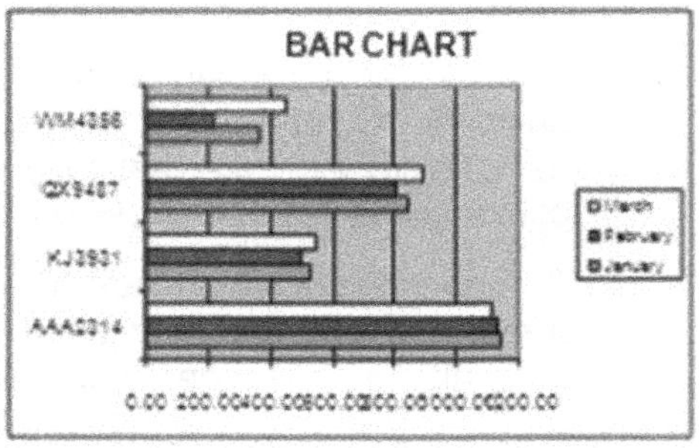

There are many variations of these types of charts such as:

- A **single bar** (or column) **chart** which represents one set of information (for example, total sales over the last five years);
- A **stacked bar** (or column or compound) **chart** which stacks single data sets on top of each other in order to form an overall single bar.

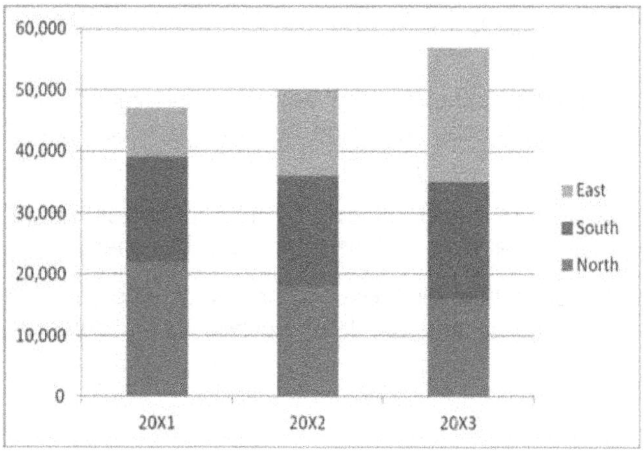

For example, the above column chart illustrates total sales over the last three years. It can be seen from the overall size of the column each year that the overall sales have been increasing. But each column is also shaded for each of the three different sales areas within this company (North, South and East). It can be seen, for example, that in the first year 'North' made up most of the sales column but by the third year 'East' made up most of the sales column. This type of chart has the advantage of the single bar chart in that the total increase in sales can be seen. But it has the added advantage in being able to see the relative proportion of sales made up by each division. However, it is very difficult to determine the absolute change in sales for each component (for example, it is very difficult to tell from the chart whether sales in 'South' have changed each year). If that information is wanted by users, then a compound bar or column chart may be of more use.

Notes – a stacked bar chart is sometimes called a component bar chart

– the same information could also be presented in the form of a stacked bar chart with the data being represented by component horizontal bars rather than columns.

- A **compound bar** (or column) **chart** combines several sets of single bar charts into one overall chart. For example, it may be used to combine the bar charts for sales of individual divisions into one overall bar chart. The stacked column chart used in the previous illustration would be reconstructed as a compound column or bar chart as follows:

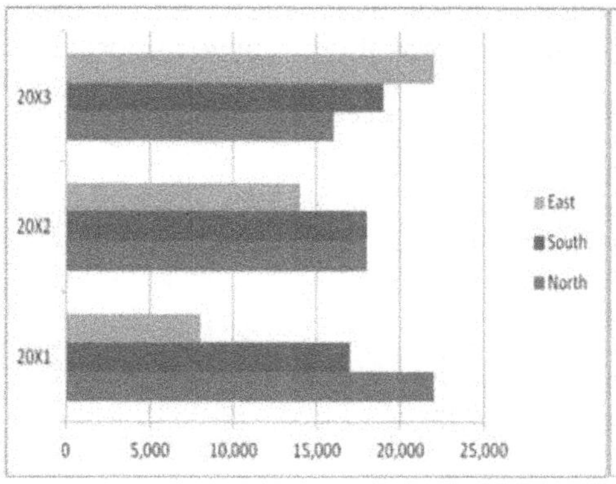

Column chart

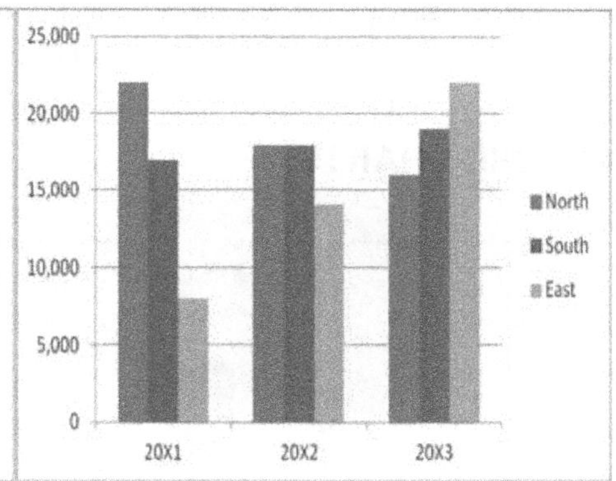

Bar chart

In a compound chart we can still see which component makes up the largest share of sales but we can now also get a better illustration of the changes which are happening for each component (for example, we can now see that 'South' has made a gradual increase each year). But we now lose data on total sales. Another problem with compound charts is that they can become too clustered and confusing if there are too many components to examine.

Advantages

- Bar and column charts can be used to represent more than two sets of data at once. For example, the axis may be, say total sales and years, whilst each bar or column could represent individual products sold.
- The information can be interpreted very quickly. From a glance at the chart, patterns can be determined and the relative height of each column or length of each bar can be observed.
- It is easy to see the relative importance of each product, say, simply by comparing the height of the column

- They are widely used tools which are therefore easily understood and communicated.
- Totals can be broken down into components for better analysis. For example, each product's individual sales could be represented by its own individual column or bar.

Disadvantages

- It is difficult to portray accuracy or precision. Bars or columns which are far apart but of a similar height are difficult to compare.
- It can look confusing if too many columns or bars are used. For example, if a company sold 15 different types of products it may be difficult to have 15 columns for each year and to also observe changes for each product over a number of years.
- If totals are broken into components then the total gets 'lost' and is difficult to determine.
- The chart will need additional information in the form of a 'key' in order to fully convey its message.
- Column charts are more common than bar charts because people are more accustomed to reading numbers on the vertical axis. The use of bar charts places numbers on the horizontal axis and the value of the numbers can become less obvious.

Suitability: Bar and column charts are best used when we want to compare more than one item over time and see their relative importance.

4.2 PIE CHARTS

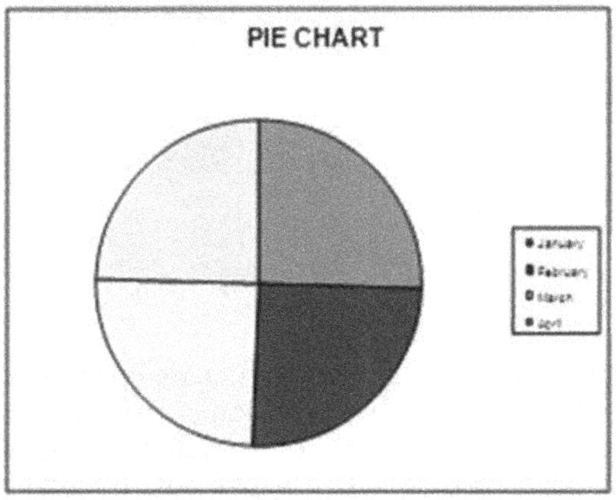

Pie charts represent proportions of a whole [example: percentage of males over 25] and does not have axes. A pie chart can only have one data series. These types of charts are most effective with a small number of data points – otherwise the chart becomes too busy and crowded.

Advantages

- The relative size of each component can quickly be assessed.
- The size of the circle (or pie) can be used to represent the overall total if we are comparing data between a number of periods.
- They can represent lots of complicated data quickly and simply.
- Again, they are widely used and understood.

Disadvantages

- It is difficult to determine exact values.
- It can become complicated if more than one pie is represented with different sizes to represent overall total value.
- They may be too simple for some users who are concerned with the details.
- It can be difficult to make distinctions when values are close together.

Suitability: Pie and doughnut charts are best used when we want to show the relative proportions of multiple classes of data.

4.3 SCATTER GRAPH (XY)

This type of graph has two value axes and no category axis, and is typically used to show the relationship of two sets of numbers. In the example below the relationship is of sales volume to sales revenue. The data points [represented by diamonds] show the intersection of the two sets of numbers

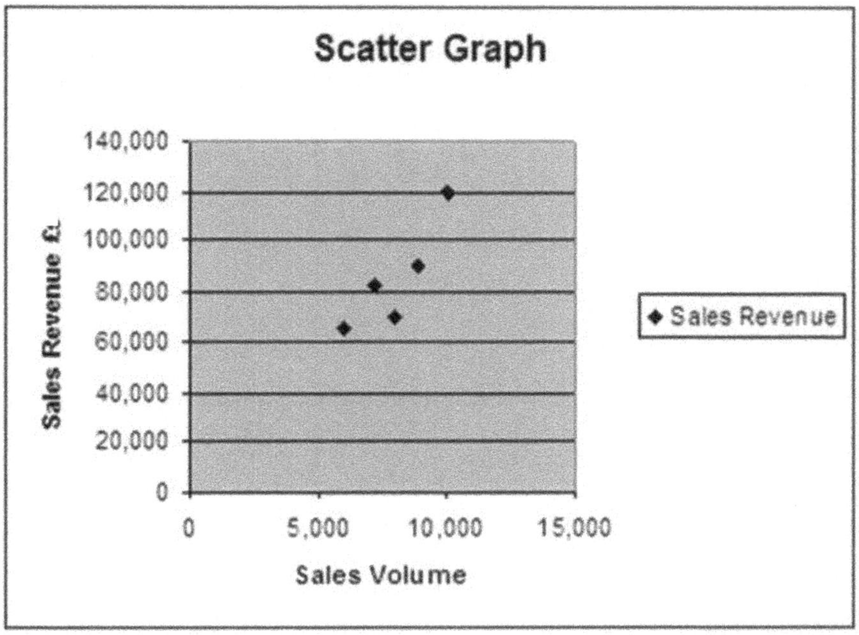

Advantages

- It can be used to quickly identify the 'direction' of the relationship between the two variables. In the example above it can easily be seen that as sales volume increases then sales revenue also, generally, increases.
- Scatter graphs can display a more varied series of data than line graphs. Data doesn't need to be at set intervals and can be both closer and further apart from each other.
- It may be the best way to illustrate a non-linear or random pattern/relationship between the variables.

Disadvantages

- Only two variables can be compared at one time.
- A user might find it difficult to interpret without further information.
- It can be difficult to assess data exactly or accurately.
- If there are only a few data points then the diagram can become misleading and less useful.
- If no relationship exists a flat line may occur which may have little value to a user.

Suitability: Scatter graphs are a good way of illustrating the lack of a relationship between variables. If data is scattered around the graph it can illustrate that the variables are not related.

4.4 SINGLE AND DOUBLE LINE GRAPHS

Line charts are used to plot continuous data and are very useful for showing trends. The more data series there are the more lines you can have on your graph.

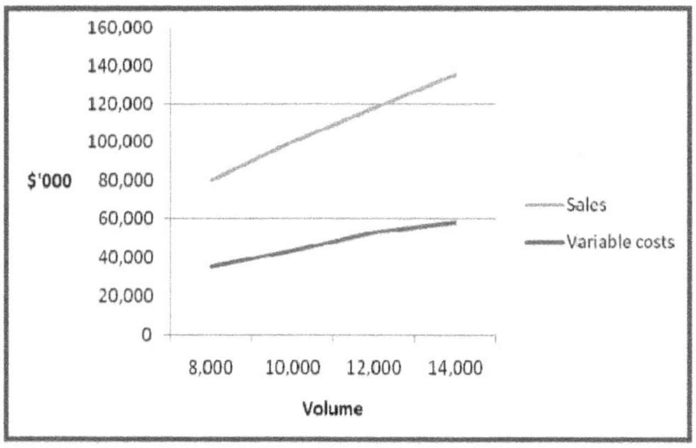

Advantages

- This helps identify the 'correlation' between the data. The straighter the points are on a line then the stronger the relationship between the data. In the example above the sales line seems fairly straight and it would therefore tell us that there is a strong, linear relationship between total sales and volume – as volume increase then total sales will also increase. With the variable cost line it appears to 'tail off' a little, and therefore the correlation between volume and variable costs is less linear.
- More than one set of data can be shown at a time, which can make comparisons easier.

- Line graphs can be used to identify trends. If, for example, there is some seasonality in sales over time, then when this is plotted on a line graph the peaks and troughs should become obvious.

Disadvantages

- It is difficult to use line graphs over very large ranges or where the 'gaps' between data observations are inconsistent. For example, in the above diagram the volume increased by a consistent 2,000 units at a time. The graph becomes less useful if this is not the case.
- When lines intersect or cross and lots of lines have been used the graph can become over-complicated and more difficult to interpret.

Suitability: Line graphs are best used for identifying trends and when there is a strong correlation between the data.

4.5 AREA CHART

An area chart displays a series as a set of points connected- by a line, with all the area filled in below the line. It is an extension of a line graph. It is used to show overall totals (the top line) as well as the components from different sources (the different shades).

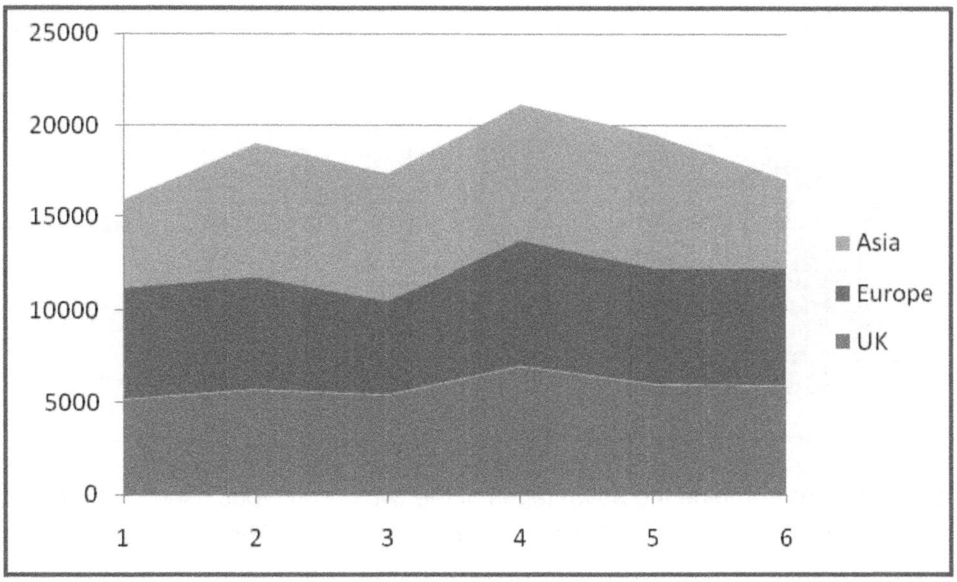

Advantages

- Both the overall total and the component elements can be illustrated.
- Trends in components and in the total can be easily identified.
- The graph illustrated uses an absolute scale to prepare the chart (i.e. the absolute total is used). A percentage scale can be used instead where the total must always come to 100% and this can be more useful in identifying the relative size of each component against each other.

Disadvantages

- Only one overall total can be displayed.
- It can be difficult to assess the relative size of each component as the absolute data is difficult to determine. For example, would a user be able to judge the amount of European sales in quarter 3 just from looking at the graph? They would be able to identify that the sales have fallen but it would be very difficult to put a definite value on the size of the fall.
- It can become confusing if there are too many components.
- Small components can be difficult to assess and add little value to the chart.

Suitability: Area charts are best used to display over time how a set of data adds up to a whole (cumulated totals) and which part of the whole each element represents.

4.6 MULTIPLE GRAPH TYPES ON ONE CHART

Also known as Combination Charts these charts must consist of at least two data series. With this chart type you can have either two graph types on one axis or insert a second value or 'Y' axis.

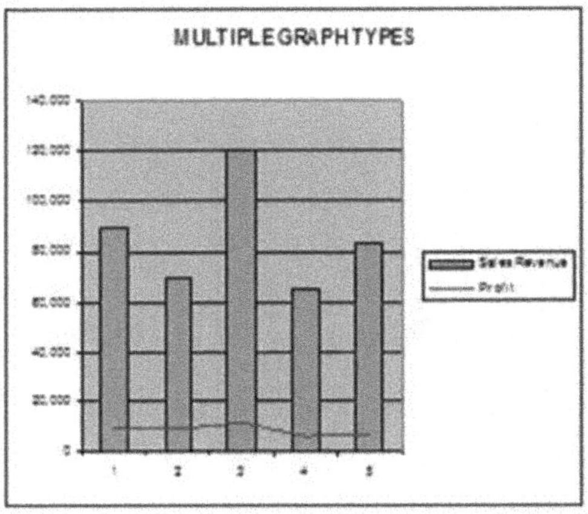

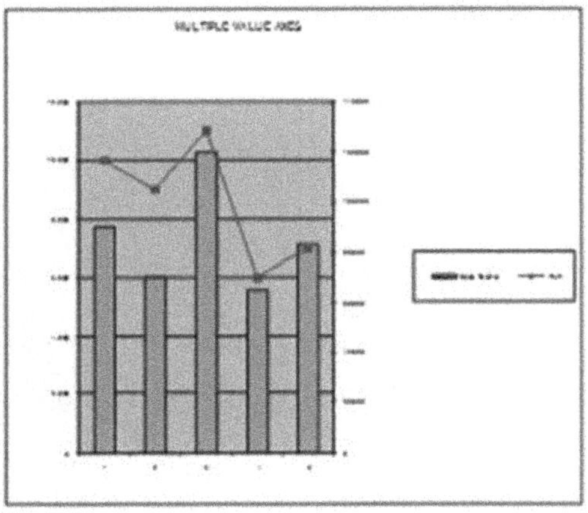

These graphs combine the advantages of the two graph types used. But they can become more confusing for users and require further explanation.

5 METHODS OF REPORTING

Methods of comparing information were considered earlier. A comparison of information will normally be requested in a particular format. This can range from an informal note through to a formal report. We will consider each of the different methods of reporting.

5.1 HOUSE STYLE

Although the basic requirements of each method of reporting will be covered in this chapter it is important to realise that each organisation will have its own style and methods of reporting. These will normally be contained in the organisation's policy manual and house styles should always be followed.

5.2 CONFIDENTIALITY

It is extremely important that the information that has been requested is sent to the appropriate person and only that person and any others that you are specifically asked to send it to. Often the information is confidential and therefore should be treated with the highest respect and care.

You should ensure that confidential information is viewed by the recipient only, bearing in mind the fact that a manager's secretary or assistant might deal with their incoming mail. If information is extremely confidential it should be marked as such or delivered in person, and each copy of the information should be uniquely numbered. If in doubt, do not pass on confidential information until you have been told specifically to do so by your manager.

5.3 CHOOSING A SUITABLE FORMAT FOR COMMUNICATING INFORMATION

A number of factors need to be taken into account when deciding on the appropriate format for communicating management information. Some of the factors conflict with each other and it is up to the person who prepared the information to weigh up the various considerations to select the most appropriate communication medium.

The factors to be considered include the following:

Speed and timing

A short memorandum can be prepared and read more quickly than a lengthy written report. Information to be discussed at a meeting must be communicated to the relevant people in time for them to read and understand it. Urgent information can be sent almost instantaneously by email.

The need for a written record

Written information is less open to misinterpretation and a hard copy is available for filing in case queries should arise at a later date.

Confidentiality

The choice of communication medium is extremely important when you are dealing with confidential information. For example with a fax there is the possibility that an unauthorised person may see the message and a telephone conversation could be overheard. Email can also cause problems with confidentiality, for example if the recipient has left their computer unattended.

Cost

Email is a very cheap and rapid communication medium but it may not be suitable for sending confidential information. Fax or post might be cheaper but could cause delays. Sending information by courier is more appropriate for confidential information but it can be expensive. Obviously the cost aspect must be weighed up in the light of all the other factors.

Distance

Email systems, for example, communicate information rapidly and cheaply over large distances whereas post and couriers are slower but provide a more secure service for confidential information.

Complexity

More complex information may be communicated more effectively through a written medium rather than, for example, through a telephone conversation. On the other hand, in a face to face or telephone conversation it is possible for the recipient to ask questions and thus for some interaction to take place.

6 A NOTE OR LETTER

Probably the most simple and informal method of reporting information to another person in the organisation is by way of a note.

6.1 NOTE FORMAT

There is no set format for a note although obviously it must be addressed to the appropriate person, be dated, be headed up correctly so that the recipient knows what it is about. Make sure you include your name so that the recipient knows who the note is from.

In most cases the information that you are reporting on will be important management information and therefore it is unlikely that a note would usually be the most appropriate format. Only use a note if specifically asked to do so by the person requesting the information.

6.2 LETTER FORMAT

A slightly more formal method of communicating information is in the form of a letter. A letter is most likely to be used when communicating with someone outside the organisation. It would be quite unusual to communicate with another person in the same organisation in this way although a letter may be appropriate if the person to whom you are sending the information works in a separate location.

A letter should always have a letter heading showing the organisation's name, address, telephone number, etc. Most organisations will have pre-printed letterheads for you to use.

The letter must also be dated and the name and address of the recipient be included before the contents of the letter are written.

The method of signing a letter will depend upon the formality of how the letter begins.

If a letter is started as 'Dear Sir' then the appropriate way to sign off the letter is 'Yours faithfully'.

However if the letter is started 'Dear Mr Smith' then the appropriate way to sign off the letter is 'Yours sincerely'.

7 ELECTRONIC MAIL

Most organisations are now fully computerised and most individuals within an organisation can communicate with each other via electronic mail or email.

7.1 FORMAT

An email must be addressed to the person to whom it is being sent using their email address. It should also be given a title so that the recipient can see at a glance who it is from and what it is about.

In terms of format of the content of the email there are no rules other than any organisational procedures that should be followed.

8 MEMORANDA

Definition A **memorandum** (or memo) is a written communication between two persons within an organisation. The plural of memorandum is memoranda.

A memorandum serves a similar purpose to a letter. However the main difference is that letters are usually sent to persons outside the organisation, whereas memoranda or memos are for communication within the organisation itself. Memos can range from brief handwritten notes, to typed sets of instructions to a junior, to a more formal report to a superior. In general a memo can be used for any purpose where written communication is necessary within the organisation, provided this is according to the rules of the organisation.

8.1 FORMAT

Many organisations will have pre-printed memo forms. In smaller organisations each individual may draft his own memoranda. However there are a number of key elements in any memorandum.

Memorandum

To:

From:

Date:

Ref:

Subject:

Body of memorandum

Signature:

cc:

Enc:

All memoranda will show who it is they are being sent to and from whom. The date and a suitable reference, for filing purposes, are also essential. The memorandum then must be given a heading to summarise what the message is about.

The content of the body of the memorandum will be discussed in the following paragraph. Whether or not a memo is signed will depend upon the organisation's policy. Some organisations insist on a signature on a memorandum; others do not.

It is highly likely that a number of copies of a memorandum will be sent out and these should be listed in the section headed 'cc'. This is an important aspect of most written communications, since each recipient will need to know who else has a copy of the information.

Finally if there are any enclosures, i.e. additional pieces of information that are being sent out with the memorandum then these should be noted under this final heading of 'Enc'.

8.2 CONTENT OF A MEMORANDUM

The details of the content and style of a memo will depend upon who is sending the memo, to whom they are sending it, the degree of formality required and the actual subject matter of the memo.

Some memos will simply be handwritten notes from one colleague to another.

If a memo is to be sent to a superior in the organisation, either showing information requested or making recommendations, then both the tone and the content might perhaps be slightly more formal.

Again if a manager is writing to junior personnel in his department his style may be of a more formal nature than if he were writing to another manager within the organisation.

Whatever the precise style and content of the memo some general rules apply:

- There should be a heading to give an indication of the subject matter.
- There should be an introductory paragraph setting the scene.
- The main paragraphs of the memo should follow in a logical order, so that the recipient clearly understands the arguments being put forward.
- There should be a summary of the main points.

9 INFORMAL BUSINESS REPORT

An informal business report sits somewhere between a memorandum and a formal business report. It is likely to have more structure than a memorandum but use less formal language and tone than a formal business report. Therefore it is likely to have an introduction, explanation of the circumstances and recommendations and conclusions. But at the same time it would normally have less scene setting information, use bullet points and lists, use personalised language and have few appendices.

These reports are often internal in nature and are used for areas such as reporting variances, making initial business proposals and exception reporting.

CONCLUSION

Management require good information to enable them to make decisions, to plan and to control the organisation. Information may be easier to use and more relevant if it is presented in a suitable format, such as a table or a graph.

KEY TERMS

Tabulation – the systematic arrangement of numerical data to provide a logical account of the results of analysis.

Pictograms – pictures or symbols which can be readily associated with the data given.

Simple bar chart – a chart in which each bar represents the variable under consideration.

Component bar chart – a chart in which each bar is made up of several component parts, which form a logical whole.

Percentage component bar chart – a chart in which the component parts are shown on each bar as a percentage of the bar total. Each whole bar represents 100%.

Multiple bar chart – a chart in which two or more related items are to be compared. The bars are placed next to each other and each represents a different item.

SELF TEST QUESTIONS

		Paragraph
1	What kind of reports might a marketing department typically produce?	1.3
2	What are the disadvantages of using an area chart?	4.5
3	When would it be suitable to use a pie chart?	4.2
3	What factors should be considered when selecting the most appropriate communication medium?	5.3
4	List the key elements to be included on a memorandum.	8.2

EXAM-STYLE QUESTIONS

1 Which of the following would not be considered a pictorial presentation?

A Enclosure

B Chart

C Graph

D Table

2 You have been asked to supply the quarterly sales figures for the last six years using a suitable pictorial representation. What might the appropriate form for such information take?

A Bar chart

B Pie chart

C Area chart

D Table

3 Which of the following methods of communication is likely to be most appropriate for complaining to the organisation's cleaning contractor about the standard of cleanliness in the sales offices?

A Memo

B Telephone

C Letter

D Courier

4 The following diagram illustrates staff numbers in X Ltd for the period April to June:

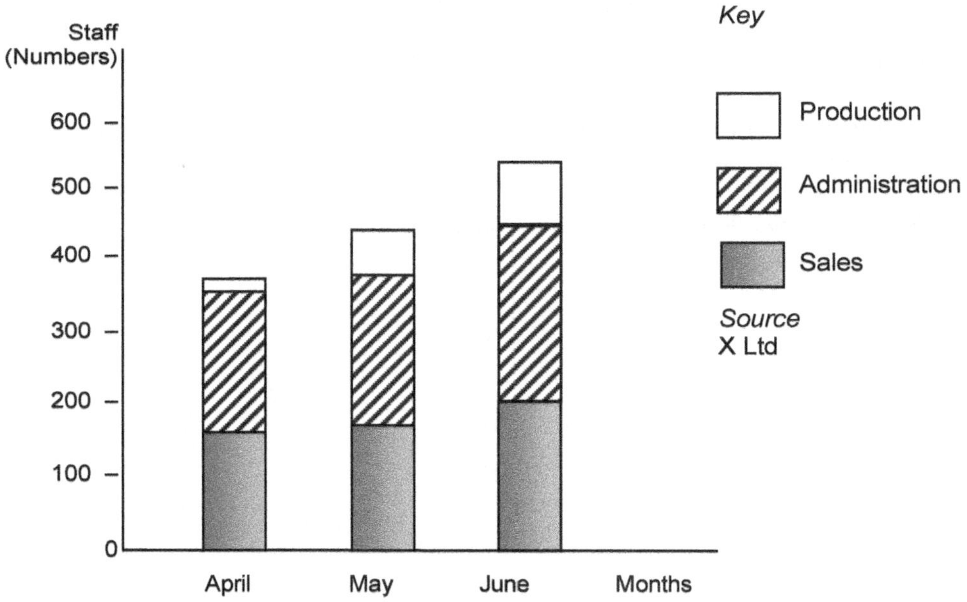

Which of the following statements are true?

A Production staff numbers have increased from April to June

B Production staff numbers have decreased in May

C Sales staff numbers have decreased in June

D Total staff numbers exceeded 500 throughout the period

5 Which of the following would not be considered when considering how to distribute a report?

A Cost

B Preparer

C Distance

D Confidentiality

For suggested answers, see the 'Answers' section at the end of the book.

ANSWERS TO ACTIVITIES AND END OF CHAPTER QUESTIONS

CHAPTER 1

ACTIVITY 1

Here are some suggestions:

1 The cost of each department (for example the ear, nose and throat department, accident and emergency, the X-ray unit, and so on).

2 The cost of carrying out different types of surgical operation.

3 The average cost of each type or course of treatment.

4 The daily cost of looking after a patient in hospital (the cost of a patient/day).

EXAM-STYLE QUESTIONS

1 **B**

Profit = revenues minus operating costs. Answer D describes an investment centre.

2 **D**

Qualities A, B and C might be desirable in some situations, but not in every situation.

3 **B**

Data is unprocessed facts. B is the only option in which some analysis has not yet been carried out.

4 **A**

Information should only be produced when the value exceeds the cost hence (i) is incorrect. Information should be relevant and timely. Information which has always been produced should be reviewed to make sure that it is still relevant and that the cost does not exceed the value. Hence (iii) is not a valid reason for producing information.

CHAPTER 2

ACTIVITY 1

According to the coding system the code is: EDSP.

ACTIVITY 2

(a) 302001

(b) 503051

(c) 301071

EXAM-STYLE QUESTIONS

1 **A**

Direct labour costs are charged (debited) to work-in-progress.

2 **D**

A cost unit is a unit of output for which costs are measured. The costs of a department are the costs of a cost centre, and the cost per labour hour and stationery costs are costs of input resources. For a business providing services to its customers, an appropriate cost unit measure is the cost per unit of service provided.

3 **A**

This transaction **increases** the asset 'work-in-progress', so debit work-in-progress; it **decreases** the asset 'materials inventory', so credit stores control.

4 **C**

When the wages are paid they will be initially recorded in wages control (Debit wages control, Credit Cash/Bank). They will then be charged out to the appropriate cost ledger account – in this case overheads, as it is indirect labour.

5 **C**

A modem is an example of computer hardware. All of the other options are examples of computer software.

CHAPTER 3

ACTIVITY 1

Cost number		*Classification number*
1	iv	production overhead
2	vii	administration overhead
3	ii	direct labour
4	vii	administration overhead
5	viii	finance costs
6	iv	production overhead
7	vi	selling and distribution costs
8	iv	production overhead
9	i or iv	Carriage inwards costs are usually included within the cost of the materials, and so are an element of the direct materials cost
10	iii	direct expenses

ACTIVITY 2

		C $		*D* $	*Total* $
Direct materials	(1,200 × $8)	9,600	(1,800 × $7)	12,600	22,200
Direct labour	(1,200 × $6)	7,200	(1,800 × $4)	7,200	14,400
Variable overheads	(1,200 × $1)	1,200	(1,800 × $1)	1,800	3,000
Total variable costs		18,000		21,600	39,600
Fixed costs					40,000
Total costs					79,600
Revenue	(1,200 × $25)	30,000	(1,800 × $30)	54,000	84,000
Profit					4,400

ACTIVITY 3

	Activity level	$
High	900	2,300
Low	(400)	(1,050)
Difference	500	1,250

Variable cost = $1,250/500 = $2.50 per unit

	$
Total cost of 900	2,300
Variable cost of 900 (× $2.50)	(2,250)
Fixed costs	50

The variable cost is $2.50 per unit and fixed costs are just $50 in total per period.

EXAM-STYLE QUESTIONS

1 **A**

Overheads are not a function.

2 **B**

Assembly workers are direct labour in a manufacturing company, plasterers are directly involved in building and audit clerks are directly involved in providing the services of their firm to clients. Only stores workers in a manufacturing business are indirect workers.

3 **A**

Direct costs are costs directly attributable to the item being costed, which can be a single unit or a batch of cost units. D may be true but is the definition of a variable cost. Direct costs will normally be charged to the Statement of profit or loss (option B), but not all costs that are charged to the Statement of profit or loss will be direct costs.

4 **B**

	Activity level million	$
High	4	6,000
Low	2	5,000
Variable cost	2	1,000

Variable cost per million units = $1,000/2 = $500 per million units.

	$
Total cost of 4 million	6,000
Variable cost of 4 million (× $500)	2,000
Fixed costs	4,000

Estimate of total cost for 5 million units

	$
Fixed costs	4,000
Variable costs (5 million × $500)	2,500
Total costs	6,500

5 **D**

The fixed cost per unit falls as output increases, but not in a straight line.

6 **D**

December costs at January price levels = $97,438/1.03 = $94,600.

	Activity level	$
High	21,000	94,600
Low	18,000	86,800
Variable cost	3,000	7,800

Variable cost per unit (January price level) = $7,800/3,000 = $2.60 per unit.

7 **A**

D is only correct if the range of volume of activity is known.

8 **B**

	$
At 5,000 units total variable cost is	12,500
Total cost is	21,100
Therefore fixed cost is	$8,600

9 **A**

	Activity	*Cost*
High	83	6,700
Low	60	5,826
Difference	23	874

Therefore variable cost is $\frac{\$874}{23}$ = $38 per unit

At an activity level of 83	total variable cost is	3,154
	total cost is	6,700
	so fixed cost is	3,546
Total cost forecast:		
For 90 units	total variable cost is (90 × $38)	3,420
	total fixed cost is	3,546
	so total cost is	6,966

10 **C**

Budgeted fixed costs = 4,000 units x ($3 + $1) = $16,000 (these won't change in February as they are fixed.

February variable costs = 5,000 units x ($4.12 + $1.36) = $27,400

Total February costs = 27,400 + 16,000 = $43,400

CHAPTER 4

ACTIVITY 1

FIFO results in later purchases remaining in inventory. The calculations are as follows.

FIFO

	Units	$	
Opening inventory	50	350	(50 units at $7)
1 Feb: Purchases	60	480	
	110	830	(50 at $7, 60 at $8)
1 March: Sales	(40)	(280)	(40 at $7)
	70	550	(10 at $7, 60 at $8)
1 April: Purchases	70	630	
	140	1,180	(10 at $7, 60 at $8, 70 at $9)
1 May: Sales	(60)	(470)	(10 at $7, 50 at $8)
Closing inventory	80	710	(10 at $8, 70 at $9)

		Sales $	*Cost $*	*Profit*
Profit on sale	1 Mar	400	280	120
	1 May	720	470	250
	Total			370

LIFO

	Units	$	
Opening inventory	50	350	(50 units at $7)
1 Feb: Purchases	60	480	
	110	830	(50 at $7, 60 at $8)
1 March: Sales	(40)	(320)	(40 at $8)
	70	510	(50 at $7, 20 at $8)
1 April: Purchases	70	630	
	140	1,140	(50 at $7, 20 at $8, 70 at $9)
1 May: Sale	(60)	(540)	(60 at $9)
Closing inventory	80	600	(50 at $7, 20 at $8, 10 at $9)

		Sales $	*Cost $*	*Profit*
Profit on sale	1 Mar	400	320	80
	1 May	720	540	180
	Total			260

Cumulative weighted average

	Units	$	Weighted average
Opening inventory	50	350	$7
1 Feb: Purchases	60	480	
	110	830	($830/110) = 7.5455
1 March: Sales	(40)	(302)	(40 at $7.5455)
	70	528	(50 at $7.5455)
1 April: Purchases	70	630	
	140	1,158	($1,158/140) = $8.2714
1 May: Sale	(60)	(496)	(60 at $8.2714)
Closing inventory	80	662	(80 at $8.2714)

		Sales	*Cost*	*Profit*
		$	$	$
Profit on sale	1 Mar	400	302	98
	1 May	720	496	224
	Total			322

Periodic weighted average pricing

The periodic weighted average price = $\frac{350 + 480 + 630}{50 + 60 + 70}$ = $8.11

The value of issues is 100 × $8.11 = $811

The closing inventory value is:

	Units	$
Opening inventory	50	350
1 Feb	60	480
1 April	70	630
	180	1,460
1 March	(40)	(324)
1 May	(60)	(487)
Closing inventory	80	649

		Sales ($)	*Cost ($)*	*Profit*
Profit on sale	1 Mar	400	324	76
	1 May	720	487	233
				309

ACTIVITY 2

Input = 1,520 kilograms × (100/95) = 1,600 kilograms.

At $8 per kilogram, the materials cost will be $12,800.

EXAM-STYLE QUESTIONS

1 (i) **A**

LIFO = 400 × $3.40 + 525 × $3.00 = $2,935

(ii) **C**

AVCO = $3.20 × 275 + $3.00 × 600 + $3.40 × 400 = $4,040

$4,040/1,275 = $3.17 per unit × 925 = $2,932

(iii) **D**

FIFO = 275 × $3.20 + 600 × $3.00 + 50 × $3.40 = $2,850

2 **A**

Issues 700 units

Receipts 700 units

So opening inventory is 400 units.

20 July issues would have been 200 @ $22

10 July issues would have been 300 @ $25

and 200 @ opening inventory value per unit

So closing inventory = 200 × $22 + 200 × opening inventory value per unit

$10,000 = 200 × $22 + 200 × opening inventory value per unit

$$\text{Opening inventory value per unit} = \frac{\$10{,}000 - \$4{,}400}{200} = \$28$$

So opening inventory = $28 × 400 = $11,200.

3 **A**

Closing inventory in units is 4,000 + 1,200 + 2,800 – 3,900 – 1,100 = 3,000

The 3,000 units in closing inventory are valued as follows.

	$
8 March receipt (100 @ $5)	500
19 March receipt (100 @ $6)	600
24 March receipt	21,000
Closing inventory valuation	22,100

4 **D**

1,100 issued made up of 100 from 8 March batch and 1,000 from 19 March batch

so (100 × $5) + (1,000 × $6) = $6,500.

5 **C**

			$ per unit	*Balance*
8 March	Received	4,000	5	20,000
15 March	Issue	3,900	5	19,500
	Balance	100		500
19 March	Received	1,200	6	7,200
	Balance	1,300	5.923	7,700
21 March	Issued	1,100		6,515
	Balance	200	5.925	1,185
24 March	Received	2,800	7.50	21,000
		3,000		22,185

6 **A**

FIFO means that the value of closing inventory reflects the most recent prices paid.

7 **C**

Date	*Receipts*	*Issues*	*Balance*		*Average cost*
			No.	$	$
1 Sept				Nil	
3 Sept	200 × $1.00		200	200.00	
7 Sept		180 × $1.00	20	20.00	
8 Sept	240 × $1.50		260	380.00	1.462
14 Sept		170 × $1.46	90	131.58	1.462
15 Sept	230 × $2.00		320	591.58	1.849
21 Sept		150 × $1.85	170	314.33	1.849

CHAPTER 5

ACTIVITY 1

Your solution should be as follows.

Use the formula:

$$EOQ = \sqrt{\frac{2C_oD}{C_H}}$$

Where:

C_o = \$40

D = 600,000

C_H = \$3

$$EOQ = \sqrt{\frac{2 \times 40 \times 600{,}000}{3}}$$

= 4,000 units

ACTIVITY 2

(a) Annual demand is 36,750.

EOQ is 3,500.

The company will therefore place an order (36,750/3,500) 10.5 times every year, which is once every $\frac{3{,}500}{36{,}750} \times 365$ days

$\approx$ 35 days.

(b) The company must be sure that there is sufficient inventory on hand when it places an order, to last the two weeks' lead time. It must therefore place an order when there is two weeks' worth of demand in inventory.

i.e. $\frac{2}{52} \times 36{,}750 \approx 1{,}413$ units.

ACTIVITY 3

$$3{,}600 - \left[\frac{500+300}{2} \times 5\right] = 1{,}600 \text{ units}$$

ACTIVITY 4

Average usage = (500 + 300)/2 = 400 units per day.

Re-order level = 500 units × 7 days = 3,500 units.

Minimum inventory control level = 3,500 – (400 units × 5 days) = 1,500 units.

Maximum inventory control level = 3,500 + 5,400 – (300 units × 4 days) = 7,700 units.

EXAM-STYLE QUESTIONS

1 **B**

Re-order when level is maximum usage in maximum lead time, i.e.:

Maximum usage: 175 per day

Maximum lead time: 16 days

Re-order level = 175 × 16 = 2,800

2 **41,200** units

ROQ + ROL – (Min. usage × Min. lead time) = 28,000 + 19,200 – (750 × 8) = 41,200

3 **C**

$$\text{EOQ} = \sqrt{\frac{2 \times 3{,}000 \times 342{,}225}{0.60}}$$

= 58,500 litres

4 **$15.500**

Re-ordering costs = (Number of re-orders pa × C_0)

$$= \frac{48{,}050 \times \$500}{1{,}550}$$

= $15,500

5 **B**

Stockouts result in lost sales and stopped production. Organisations may seek alternative supplies and have to pay a premium. Bulk purchase discounts would be lost if order quantities are below a certain level. This is not specifically related to stockouts.

6 **B**

Average inventory = 500/2 + 100 = 350 kg

Holding cost = 350 × ($6.50 × 10%) = $227.50

7 **8,000 litres**

Demand is given monthly, but for the EOQ it is needed annually = 1,000 litres x 12 = 12,000 litres

$$EOQ = \sqrt{\frac{2 \times 160 \times 12{,}000}{0.06}}$$

= 8,000 litres

8

	True	False
When using re-order level control for inventory the supply lead time is always known		✓
The economic order quantity assumes that no buffer stock of inventory is held	✓	

Supply time is unlikely to be a known constant and therefore re-order level control uses buffer stock based on maximum and minimum expected lead times.

The EOQ calculations are only appropriate if no buffer stock is held.

CHAPTER 6

ACTIVITY 1

31.5 hours × $15.86 = $499.59

ACTIVITY 2

Total weekly wage

	$
Monday (12 × $6)	72
Tuesday (14 × $6)	84
Wednesday (9 × $6)	54
Thursday (14 × $6)	84
Friday (8 × $6)	48
	342

As the weekly earnings are above $300, the guaranteed amount is not relevant to the calculations in this instance.

Conclusion The payment of any guaranteed amount is not a bonus for good work but simply an additional payment required if the amount of production is below a certain level.

ACTIVITY 3

The amount the employee will be paid will depend upon the exact wording of the agreement. Production of 102 units has taken the employee out of the lowest band (up to 99 units) and into the middle band (100 – 119 units). The question now is whether **all** his units are paid for at the middle rate ($1.50), or only the units produced in excess of 99. The two possibilities are as follows:

(a) 102 × $1.75 = $178.50

(b) (99 × $1.50) + (3 × $1.75) = $153.75

Most organisations' agreements would apply method (b).

ACTIVITY 4

	$
Basic pay (40 × $5)	200.00
Overtime (5 hours × ($5 × 1.5))	37.50
Weekly wage cost	237.50

Alternatively this could be shown as:

	$
Basic pay (45 × $5)	225.00
Overtime premium (5 hours × ($5 × 0.5))	12.50
	237.50

Conclusion This second method shows the overtime premium separately. The premium is the additional amount over the basic rate that is paid for the overtime hours rather than the total payment. This method is preferred because it enables direct costs to be separated from indirect costs.

ACTIVITY 5

Annual salary $19,500

Standard hours to be worked in the year

(52 weeks × 38 hours) 1,976 hours

Salary rate per hour $\frac{\$19,500}{1,976}$

= $9.87 per hour

Overtime rate (1.5 × $9.87) = $14.81 per hour

ACTIVITY 6

$$\text{Bonus} = \frac{40-25}{60} \times 35\% \times \$15.00$$

$$= \$1.3125$$

ACTIVITY 7

JOB CARD – 28/3JN

		$
Materials	X	
Labour		
–	making icing (3 hours × $15.30)	45.90

JOB CARD – 28/3KA

		$
Materials	X	
Labour		
–	making icing (5 hours × $15.30)	76.50

ACTIVITY 8

$$\text{Labour turnover} = \frac{200}{7{,}000} \times 100\% = 2.9\%$$

ACTIVITY 9

Preventative costs

These are costs incurred to reduce labour turnover. Examples include:

- increased wages
- training
- improved working environment.

Replacement costs

These are costs incurred replacing employees who leave an organisation. Examples include:

- advertising
- loss of output
- training.

ACTIVITY 10

$$\text{Efficiency ratio} = \frac{\text{Actual output measured in standard hours}}{\text{Actual production hours}} \times 100\%$$

$$= \frac{230}{180} \times 100\% = 127.8\%$$

$$\text{Capacity utilisation ratio} = \frac{\text{Actual hours worked}}{\text{Budgeted production hours}} \times 100\%$$

$$= \frac{180}{200} \times 100\% = 90\%$$

$$\text{The production/volume ratio} = \frac{\text{Actual output measured in standard hours}}{\text{Budgeted production hours}} \times 100\%$$

$$= \frac{230}{200} \times 100\% = 115\%$$

ACTIVITY 11

$$\text{The idle time ratio} = \frac{\text{Idle hours}}{\text{Total hours available}} \times 100\%$$

Idle hours = 50,000 hours paid – 42,000 hours worked = 8,000 hours

Total hours = 50,000

$$\text{The idle time ratio} = \frac{8{,}000}{50{,}000} \times 100\% = 16\%$$

EXAM-STYLE QUESTIONS

1 **B**

Unless the overtime has been carried out at the specific request of customer, it will be treated as an indirect production cost, i.e. factory overhead.

2 **C**

$$\text{Actual expected total time} = \frac{2{,}520}{0.9} = 2{,}800 \text{ hours}$$

∴ Budgeted labour cost = 2,800 × $24 = $67,200.

3 **B**

4 **B**

\$(62,965 + 13,600) = \$76,565. The only direct costs are the wages paid to direct workers for ordinary time, plus the basic pay for overtime. Overtime premium and shift allowances are usually treated as overheads. However, if and when overtime and shift work are incurred specifically for a particular cost unit, they are classified as direct costs of that cost unit. Sick pay is treated as an overhead and is therefore classified as an indirect cost.

5 The wage cost of this employee is **\$1,001** for the week.

	\$
Basic pay (35 hours × \$22 per hour)	770
Overtime (7 hours × \$22 per hour × 1.5)	231
Total pay	1,001

6 **A**

$$\text{Bonus} = \frac{60-50}{60} \times 40\% \times \$15.00$$

$$= \$1.00$$

7 Usefulness of each ratio:

Ratio	Capacity ratio	Efficiency ratio	Activity ratio
A measure of productivity		✓	
A measure of overall production			✓
A measure of utilisation	✓		

8 **A**

$$\text{Efficiency ratio} = \frac{\text{Actual output measured in standard hours}}{\text{Actual production hours}} \times 100\%$$

Standard hour = 60,000 units/5,000 hours = 12 units per hour

Actual output in standard hours = 60,300 units/12 units per hour = 5,025 hours

$$= \frac{5{,}025}{6{,}000} \times 100\% = 83.75\% \text{ or } 84\% \text{ to nearest whole percentage}$$

9 **B**

$$\text{Capacity utilisation ratio} = \frac{\text{Actual hours worked}}{\text{Budgeted production hours}} \times 100\%$$

$$= \frac{32}{40} \times 100\% = 80\%$$

10 The labour production/volume ratio for the period was **117%**

$$\text{The production/volume ratio} = \frac{\text{Actual output measured in standard hours}}{\text{Budgeted production hours}} \times 100\%$$

Standard hours = 3,000 units/24,000 hours = 0.125 units per hour

Actual output in standard hours = 3,500 units/0.125 units per hour = 28,000 hours

$$= \frac{28{,}000}{24{,}000} \times 100\% = 117\%$$

11 **A**

Number of leavers who were replaced = 56

Employees at the end of the year = 312 + 41 = 353

Average number of employees = (312 + 353) / 2 = 332.5

Labour turnover ratio = (56 / 332.5) × 100% = 16.8%

CHAPTER 7

ACTIVITY 1

	$
Cost	48,000
Residual value	20,250
Total depreciable amount	27,750
Expected life	3 years
Annual depreciation charge	$9,250

ACTIVITY 2

	$
Cost	48,000
Year 1 depreciation charge ($48,000 × 25%)	12,000
Carrying value (year 1)	36,000
Year 2 depreciation charge ($36,000 × 25%)	9,000
Carrying value (year 2)	27,000
Year 3 depreciation charge ($27,000 × 25%)	6,750
Carrying value (year 3)	20,250

ACTIVITY 3

$$\text{Depreciation charge} = \frac{\$20,000}{5,000\text{ hours}} = \$4 \text{ per hour}$$

Depreciation charge in year 1 = 1,800 hours × $4

= $7,200

EXAM-STYLE QUESTIONS

1 **D**

Lubricating oil would be an indirect material.

2 **B**

The production overhead control will record overheads whereas the subcontractors' fees are likely to be direct expenses. The subcontractors' fees are direct expenses and should be debited to WIP. These are not employees and therefore should not be recorded in the labour control account.

3 **A**

	$
Original cost	20,000
Year 1 Depreciation	5,000
Carrying value	15,000
Year 2 Depreciation	3,750
Carrying value	11,250
Year 3 Depreciation	2,812.50

4 **C**

The straight-line method would charge $\frac{1}{6}$ of the cost each year. The reducing balance method charges $\frac{1}{5}$ in Year 1 and the charge then reduces over the remaining years. The total cost is never written off using the reducing balance method.

CHAPTER 8

ACTIVITY 1

	Cost centres			
	P	*Q*	*S*	*General*
	$	$	$	$
Labour cost			6,500	
Supervision		2,100		
Machine repair cost		800		
Materials			1,100	
Depreciation of machinery			700	
Indirect materials	500			
Lighting and heating				900
Cost of works canteen				1,500

Note: Direct labour costs in Department P and material cost of widgets are direct production costs, not overheads – do not allocate.

ACTIVITY 2

(a) Number of actual machines or number of machine hours per cost centre.

(b) Value of machinery in each cost centre.

(c) Number of vehicles used by each cost centre or mileage of vehicles used by each cost centre.

ACTIVITY 3

(a) Neither service cost centre does work for the other.

	Total	*Cost centre P1*	*Cost centre P2*	*Cost centre S1*	*Cost centre S2*
	$	$	$	$	$
Allocated costs/share of general costs	550,000	140,000	200,000	90,000	120,000
Apportion:					
S1 costs (60:40)		54,000	36,000	(90,000)	
S2 costs (1:2)		40,000	80,000		(120,000)
		234,000	316,000		

(b) Cost centre S2 does some work for Cost centre S1. Start by apportioning the costs of Cost centre S2, then apportion Cost centre S1.

	Total	*Cost centre P1*	*Cost centre P2*	*Cost centre S1*	*Cost centre S2*
	$	$	$	$	$
Allocated costs/share of general costs	550,000	140,000	200,000	90,000	120,000
Apportion:					
S2 costs (25: 50: 25)		30,000	60,000	30,000	(120,000)
				120,000	
S1 costs (60:40)		72,000	48,000	(120,000)	
		242,000	308,000		

ACTIVITY 4

Machining:

$$\frac{\text{Cost centre overhead}}{\text{Machine hours}} = \frac{\$65,525}{7,300}$$

= $8.98 per machine hour.

Finishing:

$$\frac{\text{Cost centre overhead}}{\text{Direct labour hours}} = \frac{\$36,667}{6,250}$$

= $5.87 per direct labour hour.

Packing:

$$\frac{\text{Cost centre overhead}}{\text{Direct labour hours}} = \frac{\$24,367}{5,200}$$

= $4.69 per direct labour hour.

ACTIVITY 5

		$
Machining	3 machine hours @ $8.98	26.94
Finishing	0.9 direct labour hours @ $5.87	5.28
Packing	0.1 direct labour hours @ $4.69	0.47
Overhead absorbed in one unit of 'pot 3'		32.69

ACTIVITY 6

(a)

	Department X	*Department Y*
Budgeted overheads	$840,000	$720,000
Budgeted activity	40,000 machine hours	60,000 direct labour hours
Absorption rate	$21 per machine hour	$12 per direct labour hour

(b)

	Department X		*Department Y*	
		$		$
Absorbed overhead	(41,500 × $21)	871,500	(62,400 × $12)	748,800
Actual overhead		895,000		735,000
Over-/(under-)absorbed		(23,500)		13,800

ACTIVITY 7

(a)

		$
Total overhead cost of:	42,000 hours	153,000
Total overhead cost of:	37,000 hours	145,500
Variable overhead cost for:	5,000 hours	7,500
Variable overhead cost per hour ($7,500/5,000)		$1.50

This is the absorption rate for variable overheads.

	$
Total overhead cost of 42,000 hours	153,000
Variable overhead cost of 42,000 hours (× $1.50)	63,000
Therefore fixed costs	90,000

The absorption rate for fixed overhead, given a budget of 40,000 direct labour hours, is therefore $2.25 per direct labour hour ($90,000/40,000 hours)

(b)

	Fixed overhead	*Variable overhead*
	$	$
Absorbed overheads:		
Fixed (41,500 hours × $2.25)	93,375	
Variable (41,500 × $1.50)		62,250
Overheads incurred	91,000	67,500
Over-/(under-)absorbed overhead	2,375	(5,250)

(c)

Production overheads account

	$		$
Expenses incurred:		Work-in-progress:	
Fixed overheads	91,000	Fixed overheads absorbed	93,375
Variable overheads	67,500	Variable overheads absorbed	62,250
Over-absorbed overhead (fixed)	2,375	Under-absorbed (variable)	5,250
	160,875		160,875

Under/over absorbed overhead account

	$		$
Production overhead account	5,250	Production overhead account	2,375
		Statement of profit or loss	2,875
	5,250		5,250

ACTIVITY 8

Overhead recovery rates

	Finishing	*Packing*
Overhead / Direct labour hours	$74,000 / 12,750	$49,000 / 10,500
	= $5.80	= $4.67

January 20X4

	Finishing	*Packing*
Overhead absorbed	1,100 direct labour hours × $5.80 per hr	900 direct labour hours × $4.67 per hr
	$6,380	$4,203
Overhead incurred	$6,900	$4,000
Over-(under) absorbed overhead	$(520)	$203

Overhead control a/c

	$		$
Overhead incurred – finishing	6,900	Overhead absorbed W-I-P	
– packing	4,000	Finishing	6,380
		Packing	4,203
		Statement of profit or loss	317*
	$10,900		$10,900

*This $317 net under recovery comprises:

Finishing	$(520) under-absorbed overhead
Packing	$203 over-absorbed overhead
	$(317)

EXAM-STYLE QUESTIONS

1 **D**

A is incorrect because it refers to controllability. B is incorrect because it is describing absorption of costs. C is incorrect because it is describing allocation of costs. Only answer D refers to the process of cost apportionment.

2 **A**

Cost allocation is the process of charging a whole item of overhead cost to a cost centre.

3 **A**

The overhead absorption rate is based on budgeted figures:

$$\frac{\$258,750}{11,250} = \$23 \text{ per hour}$$

Since actual hours were 10,980, this means that overheads absorbed were 10,980 × $23 = $252,540. Actual overheads were $254,692, which means that overheads were under absorbed by $2,152.

4 **A**

		$
Budgeted absorption rate per hour		
Fixed	$94,000 ÷ 25,000	3.76
Variable	$57,500 ÷ 25,000	2.30
Total		6.06

	$
Overheads absorbed 26,500 hours × $6.06 per hour	160,590
Overheads incurred $102,600 fixed + $62,000 variable	164,600
Under-absorbed overhead	4,010

5 **C**

A relates to allocation and apportionment, B is addition, and absorption does not control overheads thus D is not correct.

6 **A**

Department 1 recovery rate = $2,400,000 ÷ 240,000 = $10 per hour

Department 2 recovery rate = $4,000,000 ÷ 200,000 = $20 per hour

Cost per IC = (3 × $10) + (2 × $20) = $70.

7 **C**

Fixed cost/unit (10,000 + 5,000 + 4,000 + 6,000) ÷ 2,000 = $12.50.

8 **D**

	Absorbed
	$
Actual overhead	138,000
Add: Over absorbed	23,000
Absorbed overhead	161,000

Hours worked = 11,500

Absorption rate per hour = $161,000/11,500 = $14

9 **C**

Answers A and B are not possible as the question states that actual and budgeted expenditure are the same. Therefore, there is no over- or under-spending on fixed production overheads. Over-absorption or under-absorption occurs when the absorption rate is a pre-determined rate based on budgeted data. Option C is correct because absorption using a pre-determined rate on above budget activity would absorb too much overheads into products.

10 **D**

	$
Actual overhead incurred	46,000
Overhead under-absorbed	1,375
Absorbed overhead	44,625
Actual machine hours	7,140
Overhead absorption rate ($44,625 / 7,200)	$6.25

Therefore budgeted hours must be $42,000 / $6.25 = 6,720 hours

CHAPTER 9

ACTIVITY 1

(a) **Absorption costing**

	$	$
Sales		48,000
Cost of sales		
Production costs (6,000 × $8)	48,000	
Closing inventory (1,200 × $8)	9,600	
		38,400
		9,600
Over-absorbed fixed overhead ((6,000 × $2) – $10,000)		2,000
Gross profit		11,600

(b) **Marginal costing**

	$	$
Sales		48,000
Cost of sales		
Production costs (6,000 × $6)	36,000	
Closing inventory (1,200 × $6)	7,200	
		28,800
Contribution		19,200
Fixed overheads		10,000
Gross profit		9,200

(c) **Reconciliation of profit figures**

	$
Profit per absorption costing	11,600
less fixed costs included in the increase in inventory (1,200 × $2)	(2,400)
Profit per marginal costing	9,200

Note: The over absorption of $2,000 does not feature in the reconciliation of the two profit figures.

EXAM-STYLE QUESTIONS

1 **D**

Without knowing the fixed overhead element in unit costs with absorption costing, we cannot calculate the profit difference.

2 **B**

When closing inventory is higher than opening inventory, profits are higher with absorption costing than with marginal costing. Closing inventory valuations are always higher under absorption costing as they include an element of fixed overhead.

3 **B**

This is a basic definition.

4 **D**

Under-absorption occurs when the amount absorbed is less than the actual overheads incurred.

5 **B**

The **under** absorbed fixed production overheads for the year were **$75,000**.

Absorption rate $= \frac{\$450,000}{900,000} = \$0.50/\text{hour}$

Absorbed overheads = 800,000 hours × $0.50/hour

= $400,000

Actual overheads = $475,000

Under - absorption = $75,000

6 **B**

Production is greater than sales, so absorption costing will have the higher profit.

Difference in profit = change in stock × fixed production overhead per unit.

Difference in profit = 2,500 units × $8/unit = $20,000.

Therefore, profit reported under marginal costing = $42,000 – 20,000 = $22,000.

7 **C**

Marginal costing does not follow the matching costing. This is an advantage of absorption costing. The other statements are all advantages of marginal costing.

8 **C**

Production is less than sales, so absorption costing will have a lower profit than the profit calculated using marginal costing.

Difference in profit = change in stock × fixed production overhead per unit.

Difference in profit = (7000 – 5000 units) × $1.50/unit = $3,000.

Therefore, profit reported under marginal costing = $56,000 + 3,000 = $59,000.

CHAPTER 10

ACTIVITY 1

JOB COST CARD

Job number: 3867	Customer name: OT Ltd
Estimate ref:	Quoted estimate:
Start date: 1 June	Delivery date: 17 June
Invoice number:	Invoice amount:

COSTS:

Materials

Date	Code	Qty	Price	$
1 June	T73	40 kg	$60	2,400
5 June	R80	60 kg	$5	300
9 June	B45	280m	$8	2,240
				4,940

Labour

Date	Grade	Hours	Rate	$
1 June	II	43	15.80	679.40
2 June	II	12	15.80	189.60
	IV	15	17.50	262.50
5 June	I	25	14.70	367.50
	IV	13	17.50	227.50
9 June	I	15	14.70	220.50
				1947.00

Expenses

Date	Code	Description	$

Production overheads

Hours	OAR	$

Cost summary:

	$
Direct materials	4,940
Direct labour	1,947
Direct expenses	
Production overheads	
Administration overheads	
Selling and distribution overheads	
Total cost	6,887
Invoice price	
Profit/loss	

ACTIVITY 2

As the machinery is used in equal proportions on three different jobs then only one third of the hire charge is to be charged to Job 3867 ($1,200 × ⅓ = $400).

JOB COST CARD

Job number: 3867	Customer name: OT Ltd
Estimate ref:	Quoted estimate:
Start date: 1 June	Delivery date: 17 June
Invoice number:	Invoice amount:

COSTS:

Materials

Date	Code	Qty	Price	$
1 June	T73	40 kg	$60	2,400
5 June	R80	60 kg	$5	300
9 June	B45	280m	$8	2,240
				4,940

Labour

Date	Grade	Hours	Rate	$
1 June	II	43	15.80	679.40
2 June	II	12	15.80	189.60
	IV	15	17.50	262.50
5 June	I	25	14.70	367.50
	IV	13	17.50	227.50
9 June	I	15	14.70	220.50
				1947.00

Expenses

Date	Code	Description	$
1 June	85	Machine hire	400
			400

Production overheads

Hours	OAR	$

Cost summary:

	$
Direct materials	4,940
Direct labour	1,947
Direct expenses	400
Production overheads	
Administration overheads	
Selling and distribution overheads	
Total cost	7,287
Invoice price	
Profit/loss	

ACTIVITY 3

JOB COST CARD

Job number: 3867	Customer name: OT Ltd
Estimate ref:	Quoted estimate:
Start date: 1 June	Delivery date: 17 June
Invoice number: 26457	Invoice amount: $7,800

COSTS:

Materials

Date	Code	Qty	Price	$
1 June	T73	40 kg	$60	2,400
5 June	R80	60 kg	$5	300
9 June	B45	280m	$8	2,240
				4,940

Labour

Date	Grade	Hours	Rate	$
1 June	II	43	15.80	679.40
2 June	II	12	15.80	189.60
	IV	15	17.50	262.50
5 June	I	25	14.70	367.50
	IV	13	17.50	227.50
9 June	I	15	14.70	220.50
				1947.00

Expenses

Date	Code	Description	$
1 June	85	Machine hire	400
			400

Production overheads

Hours	OAR	$
123	4.00	492
		492

Cost summary:

	$
Direct materials	4,940
Direct labour	1947
Direct expenses	400
Production overheads	492
Administration overheads	156
Selling and distribution overheads	78
Total cost	8,013
Invoice price	9,030
Profit/loss	1,017

ACTIVITY 4

(a) Total cost = $785 + ($785 × 0.25) = $981.25

Selling price = $981.25 + ($981.25 × 0.20) = $1,177.50

(b) Selling price = $785/0.7 = $1,121.43

(c) Selling price = $981.25/0.85 = $1,154.41

ACTIVITY 5

		$
Direct materials	120 kg @ $4 per kg	480
Direct labour	3 hours @ $18 per hour	54
	20 hours @ $12 per hour	240
Hire of machine	2 days @ $100 per day	200
Overhead	23 hours @$8 per hour	184
		1,158
Price charged		1,116
Loss		(42)

EXAM-STYLE QUESTIONS

1 **D**

$$2{,}400 \times \frac{100}{80} \times \$10 = \$30{,}000$$

2 **C**

Overheads are charged to jobs at predetermined absorption rate.

3 **D**

		$
Senior	86 hrs at $20	1,720
Junior	220 hrs at $15	3,300
Overheads	306 hrs at $12.50	3,825
Total cost		8,845
Mark-up	(40%)	3,538
Selling price		12,383

CHAPTER 11

ACTIVITY 1

Expected output = 1,900 units less normal loss of 2% = 1,900 – 38 = 1,862 units.

Actual output = 1,842 units.

Abnormal loss = 1,862 – 1,842 = 20 units.

Total costs of production = $31,654 ($28,804 + $1,050 + $1,800).

$$\text{Cost per unit of expected output} = \frac{\$31,654}{1,862 \text{ units}} = \$17 \text{ per unit}$$

Both good output and abnormal loss are valued at this amount.

These transactions should be recorded in the cost accounts as follows.

Process A

	Units	$		Units	$
Direct materials	1,900	28,804	Finished goods	1,842	31,314
Direct labour		1,050	Normal loss	38	–
Process overhead		1,800	Abnormal loss	20	340
	1,900	31,654		1,900	31,654

Abnormal loss a/c

	Units	$		Units	$
Process A	20	340	Statement of profit or loss	20	340
	20	340		20	340

Finished goods

	Units	$		Units	$
Process B	1,842	31,314			

ACTIVITY 2

Expected output = 100,000 kilos less normal loss of 6% = 100,000 – 6,000 = 94,000 kilos.

Actual output = 96,000 kilos.

Abnormal gain = 96,000 – 94,000 = 2,000 kilos.

	$
Direct materials	100,000
Conversion costs	135,000
Less scrap proceeds of normal loss	(6,000)
Production costs	229,000

$$\text{Cost per unit of expected output} = \frac{\$229{,}000}{94{,}000 \text{ units}} = \$2.436 \text{ per unit}$$

Both good output and abnormal gains are valued at this amount.

Process a/c

	Units	$		*Units*	$
Direct material	100,000	100,000	Output	96,000	233,856
Conversion costs		135,000	Normal loss	6,000	6,000
Abnormal gain	2,000	4,872	Rounding error		16
	102,000	239,872		102,000	239,872

		$
Valuation of output	96,000 kilos × $2.436	233,856
Valuation of abnormal gain	2,000 kilos × $2.436	4,872

Abnormal gain a/c

	Units	$		*Units*	$
Normal loss a/c	2,000	2,000			
Statement of profit or loss		2,872	Process a/c	2,000	4,872
		4,872			4,872

Normal loss a/c

	Units	$		*Units*	$
Process a/c	6,000	6,000	Bank	4,000	4,000
			Abnormal gain a/c	2,000	2,000
		6,000			6,000

Note that the scrap proceeds 'lost' because normal loss is less than expected is debited to the abnormal gain account (reducing the gain taken to the statement of profit or loss) and credited to the normal loss account.

ACTIVITY 3

(a) (i) Cost per kg = $122,500/7,000 = $17.50

Cost apportioned to X = 3,000 × $17.50 =	$52,500
Cost apportioned to Y = 4,000 × $17.50 =	$70,000
Total costs	$122,500

(ii) Net realisable value = 3,000 × ($150 – $30) + 4,000 × $50 = $560,000

Cost per $ of net realisable value = $122,500/$560,000 = $0.21875

Cost apportioned to X = 360,000 × 0.21875 =	$78,750
Cost apportioned to Y = 200,000 × 0.21875 =	$43,750
Total costs	$122,500

(b) (i)

	X ($)	X ($)
Sales	450,000	200,000
Less further processing cost	90,000	–
Net realisable value	360,000	200,000
Cost (from a))	52,500	70,000
Profit	307,500	130,000
Profit per unit	102.50	32.50

(ii)

	X ($)	Y ($)
Sales	450,000	200,000
Less further processing cost	90,000	–
Net realisable value	360,000	200,000
Cost (from a))	78,750	43,750
Profit	281,250	156,250
Profit per unit	93.75	39.06

EXAM-STYLE QUESTIONS

1 **B**

Total output 25,000 kg

Joint cost per kg = $\frac{\$100,000}{25,000\,kg}$ = \$4

Profit per unit of X = \$10 – \$4

= \$6.

2 **C**

	Output	*Selling price*	*Sales value*
			\$
X	5,000	\$10	50,000
Y	10,000	\$4	40,000
Z	10,000	\$3	30,000
			120,000

Cost per \$ of sales = $\frac{\$100,000}{\$120,000}$ = \$0.83

Profit of Y

	\$
Sales	40,000
Cost	33,333
Profit	6,667

3 **D**

A is incorrect. The percentage profit margin is the same if the joint costs are apportioned on sales value.

B is incorrect. Total profits will be the same whatever method of apportionment is used.

4 **D**

Statement A is correct. Job costs are identified with a particular job, whereas process costs (of units produced and work-in-process) are averages, based on equivalent units of production.

Statement B is also correct. The direct cost of a job to date, excluding any direct expenses, can be ascertained from materials requisition notes and job tickets or time sheets.

Statement C is correct, because without data about units completed and units still in process, losses and equivalent units of production cannot be calculated.

Statement D is incorrect, because the cost of normal loss will usually be incorporated into job costs as well as into process costs. In process costing this is commonly done by giving normal loss no cost, leaving costs to be shared between output, closing WIP and abnormal loss/gain. In job costing it can be done by adjusting direct materials costs to allow for normal wastage, and direct labour costs for normal reworking of items or normal spoilage.

5 **B**

In process costing, abnormal gains and losses are valued at the same cost per unit as normal good production output.

6 **A**

	Kg
Material input	2,500
Normal loss @ 10%	(250)
Abnormal loss	(75)
Good production achieved	2,175

7 **D**

	Tonnes produced	*Basis of valuation Selling prices per tonne*	*Sales value*
		$	$
W	700	40	28,000
X	600	90	54,000
Y	400	120	48,000
Z	100	200	20,000
	1,800		150,000

Total cost of production

	$
Material	75,000
Labour	24,000
Overhead (25% of labour)	6,000
	105,000

Share of joint costs based on sales value = $\frac{\text{Joint costs}}{\text{Sales value}} \times 100 = \frac{105,000}{150,000} \times 100 = 70\%$

Mineral	*Share of joint costs*	$
W	$28,000 × 70% =	19,600
X	$54,000 × 70% =	37,800
Y	$48,000 × 70% =	33,600
Z	$20,000 × 70% =	14,000

8 **D**

$$\text{Cost per tonne} = \frac{\text{Total joint cost}}{\text{Total output}} = \frac{105{,}000}{700 + 600 + 400 + 100} = \frac{105{,}000}{1{,}800}$$

= $58.33 per tonne

Hence value of closing inventory is:

			$
W	30 × $58.33	=	1,750
X	20 × $58.33	=	1,167
Y	80 × $58.33	=	4,667
Z	5 × $58.33	=	292
			7,876

Note: Inventory should be valued at the lower of cost and net realisable value. Using this method the 'cost' of W is $58.33, whereas the net realisable value (here the sale value) is $40. Clearly, inventory could not be valued at $58.33.

9 **C**

Total costs of direct materials, labour and overhead: $5,000 + $4,500 = $9,500.

Expected output = 95% of 2,000 = 1,900 kilograms

Cost per unit = $9,500/1,900 units = $5 per unit.

Value of output = 1,850 units × $5 = $9,250.

Alternatively:

Process 1 account

	Units	$		*Units*	$
Direct materials	2,000	5,000	Output to Process 2	1,850	9,250
Labour and overhead		4,500	Normal loss	100	0
			Abnormal loss	50	250
	2,000	9,500		2,000	9,500

CHAPTER 12

EXAM-STYLE QUESTIONS

1 **D**

As a non-profit seeking charitable organisation, profit would not be an appropriate measure.

2 **A**

Service costing can be used for both internal and external services and is not limited to service industries.

3 Average cost per occupied bed per day was **$9.90**

$$= \frac{\text{Total cost}}{\text{Number of beds occupied}}$$

$$= \frac{\$(100{,}000 + 5{,}000 + 22{,}500)}{6{,}450 \times 2} = \$9.9$$

4 The performance measures would be calculated as follows:

Performance measure	**Room occupancy**	**Bed occupancy**	**Average guest rate**
Total revenue divided by number of guests			✓
Total number of beds occupied as a percentage of beds available.		✓	
Total number of rooms occupied as a percentage of rooms available to let.	✓		

5 The following measures would be useful for assessing the maintenance services:

- Cost per item repaired
- Cost per employee
- Cost per square area covered

Cost per item repaired would be a key cost. Cost per employee would allow the organisation to assess the efficiency of staff and cost per square area would allow the organisation to take account of the difference in size of the departments.

The following measures would not be useful

- Profit per item repaired
- Sales per employee
- Purchase cost of the item repaired

Profit and sales per employee would not be relevant as the service is provided for free. The original cost of the item is not relevant to the maintenance service provided.

CHAPTER 13

ACTIVITY 1

Break-even point in units = $\frac{\text{Fixed costs}}{\text{Contribution per unit}}$ Break-even point in \$ = $\frac{\text{Fixed costs}}{{}^{C}/_{S}\text{ ratio}}$

$= \frac{\$5,000}{\$20} = 250$ units $= \frac{\$5,000}{{}^{20}/_{30}} = \$7,500$

Or the break even revenue can be found as 250 units (BEP) x \$30 (selling price) = \$7,500

ACTIVITY 2

(a) Unit variable cost = \$24 – \$18 = \$6. Fixed costs = \$800,000.

Break-even point in units = $\frac{\$800,000}{\$6 \text{ per unit}}$ = 133,333 units

Break-even point in \$ = $\frac{\$800,000}{{}^{6}/_{24}}$ = \$3,200,000

(b)

Budgeted sales	140,000 units
Break-even sales	133,333 units
Margin of safety	6,667 units

Margin of safety as a percentage of budgeted sales = 100% × (6,667/140,000)
= 4.8%

ACTIVITY 3

	\$
Target profit	400,000
Fixed costs	
Production	350,000
Administration	110,000
Selling	240,000
Target contribution	1,100,000

Contribution per unit = \$25 – \$10 – \$4 = \$11

Target sales volume

$= \frac{\text{Target contribution}}{\text{Contribution per unit}}$ = \$1,100,000/\$11 per unit = 100,000 units

ACTIVITY 4

	$	$
Sales price	11	12
Variable cost	8	8
Unit contribution	3	4
Expected sales demand	200,000	160,000
	$	$
Annual contribution	600,000	640,000
Annual fixed costs	550,000	550,000
Annual profit	50,000	90,000
Break-even point (units)	183,333	137,500
Margin of safety (units)	16,667	22,500
Margin of safety (% of budget)	8.3%	14.1%

Of the two sales prices under consideration for Product ZG, a price of $12 appears to be preferable.

On the basis of the estimates for variable costs, fixed costs and sales demand at each price, the annual profit would be $90,000 at a price of $12 and only $50,000 at a price of $11.

The higher price also appears to offer the lower risk with regard to sales demand falling short of the expected levels. The margin of safety would be about 14% at a price of $12, but only about 8% at a price of $11.

ACTIVITY 5

(a) Break-even point in units

$$\frac{\text{Fixed costs}}{\text{Contribution per unit}}$$

$$\frac{\$650{,}000}{\$35}$$

= 18,572 tonnes

Margin of safety = 50,000 – 18,572/50,000 × 100% = **62.86%.**

(b) Break-even point in sales value:

$$\frac{\text{Fixed costs}}{(\text{Contribution/Sales})}$$

$$= \frac{\$650{,}000}{(1{,}750{,}000/3{,}750{,}000)}$$

= $1,392,857

(c)

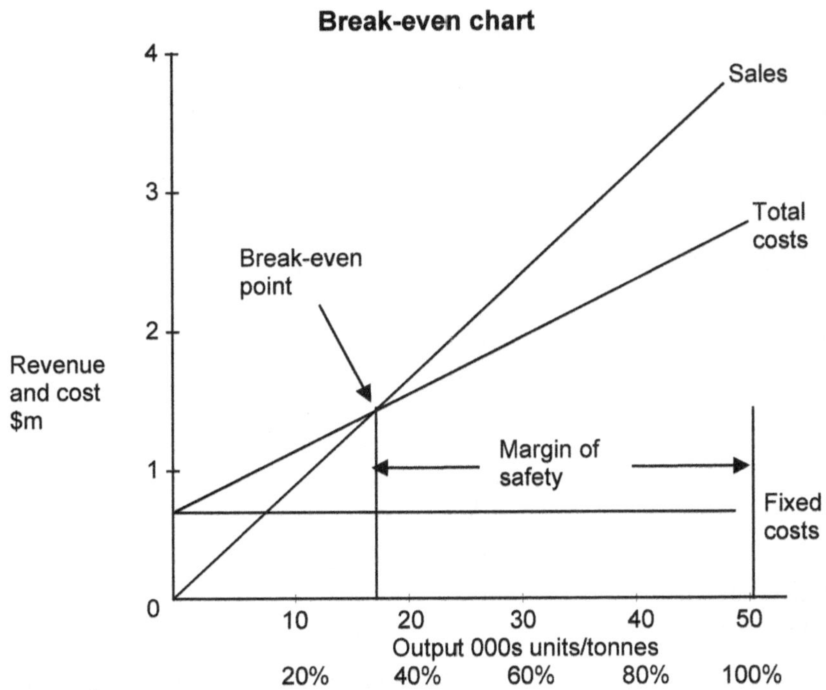

Break-even point = approx 18,500 tonnes.

Margin of safety = approx 31,500 tonnes (approx 63%).

ACTIVITY 6

(a) The first step is to calculate a variable cost per unit using the high-low method.

	$
Total costs of 70,000 units	675,000
Total costs of 55,000 units	607,500
Therefore variable costs of 15,000 units	67,500

Variable cost per unit = $67,500/15,000 = $4.50 per unit.

We can now calculate fixed costs, in either of the ways shown below.

	70,000 units	*55,000 units*
	$	$
Total costs	675,000	607,500
Variable costs at $4.50 per unit	315,000	247,500
Therefore fixed costs	360,000	360,000

Contribution per unit = Sales price – Variable cost = $10 – $4.50 = $5.50.

Break-even point = $360,000/$5.50 per unit = 65,455 units.

(b) **Margin of safety** = 68,000 – 65,455 = 2,545 units. As a percentage of budgeted sales, this is 3.7%.

(c) To achieve a **target profit** of $40,000, total contribution must be $400,000 ($360,000 fixed costs + $40,000 profit). Required sales =

$400,000/$5.50 contribution per unit = 72,727 units.

This is a higher sales volume than the 'high' level of costs used in the high-low analysis. This must raise doubts as to whether a sales volume of nearly 73,000 units and a profit of $40,000 are achievable at the current sales price and cost levels.

EXAM-STYLE QUESTIONS

1 **A**

Contribution = selling price – variable costs

= $40 – $25 = $15

2 **B**

Break-even point (BEP) = total fixed costs/contribution per pair

BEP = 100,000 + 40,000 +100,000/15

= 16,000

3 **C**

Margin of safety = Current level of sales – break-even sales =

25,000 – 16,000 = 9,000 pairs

The margin of safety can also be expressed as a percentage of the current level or budgeted level of sales.

4 **B**

C/S ratio is $\frac{312{,}000 - 124{,}800}{312{,}000} = 0.6$

so sales revenue required is $\frac{\$130{,}000 + \$75{,}000}{0.6} = \$341{,}667$

5 **A**

Contribution per unit = $\$\left(\frac{312{,}000 - 124{,}800}{52{,}000}\right) = \$3.60$

so sales units required are $\frac{\$130{,}000 + \$82{,}000}{\$3.60} = 58{,}889$

6 **C**

BEP (units) = $\frac{130{,}000}{3.60} = 36{,}111$

Margin of safety = $\frac{52{,}000 - 36{,}111}{52{,}000} = 30.6\%$.

CHAPTER 14

ACTIVITY 1

(a) Production is restricted as follows:

Machine hours	200/5	=	40 units of X; or
	200/2.5	=	80 units of Y
Materials	$500/$10	=	50 units of X; or
	$500/$5	=	100 units of Y

Therefore machine hours are the limiting factor since production of Products X and Y are most severely limited by machine hours.

(b) Benefit per machine hour:

Product X	$20/5 hours	=	$4/hour
Product Y	$15/2.5 hours	=	$6/hour

Product Y should be made because it has the highest contribution per unit of limiting factor (machine hours).

ACTIVITY 2

Product	*A*	*B*	*C*
Contribution per labour hour	$\frac{\$25}{5} = \$5.00$	$\frac{\$40}{6} = \$6.66$	$\frac{\$35}{8} = \$4.375$
Rank order	2nd	1st	3rd

Firstly make 200 units of Product B (maximum demand) and then with the remaining 300 hours make 60 units of Product A.

ACTIVITY 3

If labour hours are limited to 4,000 hours the excess cost per labour hour should be determined:

	Component B	*Component C*
Excess cost	$2	$6
Labour hours	2	4
Excess cost per labour hour	$1	$1.50

Therefore, Component B has the lowest excess cost per limiting factor and should be bought externally.

Proof

	Component B	*Component C*
Units produced in 4,000 labour hours	2,000	1,000
	$	$
Production costs	8,000	7,000
Purchase costs	12,000	13,000
Excess cost of purchase	4,000	6,000

ACTIVITY 4

The proposal reduces variable costs by $60,000 but increases fixed costs by $72,000 and is therefore not to be recommended unless the total volume increases as a result of the policy (e.g. if the supply of the components were previously a limiting factor). The increase in sales needed to maintain profit at $150,000 (assuming the price remains at $8) would be as follows:

Reduced profits at 100,000 units	$12,000
Revised contribution per unit	$3.60
∴ Additional volume required	3,333 units

ACTIVITY 5

The original cost of the material is a sunk cost, and therefore not relevant. Essentially, Zara has two choices: either to use the material for the new job, or to sell it at $3 per kg.

If the material is used in the new job, Zara will lose out on $120 that could have been earned by selling it. This means that the opportunity cost of using the material for the new job is $120, and this is the relevant cost that should be included in the price.

ACTIVITY 6

What contribution cash flow is lost if the labour is transferred to the project from doing nothing? Answer: nothing.

The relevant cost is therefore zero.

EXAM-STYLE QUESTIONS

1 **C**

Fixed costs can be relevant costs, because some fixed costs can be saved or incurred as a result of a decision.

2 **D**

The question gives a basic definition of notional cost.

3 **A**

A sunk cost is a cost that has already been incurred or committed.

4 **D**

In order to fully satisfy demand the company would need

3kgs × 100 units to satisfy demand for P =	300
4kgs × 150 units to satisfy demand for Q =	600
5kgs × 300 units to satisfy demand for R =	1,500
Total kgs of materials required=	2,400

Therefore materials are a limiting factor and products should be ranked in order of contribution per kilogram:

Product	*P*	*Q*	*R*
Contribution per kg of material	$\frac{\$10}{3\text{ kg}} = \$3.33$	$\frac{\$12}{4\text{ kg}} = \$3.00$	$\frac{\$20}{5\text{ kg}} = \$4.00$
Ranking	2nd	3rd	1st

5 **B**

Product R has the highest benefit from the use of the materials; its demand is limited to 300 units per month requiring 5 kg of material per unit, or 1,500 kg in total (300 × 5 kg). Since there is a total of 1,680 kg of material available and only 1,500 kg are used to produce Product R, there are 180 kg of material still available.

The next best product is Product P which has a maximum demand of 100 units, each of which requires 3 kg of material. The maximum quantity of Product P would require 300 kg (100 × 3 kg) but we only have 180 kg available so we can only produce:

$$\frac{180\text{ kg}}{3\text{ kg/unit}} = 60 \text{ units of Product P}$$

6 **B**

All of the available materials have now been allocated. The production plan that maximises profit is:

			Total contribution ($)
300 units of R	using	1,500 kg of material	6,000
60 units of P	using	180 kg of material	600
		1,680 kg	$6,600

7 **C**

Since the weekend working is caused if the work is undertaken the full cost is relevant:

Standard work: 125 hours @ $4/hr =	$500	
Weekend work: 125 hours @ $5/hr =	$625	$1,125

8 **A**

The weekend work results in 50 hours' time off in lieu, this with the 75 other hours worked totals 125 hours which is less than the 200 hours of idle time which are already being paid for, thus there is no incremental cost.

9 **D**

As the material is used elsewhere in the business the cost for the project should be the replacement cost of $10 per kg. So the total relevant cost is $600.

10 **$37,500**

The salaries and normal working hours are not relevant to the decision as they will be paid even if the project does not proceed. Only the overtime represents an incremental cost.

The cost of the overtime is = 60% × 5,000 hours × $10 per hour × 1.25 (overtime rate) = $37,500

CHAPTER 15

ACTIVITY 1

The $15,000 already spent on the feasibility study is not relevant, because it has already been spent. (It is a 'sunk cost'.) Depreciation and apportioned fixed overheads are not relevant. Depreciation is not a cash flow and apportioned fixed overheads represent costs that will be incurred anyway.

	$
Estimated profit	8,000
Add back depreciation	40,000
Add back apportioned fixed costs	25,000
Annual cash flows	73,000

The project's cash flows to be evaluated are

Year		$
Now (Year 0)	Purchase equipment	(160,000)
1 – 4	Cash flow from profits	73,000 each year

ACTIVITY 2

$$\text{Payback} = \frac{\$2,300,000}{\$600,000} = 3.8333 \text{ years}$$

0.8333 years = 10 months (0.8333 × 12)

Payback is therefore after 3 years 10 months.

It is assumed that the cash flows each year occur at an even rate throughout the year.

ACTIVITY 3

The payback period is calculated as follows.

Year	*Cash flow*	*Cumulative cash flow*
	$000	$000
0	(3,100)	(3,100)
1	1,000	(2,100)
2	900	(1,200)
3	800	(400)
4	500	100
5	500	600

Payback is between the end of Year 3 and the end of Year 4 – in other words during Year 4.

If we assume a constant rate of cash flow through the year, we could estimate that payback will be three years, plus (400/500) of Year 4, which is 3.8 years.

0.8 years = 10 months (0.8 × 12)

We could therefore estimate that payback would be after 3 years 10 months.

ACTIVITY 4

(a) $\$2,000 \times \frac{1}{1.08^4} = \$1,470$

(b) $\$5,000 \times \frac{1}{1.07^3} = \$4,081$

ACTIVITY 5

Year	*Cash flow*	*Discount factor at 6%*	*Present value*
	$		$
0	(25,000)	1.000	(25,000)
1	6,000	0.943	5,658
2	10,000	0.890	8,900
3	8,000	0.840	6,720
4	7,000	0.792	5,544
			+ 1,822

+ $1,822 is in fact the net present value of the project.

ACTIVITY 6

DCF Schedule (NPV method)

Discount rate 12%

Year	*Outflow*	*Inflow*	*Discount factor at 12%*	*NPV*
	$	$		$
0	(35,000)		1.000	(35,000)
1		8,000	0.893	7,144
2		9,000	0.797	7,173
3		12,000	0.712	8,544
4		9,500	0.636	6,042
5		9,000	0.567	5,103
			NPV	(994)

Recommendation

At the cost of capital of 12%, the NPV is negative, showing that the investment would earn a return below 12% per annum. On financial grounds, the recommendation is that the project should not be undertaken.

ACTIVITY 7

Using the present value table for Dennis plc machine (as cash flows are different in each year) to find discount factors the calculation of the NPV is as follows:

Year	**Cash flow $**	**Discount factor**	**Present value $**
0	(1,500)	1	(1,500)
1	900	0.909	818
2	600	0.826	496
3	500	0.751	376
		Net Present Value	190

Using the annuity table for Thompson machine (as there is a constant annual cash flow each year) the annuity factor is 2.487 and the calculation of the NPV is as follows:

Year	**Cash flow $**	**Discount factor**	**Present value $**
0	(1,500)	1	(1,500)
1 – 3	700	2.487	1,741
		Net present value	241

The Thompson machine has the highest NPV and should be chosen.

ACTIVITY 8

Year	Equipment	*Cash flow from operations*	*Net cash flow*	*Discount factor at 7%*	*Present value*
	$	$	$		$
0	(60,000)		(60,000)	1.000	(60,000)
1 – 4		18,000	18,000	3.387	60,966
5	5,000	6,000	11,000	0.713	7,843
NPV					+ 8,809

The NPV is positive, therefore the investment is financially worthwhile at a cost of capital of 7%.

ACTIVITY 9

The maximum price the investment company should be prepared to pay is the present value of the future cash flows in perpetuity. The cost of capital is 8% so the present value of the cash flows is:

$25,000/0.08 = $312,500.

ACTIVITY 10

Year	Cash flow	Discount factor at 9%	PV at 9%	Discount factor at 12%	PV at 12%
	$		$		$
0	(100,000)	1.000	(100,000)	1.000	(100,000)
1 – 5	25,000	3.890	97,250	3.605	90,125
5	12,000	0.650	7,800	0.567	6,804
			+ 5,050		(3,071)

(a) The NPV at 9% is + $5,050.

(b) The NPV at 12% is – $3,071.

(c) Using interpolation, the approximate IRR is:

$$9\% + \left[\frac{5,050}{(5,050 + 3,071)} \times (12 - 9)\%\right]$$

= 9% + 1.86%

= 10.86%, say 10.9%.

EXAM-STYLE QUESTIONS

1 **C**

$$2 \text{ years} + \left[\frac{6{,}200}{(6{,}200 + 1{,}100)} \times 12 \text{ months}\right]$$

= 2 years 10 months.

2 **B**

$$\text{IRR} = 10\% + \left[\frac{17{,}000}{(17{,}000 + 53{,}000)} \times (14 - 10)\%\right]$$

= 10.97% = 11.0%

3 **A**

If the NPV is positive, the IRR must be higher than the cost of capital. Simple payback happens earlier than discounted payback, because with discounted payback the net cash flows are reduced to a present value.

4 **D**

The value of the investment after three years (principal plus interest) =

$\$15,000 \times (1.06)^3$

= $17,865.

The interest is therefore $17,865 – $15,000 = $2,865.

5 **B**

NPV = $0

Let $x be annual rent.

Annuity factor for year 5 at 17% is 3.199.

$\therefore$ $x × 3.199 = 27,200

$\therefore$ $x = 8,502

6 **C**

The IRR (Internal Rate of Return) is the percentage cost of capital that results in the NPV being zero. For projects with an initial outflow followed by a series of positive inflows the higher the cost of capital the lower the NPV becomes. If, in this scenario, the NPV is still positive after the cost of capital has moved from 12% to 18%, then the cost of capital which gives a zero NPV (i.e. the IRR) must be higher still than 18% p.a.

7 **D**

The IRR (Internal Rate of Return) is the percentage cost of capital that results in the NPV being zero. In this scenario, this occurs when the cost of capital is 22%.

8 **B**

Depreciation is not a cash flow so needs to be added back to profit to calculate cash flows.

Depreciation on straight line basis = ($400,000 – $50,000)/5 = $70,000 per year

Year	*Profit ($)*	*Cash flow ($)*	*Cumulative cash flow ($)*
0		(400,000)	(400,000)
1	175,000	245,000	(155,000)
2	225,000	295,000	140,000

Payback period = 1 + 155/295 years = 1.53 years to nearest 0.01 years

9 **C**

The present value of a $1 perpetuity is 1/r.

The present value of the rental income is $80,000/0.08 = $1,000,000

The NPV of the investment is $1,000,000 – $850,000 = $150,000

CHAPTER 16

ACTIVITY 1

The opening receivables (i.e. amounts outstanding at the end of the last period) can be assumed to be received in this period. But the closing receivables will still be outstanding at the end of the period and have not yet been converted into cash. It means that the operational cash inflow from sales will be:

= 240,000 + 18,000 – 28,800 = $229,200

ACTIVITY 2

If you have a lot of sales, you still may not have cash, since you will always have some outstanding accounts receivable to be collected. If you put that together with the purchase of inventory and equipment, payments to suppliers for items purchased prior to the actual payment and payments on debt, you will likely have less cash – or less access to it – than you think.

EXAM STYLE QUESTIONS

1 **D**

Supermarkets tend to keep inventory turnover low and the majority of receivables will be recovered within a couple of days. Their power gives them an extended level of credit from suppliers, so that overall their working capital cycle is often negative – that is, they often receive money in before they have to pay anything out.

The band's cycle should be no more than one week long. They will have little or no inventory or payables, and the fee should hopefully be received in one week's time. A college selling material will have to buy the material upfront, for delivery on day one of the course. This will build up inventories. The government might take some extended credit to pay invoices so that the total working cycle might be a few months long.

Ships can take months to build and during that period large inventories (in the form of work-in-progress can be built up). On top of that, buyers are often large powerful companies who can take months to pay invoices so that the overall cash operating cycle can run to many months for shipbuilders.

2 The following are items that relate to an organisation obtaining finance:

- Increases in long-term debt
- Increases in equity
- Increasing current liabilities

Increases in current assets are likely to drain finance such as:

- Increasing trade receivables
- Purchasing inventory

3 **B**

Option B would impact cash and not profit as the purchase would have impacted on profit already when the goods were supplied. The other options all impact on profit.

4 **D**

Options A and B would affect both cash and profits. Option D would affect cash only. Option C would affect profits only.

5 **A**

B, C and D are capital items. A would be classified as a revenue receipt – the value of the receipt is not relevant.

6 **5** months

	Months
Raw materials inventory holding period	2
Less: suppliers' payment period	(1)
WIP holding period	1
Finished goods holding period	1
Receivables' collection period	2
Working capital cycle (months)	5

CHAPTER 17

ACTIVITY 1

(a) **Interest yield** = $\frac{4}{94.00} \times 100\% = 4.25\%$

(b) **Approximate redemption yield**

If an investor buys the stock now at $94.00 and holds it for three years until maturity, he will make a capital gain of 100 – 94 = 6 at redemption. In other words, there will be a capital gain of $6 for every $100 of stock, or for every $94 invested. This gives an average annual gain on redemption of $2 for each $94 invested, which is about 2% per annum.

The approximate redemption yield is therefore the interest yield of 4.25% plus 2%, which is about 6.25%.

ACTIVITY 2

We have $5 million to invest for 50 days. We want to invest at a fairly low risk.

There are two risks with investing in bills.

1 *Credit risk.* This is the risk of non-payment of the bill at maturity. This is non-existent for Treasury bills and very low for bank bills. We can invest in either of these types of bill, through our bank.

2 *Risk of falling market prices.* The market value of bills in the discount market will fall if interest rates go up in the next 50 days. This risk only exists if we intend to re-sell the bills before their maturity. To overcome this problem, we can ask our bank to purchase 'second-hand' bills in the discount market with a maturity of 50 days. In this way, the return on our investment will come from the payment of the bills at maturity, and we will not have to sell them in the discount market to cash in our investment.

ACTIVITY 3

A balloon loan and a bullet loan each involve a large final payment to repay a loan. The difference is the amount. A bullet is the full principal amount of the loan; no principal is paid off prior to the date of the bullet. By contrast, a balloon payment is normally less than the full loan amount and some of the loan principal is paid back prior to the date of the balloon payment.

ACTIVITY 4

Bank overdrafts offer flexibility when the amount of finance required is unknown. The cost of this flexibility, however, is higher interest rates than those charged on bank loans. Overdrafts should therefore be seen as a short term source of finance.

Bank loans offer a definite amount of finance but have no flexibility. They should be used when the amount of expenditure is certain and the requirement is likely to arise over the longer term.

In this scenario, the cost of the machine is known and the investment is for the long term, so a bank loan would appear to be more appropriate than a bank overdraft.

EXAM STYLE QUESTIONS

1 **A**

2 **C**

The production department would be responsible for utilising labour and the personnel department would have responsibility for recruiting and training them. The finance department would be responsible for paying them. Paying staff is not a responsibility for the treasury department.

3 **B**

Options B, C and D all refer to equity, but only option B involves making an investment.

4 **B**

5 **B**

The redemption yield is equal to the interest yield added to the redemption gain.

The interest yield on the stock is calculated as a % of market value as follows:

= 8/98 × 100 = 8.16%

If an investor buys the stock now at $98.00 and holds it until maturity, he/she will make a capital gain of 100 – 98 = $2 at redemption (the stock will repay $100 in one year's time for an investment of $98 now). This gives an average annual gain on redemption of $2 for each $98 invested, which is about 2% per annum.

The approximate redemption yield is therefore the interest yield of 8% plus 2%, which is about 10%.

CHAPTER 18

ACTIVITY 1

Workings: Receipts from credit sales

			Cash receipts	
Sales month	*Credit sales*	*July*	*August*	*September*
	$	$	$	$
April	60,000	6,000	–	–
May	64,000	19,200	6,400	–
June	50,000	30,000	15,000	5,000
July	60,000		36,000	18,000
August	65,000	–		39,000
September	75,000	–	–	–
Total credit receipts		55,200	57,400	62,000

Total cash receipts	*July*	*August*	*September*
	$	$	$
Receipts from cash sales	4,500	4,500	5,000
Receipts from credit sales	55,200	57,400	62,000
Total receipts	59,700	61,900	67,000

ACTIVITY 2

	January	*February*	*March*
Sales quantity	400	450	420
Less: Opening inventory	(100)	(150)	(120)
Add: Closing inventory	150	120	180
Production in units = units purchased	450	420	480
Cost of purchases at $2 per unit	$900	$840	$960

Payment in March		$
For January purchases	(60% of $900)	540
For March purchases	(40% of $960)	384
Total payments for materials		924

ACTIVITY 3

(a) **Tutorial note:** Inventory is used up by material usage, and by closing inventory. This usage is made up partly from opening inventory. The balance must be made up from purchases. This situation is shown in the solution following.

	June	*July*	*August*
	$	$	$
Material usage	8,000	9,000	10,000
Closing inventory	3,500	6,000	4,000
	11,500	15,000	14,000
Less: Opening inventory	5,000	3,500	6,000
Purchases	6,500	11,500	8,000

(b) **Tutorial note:** The main points to watch out for are sales receipts and overheads. Tackle sales receipts by calculating separate figures for cash sales (10% of total sales, received in the month of sale) and credit sales (90% of **last month's** sales). For overheads, remember that depreciation is not a cash expense and must therefore be stripped out of the overheads cash cost.

Cash budgets, June – August

	June	*July*	*August*
	$	$	$
Receipts of cash			
Cash sales	4,500	5,000	6,000
Credit sales	29,500	40,500	45,000
	34,000	45,500	51,000
Cash payments			
Wages	12,000	13,000	14,500
Overheads	6,500	7,000	8,000
Direct materials	6,500	11,500	8,000
Taxation	–	25,000	–
	25,000	56,500	30,500
Surplus/(deficit) for month	9,000	(11,000)	20,500
Opening balance	11,750	20,750	9,750
Closing balance	20,750	9,750	30,250

EXAM STYLE QUESTIONS

1 **C**

Receipts:

Month	*Total*	*Jan*	*Feb*
Sales	$	$	$
Opening receivables	80,000	60,000	18,400
January	70,000	14,000	35,000
February	70,000		14,000
Total	450,000	74,000	67,400

2 **D**

From working in answer 1

3 **B**

Payments to suppliers

Purchases are 75% of sales value.

Purchases in December and January, for sales in February and March, will be 75% of $70,000 = $52,500 each month.

Purchases are paid for one month in arrears. So the December and January purchases will be paid for in January and February.

4 **B**

Cash expenses are $8,500 each month less $500 depreciation = $8,000 each month.

These include rental costs of $2,000 each month, which are payable in June.

Cash expenditures are therefore $8,000 – S2,000 = $6,000 each month in January. The payment for the van loan is a normal cash expense that would be included as part of the distribution costs.

5 **C**

The monthly total fixed cost is $75,000/12 = $6,250

Of this, 10% ($625) is depreciation and won't affect the cash payment.

The remainder will be the monthly budgeted cash payment

= $6,250 – $625 = $5,625

6 **B**

	1	*2*
Sales (Units × $10)	15,000	17,500
Paid in month – 20% × 0.98	2,940	3,430
45% in the following month		6,750
25% in 3rd month		
Sales Receipts	2,940	10,180

7 **A**

Production	*1*
	units
Required by sales	1,500
Opening inventory	–
	1,500
Closing inventory (20% × following month's sales)	350
Production	1,850

8 **C**

The centred moving average will match up exactly with a quarterly period each year allowing for the calculation of the seasonal variation each quarter.

CHAPTER 19

ACTIVITY 1

The standard price of the material is $5 per litre and the actual price paid is $4.90 (($5 × 98%). This will lead to a favourable total materials cost variance because less will be spent on materials than expected.

ACTIVITY 2

The budgeted price was $4.00 and the actual price was $4.25 per metre. Therefore there is an unfavourable or adverse total materials cost variance because more will be spent on materials than expected.

ACTIVITY 3

For each batch of the product 15 millilitres is now required compared to the budgeted usage of 10 millilitres. This gives rise to an adverse total materials cost variance of 5 millilitres per batch.

ACTIVITY 4

Original budget (1,000 × $7.20) = $7,200

Flexed budget (940 units × $7.20) = $6,768

(a) Materials activity (volume) variance = original (fixed) budget – flexed budget

Materials activity variance = $(7,200 – 6,768) = $432 favourable

(b) Variance due to changes in purchase price and/or efficiency of usage = flexed budget – actual costs incurred

Variance due to other changes = $(6,768 – 6,240) = $528 favourable

(c) Materials total variance = actual costs incurred – original (fixed) budget

Materials total variance = $(6,240 – 7,200) = $960 favourable

ACTIVITY 5

Total direct labour cost variance:	$
Flexed budget for direct labour for actual output	
(100 units × $30 per unit)	3,000
Actual cost	3,660
Variance	660 (A)

ACTIVITY 6

The actual cost of labour will be $13.12 per hour ($12.80 × 1.025) causing an unfavourable or adverse total labour cost variance because labour costs will be higher than expected.

ACTIVITY 7

Each unit has actually taken six minutes to produce rather than the budgeted time of five minutes. Therefore, there will be an unfavourable or adverse total labour cost variance because the labour force will be working less efficiently than expected.

ACTIVITY 8

(a) Sales activity (volume) variance

This is the difference between the flexed sales revenue budget and the original budget.

Sales activity variance = (8,000 × $8) – $80,000 = $64,000 – $80,000 = $16,000 (A)

(b) Selling price variance

Actual selling price = $68,000/8,000 = $8.50 per unit

Budgeted selling price = $8 per unit

The selling price was therefore $0.50 more than expected and therefore there is a favourable selling price variance of 8,000 × $0.50 = $4,000 (F).

(c) Total sales variance

This is the difference between the original sales revenue budget and the actual sales revenue earned = $80,000 – $68,000 = $12,000 (A).

Proof: sales activity budget + selling price budget = $(16,000 (A) + $4,000 (F)) = $12,000 (A)

EXAM-STYLE QUESTIONS

1 **B**

If the original budgeted labour rate was set too low this would contribute to an adverse direct labour cost variance, since actual costs are likely to be higher than budgeted.

2 **D**

The budgeted material cost per unit is $2,625/700 = $3.75

720 units should cost	$2,700
But they did cost	$2,628

There is a favourable variance of $72

3 **B**

Inexperienced labour using more material would result in an adverse material variance. All of the other causes would or could result in favourable material variances.

4 Action taken to correct deviations or to revise the budget if appropriate is an example of **feedback** control

5 **D**

The flexed budget for the revised direct material cost based on actual production is:

$$\frac{9{,}000 \text{ units}}{8{,}000 \text{ units}} \times \$48{,}000 = \$54{,}000$$

The activity (volume) variance is the difference between the original (fixed) budget and the flexed budget i.e. $48,000 – $54,000 = $6,000 adverse. The variance is adverse because more units were produced compared to the original budget. This means that more direct material costs were incurred.

6 The flexed total cost budget for the period would be **$380,000**

	Original budget	*Flexed budget*
	$	*$*
Budgeted variable costs	150,000	300,000
Budgeted	80,000	80,000
Total sales variance	230,000	380,000

7 **D**

The other changes might explain other variances caused by changes in rate or efficiency. But the labour activity (volume) variance simply reflects changes in labour caused by changes in activity.

8 The selling price for the period is **$80,000** and it would be **favourable**

The actual selling price per unit was $1,680,000/800 = $2100 per unit. This means that the selling price was $100 per unit more than budgeted. Multiplying this by the actual quantity sold, the **sales price variance** = 800 × $100 = $00 (favourable). The variance is favourable because the selling price per unit was more than the original budgeted price.

9 **A**

The other reasons are valid reasons. But the direction of the variance is not normally a valid reasons – favourable variances can highlight that a process is out of control just as much as adverse variances can.

CHAPTER 20

EXAM-STYLE QUESTIONS

1 **A**

Enclosures are additional pieces of information that are sent out with the memorandum or letter.

2 **A**

A bar chart shows not only the actual amount of the data but also the relationship between the various items of data, for example the sales in each year. When using bar charts it is easy to compare the amount of sales achieved each year. A table is not a picture.

3 **C**

A letter provides written evidence of the complaint and is less open to misinterpretation or being overlooked than a verbal conversation on the telephone. A memo is not formal enough for a complaint and a courier would probably be unnecessarily expensive.

4 **A**

The area covered by production numbers has increased month to month, as has the sales staff numbers. Total staff numbers did not exceed 500 until June.

5 **B**

The nature of the person who prepared the report would not normally be considered when deciding upon how the report should be distributed.

INDEX

K

L

M

N

O